"*Announcing the Kingdom* takes the reader on a panoramic tour of the Kingdom of God from Genesis to Revelation. A theology of mission centered on the Kingdom, it intersects biblical exegesis with missiological reflection to produce a solidly evangelical and relevant understanding of mission for Christians who want to share the good news in today's troubled world."

—Gary B. McGee,
Assemblies of God Theological Seminary

"Until now there has been little in-depth analysis of the Bible from a missiological perspective. In this book, a premier mission theologian offers a thought-provoking study of the heart of God for the nations that covers the whole of Scripture."

—Robert L. Gallagher,
Wheaton College Graduate School

"In an age when theologies of mission can be reductionistic in focus and concern, Glasser expounds the biblical revelation with detail and diligence. *Announcing the Kingdom* analyzes the Kingdom theme from Genesis to Revelation and along the way engages other issues of importance in contemporary debate, such as the centrality of social justice to holistic mission, the question of Jewish evangelization, and the fate of those who do not believe. This volume is a testament to a significant career and a rich foundation for continuing reflection on Christian mission."

—M. Daniel Carroll R.,
Denver Seminary

"*Announcing the Kingdom* challenges biblical scholars to look outwardly and to think missionally and challenges missiologists to base theory and experience in exegesis and biblical theology. While one may not agree with every detail of this theological reconstruction, all will profit immensely from the careful attention given to the biblical text in understanding the central place that mission plays in God's historical plan of establishing the Kingdom of God. This work will be used with great profit in biblical theology as well as missiology courses."

—Michael J. Wilkins,
dean, Biola University

"Written from a lifetime of teaching and practice, Arthur Glasser's *Announcing the Kingdom* tackles three theological deficiencies in Christendom: the role of the Kingdom of God, the missional nature of Scripture, and the integrative character of the sacred storybook from Genesis to Revelation. Conveyed through humble and honest scholarship, this welcome text tracks the unfolding revelation of the triumphant Kingdom of God that demands a call to conversion of all peoples."

—Tom A. Steffen,
Biola University

"Art Glasser, an esteemed member of an elite group of modern missionary statesmen/theologians, has drawn on years of biblical scholarship and mission experience to give the church a great gift. *Announcing the Kingdom: The Story of God's Mission in the Bible* is the essential book for new generations wishing to engage in mission on the sure foundation of biblical truth. Focusing on the scriptural pervasiveness of Jesus' favorite subject, Glasser and his talented disciples show plainly that the Kingdom of God is the dominant theme linking the task of mission in both Testaments and make a strong case that it is the one theme upon which it is possible to build a comprehensive biblical theology of mission. Because of their labors, missions in a new millennium has a great new tool for understanding its task, and it will no doubt be and do better because of their efforts."

—Gary Corwin,
SIM (Serving in Mission)

ANNOUNCING THE KINGDOM

THE STORY OF GOD'S MISSION IN THE BIBLE

ARTHUR F. GLASSER

WITH CHARLES E. VAN ENGEN,
DEAN S. GILLILAND, AND SHAWN B. REDFORD

FOREWORD BY PAUL G. HIEBERT

Baker Academic
Grand Rapids, Michigan

Published by Baker Academic
a division of Baker Publishing Group
P.O. Box 6287, Grand Rapids, MI 49516-6287
www.bakeracademic.com

Printed in the United States of America

Library of Congress Cataloging-in-Publication Data
Glasser, Arthur F. (Arthur Frederick), 1914–
    Announcing the kingdom : the story of God's mission in the Bible / Arthur F. Glasser
  with Charles E. Van Engen, Dean S. Gilliland, and Shawn B. Redford ; foreword by
  Paul G. Hiebert.
        p.   cm.
    Includes bibliographical references (p.).
    ISBN 10: 0-8010-2626-1 (pbk.)
    ISBN 978-0-8010-2626-3 (pbk.)
    1. Missions—Biblical teaching. I. Title.
  BV2073.G54 2003
  266—dc21   2003040099

Contents

Part 6   God's Mission Extends to the End of Time

Foreword

One of the hallmarks of modernity is the fragmentation of life into different spheres: public and private; economic, social, political, and religious; rich and poor. This fragmentation is reflected in the university, with its many disciplines and narrow specializations. With this fragmentation has come the loss of any sense of the dramatic story underlying all history.

There are attempts to recapture this story. If we ask Marxists what is going on, most lay out a story of oppression by the bourgeoisie and a revolution that will restore righteousness on earth for all. Many scientists outline a story of evolution and the triumph of reason. But these attempts are rapidly losing their credibility, and most of us are left to live in a world of highly specialized knowledge and no integrating cosmic story.

The same is true for many Christians. Reginald Bibby documents what many of us know from experience. Most Christians have a smorgasbord theology—based on the study of specific biblical passages in sermons, Sunday School classes, and Bible studies—which answers certain questions and focuses on individuals and their needs. Most Christians talk about personal salvation and what God has done for them in their lives. They have a theology of worship and fellowship, of health and prosperity, and of care for the needy. But they have little in their thinking for a world full of diverse peoples, of an earth caught up in the evils of sin, of a history from before Creation to eternity, or of the reason for their existence in such a world.

In seminaries, too, this fragmentation and specialization has taken its toll. Great care is given to the detailed study of one biblical passage or another, of one biblical hero or another, and of what the Gospel means to us in our lives today. We have a doctrine of God, of sin and personal salvation, and of divine healing and provision. We have a fragmented story—of Jesus, Ruth, David, Mary, and Peter. No longer do we see ourselves as part of a movement far greater than ourselves and a universal history that gives meaning to our lives because it shows us our place in a cosmic story.

In this masterpiece of reflection based on many years of global ministry, teaching, and reflection, Arthur Glasser draws together the many strands of Scripture and gives us again a great vision of the unity of all history. He examines the themes of King and Kingdom as these run through Scripture. He shows that all of Scripture points to the fact that God is a missionary God, that the church is to be a missionary community, and that God's people are to be missionary people. He shows us that mission is at the center of God's great plan, not only of redemption, but also of Creation. He reminds us that this mission is God's mission, that it is much bigger than the little worlds in which we minister, and that it includes not only the salvation of individuals and the redemption of the church but also the reestablishment of God's Kingdom of righteousness, peace, and justice in a new heaven and a new earth. If we as God's people truly meet God, we cannot not be a missionary people, and the church cannot exist apart from mission. Our ministries take on meaning not because they are deeds of witness and service, important as these are, but because they are part of the great mission of God.

Glasser provides a coherent view of the Kingdom running through all of Scripture. In doing so, he brings together Old Testament and New Testament, Jew and Gentile, theology and mission. He shows how God's people, Israel, are important in God's mission plan, but that the Kingdom includes all people.

For those of us who had the privilege of studying under and working with Arthur Glasser, this volume is most welcome. Arthur Glasser's teachings and writings have been life transforming for many of us. For the greater church and for missions this book is very timely. In missions and in the larger church, we live in a time of fragmentation—of substituting theologically founded mission with aimless activism. We need to pause and take stock of where we are going. We need to recapture the vision of mission that runs through Scripture, and use that as the basis for the motivation and methods we use in mission outreach.

If the church recovers a vision of mission as seen in the Bible, it will be revived. If in Christian missions we recover that vision, we will be freed from the tyranny of activism and human-centeredness and recover the long-range perspective and coherence that we now lack. We will joyfully participate in God's mission because we have met a missionary God, and because he has sent us into the world to proclaim salvation, righteousness, justice, and peace.

The danger is that we will do with this work what we do best as moderns. We will classify it, label it, and send it to the right department in church or seminary for action. We will be satisfied that the job will get done if it is assigned to the right people. And then we can get on with the important things in our everyday lives. But church history is a warning. When a church loses its missionary vision, God raises up a new church to carry on the task. Jerusalem, Antioch, Ephesus, Constantinople, Rome, Scotland, Germany, England, and North America have been centers of mission outreach. But when they lost that vision they became peripheral to God's great mission. Today God is raising up young churches around the world who see mission as their central reason for existence on earth because in worship they have met a missionary God and heard his call to proclaim his Kingdom to a lost and needy world. The question is whether the Western churches will be part of that movement, or another side branch in the history of the Kingdom. But Glasser's call goes deeper—to each one of us as God's sign and witness to that Kingdom. In that sense this is a dangerous book, for when we know the truth and hear God's call, we must respond—either with obedience or indifference.

PAUL G. HIEBERT

Preface

Announcing the Kingdom: The Story of God's Mission in the Bible represents a lifetime of thought, Bible study, missionary experience, and missiological teaching by one of the premier missiologists of the last half of the twentieth century. During the past fifty years, there have been few works that have dealt in-depth with a missional reading of the Bible. Yet of those that do exist, in many cases the biblical analysis has been done by Bible scholars with little background in missiological thought or praxis. In other cases missiologists with little background in biblical studies have tried to derive biblical foundations for their missionary perspectives. In this volume Arthur Glasser uniquely couples a careful and in-depth approach to the Bible with a broad understanding of missiological reflection and missionary action.

The purpose of this book is to offer the reader a biblical study of the Kingdom of God and the worldwide mission of God's people. One of the most basic aspects of mission theology has to do with the relation of the Bible to mission theory and practice. Initially one would think that this would be obvious. Such is not the case. In each generation there is a need to reflect again on the way the church embraces or exploits the scriptural understanding of mission.

In Arthur Glasser's words:

> Only if the church understands the full biblical revelation of God concerning the mission of God's people, stimulated by confronting Scripture with today's questions, will they be responsibly challenged to offer to God the devotion of heart, strength, time, and resources essential to its completion. This means listening to the Old Testament witness as well as to the New Testament. . . . All Scripture makes its contribution in one way or other to our understanding of mission. This is our thesis. In our day evangelicals are finding that the biblical base for mission is far broader and more complex than any previous generation of missiologists appears to have envisioned. . . . It has become increasingly difficult to defend the modern missionary movement by supplementing this concern with appeals to the Great Commission (Matt. 28:18–20), in the tradition of William Carey and Hudson Taylor. Nor can greater credibility be gained by broadening the base through appealing to proof-texts carefully selected to

support such related themes as the sending character of God, the compassionate compulsion of the Spirit, the example of the apostolic church, and the relation between missionary obedience and the second coming of Christ. . . . An overall approach to Scripture must be undertaken that will allow each part to make its contribution so that the total concern of God for the nations might be understood. To develop such an approach is our concern in this book. (Glasser 1992: 26–27)

In this study our objective is to explore the emergence and development of the Kingdom of God motif within both the Old and the New Testaments taken as a whole, in order to understand more deeply God's mission through God's people in God's world. This, in turn, will give us new wisdom and insight as to what should be the church's mission in a new millennium.

Our mission is none other, no more nor less, than participation in Jesus' mission. To state it negatively, when it is not Christ's mission, it may be colonial expansion, church extension, proselytism, or social services—but it is not mission. Our mission is biblical mission only when it is centered in Jesus Christ. As Art Glasser has said, "The gospel has at its heart the affirmation that Jesus Christ alone is Lord and that he offers to enter the lives of all who come to him in repentance and faith" (Glasser 1984: 726).[1]

The authors of this book have used an earlier draft of this volume with great benefit for several years in courses in biblical foundations of mission at Fuller Seminary's School of World Mission. Nearly two hundred students have read the book each school year and have consistently acclaimed it as the most profound, helpful, and provocative book relating Bible and mission they have ever read.

A Kingdom of God perspective has been one of Arthur Glasser's major contributions to missiology. Drawing from the works of George Ladd, Herman Ridderbos, Oscar Cullmann, and others, Glasser's Kingdom of God paradigm has done at least four things for missiology.

First, the Kingdom of God concept broadens missiological reflection beyond a predominantly individualized and vertical understanding of salvation to a holistic view of the interaction of church and world.

Second, Glasser's Kingdom missiology breaks the impasse between evangelism and social action that has plagued Protestant evangelicals.

Third, Kingdom of God missiology creates the possibility of new conversation among evangelicals, representatives of the conciliar movement, Roman Catholics, Orthodox, Pentecostals, and charismatics.

Fourth, Glasser's own personal pilgrimage made him deeply aware of the social and political implications of the Kingdom of God that challenges all governments, all forms of racism, all social structures that would seek to deify themselves.

---

1. In another place Glasser says, "In recent years evangelicals have become increasingly concerned to become more comprehensively biblical in their understanding and performance of the Christian mission. . . . They are determined as never before to keep his redemptive work central, for by his substitutionary death and bodily resurrection he alone provides access for sinful human beings into the presence and fellowship of God" (Glasser 1985: 9).

Born in 1914, the year that World War I began, Arthur and his wife, Alice, saw tremendous changes take place in the way Christian missions are done. Yet throughout all those changes, their vision of the essential motivation and goal of Christian mission remained focused. As Art Glasser once wrote, "There is but one acid test that should be applied to all activities that claim to represent obedience in mission. Do they or do they not produce disciples of Jesus Christ?" (1974: 8). Here Glasser was echoing Donald McGavran's conviction on which Fuller's School of World Mission (SWM) was founded. McGavran understood mission "as an enterprise devoted to proclaiming the good news of Jesus Christ, and to persuading men and women to become his disciples and responsible members of his church" (1990: 23–24). McGavran believed this was the primary basis on which ministry formation should be evaluated (1989: 22–26).

Graduating from Cornell University in Civil Engineering in 1936, Art felt that God was calling him to full-time cross-cultural missionary service. After graduating from Faith Theological Seminary in 1942, Glasser joined the Navy as a chaplain in the First Marine Division, which saw fierce fighting in the South Pacific in 1943 and 1944. After the war, Art and Alice Glasser joined the China Inland Mission (CIM), and were a part of the first group of candidates accepted by CIM after World War II. In 1946 they were sent to China. In their first missionary prayer letter, dated December 28, 1946, the Glassers wrote, "There are two basic reasons why we are on our way to China. First, as Christians, we owe to the One who died for us the obedience He demands of all His disciples, since He has placed upon us the solemn obligation to 'go into all the world and preach the gospel to every creature.' And secondly, we are going to China because of the appalling need of that tragic land which has one quarter of the world's population."

After the Communist takeover of China in 1949, Art taught for several years at Columbia Bible College in Columbia, South Carolina. In 1955 Glasser was appointed assistant home director of CIM, by then called the Overseas Missionary Fellowship (OMF). He and Alice lived for several years in Singapore. In 1960 he became the home director of OMF. During those years Glasser was the editor of *China's Millions,* later called *East Asia's Millions.* In 1969 Glasser resigned his position with OMF to study for a year at Columbia University in New York. From the 1940s until the late 1960s Glasser was also heavily involved with Erik Fife and others in the Urbana Missionary Conferences of the Foreign Missionary Fellowship of InterVarsity. In 1970 Art was invited by David Allan Hubbard to become the second dean of the School of World Mission, following Donald McGavran. He served as dean from 1971 to 1980. Drawing from his lifelong passion for Jewish evangelization, Glasser founded the Judaic Studies Program in the School of World Mission. During more than sixty years, God has used Art widely with his various gifts as missionary theologian, mission statesman, theological educator, mission executive, mission mobilizer, evangelist, writer, editor, and speaker. Today Art and Alice make their home in Seattle, Washington.

The other names that appear on the cover of this book are those of three "generations" of disciples who have been transformed by Arthur Glasser's missiology.

Dean Gilliland served as a missionary, teaching and training church leaders in Nigeria for many years. In 1977 he was invited by Art Glasser to join the faculty of the School of World Mission at Fuller, where he now teaches contextualization and Pauline theology of mission. Chuck Van Engen studied mission theology and church growth with Art in 1972 and 1973, prior to going as a missionary to Mexico. At Art Glasser's insistence, Chuck joined the School of World Mission in 1988, at which time Art promptly handed over to him a course called "Biblical Foundations of Mission," for which the primary textbook was an early draft of this book. In the mid-1990s Shawn Redford began his studies at Fuller and has been a follower of Art Glasser's missiology ever since. Chuck and Shawn now team-teach "Biblical Foundations of Mission," and they use this book as the primary resource to help students understand God's mission as it takes place from Genesis to Revelation.

Our prayer is that you, our reader, will allow this unique work to serve as a focusing lens through which you can read the Bible with new missional vision. And once you look through this lens, we pray you will rejoice with us in the amazement and wonder we have experienced in seeing the kaleidoscope of ways in which God's mission advances through Scripture. We are all indebted to Arthur Glasser for giving us new eyes to see God's mission in the Bible.

PART 1

GOD'S
MISSION
IN THE
BEGINNING

1

The Whole Bible
Is a Missionary Book

Introduction

The whole Bible, both Old and New Testaments, is a missionary book, the revelation of God's purpose and action in mission in human history. The Old Testament was the Bible of the apostolic church. Because Jesus Christ accepted it as the Word of God, his disciples could not but follow his example. Although the Old Testament is the Word of God primarily to Israel, its value does not lie only in the way it anticipates the New Testament's announcement of the Messiah of Israel and the Savior of the world. It is in fact revelation in the same sense as the New Testament, for it reveals the mighty acts and gracious purposes of God on behalf of his people and the world he created for them. Both testaments are organically related in a dynamic and interactive relationship. In both, God acts through God's Son. In his development of this interrelationship, George A. F. Knight states:

> We might employ St. Paul's declaration in 2 Cor. 5:19, . . . (alternating two words, to show) the essential contents of the Old Testament . . . : "God was in Israel, seeking to reconcile the world unto himself." "In Israel" God did not succeed in redeeming the world. It remained for him to act "in Christ" in order finally to draw all (people) unto himself. (1959: 8)

On this basis we can say with confidence that "the central theme of the Old Testament is the revelation of the redemptive activity of God in and through the Son, Israel" (Knight 1959: 9). This means that all aspects of the Old Testament, particularly those concerning Israel, should be seen as related to God's worldwide, redemptive purpose.

The Two Testaments: Continuity and Discontinuity

In this study our objective is to explore the emergence and development of the mission of God in both the Old and the New Testaments. In pursuing this goal we shall seek to identify with the writers of the New Testament who assumed the essential continuity between ancient Israel and the church. On the one hand, they saw the church as the people of God called to reach out to Gentiles as well as Jews. This calling began when the community of faith was first formed with God's choosing Abraham and Sarah. On the other hand, in appropriating God's gift of grace, the Jewish writers of the New Testament also saw significant discontinuity between themselves and the nation of Israel. The New Testament expression of the people of God was born at Pentecost not of the flesh (through physical descent) but of the Holy Spirit. "The Church is thus also regarded as the Community of the Resurrection" (Knight 1959: 350).

This being so, the New Testament people of God need the Old Testament—every word of it! Gentile Christians dare not assume that they have taken over all the promises God made to ancient Israel, leaving only curses on the Jewish people. In contrast, Christians must see themselves as having been grafted into the stock of Israel's covenant relationship with God, to "share in the nourishing sap from the olive root" (Rom. 11:17), and this has been solely because of the grace of God. According to the Scriptures there is only one people of God, only one community of faith.

When Christians recognize that both the Old and the New Testaments are the Word of God, they bind themselves to the Scriptures in the deepest sense. This demands a deep concern with God's creation and God's rule, with the first things and the last things, with the divine image in all people and the law of God for all people, with holiness and sanctification, with civility and humanization, with ethos and culture, with society and marriage, with history and the state (Van Ruler 1971: 88).

Therefore, we challenge the appropriateness of words like "old" and "new" to distinguish the two sections of the Bible. Although these terms are biblical, they point up the need to be aware of the precise sense in which the "old covenant" is old and the "new covenant" is new. The tragedy is that all too frequently it is assumed that the "old" has been annulled by the "new" and that one can regard the "old" as merely preparatory or, at best, as "the law put in charge to lead us to Christ" (Gal. 3:24).

Jewish people are particularly offended by this designation of their Scriptures as "old." Malachi, they would argue, is on their side when God speaks through him, saying, "I the LORD do not change. So you, O descendants of Jacob, are not destroyed" (Mal. 3:6). Jews would also rightly contend that the covenant God ratified at Sinai is forever settled in heaven. It is eternal and unending. It is no wonder, then, that down through the centuries Judaism has utterly repudiated any idea of a "new" covenant that regards God's earlier covenantal activity as "old."

The phrase "old covenant" occurs only once in the New Testament (2 Cor. 3:14), and "new covenant" occurs six times (excluding Mark 14:24). What is more, the term *new covenant* appears in the Old Testament (for example, in Jer. 31:31). No real resolution is achieved by identifying the Old Testament as "law" and contrasting it with "grace" through quoting with finality John 1:17 ("The law was given through Moses; grace and truth came through Jesus Christ"). The revelation at Sinai was verbal in the fullest sense, and the eternal Word was fully incarnate in Jesus Christ. Both parts of the Bible are of the same essence. Together they constitute the Word of God. This Word of God, however, is characterized by the progressive unfolding of divine revelation, "for God was pleased to have all his fullness dwell" in Jesus Christ.

Interdependence of the Old and the New Testaments

The New Testament is incomprehensible without the Hebrew Scriptures, for it is intimately related in direct quotations and common themes, in terminology, and in the fullness with which it portrays the God of Abraham, Isaac, and Jacob. Easter is both chronologically and theologically related to Passover as are Pentecost (Lev. 23:16) and First Fruits (Lev. 23:9–21). Indeed, at every level, ranging from assumptions to thought forms, idioms, and hopes, the New Testament is impossible to grasp apart from its Old Testament rootage. Hence, we endorse Knight's suggestion, following 2 Corinthians 5:19, that the essence of the Old Testament is that "God was reconciling the world to himself." In Israel, however, he could not succeed because of the failures of the people of Israel. It remained for him to act "in Christ" in order to draw all peoples to himself (1959: 8).

However, one cannot remain in the Old Testament without becoming restless and sensing a need for something that the Old Testament by itself cannot provide. This restlessness finds focus in the need to turn to the New Testament and rejoice in its record of the dawning of the messianic age. In the study of the Old Testament there is a longing for multiple assurances that all will be well in the end. There is hope that all creation will witness the final vindication of God, fully triumphant in the midst of his creation, having banished from it all that was contrary to God's will. Furthermore, the Lord God will be gloriously satisfied when he receives something vastly different from the fitful obedience of a small remnant of Israel, admittedly only one small segment of the human race. He will then be loved and served by a people drawn from all the nations, eager to live under his direction and for his glory.

We must keep in mind that the Old Testament was given to the Israelites. As Christians we hear its message through Christ, who has given it to us. Indeed, we are obliged to refer each Old Testament text to the New Testament for a verdict, whether it is ratification, modification, or judgment. Again and again, however, we will find that many essential perspectives and features of our biblical faith are not explicitly developed in the New Testament because the Spirit of God has already adequately developed them in the Old Testament. This fact in itself helps establish the reality of the continuity of the people of God before Christ and after Christ. For instance, the Psalms guide us day by day in our worship, and the prophets make us conscious of our social responsibilities to our generation (Bright 1967: 204). But the surprises within the New Testament are essential to our understanding of how God will ultimately and completely fulfill the unrealized expectations of Old Testament faith. Christians find their rootage in both the Old Testament and the New.

The Old Testament is the backdrop for our heritage of faith—but before Christ (B.C.). It is the record of the dealings of our God with God's people and is a revelation of his Word to them—but before Christ. It is filled with material that speaks to issues that confront the church in the New Testament as it breaks into new frontiers of missionary advance where people live in large measure in B.C. situations. These situations mirror the predicament that characterizes the human condition. As John Bright writes:

> The Old Testament rightly heard, places me in my B.C. dilemma, shows me the wreckage of my B.C. hopes, and thereby creates in me the readiness to hear of some better hope—beyond all B.C. The proper conclusion of Israel's history is Jesus Christ. (1967: 208–9)

A hermeneutic that silences parts of the Old Testament, or enables us to hear only its easy parts, or arbitrarily confines the total biblical revelation or any particular subject to New Testament passages, will not do. "Every Old Testament text, if rightly heard, has its word for us today" (Bright 1967: 212).

Because of the historical character of revelation, we find many ideas in the Old Testament that are not directly applicable to the people of God today. Some might even say that Jesus also gave some instructions to his disciples that no longer can or should be taken literally. There are those who contend that much in Scripture may be passed over with no resultant loss. This is far from true. Each and every section of Scripture, if permitted to speak for itself, will reveal lines of truth, such as law and grace, promise and exhortation. These themes are relevant to the people of God today in every culture and every circumstance of life. Toward the end of his ministry, the apostle Paul could confidently affirm that "all Scripture" (every part of the Old Testament corpus) is "useful for teaching, rebuking, correcting and training in righteousness," because all is "God-breathed" (2 Tim. 3:16). He concluded that thereby the servant of God is "equipped for every good work" (v. 17).

The Old Testament as Expectation of the Kingdom

God's right to reign and rule over all of creation and over all the peoples of the world must be unequivocally understood. This brings together the message of Old and New Testament narratives because the Kingdom of God is one of the central, overarching themes of the Bible. Although it is explicitly a New Testament theme, we are deeply persuaded that the Old Testament can also be understood from this perspective. In the Old Testament God discloses himself and his outgoing activity in a variety of ways. As *Creator* he established the world and filled it with his creatures. As *Governor* he watches over it for his good pleasure. As *Redeemer* he reveals his forgiving love for his people. And as *Revealer* he points the way to his ultimate purpose for them, as Isaiah vividly described:

Since you are precious and honored in my sight,
    and because I love you,
I will give men in exchange for you,
    and people in exchange for your life.
Do not be afraid, for I am with you;
    I will bring your children from the east and gather you from the west.
I will say to the north, "Give them up!"
    and to the south, "Do not hold them back."
Bring my sons from afar
    and my daughters from the end of the earth—
everyone who is called by my name,
    whom I created for my glory,
    whom I formed and made. (43:4–7)

The Old Testament is replete with statements of this sort. There is a future for Israel, the people of God descended from the patriarchs: Abraham, Isaac, and Jacob. But this future is not unrelated to God's redemptive purpose for the Gentile nations. Following the redemptive work of the Holy One of Israel, Isaiah also prophesied that there would come a day—the day of God—when the nations will be drawn to Zion:

Many peoples will come and say:
"Come, let us go up to the mountain of the Lord, to the house of the God of
    Jacob.
He will teach us his ways
    so that we may walk in his paths."
The law will go out from Zion,
    the word of the Lord from Jerusalem.
He will judge between the nations
    and will settle disputes for many peoples.
They will beat their swords into plowshares
    and their spears into pruning hooks.
Nation will not take up sword against nation,
    nor will they train for war anymore. (2:3–4)

The apostle Paul centuries later confirmed this when he stated that God's purpose was to "bring all things in heaven and on earth together under one head, even Christ" (Eph. 1:10). The Old Testament affirms again and again that God desires to destroy all evil and bring to an end every grief that plagues humankind. Without its contribution to our understanding of the eternal purpose of God with respect to individuals and nations, the New Testament portrayal of the "already," the "not yet," and the "consummation" of the Kingdom will appear incomplete. The revelation of the love of God in Christ cannot be fully grasped apart from the Old Testament. Even the lordship of Christ can be best understood when it is informed by Old Testament concepts of kingship.

God's rule is both universal and covenantal. Since God created the heavens and the earth by his word and the first human couple in his image, it was inevitable that from that time onward God would exercise a loving and providential care over his creation. This can be described as his universal kingship. God is the source of all authority, and he has decreed that he will ultimately triumph over all things, particularly the nations: "All the ends of the earth will remember and turn to the LORD, and all the families of the nations will bow down before him, for dominion belongs to the LORD and he rules over the nations" (Ps. 22:27–28). The New Testament also teaches the universal rule of God. Jesus Christ is described as "the ruler of kings on earth" who in the last day will be fully revealed as the Lord our God, the Almighty One who reigns (Rev. 1:5, 8; 19:6).

However, in the Old Testament we also find God's kingly rule identified with a particular people with whom he established a special covenantal relationship—the seed of Abraham, Isaac, and Jacob. He constituted them as his peculiar possession after liberating them from Egyptian bondage and securing their willing acceptance of his covenant at Sinai (Exod. 19–20). From that time onward his moral governance over them embraced the pledge of guidance and provision, instruction and blessing. If they obeyed, they could count on his faithfulness to his covenantal commitment. If they became rebellious and disobedient, they could anticipate his chastening. Over the years he disclosed himself to them by "mighty acts" and "spoken words." They came to understand that his rule was spiritual and irrevocable and included the guarantee of an imperishable national existence, a messianic expectation, and an eternal salvation to those who turned to him. When God prophesied through Daniel that "the saints of the Most High will receive the kingdom and will possess it forever . . . and ever" (7:18), he sent the Israelites' minds soaring. Here was an unconditional promise of ultimate triumph under the banner of "one like a son of man" (7:13). He would enable them in the last day to share in God's final victory. Understandably, the Jewish people have never forgotten this promise!

Hence, in the Old Testament it is not uncommon for God to be addressed by people as their King (Ps. 10:16). They regarded God as enthroned in their midst, dwelling between the cherubim in the innermost sanctuary of the tabernacle, and later in the Temple in Jerusalem (Num. 7:89; Isa. 37:16). His throne was "the mercy seat." God's presence there pledged his faithfulness to his covenant. They would triumph over their enemies!

There is both differentiation and intimate correlation between God's universal rule and God's kingly rule over God's people. As *Creator* and *Redeemer* he will finally and fully triumph in human history. As a God who is faithful to his covenants, God will bring his people to their "golden age of salvation." These are interrelated and in sequence. First, the Israel of God must be a redeemed people. Second, the nations that have long resisted God's will must be totally divested of their pretensions, their autonomy, and their dominion. Third, the ruin and downfall of all God's enemies are prerequisite to his being established as "King of kings and Lord of lords" (Rev. 19:16). Fourth, it is only at the last day—the time of God's final judgment—that "they will call Jerusalem The Throne of the LORD, and all nations will gather in Jerusalem" (Jer. 3:17). And finally, following this eschatological summons of the nations to seek the Lord and give account of themselves, the people of God will see "new heavens and a new earth" (Isa. 65:17). Only then will they enjoy the enduring peace and justice people have sought and the economic security that has eluded human striving (Mic. 4:3, 4).

Despite this oft-repeated prospect of the final triumph of God in human history, the record of the Old Testament represents almost unrelieved failure on the part of Israel. The kingly rule of God met with little appreciation and even less response. God lavished love on his people but received little in return. They did not find it congenial to their self-interest to live under God's direction and for his glory. They were constantly tempted and overcome by rival claims to knowledge, security, and power attractively packaged in ancient cultures and dominated by enslaving idolatries. Again and again they brought catastrophe upon themselves through worshiping the gods of neighboring peoples and thus departing from the living God. They only survived by God's grace. Each successive divine deliverance revealed God's faithfulness and his power as *Liberator, Healer,* and *Guardian.* Over the years they were taught what is demanded of those who would confess him as their *Sovereign King.*

We cannot adequately understand the Old Testament unless we take into account the full measure of this record of failure. We must ponder deeply the somber details of Israel's persistent apostasy and from this perspective review the hopes and expectations so vividly set forth by the prophets: God will ultimately realize his covenantal goal for God's people. Through this hope we can begin to appreciate the uniqueness of Jesus Christ. He is the "other Israel." By a totally obedient life, a truthful witness to his generation, and a substitutionary atoning surrender of his life in death, Jesus Christ establishes a new and unbreakable covenant of grace and salvation that will embrace all the nations (Jer. 31:31–34; Ezek. 39:24–28). He makes possible the ultimate triumph of God in history.

Axioms Linking God's Mission in the Old and the New Testaments

Seven major axioms in the Old Testament are primary to the Bible's unfolding of God's mission in the Bible. They can be traced within the record of God's response to Israel's troubled history as God's people. Each one is an intimation of what will be developed in fullness in the New Testament. Understanding these themes is essential to a unified biblical grasp of God's mission in the Bible. These themes will be kept before us as underlying motifs that span the two testaments.

God is sovereign in his kingship.

God's rule over individuals and nations is always righteous and just. Indeed, whatever he does is a reflection of his character. God's power and goodness, holiness and justice, patience and mercy are always prompted by a loving concern for the best interests of his creatures. No one convinced of the reality of God is likely to become preoccupied with second causes. It is only with God that God's people have to deal. He is the moral *Governor* of the universe and "will reign for ever and ever" (Exod. 15:18).

The absolute reign of God over the Kingdom he created and the human beings who care for one another and for the created world depicts both the divine ideal and will as well as the painful truth of the Old Testament. A secularizing and rebellious Kingdom people thwarted God's rule. The demand for an earthly king and the behavior of the people under the rule of the earthbound kings set the stage for the new covenant when Jesus would walk among humans and would declare a new covenant in his blood.

In the New Testament God reestablished his right to rule. In the new era, God's sovereignty focuses on Christ's lordship. The sons and daughters of the Kingdom will proclaim Jesus as Lord: "We do not preach ourselves, but Jesus Christ as Lord" (2 Cor. 4:5). This is the heart of the good news of the Kingdom (Rom. 10:9–10). Jesus is the vice-regent of the Father. Through the cross he conquered all his foes and obtained salvation for his people. He now works through them by the power of the Holy Spirit. His present rule over the redeemed foreshadows his ultimate rule over all, over "a new heaven and a new earth." It follows then that the worship of all other gods is utterly abhorrent to him and hence totally futile. He is Lord of all.

God's sovereign rule demands personal commitment.

Those who would acknowledge God to be their God must personally commit themselves to him and to his righteousness. He has decreed no acceptable alternative other than this commitment: that those who bear his image should love him with all their heart, soul, strength, and mind. Furthermore, this relationship has been sealed by a covenant that he initiated and keeps. There can be no kingdom without subjects, and the righteous God demands righteousness on the part of all who would be in covenantal relationship with God. God pointedly states that he rejects those whose lives reflect gross ethical waywardness and misplaced religious practices. In God's judgment this reflects their having put out of their minds all recollection of God's past gracious care, interventions, and deliverances on their behalf and their determination to remain indifferent to his right to rule over their lives as they face the future.

In Micah 6 we find God contending with God's people because they had forgotten his saving acts on their behalf and what it means to walk humbly with God. They were indignant that he was not satisfied with mere external religious activities and ritualistic sacrifices. But this prophet reminded them that the Lord requires his redeemed "to act justly and to love mercy and to walk humbly with your God" (Mic. 6:8).

The New Testament emphasizes the necessity of accepting Christ's lordship by grace through faith. It calls for a covenant commitment to God similar to that found in the Old Testament. The New Testament points to the new birth, the inner witness of the Holy Spirit, and its outward expression in love and Kingdom service. Only those who are truly "new creatures in Christ" will enter the Kingdom of God. Indeed, any who do not have the Spirit of Christ do not belong to him (Rom. 8:9). All are commanded to be filled with the Holy Spirit; to disobey is to step deliberately out of the will of God (Eph. 5:18). And those who profess his lordship but whose lives do not reflect his values and perspectives are challenged to examine themselves and see whether they are truly his (2 Cor. 13:5).

God's subjects must constitute a "servant" community.

God is not concerned solely with individuals but with families, peoples, and nations. He presses social obligations on his redeemed people (the Sinaitic legislation). He delights to dwell in their midst, that through them God's rule might extend to all aspects of their social order. Furthermore, God intends that they be a "light for the Gentiles," and his salvation may reach "to the ends of the earth" (Isa. 49:6). He reveals himself as opposed to racism, nationalism, sexism, and all other "isms" that demean people. He stands against aggressive war, enforced poverty, the abuse of political power, and the neglect of "the stranger within the gates." Indeed, the Old Testament often surprises us by suggesting viable approaches to many of the contemporary problems confronting the church today. God is concerned for social justice. He is strangely moved at the cries of the oppressed, particularly when God's people collectively make neither effort nor sacrifice to relieve their anguish.

This spirit of service and openness is to be one of the distinguishing marks of God's subjects as they live out their understanding of the Bible's vision of *shalom*, watched by the peoples of the earth. The messianic hope envisions a new people. The new people are those who anticipate the coming of the one who will set up a new community of those who accept the role of the Suffering Servant. Jesus spoke of this radical departure from the past to the future when he distributed the cup and the bread with his disciples as a sign of the New Testament made possible by his blood.

The Old Testament community of the King becomes the New Testament body of Christ.

The people of God, as custodians of the keys to the Kingdom, will share a new togetherness as members of the New Testament church. They possess a common life within the context of individual participation in Jesus Christ. This is expressed through corporate worship, mutual sharing, united confession, and outgoing service. They guard their corporate wholeness through faithfully dealing with sin in their midst (Acts 5:1–6). They live by prayer and the confession of sin. Although the church as Christ's body is of divine creation, Christ alone can gather together the redeemed. The church's structured presence is a flawed mixture of God's grace, human fallenness, and demonic penetration. Its only glory is the presence of Christ in its midst, realized by faith.

God's people are called to mission.

God's sovereign rule will ultimately bring to light his lordship over all peoples. It is in the blessings promised to the nations through Abraham (Gen. 12:3) that the future begins. Where Israel failed, the church is given the mandate to "fill up . . . what is still lacking in regard to Christ's afflictions, for the sake of his body, which is the church" (Col. 1:24). Nothing is more important in the divine order for the church than mission into the world.

In the New Testament the church will be called to mission locally and globally. This mission arises from Christ's redemptive victory and his gathering of a "Kingdom community" by the proclamation of the gospel in word and deed. Its explicit details are striking endorsement and supplement to the Old Testament injunction "to act justly and to love mercy and to walk humbly with your God" (Mic. 6:8). Only after Pentecost do the people of God consciously begin to sense that they possess a universal faith for all nations. They begin to go beyond the bounds of Israel to the Gentile nations and proclaim the good news of the Kingdom by word and deed. Their central and irreplaceable task is to persuade all peoples to become Christ's disciples and reflect in their lives, speech, and service all the dimensions of the Kingdom that Christ will reveal in power and glory on the last day. Those who believe will be incorporated into the communal life of local churches—permanent centers of fellowship, worship, training, and further outreach.

The New Testament shows that Christ's second coming has a relationship to mission, for the Lord is not willing that any should perish but that all should come to repentance (2 Peter 3:9). The apostle Paul emphasizes that a key aspect of mission involves restraining the advance of the Antichrist (2 Thess. 2:1–8).

God will ultimately triumph. The future is his. The New Testament is explicit on this point. In Paul's words: "[God] has set a day when he will judge the world with justice by the man he has appointed. He has given proof of this to all men by raising him from the dead" (Acts 17:31). Only when this worldwide task has been completed to his satisfaction will the end come (Matt. 24:14).

God's sovereign rule will be relentlessly resisted and opposed by his people, by the nations that do not know him, and by the unseen "powers."

Meanwhile, as the church carries out its mission to the nations, conflict will continue because the performance of mission will involve suffering. The mission of the church will be relentlessly resisted and opposed by the peoples and nations that do not acknowledge Christ's lordship and particularly by the "powers and authorities."

One feels the humiliation of God. The Old Testament records that his gifts are either despised or irresponsibly squandered. His love is lavished on an ungrateful people, for his will was opposed again and again. This discloses the inveteracy of human evil. God knows the full measure of human ignorance, apathy, selfishness, greed, and cowardice. Amazingly, God is never overcome by evil, although he often bears the shame of the failure of his people (Jer. 34:16; Ezek. 39:7).

It was deep in the messianic vision that the Servant would suffer for the salvation of his people. Through his death and resurrection, Jesus Christ conquered the powers. Though we know the final outcome of Christ's victory over all evil, sin, and death, in this time between Christ's ascension and Christ's second coming opposition, suffering, and conflict remain the model of discipleship to which Jesus the Messiah calls his church. Conflict is inevitable. It arises from the cosmic struggle that was inaugurated on the cross when the messianic Christ disarmed the "powers and authorities" (Col. 2:15).

The New Testament is replete with the record of conflict and suffering arising from the spiritual warfare precipitated by the advent of the Kingdom. Jesus himself experienced the world's rejection and the devil's fury and learned obedience through what he suffered (Heb. 5:8). In much the same way, the church, claiming the victory of Christ over the powers (Col. 2:15), will nonetheless experience the sifting of Satan (Luke 22:31) and the testing of fire (1 Peter 1:6–8). And in that suffering the church is perfected, the better to perform its mission. This process will continue and even intensify toward the close of the age. Even so, there will be no diminishing of the church's responsibility to fulfill its mission to the nations.

The direction of God's sovereign rule is always into the future.

God is never totally preoccupied with the present. Again and again his prophets pointed to the coming day of God, when his righteousness would be fully triumphant, when "the earth will be filled with the knowledge of the glory of the LORD, as the waters cover the sea" (Hab. 2:14). He is the God of hope, of victory, and of personal salvation. His ultimate goal for human history is never lost sight of. For this reason, despite the dark shadows that cover most of Old Testament history, he always had a remnant of his people facing forward, looking for "the consolation of Israel" and "the redemption of Jerusalem" (Luke 2:25–38). They were sustained by the conviction that the redemptive purpose of God would finally be realized and that his Kingdom would then be fully established.

We shall find that the Old Testament constantly looks forward to something beyond itself. This should challenge us to take particular note of each specific line of thought that yearns for "more to follow." This exercise will confirm to us the fact that only the New Testament makes the Old Testament fully intelligible.

Again and again the New Testament will sound the note that God's redemptive purpose will be fulfilled in Jesus Christ, who as Alpha and Omega initiates and will consummate human history. He will succeed in calling out a completed people from the nations. And "[God] will judge the world with justice by the man he has appointed. He has given proof of this to all men by raising him from the dead" (cf. Acts 17:30–31 with Matt. 25:31–32). This is the "blessed hope—the glorious appearing of our great God and Savior, Jesus Christ" (Titus 2:13). When Christ returns, the church in its completeness will know that its missionary purpose has been finally realized. The Kingdom of God will then come in power and glory and thereby usher in "a new heaven and a new earth." The climax of Christ's redemptive purpose will take place "when [all things are subjected to God], then the Son himself will be made subject to him who put everything under him, so that God may be all in all" (1 Cor. 15:28).

Conclusion

The stage is now set for our examination of the whole Bible as a missionary book revealed by a missionary God who creates and calls a special people to participate in God's mission to the nations (Gen. 12:1–3; 1 Peter 2:9–10). We continue in the next chapter, then, with a closer look at the biblical account of primeval history.

2

God Creates the World, and Humanity Rebels

Introduction

We divide the canonical Scriptures into three sections: the first concerns primeval history, starting with Creation and concluding with the judgment at Babel, which scattered the human race throughout the earth (Gen. 1–11). We use the term *universal* to characterize this section, for during this period the human race is one in Creation, Fall, judgment, and dispersion. The activity of God is universal. When Adam and Eve sinned, the whole human race sinned. When the Flood came, it was a universal judgment. When God made a covenant with Noah and his family, the covenant embraced the entire human race. No person escaped God's language-related judgment arising from the rebellious attempt to oppose God at Babel.

The second section of the biblical narrative (Gen. 12 through Acts 1) is designated particular history and is almost solely concerned with God's dealings with Abram (who became Abraham) and his descendants via Isaac and Jacob (Gen. 12–50). It then traces the centuries of Israel's experience as a nation, beginning with its liberation from Egyptian bondage and continuing to its eventual transformation into a powerful monarchy. This period is followed by Israel's tragic division into two competing kingdoms. Because of spiritual apostasy, the larger kingdom (Israel) experienced God's judgment and was destroyed by Assyria. Its people were scattered among the nations, never to be reunited. The smaller kingdom (Judah) wandered away from God and likewise experienced divine judgment. The Babylonians were God's instrument of judgment. Many from Judah who survived were taken as captives to Babylon. Seventy years later they were permitted to return to their ruined land. Some responded, and the Old Testament concludes with a brief review of their subsequent experience, particularly God's ministry to them through what are known as the postexilic prophets. Then followed four hundred years of silence, the intertestamental period. The New Testament begins with the coming of the Messiah to Israel, as depicted in the four Gospels. This second section concludes with Jesus' redemptive death, burial, resurrection, and ascension.

The third section of the Scriptures commences with the coming of the Holy Spirit on the day of Pentecost (Acts 2). With this event the biblical record reverts to dealing with universal history—for the scope of gospel proclamation is universal in its intent. As Peter announced to Jews and proselytes on the day of Pentecost: "The promise is for you and your children and to all who are far off—for all whom the Lord our God will call" (Acts 2:39). This note of universality continues to the end of the New Testament with its promise of "a new heaven and a new earth" (Rev. 21:1). The eschatological consummation of human history finds the water of life streaming from the throne of God and bringing healing to the nations. "His servants will serve him. They will see his face, and his name will be on their foreheads. There will be no more night. They will not need the light of a lamp or the light of the sun, for the Lord God will give them light. And they will reign for ever and ever" (Rev. 22:3–5).

Primeval History: An Overview

Genesis begins with God but offers us no description of him. Although the whole Old Testament is about God, it will tell us nothing of what he is like in himself. Actually, in himself God is unknowable. We only learn what he is like by pondering what he has revealed through his creation, his speech, and his mighty acts in human history (Heb. 1:1). "If God kept silence, man would know nothing about him" (Jocz 1961: 28). That God both speaks and acts is the deepest conviction of the biblical writers.

As a result we will not use a scissors-and-paste approach to the Old Testament, arbitrarily fabricating from random texts a system of theological ideas. Rather we shall "follow in historical sequence the development of the relationship between the living God . . . and that empirical people whom God has chosen" (Knight 1959: 18). And since only those who believe can ever hope to understand (John 7:17), we will "put ourselves alongside the people of Israel of old and thus seek to enter ourselves into their experience of meeting with God" (Knight 1959: 19).

Genesis begins with the origins of the world and of the human race (chaps. 1–2) and follows with five separate narratives: the Fall (chap. 3), Cain and Abel (chap. 4), the sons of God (6:1–4), the Flood (6:5–9:28), and the tower of Babel (11:1–9). These narratives are interspersed with three genealogies: the generations of Adam (chap. 5), of Noah (chap. 10), and of Shem (11:10–26).

Two opposite progressions are at work: "God's orderly creation with its climax in (humanity) as responsible and blessed being(s), and then the disintegrating work of sin" (Kidner 1967: 13). Von Rad speaks of "the spread of sin, spread of grace" motif (1972: 152–53). Sin continued to escalate and to spread and eventually brought the world to "the brink of uncreation" (Clines 1976: 133). It started with the Fall, bringing humankind to total alienation from God. Its escalation process began with a man (Adam) making disparaging remarks about his wife, whom he had earlier called "bone of my bones and flesh of my flesh" (2:23), to murder (Cain), to reckless killing (Lamech), to titanic lust (sons of God with the daughters of men), to total corruption and violence (before the Flood), and finally to the complete disruption and scattering of the race (Babel). In response God punished with increasing severity, but not without displaying his mercy. He is the God of grace as well as the God of judgment. God's response at Babel involved both grace and judgment, leading to the preservation but also to the fragmentation of the human race. Babel set the stage for God's gracious call of Abram. By this call he established a covenantal relationship with one particular segment of the human race. This marked the beginning of his mighty acts on his people's behalf; these interactions of God with creation and humankind outline what is commonly called "salvation history."

How are we to understand this record of primeval history? It should not be regarded in the modern sense of objective, factual reporting, since no human witnessed the Creation, nor do we have evidence that any antediluvian person or persons could have recorded and preserved the facts over this incredibly long history. Nor can we presume that someone on his or her own utilized whatever oral traditions were available and produced this record. It is highly improbable that merely by meditating on the nature of the world, on humanity, on the fact of sin and evil with the consequences of alienation and separation from God, the author was led to true conclusions about the beginnings of things and finally stated them in the language of his day. Rather, this story involves God's self-disclosure, for speech is ever God's fundamental activity. Naturally, with the call of Abram and the unfolding of God's revelation to Israel, the authors of all subsequent Scripture were in touch with Israel's repository of family records, ideas, and concepts. Even so, their impulse to write was not of human initiative, but rather they "spoke from God as they were carried along by the Holy Spirit" (2 Peter 1:20–21).

Creation

The church in every age must proclaim earnestly the existence of God, the Maker of all things visible and invisible. It must celebrate his being and rejoice that he rules over all that he has made (Ps. 47–49). It must confess with humility that nothing deserves to be. The fact that the Creation took place is an expression of the freedom of God: God's sovereignty and grace, wisdom and power, and perfection. God's subsequent activity in preserving creation and in redeeming his people also reflects God's gracious character.

It is quite incredible to postulate that no God exists—as Creator and superintending Providence—and that the universe and everything in it is either a temporary, worthless illusion (such as maya in Hinduism) or that it came of itself (secularism). It would then follow that all sense experience is meaningless and irrelevant; that "eternal matter" possesses a conscious and deliberate capability ("natural selection"); and that the "tooth and claw" war that characterizes all animate creatures is the excellent way whereby perfection and goodness are to be achieved ("the survival of the fittest").

God's Self-Revelation in Creation

Creation took place as the initial event in space-time history, the beginning of the self-disclosure of God. The author of Genesis sought to demonstrate the power of God through making his word coequal with his deed: "He spoke, and it came to be; he commanded, and it stood firm" (Ps. 33:9). The material universe is the creation of his word; he is its Master and Lord and is transcendent to it. "By faith we understand that the universe was formed at God's command" (Heb. 11:3). Only through Jesus Christ, the Word made flesh, will we be able to comprehend the mystery of God's creative activity, as well as the goal and ultimate meaning of creation itself (John 1:1–18; Col. 1:15–20; Heb. 1:1–4; de Dietrich 1960: 27). We will find that all that God has made belongs to him and to him alone. Therefore, God, the Creator, is in full control of history.

Irresistibility and perfection marked God's creative activity. His omnipotence and omniscience combined to produce a universe that functions in an orderly and glorious fashion, an earth that is infinitely complex yet harmonious. Beholding such beauty and interdependence, God himself was pleased with what he had accomplished. And a heavenly chorus agreed! "You are worthy, our Lord and God, to receive glory and honor and power, for you created all things, and by your will they were created and have their being" (Rev. 4:11). Again and again, in the unfolding of the sequence of his creative acts, we come upon his sense of delight: he "saw that it was good" (Gen. 1:4, 10, 12, 18, 21, 25). Even more frequent in this record is the phrase "according to its kind" (ten occurrences). This language calls attention to God's desire that his creation not only reflect order but that it also contain great variety and diversity. Indeed, the scientific enterprise is built upon this reality; what God has made is capable of being rationally understood and hence can be mastered conceptually.

But when the record focuses on the creation of people, we do not read "God created man, each according to its kind." Although there is the appearance of differentiation in maleness and femaleness, this does not constitute different "kinds." The unassailable unity of the human race exists by virtue of its having been made in the image of God. Only after a divine decision was announced and achieved in the midst of the heavenly assembly (Gen. 1:26) to create this uniqueness, do we find God's concluding approbation: "It was very good" (Gen. 1:31).

Over the centuries the Israelites came to rejoice in God's creation. They brought forth songs of praise, particularly for the wisdom that prompted the display of such perfection (Ps. 8:1–9; 19:1–6; 29:1–11; 33:6–9; 95:1–5; 96:1–13; 147:8–9; 148:1–14; particularly Prov. 8:22–31). The Israelites were moved to worship God because of the ways in which creation reflected God's character. The apostle Paul would later affirm that the invisible nature of God—his eternal power and deity—are clearly perceived in the things he has made (Rom. 1:19–20).

To ancient peoples and to many animistic societies today, all sorts of spirits, powers, and divinities inhabit nature. But the biblical witness utterly refutes this. Nature is not to be worshiped; it is completely devoid of divinities. Rather, God stands totally outside of all that he has made and calls attention to the manifold ways in which every detail speaks of him. The Psalms articulate this again and again (e.g., Ps. 18:11; 29:3–5). Psalm 104 is almost completely devoted to nature. As agriculturalists, the Israelites expressed gratitude for rain, for grass for their cattle, for wine to bring cheer, and for olive oil to make their faces shine. Not only are cattle, vineyards, and fields of grain useful, but strangely, God also made wild donkeys, storks, wild goats, conies, lions, and even whales. Indeed, the sea teems with things innumerable, and all are the objects of his care. Lions "seek their food from God" (v. 21). He feeds the ravens, makes light his garment, speaks in thunder, dwells in clouds, causes volcanoes to erupt, and makes winds his messengers. Indeed, all nature reflects in myriad ways the living God and prompts the psalmists again and again to sing his praise (Ps. 65:9–13; 147:8–9).

But there is a side to the Creation account that gives us a deep sense of pause. In some of the exalted language later used to call all beings to praise God for what he has created, we find allusions to opposing powers of darkness that were overcome to some degree when he brought into existence ex nihilo (from or out of nothing) the heavens and the earth. The Genesis account only alludes to the impenetrable darkness that reigned "over the face of the deep" and the fact that the earth itself was "without form and void." Yet the Holy Spirit brooded over this chaos (Gen. 1:2)! Later passages in Scripture partly lift the veil, and we find stark references to strange symbols and existences such as "Leviathan" (Ps. 74:12–17; Isa. 27:1). Did hostile powers seek to thwart God? If so, they were utterly powerless to resist his succession of creative fiats. In some sense not clear to us, God's creative expressions in word and deed established the beginnings of order in the world. The chaos was not abolished so much as tamed, even domesticated. This taming process began with the creation of light and its inevitable separation from darkness. This set the stage for the subsequent creation of sustainable life on the planet.

This confronts us with a second mystery. When God acts alone, irresistible power, perfection, goodness, and glory characterize all his acts. As a result, he seems to have effortlessly set the stage for the unfolding of all of history. And we are confident that his wisdom and power will not be diminished in the redemptive sequence that is to follow. Having created the human race, he accommodates himself markedly to the freedom he deliberately grants human beings. As before, he remains hidden. But to achieve fully his forthcoming redemptive purpose and to continue thereby the process of self-disclosure, frequent condescension on his part is necessary. In this way God reveals himself as he truly is. Even the cross would be necessary as the ultimate display of what his love is like (Rom. 5:8). God never ceased to remind Israel, and later the church, of the availability of his wisdom and power in his care for his people. Yet they would only know of his capacity to intervene powerfully on their behalf when they actively looked to him in faith. Unfortunately, both Israel and the church have proved to be wayward peoples. Over the centuries God only infrequently intervened to remind his people that he is Creator as well as Redeemer. Such passages as Ezra's reflecting on God as Creator and Deliverer are few and far between (Neh. 9:6–37). Only in the last book of the Bible is the full potential of his divine activity gloriously manifested.

The God who worked by his Spirit to transform the formless and uninhabitable earth into something well balanced, pleasing, and potentially useful has thereby revealed a standard of order and peace in the light of which the subsequent rebellion and misery of the human race should be interpreted. There is no validity to the contention that sin is an illusion and that the present condition of men and women worldwide reflects something other than their tragic alienation from God.

The centrality of the doctrine of Creation is a biblical given. A case in point: Job never had an adequate conception of God until confronted by the marvels of God's creative work and his providential care over all that he had made (38:1–4; 42:5–6).

> Creation is the premise of all sovereignty, all grace, the grace of law, the grace of order, the grace of election, the grace of justification, sanctification and eternal life. "Is it not lawful for me to do what I will with mine own?" (Matt. 20:15). These words of the parable are put in the mouth of the owner of the vineyard, but they clearly instruct us about God. (Ingram 1975: 213)

Furthermore, the God who creates and redeems is dynamic, continuing to work positively, powerfully, and purposefully among all peoples, ever pointing the way to necessary changes and adaptations. This is the meaning of Jesus' witness: "My Father is always at work to this very day, and I, too, am working" (John 5:17). This counters a static view of human existence that tolerates stagnation and is devoid of concern for growth and development. Furthermore, the God who creates is supreme and unique, and he constantly discloses himself as such: "There is no God apart from me, a righteous God and a Savior; there is none but me" (Isa. 45:21). As a result he regards the service of other gods with abhorrence. God specifically forbids it. In this connection, no segment of the human race is exempt. He has jurisdiction over all, and all are accountable to him.

It is significant to note the place and function of Creation in the praying and evangelistic preaching of the early church (Acts 4:24; 14:15; 17:24–27). There is a sense in which the Creation story is the first element of the Christian gospel. It is "good news" to find personal identity in the fact that one has been created by God. Ferdinand Hahn is correct when he points out that the apostles' preaching to the Gentiles presupposes "not the covenant with and the promises to the Fathers, but the care of the Creator" (1965: 135).

The Nature of Human Beings: Male and Female

The Creation account does not provide us with a comprehensive answer to the mystery of the nature of humans: "He created them male and female" (Gen. 5:1–2). However, their dual origin is clearly stated. Adam was "formed . . . from the dust of the ground" (2:7). Eve was fashioned from "one of the man's ribs" (2:21). Both were created in the image and likeness of God (1:26–27). Human beings thereby became whole psychosocial organisms, not merely souls trapped in physical bodies. Although constituted with all other creatures as completely dependent upon their Creator, humans receive the breath of God and are capable of intelligent interaction with God, endowed with the freedom to obey or disobey him. Humans are thus portrayed as created specially to be in a unique relationship with their Creator. Thus, humans are to love the Lord their God with all their heart and with all their soul and with all their strength (Deut. 6:5; 11:1, 22; Matt. 22:37; Mark 12:29; John 10:30).

Stress should be placed on the nonmaterial nature of human beings: they are *discursive* (employing language and reason), *technological* (making tools and using them), *social* (drafting laws and establishing associations), *historical* (concerned with cumulative tradition), *esthetic* (creating nonutilitarian decorations and enjoying them), *ethical* (sensing the importance of moral values), and *religious* (reaching out to the unseen world). We would emphasize their capacity for knowing God. Their very essence is an incurable religiosity: a hunger for relationship with what is transcendent and an eagerness to reflect to some degree God's nature and likeness (Calvin 1960: 43–47). They can be expected to find greatest satisfaction in the sort of activity that not only stimulates the creative faculty and develops individual potential but which also particularly seals this relationship. This follows because the human race was created to serve in God's presence, under his kingly rule, and for his glory in a self-conscious and self-discriminating fashion.

Human beings are sexually differentiated. It is significant that the only specific explanation of the image of God is that it exists as "male and female" (Gen. 1:27). "The primeval form of humanity is the fellowship of man and woman" (Jewett 1975: 36). In other words, the dynamic interaction and fellowship between men and women is a fundamental reflection of the divine image. We cannot conclude that the woman was inferior, either by nature or by function. That she was created to be man's "helper" (Gen. 2:20) does not mean that she must be "subject" to him. The word *helper* is used elsewhere of God as Israel's "help and shield" in time of trouble (e.g., 1 Sam. 7:12 and Ps. 33:20). "It describes a relationship of mutual interdependence, rather than the woman existing for the male's convenience, or as his underling" (Kuhns 1978: 17). God's ideal is that human beings enjoy positive social interaction and ongoing cooperation with one another in spontaneous obedience to the will of God. Only thereby can they truly incorporate the image of God. Further, and much later, Paul would point to the appropriate and healthy relationship of man and woman within marriage as a metaphor for understanding the relationship of Christ and his bride, the church (Eph. 5:23–33). The significance of a person's individual identity and sexuality can only be apprehended through realizing what one is and means to the other person whom one complements sexually. The mystery of manhood and womanhood and their interrelation is so basic to the social existence of human beings that even at the outset of the biblical revelation one begins to anticipate that severe strictures will be made against any form of sexual perversion.

In their complementarity and mutuality Adam and Eve formed what is generally referred to in the Creation account as a human being (Gen. 5:2). Yet, despite the face-to-face intimacy of the life imparted by God (2:7) and the security of a garden (2:8), they needed the recognition of others and the affection of family and friends. To state this is to confront the mystery of culture.

Obviously, the reality of cultural phenomena has missiological significance. Since.all human conscious experience is conceptual, it will always be clothed in cultural forms within specific social and historical situations. This means that a person's faith in God will always be cast in concepts that are cultural in form. Faith cannot exist as a "pure reality" devoid of cultural form. And no cultural form is normative.

But there is more to culture than this. Inherent in any specific culture is the phenomenon of the institution. By this we mean a body of juridical rules oriented toward a common goal, constituting an enduring entity independent of (human) will, and imposing itself on (humans). No research has developed a completely convincing rational explanation for the origin of such institutions as marriage, the state, the nation (originally the clan or tribe), property, or commerce.

When asked, "What is the essence of a person's humanity?" we should reply that it is the sense of responsibility to others and the urge to seek relationship with God. All human beings were created for social involvement and free response to God. One should not say that the image of God was "lost" in the Fall (Gen. 9:6; James 3:9). One cannot remove the image of God from people and still have what the Bible means by being human. When God looks at human beings, he sees his own nature. He also sees finitude and incompleteness. God has ordained that men and women are to love him freely and be his representatives in the world. Only through the gospel will this be fully realized. Indeed, only through Jesus Christ—"the image of the invisible God" and "the second Adam"—will the real meaning of human life be revealed (Rom. 8:29; 1 Cor. 15:47–49; 2 Cor. 3:18; Col. 1:15; de Dietrich 1960: 28). In contrast, secular humanists have little philosophical basis for their exalted words about the dignity of the human race.

The Creation account is of such universal significance that one is pressed to conclude that it is the inalienable right of all people to know the God whose image they bear. Surely God desires that those who know him should share with those who do not know him the reality of God's existence and nature. The Great Commission explicitly expresses what the Creation account implies.

Threats to the Common Ancestry of All Peoples

All peoples are seen in Genesis as having originated at Creation in Adam and Eve, descending from a common ancestor and thus belonging to the same extended family. In Scripture this reality is mentioned again and again. Hence, reflection on the nature of humankind must include reference to the destructive dimensions of nationalism, a profoundly elemental force in human affairs today. On the basis of the Genesis account no people or race should regard itself as superior in origin or essence. It is rather striking that the Old Testament regards human beings as constituting one great family. The unity of the human race is an unassailable reality. "The Old Testament knows nothing of races which are 'naturally inferior' or unworthy of designation as human. . . . The dividing wall between Greeks and barbarians, or between master races and slave nations, which was never wholly overcome in the ancient world, is completely foreign to it. . . . As mankind appears at the beginning of Israel's records as a single entity, so too, in Israel's view of the future, mankind appears as the united community of nations receiving God's new world, and thus returning to their origin" (Eichrodt 1951: 36).

However, down through the centuries this unity has been selfishly forgotten and brutally attacked either because of a perverted sense of individual freedom from all social responsibility or because of the indulgence of irrational group loyalties that generate destructive wars. These two pressing dangers must be exposed.

First, there is the threat of individualism. When individuals become preoccupied with themselves, they increasingly regard with indifference their societal duties. This self-centeredness was the dominant flaw in Cain: "Am I my brother's keeper?" (Gen. 4:9). Again and again in the Scriptures, God called his people to participate willingly in all the natural forms of society: marriage, family, community, and the state. Their involvement in the enrichment and extension of the divine order of these creation ordinances and their shaping of what God would have a "holy people" be in the world would later form part of the essence of "the gospel of the kingdom." The people of God are to love their neighbors as themselves (Lev. 19:18).

Second, the dangers inherent in nationalism militate against the Bible's view of the common ancestry of all human beings. On the surface one might define nationalism as the self-conscious assertion by a people of its own individuality in relation to other peoples. Christians must be supportive of the hungering of formerly subjugated peoples for self-expression and self-determination. However, this can degenerate into a new obsession with human power. Militant nationalism can easily become a tangle of myths and actualities, truths and errors, and begin to assert itself aggressively, even to the point of precipitating aggressive war. This form of national exclusiveness and cultural arrogance appears on the surface to meet certain fundamental needs of people: their desire for purpose in life, for individual significance, and for personal security—all gained through losing themselves in a cause greater than themselves. But within any nation or racial enclave it soon becomes a demonic force through discrimination against minority peoples within its borders and persecution of citizens whose loyalties extend beyond their political boundaries. This form of exaggerated nationalism eventually results in the oppression of anyone who challenges its presuppositions. Militant nationalism is especially challenged by those whose sense of loyalty and obligation extend beyond racial and political fidelity. Those who embrace all members of the human family must call it into question. These issues constantly raise tensions between the church and the state.

One major problem that missionaries have great difficulty resolving is their unconscious or sometimes even conscious assumed sense of racial or cultural superiority. There is a sense in which all Christians are prone to ethnocentrism—and it remains, strangely, the sin they never confess. They can be easily seduced by the blandishments of the nationalists that entice them into participation in discrimination, exploitation, aggression, and war. A love for country consonant with Scripture must keep central a respect for all peoples, because all bear the image of God. One's national loyalty must never condition one's primary loyalty to God. One has only to read the Psalms with their glorification of "the world-embracing Kingship of the God of Israel" and note the care with which room is allowed "in the worship of God for the thought of the universal Kingdom of God (Ps. 93; 96; 97; 99)" (Eichrodt 1951: 39).

The Cultural Mandate

The first obligations God placed on Adam and Eve made explicit certain activities already built into their very essence as human beings. These activities primarily embraced their social existence: marriage (completing humanity and procreating), work (subduing, tilling, guarding), and government (ruling). God's key words are: "rule over," "work . . . and take care of," and "name" the creatures (Gen. 1:26–27; 2:15, 18–25). These commands mark the beginning of a stream of obligation—a mandate for family and community, law and order, culture and civilization, and ecological concern that widens and deepens as it courses through Scripture. By it God calls all who bear his image to the role of vice-regents over this world, to participate responsibly in this task.

It is not surprising then that in creating the human race in his image, God imparted to humans his own creative instinct. This instinct is admittedly secondary and derived, for it is limited by one's potential capability and the availability of materials with which to express this creative function. Furthermore, this instinct must be uncovered, trained, and then used in the service of others and not for self-aggrandizement. It follows that this creative possibility must be proclaimed and effort put forth to assist one and all in its exercise on behalf of others. Only thereby can we be assured of God's concern for the well-being of all (Lev. 19:18, 34; Ps. 8:5–8).

This fact confronts us with a major issue concerning the Kingdom of God—the cultural mandate (Gen. 1:28). As the human race extended its control over the earth under God's direction and for his glory, it encountered resistance. The existence of a serpent that would later tempt Eve (3:1–5) indicates that since Creation "the powers" have sought to usurp God's rule over the earth and that God's intent in Creation was to call forth a people who would participate with him in its reclamation. Indeed, God's placing Adam "in the Garden of Eden to work it and take care of it" (2:15) takes on significance when we realize that the Hebrew word for "keep" (*šāmar*) is a military term. This world needs to be guarded lest its rivers and air be polluted, its forests and minerals depleted, and its living creatures ruthlessly destroyed. Ecological responsibility comes within the cultural mandate.

Psalm 8 reinforces the relevancy of the cultural mandate. The question is raised: "What is man that you are mindful of him, the son of man that you care for him?" (v. 4). In response, attention is called to the majesty and dignity of every human being: "You made him a little lower than the heavenly beings and crowned him with glory and honor" (v. 5). Then follows specific reference to this mandate:

> You made him ruler over the works of your hands;
>   you put everything under his feet:
> all flocks, and herds,
>   and the beasts of the field,
> the birds of the air,
>   and the fish of the sea,
>   all that swim the paths of the seas. (vv. 6–8)

The totality of human existence and the physical world comes within the concern of the cultural mandate. But not quite! We shall find that the Bible again and again speaks of sin in terms of injustice, oppression, and exploitation. Hence, it is significant that whereas the cultural mandate commands that people subdue and have dominion over everything on the earth—whether animate or inanimate—human beings are excluded.

Actually, people lose their true humanity when they take to themselves the role of God. Marxist atheism was nowhere more blatant than in Marx's claim: "Man is the highest being for man." Such a dogma encouraged Marxist rulers to believe in their autonomy. They felt free to function without the restraint that comes from submission to God. Inevitably, the suffering that they have caused has been incalculable.

To summarize, at the beginning of Genesis we find the cultural mandate clearly distinguished from the redemptive purpose that God began to unfold after the fall. The former calls all men and women to participate in the work of civilization. The latter will represent his gracious work to reconcile a fallen human race to himself. In terms of obligation it calls the people of God to participate with him in making Christ known "in the whole world as a testimony to all nations" (Matt. 24:14). When Jesus inaugurates the Kingdom of God, these two mandates will fuse into one fundamental task. The New Testament does not separate evangelism from social responsibility. "The routine of participation in human civilization is the very arena of obedience to God" (Walhout 1963: 520).

The Fall

The primeval paradise was characterized by beauty, utility, and the moral test symbolized by "the tree of the knowledge of good and evil" (Gen. 2:16–17) that was forbidden to Adam and Eve. The tree was set before them as an alternative to discipleship. Would they choose to remain in face-to-face relation with God as his vice-regents over the earth? Or would they choose a separate existence to be self-made, wresting their knowledge, satisfaction, and values from the created world in defiance of the Creator? Adam and Eve chose the latter alternative.

The Tempter

The Bible provides no philosophical or speculative account of the ultimate origin of evil. It is also silent concerning the creation of beings within the spirit world. We are pressed to assume that there must have been a rebellion within that segment of God's created order prior to the fall of the human race. This leads us to conclude that when Satan sought to deceive Eve, the larger universe must have been filled with darkness and riddled with a spirit of rebellion against God. Even so, evil was not created by God or allowed to exist outside of his control. Nevertheless, it is an active demonic power, possessed by an incomprehensible hatred toward God (Childs 1970: 49).

However, the dominion God originally granted to humans did not extend to the world of spirits—the good and the evil. This is the more interesting when one considers, first, that it was an evil spirit that occasioned the Fall and, second, that the spirit world occupies considerable prominence in the New Testament as both beneficial to the people of God (angels, Heb. 1:14) and antagonistic to them (demons, Eph. 6:12).

The Temptation

It is rather significant that we are not told why Satan, in the guise of a serpent, first sought to disrupt the relationship between Eve and God. An ancient Jewish midrash states that he longed for her personally. He thought, "I will be king of the earth. I will walk tall and be honored. I will eat the finest foods of the world. I will wed Eve. Then I will destroy Adam." Hence, Satan's primary objective was to get Eve to question the seriousness of God's specific instruction (permission vs. forbiddance) respecting the fruit of two central trees in the garden (Gen. 2:16, 17), thus discrediting God in her eyes.

Once achieved, the rest would be easy. God's Word must be so subtly reconceptualized that Eve would begin to question whether God really had her best interests at heart (Gen. 3:1–5). Soon she "saw that the fruit of the tree was good for food and pleasing to the eye, and also desirable for gaining wisdom, [so] she took some and ate it" (3:6). Adam abruptly followed her example: his sin was more deliberate. Together they usurped God's prerogative and made themselves the masters of good and evil. They set themselves up as autonomous deities "knowing" (that is, deciding for themselves) what was "good and evil" (Jocz 1961: 44). They thereby abdicated their role as God's vice-regents in this world, rejected all responsibility to care for and control God's creatures, and refused to carry out the cultural mandate under God's direction and for his glory. They thrust God from the center of their existence, enthroned themselves, and began to use this world to further their own ends.

The Resulting Death Process

God had been very explicit in stating what would result from any violation of his ruling concerning the forbidden fruit of the tree of the knowledge of good and evil:

"for when you eat of it you will surely die" (Gen. 2:17—literally, "dying you shall die"). As a result, a death process began in Adam and Eve, a sickening that would eventuate in their physical death ("to dust you will return," 3:19). This tendency would corrupt and disrupt their relationships with God (3:10), between man and woman (3:12), between Cain and Abel (4:8), and with the environment (3:17–19). Their marriage relation would become vulnerable to the pressure of lower drives ("desire" and "domination"). Life in a cursed world would take on an unending bitterness. Making fig leaves to hide the shame of their nakedness (3:7) was a far different use of human ingenuity than was first intended or expected.

The Impact of the Fall on Women

The Fall brought about the gradual decline of the place of women in society. In their primeval innocence, nothing separated Adam and Eve: "The man and his wife were both naked, and they felt no shame" (Gen. 2:25). There were "no barriers, no secrets, no regrets, no facades, no intimidations, no status distinctions, no suspicion" (Eller 1973: 21). However, after they sinned they became conscious of their separation from God and "hid from the LORD God" (Gen. 3:8). They also began to sense their separation from each other and became ashamed of their nakedness (3:7). Sex roles became increasingly rigid. The response of God to their excuses and disobedience included a detailed series of predictions of what would inevitably result from the divisions that would overtake them (3:16–19). Women would become increasingly burdened and passive, as a result of their priorities of childbearing and nurturing. Men would become aggressive as they sought to make the "cursed" earth productive. Inevitably, the more they drifted apart, the less they would understand each other. Concerning this, Lois Clemens summarizes:

> In most human cultures, the woman is considered a lower human being than the male, less wise, less intelligent than he, and lacking in many of his capabilities and abilities. It is evident that when the woman must be the cricket on the hearth caring for the young while the man is the eagle on the wing broadening his experiences and increasing his observations, her limited experiences make her appear less highly endowed than man. (1971: 21)

The Downfall of Satan

When Eve confessed that the serpent had deceived her and that in her confusion she had deliberately broken God's commandment about the forbidden fruit, God turned to the serpent and called down on him a sweeping curse. Henceforth the serpent's role would be beneath that of all cattle and all wild animals. He would not be anyone's king. He would crawl on his belly rather than stand tall, he would eat dust rather than the finest foods, and an abiding enmity would forever exist between him and the woman, between her seed and his seed (Gen. 3:14, 15a). The two would come to a final encounter in which the "seed of the woman" would suffer, but the "seed of the serpent" would be totally destroyed (v. 15b).

This intimation of conflict and triumph with its focus on "the seed of the woman" long engaged the reflection of Christian scholars in the early church. Some contended on the basis of New Testament theology that one must predicate a "fuller sense" (*sensus plenior*) that was not apparent initially but which existed in the mind of God when this judgment on Satan was first uttered. Significantly, the Jewish translators of the Septuagint in the third or second century B.C. rendered "the seed" as a masculine, singular pronoun: "He will crush your head" (Gen. 3:15). By this decision they unwittingly provided evidence of the intensification of messianic expectations among the Jews in the centuries immediately preceding the birth of Jesus. This expectation was reiterated by Irenaeus (A.D. 150–200). Irenaeus underscored the fact that because Christ had been born of the Virgin Mary, he would therefore be able to overcome Satan at the cross. He quoted Galatians 4:4 to substantiate this. But the only statement in the New Testament about Satan being crushed represents God as yet to accomplish this (Rom. 16:20).

Although rabbinic Judaism teaches that Adam through the Fall lost the image of God (Wilson 1989: 126), it tends to downplay anything as severe as "original sin." Whereas Protestant theologians are not fully agreed as to what "the seed of the woman" refers, Luther pointedly identified it with the virgin-born Christ, whereas Calvin saw only God's promise of victory over all evil, whether Satanic or human. We should stand back from this argument and affirm the truly "good news" that the evil spirit that controlled the serpent will not have the last word in human history. The New Testament is emphatic in stating that this promise of final victory will be achieved by Christ even though the Hebrew text cannot be made to predict that "the seed of the woman" applies to him alone.

When Christ came to "save his people from their sins" (Matt. 1:21), the natural expectation was that he would deal with evil in its totality. This truly happened. He took to himself the totality of human sin and received in himself the fullness of God's righteous judgment of that sin (Rom. 5:16). In addition, at the cross he also conquered all evil "powers and authorities" (Col. 2:15), including the intruder, "that ancient serpent, who is the devil" (Rev. 20:2), the one who spoiled and soiled a world that was initially "very good" (Gen. 1:31). Jesus the Christ demonstrated the reality of the conquest of all evil by his bodily resurrection from the dead on the third day. That first Easter was the greatest event in all salvation history. As a result we can hold firmly to two certainties: (1) although enmity will character-ize the relation between "the seed" and the fallen spirit world, the Kingdom of God will be fully and finally established in the last day; and (2) Jesus' resurrection from the dead enables the people of God today to confess that on the other side of physical death they "will be with the Lord forever" (1 Thess. 4:17), possessing "eternal life" (John 3:16; 6:47).

God's final judgment was to expel Adam and Eve from paradise. This was an act of mercy, for his universe could not tolerate an "eternal life in sin," nor could its misery be endured. They could not return to the garden, even if they had wanted to. Henceforth, whether they or their descendants would ever enjoy happy fellowship with God depends entirely upon God. From this time onward, all human labor acquired a bitter dimension in the divine discipline (Gen. 3:17–19). God's judgment includes sweat in connection with humanity's wresting nourishment from a reluctant soil. The rest of the Bible unfolds the manner in which God, while not condoning the rebellious pride of men and women nor leaving their sin unpunished, will seek the objective God had in view for them from the beginning.

Intimations of Grace

Despite the darkness of this record of the entrance of sin and rebellion into the beginnings of the human family, we find encouraging intimations of the grace of God. The first evidence of God's continuing concern for human beings is to be found in what God did shortly after humanity's rebellion had taken place. Noting the sense of shame that overtook Adam and Eve and considering their efforts to cover their nakedness with aprons of leaves, God came to their rescue with garments of skins he made for them. God then proceeded to clothe them (Gen. 3:21). We can readily imagine the awe that might have overtaken these two—and their gratitude for his undeserved kindness to them.

But what would they have learned from this kindness? Would it be far-fetched to infer that as they were being driven from Eden into the unknown world beyond, this provision of adequate clothing somehow stirred them with a measure of hope about what lay ahead? If God was mindful of the need to cover their nakedness, was it not possible that he might do other things to assure them of his continuing concern for them? Did he thereby legitimize the slaughter of animals and the possibility of using their flesh for food and their skin and hides for leather goods as well as for clothing? Though such questions are stimulated by the text, they cannot be answered from the information given to us in the Genesis narrative.

Cornelius Van Til develops his reflection on the Fall by underscoring the realities of universal sin and inevitable death but goes on to suggest that by the common grace God lavishes on all peoples, God

> restrains the destructive process of sin within mankind in general and enables people, though not "born again" (through God's "special grace"—Titus 2:11–14), to develop the latent forces of the universe and thus make positive contributions to the cultural mandate given through the first man Adam, in Paradise. (1962: 374)

Had God's "common grace" not been widely operative from the Fall onward, the human race would have long since destroyed itself.

We should thank God for the many decent, public-spirited people in all human societies. We rejoice that God has enabled them to utilize economic, political, educational, aesthetic, and other means to abate the destructive forces of evil. At the same time we should never underestimate the profound seriousness of sin or its terribly destructive tendencies in all societies and among all peoples. Citizens of the Kingdom should take the lead in their support of all forms of effective social service, praying all the while, "Your kingdom come, your will be done on earth as it is in heaven" (Matt. 6:10).

Cain and Abel

This somber account reflects the fallenness of the human heart (the flesh) and the seductive aspects of human civilization (the world). Cain worshiped in arrogance and Abel in faith. Jealousy erupted into premeditated murder. Cain judged that he had the right to dominate his brother and killed him. He then went on to disclaim all responsibility for him: "Am I my brother's keeper?" (Gen. 4:9). His fallenness was thereby confirmed by his conduct. In response God showed himself to be concerned for both the innocent victim and the impenitent sinner. He is the God of justice as well as the God of mercy. From now on Cain the fugitive would bear a protecting mark (4:12, 15).

Lamech's taunt song (Gen. 4:23–24) reveals the escalation as well as the progress of sin. Whereas Cain had committed only one murder, Lamech gloried in reckless killing. At this point the narrative abruptly turns from all further reference to the line of Cain. Should we see in this the beginnings of the phenomenon of individuals so hardening their hearts that they put themselves beyond the pale of God's redemptive outreach?

On the other hand, we should seriously consider the fact that despite their alienation from God, the Cainites in their cultural development ranged from agriculture to husbandry, from science to art, and from music to metallurgy (Gen. 4:17–22). Although one might feel God should have had nothing to do with this violent and warlike people, it is significant that in later years God made much use of Cainite techniques for his people. His endorsement extended from their seminomadic existence to their settling in cities and developing arts and crafts. The thrice-repeated phrase—"he was father of all such"—acknowledges a genuine cultural indebtedness and prepares us to accept for ourselves "a similar indebtedness to secular enterprise; for the Bible nowhere teaches that the godly should have all the gifts" (Kidner 1973: 78).

Conclusion

Flowing directly from the account of Cain and Abel, the closing section of Genesis is briefly taken up with relating the story of their descendants and families, along with general comments about their moral character and cultural and societal development (4:17–22). Then rather abruptly the account switches back to Adam and Eve. When this couple was one hundred and thirty years old, God gave them a son, whom they named Seth (literally, "Appointed"). Attention is particularly focused on Eve's comment on this occasion. "God has granted me another child in place of Abel, since Cain killed him" (v. 25). Did this statement grow out of her prolonged reflection on what God had earlier said about the conquest of evil through the woman's zeal (3:15)? Would something new replace Cain's line? We cannot presume to know what was on her mind. But we must note that in the beginnings of the line of Seth, we encounter a remarkable comment that "at that time men began to call on the name of the LORD" (4:26).

Despite this engaging thought, the next section of Genesis largely focuses on the continuation of humanity's progressive deterioration in its ongoing bondage to sin and evil. In the next chapter we are made increasingly aware of the universality of human sinfulness.

Humanity's descent into evil develops to such a degree that God came to the point of repenting of ever having made the human race (Gen. 6:6). But not entirely so, for in the midst of two severe judgments we find the groundwork being laid for the beginning of God's redemptive plan for all nations.

3

God Judges Humanity
The Flood and Babel

Introduction

With this chapter the cosmic conflict between God's sublime purpose for humankind and Satan's "dominion of darkness" takes on new dimensions. First, we are confronted with Seth's lengthy genealogy, culminating with such notables as Enoch, who "walked with God"; Methuselah, who lived for "nine hundred and sixty-nine years"; and Noah, a "righteous man, blameless in his generation," and the father of Ham, Shem, and Japheth. Noah's father gave him this name ("Rest") in expectation that he would "comfort us in the labor and painful toil of our hands" (Gen. 5:29). Little did he anticipate the radical way in which Noah would serve God and further the divine purpose for the human race.

The tragic refrain of this lengthy genealogy is the repeated phrase "and he died." Despite their great longevity, these antediluvians (that is, those who lived before the Flood) all eventually died. But there was one exception: "Enoch walked with God; then he was no more, because God took him away" (Gen. 5:24). By this break in the dreary evidence of human mortality, we not only find the possibility of personal relationship with God (see also Noah in Gen. 6:9) but also, by implication, existence beyond physical death. Derek Kidner states that the phrase "God took him" left its mark on the Old Testament. He finds parallels in Psalm 49:15 and 73:24 and then adds, "As Enochs and Elijahs were rare, this hope did not easily become general, but at least twice the gates of Sheol had not prevailed" (1967: 81). We will find that the word *salvation* in its later use refers primarily to all that the believing people of God experienced. They know the "goodness of the LORD in the land of the living" (Ps. 27:13). Yet this record of the translation of Enoch must have convinced many that death could not negate God's continued care of all peoples. We recall the confession, "Whom have I in heaven but you? And earth has nothing I desire besides you. My flesh and my heart may fail, but God is the strength of my heart and my portion forever" (Ps. 73:25–26). The believing Israelite could draw from this ancient record intimations, even anticipations of life after death as a conscious ongoing existence with Yahweh, the Lord (Aldwinckle 1982: 19–31). But Karl Hartenstein would also have us understand that these very old stories of sinful rebellion against the Creator underscore

> the fundamental fact upon which the whole world of human religion has been built up. Religion . . . means the deification of man and therefore the humanization of God. The "ego" of the creature has asserted itself against the holy will of God and has freed itself from the bonds of freedom into which it has been created. The effect of this basic fact has ended in the slavery of [humans] to the spirits and demons, to sin and death. That is the comprehensive view of the Bible with regard to humanity, that behind all human thought and decision there lies the initial decision against the Lord, the religious revolution against the holy God. (1939: 124)

The apostle Paul later develops this theme theologically in his epistle to the Romans (1:21–32). What shall we say about this cryptic passage (Gen. 6:1–4) with its record of evil: the spirit world penetrating the world of fallen human beings and intermingling sexually with them? Final identification of "the sons of the gods" is impossible. They may represent sinful Sethites, but this seems improbable. We tend with Hartenstein to think of them as fallen angels who "did not keep their positions but abandoned their own home" (Jude 6). The account breathes the atmosphere of ancient myth with its unrestrained polygamy, reminding us, as in Greek mythology, of the love adventures of Apollo or the legends of Hercules. Should we see in this the activity of Satan, through the pollution of women, attempting nothing less than the degradation of the entire race so that the promised seed of the woman (Gen. 3:15) would be nothing less than the offspring of that which is demon-possessed? If so, we would then perceive God's mission through God's people as standing firmly and proclaiming loudly against any such dehumanization of women, the poor, and the marginalized.

Of one thing we can be sure. This portrayal of willful sin demonstrates that God gives his creatures freedom to oppose his will—so greatly does he prize freedom (Knight 1959: 197). The tragedy is that this freedom often leads to flagrant sin, the sort that the later Sinaitic sacrificial system will not cover (Num. 15:30; Ps. 19:13).

The Wrath of God

In the biblical record of the manner in which the living God made himself known to his people, the phrase "wrath of God" occurs again and again. Hebrew possesses more words (nine in all) than English to represent this reality. It is significant that the Bible does not use the dichotomy of saying that his wrath was directed against human sin, whereas his love for sinners remained unchanged. There is a sense in which he hates "all who do wrong" (Ps. 5:5) yet at the same time "wants all . . . to be saved and to come to a knowledge of the truth" (1 Tim. 2:4).

The Old Testament is a book of judgment. Because God is both holy and just, he must judge those who violate his laws. Only thereby can he uphold his integrity. He plays no favorites: his people do not escape. Both Israel and Judah were removed from the land that God had given them at the time of the Assyrian and Babylonian invasions—catastrophes second only to the Flood in severity and extent. This should make us conscious of the peril faced by those nations who do not acknowledge God (Jer. 25:15–33). God's wrath fell upon Israel for its breach of covenant (Lev. 10:1–2; Num. 16:33, 46–50) and for its mistreatment of the minority peoples in its midst (Jer. 7:6–7; 22:3–5; Ezek. 22:7–16; Zech. 7:9–14). And judgment fell upon non-Israelites for their oppression of his chosen people (Ezek. 36:5). Judgment will fall on those who reject Jesus Christ (John 16:8) and upon the Gentile nations in the great day of judgment: the day of the Lord (Isa. 2:10–22; Jer. 30:7–8; Joel 3:12ff.; Obad. 3ff.; Zeph. 3:8ff.; Schoonhoven 1966: 33).

The Flood

The Flood is a significant and vivid pictorialization of this wrath. The antediluvian race sank into utter depravity and violence (Gen. 6:5, 11). Eventually, even the Sethites, who had begun "to call on the name of the Lord" (4:26), also became defiled. After a long period of warning, the Flood came upon this decadent people, and the world of Genesis abruptly came to an end. We should note that

> the record neither affirms nor denies that man existed beyond the Mesopotamian valley. Noah was certainly not a preacher of righteousness to the peoples of Africa, India, China or America—places where there is evidence for the existence of [humans] many thousands of years before the flood. The emphasis is upon that group of cultures from which Abraham eventually came. (Ramm 1954: 239–40)

This first judgment has profound implications for a biblical understanding of the mission of the church. First, the whole world lies under the curse of the sin of humankind, which encourages people to imagine they can live independently of their Creator.

Second, God's wrath is introduced in Scripture as the permanent, unchanging expression of his heartfelt reaction to all that is contrary to his holy love. Only the spirit of the Antichrist could be behind the impulse to remove from gospel proclamation the obligation to proclaim, "God . . . commands all people everywhere to repent" (Acts 17:30). But how should people be brought to repentance? Christians have invariably and truthfully claimed: by prayer and the proclamation of the law that makes people conscious of their sin (Rom. 3:20) and especially by pointing them to the "goodness of God"—displayed on the cross of Christ—which "leads you toward repentance" (Rom. 2:4).

Third, whereas God may cease to strive with any particular generation of sinful people when they go "too far" in resisting him, this does not mean he desires the total destruction of the human race. A new world was anticipated with the introduction of Noah and his family. And finally, although only Noah is described as "righteous before God," we should see significance in the grace of God that brought deliverance to his household (Acts 16:31; 1 Peter 3:20). One is reminded of those occasions in Acts when whole households believed and were baptized (Boer 1961: 161–85).

The Universal Noahic Covenant

Inasmuch as the concept of covenant dominates Scripture, we would expect it to be introduced early in the record of God's dealings with people. Not only did God take Noah into his confidence when he decreed the judgment of a society that was destroying itself (Gen. 6:13), but he also promised to establish a covenant (6:18) that pledged to deliver Noah and his family and would involve their participation in a new life beyond the Flood. Noah willingly accepted this by faith (Heb. 11:7). God followed with instruction regarding the ark, the animals, and the time to seek its shelter. We note Noah's impressive obedience (Gen. 7:5, 9, 16). When all had been completed, it was with fatherly concern that "the Lord shut him in" (7:16).

After this judgment had ended, God "remembered" Noah, caused the water to abate, and brought the ark safely to Ararat. Noah expressed his gratitude for this deliverance through offering God sacrifice and worship. God graciously responded with what is known as the Noahic covenant, with its unconditional promise of no future worldwide catastrophe until the last day (Gen. 8:21–22; 9:11; 2 Peter 3:7). The rainbow was appointed as a visible and reassuring sign to remind everyone of this promise (Gen. 9:12–17). Although we are made aware in the narrative of the distance that separated Noah from God, we discern in this covenant the beginnings of a new sequence in God's dealings with humankind. Ultimately they will eventuate in "a new heaven and a new earth" (Rev. 21:1) in which a redeemed people will enjoy forever his presence, friendship, and service.

The Noahic covenant has mission implications of first magnitude. First, we note the sovereign reaching out on God's part in his mysterious selection of Noah for salvation and service. Noah was of the line of Seth. He possessed a measure of godly heritage and gave sufficient response to God to be "found righteous before him." And yet he was a man of flawed character (Gen. 9:20–21). Biblical theology postulates the reality of God's unconditional election and sovereign call. No other dimension of his activity so humbles the people of God. Furthermore, it provokes great tension between them and the world. Jesus referred to this when he stated: "If you belonged to the world, it would love you as its own. As it is, you do not belong to the world, but I have chosen you out of the world. That is why the world hates you" (John 15:19). This reality—divine election—is deeply woven into the fabric of salvation history and must be proclaimed as "good news." But this is only possible if one rejects the unbiblical notion that long before the foundation of the world God willed some to be saved and others to be damned. The essence of the gospel is that Jesus Christ is God's elect (Eph. 3:11). Election must not be construed as God's selectivity whereby some are predestined to eternal life and "the reprobates" are predestined to eternal damnation. The gospel must be freely preached as good news for all peoples everywhere, or it is not good news at all (Daane 1973: 177–205)!

Second, the essence of the biblical concept of covenant is "Obey me, and I will be your God and you will be my people. Walk in all the ways that I command you, that it may go well with you" (Jer. 7:23). God's participation in a covenant is predicated upon his faithfulness. In and through the Flood—a dramatic portrayal of his wrath against sin—he remained faithful to his creation and to his elect.

Third, unlike later covenants, God's pledge to Noah included all peoples and implied his provision of "common grace" for their continued enabling to carry out the cultural mandate (Gen. 9:1–7). He sought to restrain the violence that had corrupted the earth (6:11) by a prohibition against murder (9:5–6). By this he linked the beginnings of a specific revelation of "divine law," its validity and penalty, with the sacredness of human life. With this is included his great concern for justice in society (9:6). All life comes from God and remains his. This includes a taboo against blood, which will take on great significance in the Levitical holiness code (Lev. 17–26) and will become a basic redemptive principle (Heb. 9:11–10:18). Its normative character will be found inherent in apostolic preaching (Acts 15:20; 21:25; etc.).

Finally, Noah's oracle (Gen. 9:25–27) concerning his sons uses the conventional name (Yahweh: Lord) in connection with Shem (9:26) and intimates that salvation history will be worked out through this branch of Noah's descendants. In this we confront again the principle of God's sovereign selectivity. The oracle concerning Japheth (9:27) is obscure but exciting. Whereas the Old Testament is silent about Japhethites actually dwelling in Shem's tents, the New Testament repeatedly predicts a vast ingathering of Gentiles through the gospel that was initially offered to the Jewish people (Matt. 8:11; Rom. 1:16; Eph. 3:6; Rev. 5:9–10).

Rabbinic Judaism has long contended that the Jewish claim to divine election did not mean that God had rejected the nations. Indeed, the nations are spoken of as "Noachides," meaning that they are regarded as "equally righteous before the Lord so long as they keep the Noachide commandments which represent the basic principles of morality and social responsibility" (Talmage 1975: 6). These commandments were subsequently amplified by the rabbis to embrace a "Torah for Gentiles" with particular stress laid on refraining from (1) idolatry; (2) incest and adultery; (3) bloodshed; (4) blasphemy; (5) injustice and lawlessness; (6) robbery; and (7) inhumane conduct, such as eating the flesh of a living animal (Rosenberg 1986: 87 and Wilson 1989: 49). Sadly, the confidence with which rabbis affirm the application of the Noahic covenant to all peoples has not been matched by any mission activity on the part of the Jewish people to the Gentile nations.

Today, when rabbinically informed Jewish people discuss with Gentiles social and political problems of national and international concern, they tend to use the Noahic tradition of universal human ethics as their frame of reference. Significantly, they regard the Sinaitic covenant that God made with the Israelites as a distinct complement to the Noachide laws. Through obeying its laws, however, the Jewish people gain a separate identity that sets them apart from the nations of the world (Breslaner 1984: 199). Actually, the suggestion of a "Torah for Gentiles" based on rabbinic additions to the Noahic covenant has little meaning for those Jews or Gentiles who confess that Jesus Christ is the Lord of creation and Savior of the world. To the rabbis, such a confession is nothing less than "idolatry" (calling a man "God") and involves the irrevocable breaking of the first Noachide commandment.

The Table of Nations

The Noahic covenant stipulated that the whole earth be repeopled by the descendants of Noah. This would involve separation and scattering, the formation of clans, tribes, and nations, and the apportioning of the world to receive them. Before recording the judgment (chap. 11) by which the divine purpose was enforced, Genesis gives us a partial genealogy of the different peoples that came from Noah's three sons. In this table of nations (Gen. 10:1–32), we find evidence of God's superintending providence: "In the past, he let all nations go their own way" (Acts 14:16). Paul later expressed on Mars Hill, "From one man [God] made every nation of men, that they should inhabit the whole earth; and he determined the times set for them and the exact places where they should live" (Acts 17:26). Here is a radical break with anything mythic regarding the nations that inhabit the earth. True, not every nation later mentioned in the Old Testament is found here, but we may rightly conclude that the unity of the human race is underscored. Significantly, the families of Japheth (Gen. 10:2–5) and Ham (10:6–20) are mentioned first. Since the subsequent focus of the Old Testament is on the family of peoples rooted in Shem, the record concludes with their diversity (10:21–30).

It is striking that Israel is not mentioned directly and is only "represented . . . by a name that is completely neutral for her faith and sacred history—Arpachshad!" (Von Rad 1961: 141). Israelites should never claim that they are any different from other peoples. Indeed, their prophets would remind them again and again that they are not fundamentally superior by birth or history (e.g., "your ancestry and your birth were in the land of the Canaanites; your father was an Amorite and your mother a Hittite," Ezek. 16:3). Hence, we should conclude from this table of nations that the universal concern of God is ever dominant in his thought. Von Rad comments further:

> Israel looked at herself in the midst of the international world without illusion and quite unmythically. What Israel learns and experiences of Yahweh occurs exclusively within the realm of history. For biblical theology the inclusion of the table of nations means a radical break with myth. (1961: 141)

The Tower of Babel

The record of the first human attempt to create a universal kingdom (Gen. 11:1–9) is filled with pathos and tragedy. Fallen humanity revealed its insecurity, vanity, and self-centeredness by disobeying God's command to scatter and populate the earth. The descendants of Noah were determined to maintain their primeval unity, based on one language, a central living space, and a single aim (B. Anderson 1977: 63). Their determination to build the tower points to both arrogance and futility: something akin to striving for the impossible ("a tower that reaches to the heavens," 11:4). Had they scattered as God intended, they might have gradually and peacefully divided into diverse linguistic and cultural groupings. This would inevitably have resulted as each separate geographical situation prompted the creation of its own distinctive vocabulary. One must not forget that all living languages undergo continual change, and "this change takes place in both their phonological and their grammatical structures" (Beals 1977: 524).

But God deliberately frustrated the builders. He so accelerated the inevitable process of linguistic change that discord and tension filled their ranks, and the separate families fled from one another. The tower was never finished, and the world eventually became a "babble" of many tongues (at least six thousand!). From this time onward the kingdom of Babel (Gen. 10:8–9) would increasingly reflect the spirit that rebels against God.

When one reads the Babel story in its literary context alongside chapter ten of Genesis, with its record of the diversification of humanity, one finds no basis for the simplistic view that ethnic pluralism is merely God's judgment on human sinfulness. The linguistic diversification at Babel is presented as God's merciful way to avoid destroying the whole human race determined to rebel against him. In the Noahic covenant God had promised never again to do that. Diversity is not without its positive dimensions. Eschatological portrayals of the consummation of God's redemptive purpose focus on human unity within diversity rather than on a homogenized unity of disparate peoples (B. Anderson 1977: 64, 68). This became initially apparent on the day of Pentecost (Acts 2:1–13). Through the outpouring of the Holy Spirit, God initiated the transition from particularity (Israel) to universality (Gentiles as well as Jews). This marked the beginnings of a truly universal kingdom, "the first token of which was the gift of tongues, which pointed forward to the reunion of the nations, when the promise would be fulfilled that they should all be gathered into the tents of Shem" (Edersheim 1949: 64, in reference to Gen. 9:27). Significantly, the emerging church became increasingly an entity that was enriched through the diversity within its unity.

In the Babel story we uncover themes, old and new, that inform our theology of mission. First is the reminder that there is a limit to God's grace. In our day, when much theological discussion focuses on the welfare of people to the neglect of serious reflection on the holiness of God, the impression is given that God is virtually indifferent to sinfulness. The popular thesis is that, despite all evil conduct and indifference to him, God can be counted on to respond with more grace, more goodness. Not so. As with the Flood, so also here God reveals himself as a God of judgment. This should heighten our sense of conviction and urgency: "The whole will of God" must be proclaimed (Acts 20:27). Today is "the day of salvation" (2 Cor. 6:2). Tomorrow, "each of us will give account of himself to God" (Rom. 14:12).

Second, a theology of mission whose focus is "to bring together [the scattered children of God] and make them one" (John 11:52) must come to terms with the implications of this judgment. The difficulties of cross-cultural evangelism and the complexity of appreciating cultural and linguistic diversity need to be recognized. Equally important is the obligation to express the church's essential unity in Christ. At Babel God was deeply involved in fracturing the human race, shattering its unity, and scattering people over the face of the earth, even though this was also an act of grace in preserving the lives of those present at Babel. God's mission through the church will seek to reverse the fragmentation that came at Babel. He will create a unity out of human diversity that will be not so much a homogenized oneness as a unity that preserves diversity. In Christ, a new humanity will be created, and the old dividing walls of hostility will be abolished (Eph. 2:14–22). In the closing book of the canon, we read that in the new heaven and new earth the apostle John speaks of God dwelling with "his people" (Rev. 21:3).

Third, it is a fundamental human desire to "make a name" (Gen. 11:4). This tendency exists today in the nationalistic aspirations of peoples. How frequently we have seen nations give way to idolatrous exaltation of themselves and then become hostile toward other peoples. The people of God must expose the idolatry latent in nationalism. The church that tolerates nationalist tendencies will be defective in its prophetic witness or at best will be paternalistically destructive in its missionary outreach.

Fourth, the descendants of Noah did not profit from the warning of the Flood that a holy God is concerned with the conduct of his creatures and must punish all disobedience to his will. People appear to learn little from history. Scripture discourages all minimizing of the terrible reality of sin and the alienation from a holy God that it has brought to the human race.

Conclusion

We gain from this record of primeval history much insight into the God who is, who creates, who speaks, and who rules. He begins the disclosure of himself as the sovereign Creator: gracious, orderly, and progressive in his activity—first, in creating the universe and finally in creating humans: "male and female." The primary mandate he places on the human race is to accept responsibility for this world. Neither transitional device nor apology is used to link this record of primeval history to Israel's fathers, the patriarchs (Gen. 11:27–32).

The theme of Genesis 1–11 is that the human race in its fallenness tends to destroy God's good creation. And yet God demonstrates that he is the God of grace as well as the God of judgment. No matter how sinful people become and how severe God's punishment, his grace never fails to provide a fresh start. God is irrevocably committed to his creation. When one reflects on what the human race did at Babel by giving way to the Promethean impulse to storm the heavens and totally resist God's purpose that men and women multiply, fill the earth, and subdue it under his direction and for his glory, we can only marvel at the mitigation of his righteous indignation. We are grateful that he did not totally abandon the human race.

There is a tendency among biblical scholars to forge too close a link between the Kingdom of God concept as articulated by Jesus and the Davidic kingship (e.g., Bright 1953: 19). As a result earlier portions of Scripture are passed over as possessing little relevance to one's understanding of the Kingdom. Actually, these first chapters of Genesis confront us with the essence of God's absolute and dynamic rule over his creation, particularly over the human race, the appointed vice-regents of his world. He exercises his sovereign and creative authority by speaking: he speaks and things happen. Moreover, he also speaks through events. These events are not isolated from space/time realities in order to reflect timeless, eternal truths. Rather, they are part of the movement of human history. For this reason we are reluctant to regard the *tôlēdōt* ("generations of") subsections in Genesis 1–11 as different from other sections that identify by name the several family records making up this first book of the Hebrew canon (5:1; 10:1; 11:10, 27; 25:12, 19; 36:1, 9; 37:2). This means we find no justification for regarding the details of Genesis 1–11 as of a different order than the rest of Genesis. As a result we have been unwilling to interpret this portion mythologically or existentially, that is, as reflecting propositional truths unrelated to actual historical events. God's self-disclosure begins with Creation. The Fall actually took place. Cain was a murderer. There was a flood and a righteous man named Noah. And in the ancient world one could visit the ruins of a massive, unfinished tower.

From this account of Creation and Fall, we must draw certain presuppositions without which all subsequent reflection on mission will be invalid. First, the God who created human beings should be the object of their worship and thanksgiving. That the great majority appears unthankful for life, health, and food betrays their alienation from him. Second, since the human race lives in ignorance or defiance of God and his law and since God is a seeking God (Gen. 3:8–9), we would expect him to superintend history from this time forward, not for human contentment but to restore the order he originally intended for all who bear his image. Third, the goal of mission should not be so narrowly conceived that it focuses solely on the humanization of society and tends to overlook or minimize God's call to all people everywhere to repent (Acts 17:30).

Fourth, down through history and throughout the world scholars have traced the noble efforts of millions who sought to correct or ameliorate the raw edges of their cultures. We have earlier called attention to the presence of "common grace" in all societies—as well as to the presence of evil. This should give us hope: God has not totally abandoned the human race. His redemptive purpose will not be ultimately frustrated by the evil in the world.

Fifth, some scholars regard the unfolding of the story of Israel as evidence of dynamic and positive religious evolution. But despite all God subsequently did to hold before this people the truth concerning himself and his instruction (Torah) for their lives, their sinfulness culminated in the Judaism that destroyed Jesus—to its own loss and cost.

And finally, Christians should not look askance on human civilization, with its social patterns and political institutions, as the undisputed domain of the devil. They must contend against all that seeks to dehumanize people. Only thereby will they reflect by word and deed the fullness of the good news of the Kingdom.

In this connection the dimension of political involvement becomes inescapable when one deliberately enters the following sequence of thought. When a person sins, someone else is inevitably hurt. Sin always has social consequences, whether great or small, depending on the person sinning. One cannot sin ever so secretly without influencing the quality of one's relations with others, particularly those within his or her inner circle. When the leader of a nation sins, catastrophe may come to its citizens. On the basis of this, we should conclude that to love one's neighbor as one's self (Lev. 19:18; Matt. 22:39) necessitates involvement in activity that seeks to curb the power of political leaders through appropriate checks and balances. To be apolitical is hardly consonant with the will of God.

As we move forward now to the story of Abraham, we will see the further development of many of the major themes described embryonically in Genesis 1–11. God's mission takes a radical turn from dealing directly with the whole human race to dealing instrumentally through one extended family for the sake of all the families of the earth.

4

God Calls the Patriarchs
to Be a Blessing for the Nations

Introduction

Primeval history came to an end when God utterly frustrated the first human attempt to establish a centralized world empire. At Babel his judgment was linguistic confusion. By the scattering of peoples that resulted, he set the stage for two radically different movements. One quickly emerged in the form of competing cultural and political entities. In the centuries that followed, human history would be littered with the wreckage of a dreary succession of futile though costly efforts to create world empires in defiance of God.

The other movement represented God's need for a servant people to whom he might reveal his redemptive purpose for the nations and whom he might recruit as his means for achieving this end. When he elected, then called Abram out of Ur of the Chaldeans, we are confronted with the beginning of salvation history. At its outset God decreed that the whole people of Israel would be recipients of the promises given to Abraham (Gen. 15:4; 35:10–11; Heb. 7:5). In so doing, God deliberately turned away from humanity in the collective sense. Through this one person and a particular line of his seed, Isaac, God took steps to achieve a redemptive and regal purpose that would gather momentum and grow within world history, though always somewhat separate from it.

Genesis 12–50 contains the germinal story. These chapters record significant events in the first four generations of patriarchs in two distinct cultures (Canaanite and Egyptian). We will not explore the details of the spiritual pilgrimages of Abraham, Isaac, Jacob, and Joseph, even though the record contains much insight and instruction with respect to the idea of mission. These narratives deal with the activity of God as he sought to overcome their unbelief, deepen their commitment, frustrate their adversaries, impart spiritual vision, and intervene on their behalf. Our concern will be to note the successive steps by which the narrative moves from a single individual to a family, to a tribe, then to a cluster of tribes. This sets the stage for the Exodus from Egypt, when the children of Israel became the liberated people of God, united in worship and in the consciousness that they belonged uniquely to him. It was only then that they were free to move toward their destiny in the Promised Land. It is through reviewing their particular history that we discover relevant themes of God's mission through the people of God. These emphases will, in turn, inform our understanding of the Kingdom.

So then, Abraham's election and God's covenant with him represent the first expression of God's redemptive concern for all nations. As a result, Abraham should be regarded as "the pioneer in mission," the spiritual forefather of all the people of God scattered throughout all the races of humankind. In his discussion of the call of Abraham, Bengt Sundkler affirmed that it is "the task of mission to break the curse and replace it by understanding and unity." He then adds: "When Abraham left his home in faith, knowing nothing of the future, he took the first decisive step along this road" (1965: 12).

The Call of Abraham

> The LORD had said to Abram, "Leave your country, your people and your father's household and go to the land I will show you. I will make you into a great nation and I will bless you; I will make your name great and you will be a blessing. I will bless those who bless you, and whoever curses you I will curse; and all peoples on earth will be blessed through you." (Gen. 12:1–3)

It was God's choice to elect Abram with a view of eventually making a covenant with him (Abraham) to become "a father of many nations" (Gen. 17:5). This dual act, election and covenant, can be comprehended only in terms of his 'ahăbâ (his election-love) and his ḥesed (his covenant-love). Norman H. Snaith has drawn out the difference in these terms. God's 'ahăbâ (election-love) for Israel is an "unconditioned sovereign love" (1944: 134). God chose Israel because he willed to do so (Deut. 7:6–8). But the ḥesed ("conditional covenant-love") that God pledged to Israel through Abraham includes the following postulates: God existed before Israel, meaning that if he once existed without them, he could do so again. And if he chose them, he could also reject them. Abraham's God differed from all other gods in the demands he made upon his people as their part in the covenant (1944: 108). The word ḥesed is invariably given the English equivalent of "mercy"/"loving kindness," and when used in reference to human activity, it signifies the sort of love and duty toward God whereby the people of God live in accordance to his will.

But ḥesed has a strikingly different meaning when used in reference to divine activity. Despite all the varied shades of meaning ("firmness and steadfastness," "loving kindness and mercy," "eagerness, ardor, and intense devotion"), it is always placed within the framework of a covenant. The prior existence of a covenant provides the stage on which ḥesed may be given concrete reality. God's faithfulness as such is unconditional (Rom. 3:3), yet it is always given concrete expression by God in the context of covenant. God's unconditional love for Israel prompted him to make a covenant with Abraham. But it will be his *ḥesed* that makes possible the continuance of this covenant. The Scriptures emphasize that "the LORD set his affection on your forefathers [the patriarchs] and loved them, and he chose you, their descendants, above all the nations" (Deut. 10:15). No merit or quality prompted the decision (7:7–8).

Genesis 12 begins with the living God, later known as "the God of Abraham, Isaac, and Jacob," acting in sovereign freedom and calling Abram and Sarai, his wife, to leave Ur of the Chaldees (Acts 7:2–4). He called in grace and promised his blessing. This constituted the first step in the sequence that would eventually lead to the full disclosure of what the salvation of God is all about. Because God made absolute demands, Abram and his wife, Sarai, must leave their family, kindred, and gods and live by faith in accordance with certain specific promises that imply the faithfulness and deliverance of God (cf. 12:1–3 with Heb. 11:8–16). This would mean that they must live consciously under God's judgment as well as under his blessing.

It is often noted that the election of Abraham and the other patriarchs was primarily related to function. They were to fulfill the role of being within the line of succession, leading to Christ, "the seed of Abraham" (Gen. 3:15 and Gal. 3:16). However, although the story does not say they were explicitly elected only to eternal redemption as such, it does emphasize that they were brought into a dynamic relationship with God and they came to know God in such a way that their redemption is assumed (cf. Gen. 22:15–18 with Heb. 11:19).

Derek Kidner rightly observes: "On the ultimate aspect of salvation, deliverance from death, the last enemy, Genesis has only faint [hints]" (1973: 41). The central hope that God's grace provided was traced to his selection of a chosen people and his pledge that they would possess a land of his choice and bring blessing to the nations. That this elect people became both the recipient and the channel of divine blessing would seem to indicate that "the seed of Abraham" is more than God's vehicle for a later redemption. At this point, however, God's election should be primarily understood as "separation unto service." Later, the seed will be described as "holy" (Isa. 6:13), and this carries the implication that the blessing embraces being "appointed for eternal life" (Acts 13:48).

We read that God spoke to Abraham (Gen. 12:4). We do not know the actual form of his speech. Then we note that the Lord "appeared" to him (lit., "let himself be seen by Abram," 12:7). Does this mean something more than mere speech? This word is repeated in Genesis 17:1, and in 17:22 it states that when God "had finished speaking with Abraham, God went up from him"—and Abram's name was changed to Abraham in the process (17:5). Were these "theophanic" events? We do not know. Suffice it to say they diminish in the record of Isaac (26:2, 24), are less frequent in the life of Jacob (28:13; 35:9), and are totally absent in the account of Joseph. More often it is by "the angel of Yahweh" (or of God) that revelatory material comes to the patriarchs (16:7; 22:11, 15; 24:7, 40; 31:11; 48:16). But of one thing we can be sure. The Word of God was heard, and Abraham obeyed it.

Abraham's discipleship was built upon the premise that when God speaks, his word is to be obeyed. This is normative for historic biblical Christianity. Some scholars have a philosophical reluctance to believe that God speaks as well as acts. The classical defense of this perspective is *God Who Acts* by G. Ernest Wright (1952), with its overworked thesis that truth is to be "inferred" from what are judged to be God's "mighty acts" in "holy history." This reduces the Bible to something far less authoritative than what it claims to be: "the Word of God." Evangelical Christians have always been at variance with scholars who are overly enthusiastic about God's activity in history. Evangelical Christians would support the thesis that God acts, but they generally conclude that knowledge about God is possible only through hearing God's revelation as and when God has spoken.

The Abrahamic Covenant

> I will make you into a great nation and I will bless you; I will make your name great, and you will be a blessing. I will bless those who bless you, and whoever curses you I will curse; and all peoples on earth will be blessed through you. (Gen. 12:2–3)

These are the words that God addressed to Abram while he was in Ur. Over the years God amplified to him certain details but without any basic alterations. These further revelations followed Abram's separation from Lot (Gen. 13:14–18), his refusal of public identification with the king of Sodom (14:21–24; 15:4–5, 18–21), and his acceptance of God's decision that Ishmael would not be in the line of promise (17:4–8, 16, 19). We must call attention to their dominant themes.

Spiritual Blessing for the Nations

The salvation of the nations was God's ultimate motivation in making Abraham's name great and in being the God of Abraham's innumerable progeny. This universal purpose totally dominates the covenant. Even beyond the passages listed in the preceding section, God stresses in various ways his promise of hope for the nations of the world (Gen. 18:17, 18; 22:18; 26:4; 28:14). Centuries later the apostle Paul calls this promise nothing less than the gospel: "The Scripture foresaw that God would justify the Gentiles by faith, and announced the gospel in advance to Abraham: 'All nations will be blessed through you'" (Gal. 3:8). The salvation of humankind by faith in Jesus the Messiah was at the heart of God's redemptive purpose from before the foundation of the world (Eph. 1:3–10). God has only one gospel for the human race. It is available only in and through Jesus Christ. Whether Jews or Gentiles, those who seek God through faith in Christ Jesus will find God and will become "sons of God" and "Abraham's seed, and heirs according to the promise" (Gal. 3:26–29).

Specific Homeland for Israel

Among the Jewish people nothing exceeds their passionate love for the land of Israel. Unquestionably, this is one of their most ancient and persistent concerns.

To the patriarchs God gave what might be described as "sacred space," a place of order and blessing. Beyond its frontiers lay the world of chaos, the realm of alien spirits. As the Old Testament record unfolds, we find Israel described as being at the very center of the earth (Ezek. 38:12), Jerusalem as the center of Israel, and Mount Zion the center of Jerusalem with the Temple on its summit (Davies 1974: 8).

Only in the land would Yahweh abundantly give a variety of material gifts to his people. He would promise to care for it directly by providing rain in season. The soil of Israel would only be refreshed with water by divine decree, a point that Deuteronomy 11:10–12 makes abundantly clear. The land would never be defined with geographic precision, as any comparative reading of all pertinent passages readily indicates. Hence, one might argue that Israel is an idea as well as a territory. But what is significant is that behind Israel's existence and tenure of the land was the divine purpose for the nations.

At Sinai and later on the plains of Moab (recorded in Deuteronomy), God would give his people not only regulatory commands for their occupation of the land but also conditional promises concerning its retention. Of all the promises made to the patriarchs, none is as prominent or as decisive as the promise that all the nations would be blessed through Abraham's seed. This theme would remain prominent throughout the Old Testament but would be remarkably transformed and universalized in the New Testament.

Israel's Treatment by the Nations

God loves his people. Those who mistreat them touch "the apple of his eye" (Zech. 2:8) and cannot escape divine retribution. As a result, a note of finality was associated with the conduct of any person or people toward Abram's seed: "I will bless those who bless you, and whoever curses you I will curse; and all peoples on earth will be blessed through you" (Gen. 12:3).

At first glance, blessing and cursing would be understood in material terms, but the promise also has redemptive overtones. In Jesus' parable of the last judgment (Matt. 25:31–46), he identified himself with his people and pronounced blessing or judgment on "all the nations" (25:32) depending on how these nations have treated "one of the least of these brothers of mine" (25:40). We have here further intimation of the centrality of Israel in God's determination to bless the nations. Israel is never marginal to God's providential care of the nations. History is replete with evidence that the rise or fall of nations has often been contingent on their treatment of the Jewish people.

God's Presence and Power

When God commanded Abram to leave Ur, God also promised to be involved in Abram's journey. The phrase "I will" appears numerous times in God's promises to Abram. The implication is that the presence and power of God would be fully operative in the centuries to follow and that God's faithfulness to the covenant would become increasingly apparent. It further means that if anyone would serve

God, a radical reorientation must take place in his or her life in order to be truly related to God's will and his power. Almost immediately God enrolled Abraham in a school of discipleship and began this process of transformation. All who later sought to become involved in the Kingdom of God in the New Testament would discover that they too must come under this same training.

We shall find that all the significant events in Abram's life took place through the miraculous activity of God accomplishing what God had promised. The focus is not on what Abram was to do for God but on what God was to do through Abram. In this connection, we read God's characteristic name: El Shaddai (Gen. 17:1; 28:3; 35:11; 43:14; 48:3, and possibly 49:25). Its meaning has been variously interpreted to mean "he who is sufficient" or "the all-powerful One." Over the years, Abram grew in his understanding of God and increasingly allowed God to work out all things on his behalf, according to God's will. In this way Abram gained the assurance that his God would overcome all opposition to God's purpose. At this point Abram's relationship with God was solidified to such an extent that his name was changed to Abraham (17:5).

The Sign of the Covenant

The only possible response Abraham could make to the amazing covenantal relationship with God was to surrender to God unconditionally, with humility accepting God's terms. He did this when he was ninety-nine years old (Gen. 17:1–3). It was then that God demanded that Abraham and his people bear a visible sign of their covenant obligation to obey him. This sign was circumcision. To refuse this sign was tantamount to breaking the covenant (17:14) and deliberately rejecting the fact that God had brought him and his seed into this special relationship. Circumcision was to be a permanent reminder to Abraham and his descendants that they were to be a "holy" (set apart) nation. This external sign demonstrated acceptance of the covenant and incorporation into the believing community that was committed to it. Inevitably, it also included Abraham's family, as well as "all those born in his household or bought with his money" (17:23). By his faith and obedience Abraham thereby began to be a blessing to others, as God had promised. Prophetically, the circumcision of Abraham and the males in his household pointed beyond the physical seed of Abraham to what the apostle Paul meant when he affirmed that all those who belong to Christ are "Abraham's seed" (Gal. 3:29).

Abraham's Discipleship

God called Abraham because God loved Abraham (Deut. 4:37; 7:6–8). This was a jealous love. God wanted a particular people for his own possession. This was his indisputable right. God sealed his decision with a formal covenant that possessed legal validity and would be eternally operative. Although covenants were widely known throughout the ancient world, the idea of a single deity initiating a covenant with a particular person and his family was unknown among the religions and cultures of Abraham's day.

God would subsequently direct the life of Abraham in such a way that his faith would develop as the narrative unfolded. God would not violate the freedom granted Abraham and reduce him to a puppet on a string. Abraham must come to understand his fallenness and waywardness if he was to truly discover for himself the grace and forgiveness of God. He must go through many prolonged trials and learn obedience through suffering the consequences of disobedience.

Abraham and Mission

At first Abraham was seen as a quiet sojourner, a man of peace, a pilgrim, obscure and unknown. His lifestyle was that of a rich and religious Bedouin with a sizable retinue of followers. When strife broke out between his herdsmen and those of his nephew Lot, he was magnanimous and generous, and the land under his direction was peacefully divided between them (Gen. 13:1–13). This was pleasing to God, for he then granted him enlarged understanding of the extent of the Promised Land and the size of his progeny (13:14–18). In the narrative we can see five principles that undergird all mission activity in relation to Abraham.

Mission and Secular Involvement

We are told in Genesis 14 that the whole region was caught up in something that has a familiar ring. A coalition of neighboring powers was making war against another coalition of nations (Von Rad 1961: 170). Here is the first impingement of salvation history on the larger historical context. In the ensuing conflict Lot and his family were taken hostage. Whereas at first Abraham had avoided involvement in the struggle, this catastrophe galvanized him into action. With great energy he quickly raised a striking force (his "trained men"), conducted a daring raid, displayed martial prowess in battle, and brought about a smashing victory (Gen. 14:15–16). He then sought to return to his pilgrim way, but all was changed. He now found himself facing unexpected issues and terrible temptations as a result of this new mission paradigm: mission through conquest. This form of mission becomes all too familiar later on in the history of the Christian church.

On this occasion Abraham as heir and lord of the land stood against pagan evil. We find in this account intimations of truths yet to be revealed; especially poignant is the fact that a stranger named Melchizedek pointed out to Abraham that it was "God most high" rather than Abraham's military skill that gained for him this victory (Gen. 14:20). Scripture would increasingly emphasize the principle that human anger "does not bring about the righteous life that God desires" (James 1:19). The sword does not advance the Kingdom of God.

Mission and "Melchizedek People"

Shortly after Abraham became involved in the war to rescue Lot, he had a most unexpected encounter with a Canaanite king-priest named Melchizedek of Salem. His name and title pointed to kingship in the realm of righteousness and justice and of priesthood in the realm of access to God and worship. He was the first to bless Abraham—what God had promised (Gen. 12:2)—and he offered him bread and wine. In a memorable fashion he blessed the God who had made victory possible (14:19–20). When Abraham sensed that this king-priest's authority came directly from God, he spontaneously placed at his feet a tenth of all the treasure gained in battle (14:20). With equal discernment he turned aside the king of Sodom's offer of loot and refused to be ensnared by wealth (14:21–24).

We should underscore the importance of Abraham's positive response to Melchizedek's blessing, for it reveals that Abraham was increasingly receptive to opening his heart and mind to the unconditional acceptance of God's will for his life. We are not surprised to find shortly thereafter that the Lord came to him in a vision and spoke words of commendation and comfort: "Do not be afraid, Abram. I am your shield, your very great reward" (15:1).

When the people of God are in mission, they need to be alert to the possibility of encountering "Melchizedek people" in the course of their missionary service. Count Von Zinzendorf (1700–60), who brought mission obedience to the Moravian movement, called them "Cornelius souls" (Acts 10). People like Melchizedek may worship the same God of Abraham, Isaac, and Jacob, though they may never have heard the name of Jesus Christ. We should not deny the possibility of God's surprises, for he is most eager to draw people to himself (Schattschneider 1975: 75–78).

Mission and Prayer

When God announced judgment on Sodom, he sought to involve Abraham in a distinctly priestly role in relation to God's mission. This provides us with insight into an unexpected aspect of God's nature (Gen. 18:17–19). He began by drawing near to Abraham (18:22), the one through whom he had chosen to bless the whole world (12:3). This was precipitated by the deepening of Abraham's prayer fellowship with God. Their relationship was such that God had taken Abraham into his confidence. God had "known" Abraham and had set his affection on him. God expected some form of response. What followed was a remarkable display of what the apostle Paul later challenged Timothy to do, that is, to intercede so that the missionary purpose of God might be furthered (1 Tim. 2:1–6).

In response Abraham accepted the rightness and range of God's justice and sensed the priestly role he must then assume. Abraham presumed on God's grace and mercy and took on the difficult task of pleading for Sodom. In this portrayal of a solitary person standing between God and a wicked people, we see a foreshadowing of the ideal posture of the missionary and the mission-minded church. Missionary churches that follow the model of Abraham's intercessory prayer will find confirmation in Joel 2:17:

"Let the priests, who minister before the LORD, weep between the temple porch and the altar. Let them say, 'Spare your people, O LORD. Do not make your inheritance an object of scorn, a byword among the nations.'"

Mission Demands Attraction

Missiologists use the terms *centripetal* and *centrifugal* to describe complementary mission methodologies. They contrast Christian presence that wins people by attraction (centripetal) with deliberate efforts to win people through proclamation and persuasion (centrifugal). In this connection we should note that the promise to the patriarchs was, "By you all the nations will bless themselves/be blessed." On the basis of the variation in Hebrew form (Gen. 22:18 and 26:4 are reflexive, and 12:3, 18:18, and 28:14 are passive), Bengt Sundkler comments:

> Centripetal [universality] is actualized by a messenger who crosses frontiers and passes on his news to those who are afar off; centripetal [as if drawn] by a magnetic force, drawing distant peoples into the place of the person who stands at the center. (1965: 14, 15)

The dominant Old Testament emphasis is centripetal. Only occasionally does one encounter centrifugal overtones. This means that we find almost no evidence in the Old Testament of Israelites putting forth effort to share their knowledge of God with the neighboring nations.

Throughout Israel's history there were times when outsiders were attracted by the example of godly Jews and deliberately took steps to come within the circle of the blessing of Yahweh (e.g., Ruth 1:16–17; 1 Kings 10:1–13; 2 Kings 5:1–19; hence the prayer of Ps. 67:1–2). Several eschatological passages from the prophets state hundreds of years later that in the last day the nations will encourage one another to seek the God of Israel (e.g., Zech. 8:22–23).

Mission and Passivity

This centripetal emphasis can be abused and the nations forgotten. As we move deeper into the Old Testament, we will see that the vision of worldwide spiritual blessing through Abraham's seed did not become increasingly more vivid in the consciousness of the people of God. It virtually disappeared in the long interval between the patriarchs and the monarchy, apart from Exodus 19:5–6, when the Israelites were called to become "a kingdom of priests" standing before God on behalf of the nations. However, it reappeared with increasing frequency in the Psalms and the prophets. Even so, "at its faintest it always imparted some sense of mission to Israel; yet it never became a program of concerted action until after the Ascension and the descent of the Holy Spirit on the day of Pentecost" (Kidner 1973: 114).

While it is true that "Israel never felt the need to include the salvation of the non-elect within a theological synthesis of its major doctrines" (Senior and Stuhlmueller 1983: 9), this is the tragedy of Israel itself, not the fact that God was unconcerned or that the Old Testament is totally silent on this matter. Both Israel's separation from the nations and the ultimate centrifugal responsibility to it of Abraham's seed will be seen as necessary, as we move into the complex but not discordant world of Old Testament revelation.

Abraham's Descendants as Instruments of God's Mission

Although the focus of Genesis 12–50 is primarily on Abraham and only secondarily on his descendants, the record of the other patriarchs is likewise replete with missiological significance. True, they are starkly portrayed as rather flawed in both character and obedience. They frequently failed and were often plagued with inner doubt, so much so that they often vacillated between obedience to God and the service of themselves. But they experienced God's grace again and again, for his dealings with them always reflected God's concern to keep faith with the covenant. In the story of the patriarchs, we read intimations of the progression of the mission task and the virtues required to accomplish God's mission.

Isaac and Servanthood

Isaac is often dismissed as colorless and petty, lacking in greatness, and is even chided for liking savory food (Gen. 25:28). But we should not overlook the two dominant features of his life: his birth and marriage. First, with respect to Isaac's birth, Abraham had been severely tested because the promise that a son would be born through Sarah was essential. Isaac was born when Abraham was one hundred years old. One can only imagine the limitations such an age would have. Isaac's birth was possible only through the miraculous intervention of God. When Isaac was weaned, his brother Ishmael mocked him and made him the object of unholy laughter (21:9), thereby unwittingly demonstrating that these two brothers represented two different worlds. The Old Testament has by and large represented Ishmael as being outside the stream of Israel's redemptive history (16:12; 21:20–21). Ishmael's "restless existence is no pilgrimage, but an end in itself, his non-conformism is a habit of mind, not a light to the nations" (Schattschneider 1975: 127).

The second significant feature of Isaac's life is his marriage. His birth was a miracle, and while still a youth it seemed he must die. But God preserved his life, and through him the promised line continued. Isaac's role in God's mission made his marriage important. Again we find evidence of God's miraculous intervention in the selection of Rebekah and the love that followed Isaac's considerate and courteous treatment of her (Gen. 24). That for twenty years she remained barren caused Isaac much prayerful concern, and once again God's miraculous intervention was essential to the continuance of the promised line, although their twins (Jacob and Esau) developed into mutually hostile peoples.

Isaac is portrayed as the embodiment of the servant role. We see him as the unprotesting victim who carries the wood on which he is to be slain (Gen. 22:6), as the patient son of his father who does not marry until late in life ("forty years old," 25:20), as the fervent intercessor who wanted the chosen line to continue

(25:21), and as the peaceful, reasonable person who finds himself caught between hostile peoples in their oases and cities and the waterless countryside where he is unable to find pasturage for his flocks. All these factors model for us the servant role God would have his people adopt in our day. And yet we must not forget Isaac was also weak in character, being both deceptive and fearful (26:1–11). Only Christ is the perfect Servant!

Jacob and Priorities

We should not be surprised that almost a quarter of the Book of Genesis is devoted to Jacob. He, and not Abraham, became the father of the chosen people. His descendants called themselves by his name, Israel (Jacob frequently occurs in parallel form in Hebrew poetry). He was born clutching the heel of his elder twin, Esau (Gen. 25:26), and acquired the name "He Who Clutches," although this nuanced into "Supplanter" because of his pursuit of the rights of the firstborn. He enticed Esau to sell his birthright for a meal (25:29–34), deceptively obtained the irrevocable blessing of his father Isaac (27:18–29), and had to flee when Esau discovered this (27:34–37). This flight leads to his being granted a vision at Bethel in which the promise given to Abraham was confirmed to him along with the promise of divine protection (28:10–17). Consider Jacob's conflicts with Laban, his polygamous marital confusion, the birth of eleven sons and one daughter, and the protracted barrenness of his beloved Rachel. Jacob both knew and caused much personal pain.

Understandably, when God ordered him to return to the land (Gen. 31:3), he obeyed without hesitation. On the way home the fear of Esau made Jacob desperate. God graciously met him at Jabbok and attempted to prevail over his stubbornness. In the encounter Jacob's hip was dislocated, a reminder to Jacob for the rest of his life of his struggle with God. This opened Jacob's eyes to divine realities, causing him to turn to God and receive the divine blessing that he now desired above all else. This event was regarded as Jacob's deliverance "from all harm" (48:16).

Despite this strange, belated victory, Jacob was the most complicated of the patriarchs, being at one and the same time a prodigy, an impostor, an entrepreneur, and a liar. All his terrible flaws notwithstanding, Jacob had a sense of priority that is worthy of emulation. It surfaced at Jabbok. Although we cannot accept the manner in which Jacob sought to receive the spiritual dimensions of the covenant, we admire the dogged persistence with which he struggled. He clung to the presence and promise of God despite a painful awareness of his own deficiencies. He reached out to God, reminding God of the promises he had made earlier: "You have said" (Gen. 32:9, 12). He would not let the stranger go at Jabbok unless the stranger would bless him (32:26). For this tenacity alone he is commended with the name "Israel" (Hos. 12:4). This name emphasizes the reality that he has "struggled with God and with men and [has] overcome" (Gen. 32:28). What an amazing commendation: Jacob's descendants, the Israelites, have had privilege ever since. They too can "strive with God."

Joseph, Servant of God and Pharaoh

Genesis 37 through 50, with the exception of chapter 38, are devoted to the story of Joseph. Various suggestions have been made to explain why the author devoted so much space to detailing the train of events that would eventuate in "the offspring of Jacob," seventy persons in all, leaving the land of promise and dwelling in Egypt (Gen. 46:27; Exod. 1:5). It is reasonable to conclude that early in God's disclosure of himself to his people as the God of Providence, they would need to be given an almost classical presentation of the way in which God would seek to overrule in the lives of their families. They would understand the rivalries among Jacob's own children and the problems that these led to. But they would also stand amazed at the unerring way in which God brought Jacob's extended family under Egyptian domination to set the stage for the ultimate event in that period of their history—the Exodus. This detailed record must have confirmed to them in meaningful ways the implications of their divine election and God's abiding faithfulness to his covenanted promise to them.

In general, the patriarchs wielded no authority over others; they merely exerted influence. They were called to a pilgrim way and sensed no call to be social critics or to seek office (contrast Lot in Sodom, Gen. 19:1, 9). They obeyed local laws and conformed to local customs (21:30; 26:15–22; 14:13; 23:4ff.; 33:19). But they disapproved of marrying into Canaanite families (24:3; 26:34) and disassociated themselves from flagrant immorality (14:23; 24:3).

The exception is Joseph. The record is completely silent as to any flaws in his character or obedience to God. Perhaps because he was the favorite son of his father, his brothers envied him and sold him into slavery. But we encounter no bitterness. He refuses to commit adultery with Potiphar's wife because of his desire to be obedient to God and is unjustly imprisoned for seven years. His promotion to the civil service of Egypt was unsought, though he displayed no hesitation in accepting political responsibility when it was unexpectedly offered to him. He devoted his energy and wisdom to promoting Egypt's interests as well as those of the people of God. He demonstrated the possibility of being the servant of both Pharaoh and God. We might, in fact, summarize the social responsibility of all the patriarchs as follows: human rules were upheld as divine ordinances; political leaders were regarded as God's servants; and the people of God were "aliens and strangers" (1 Peter 2:11) as well as "cooperative citizens" whose "doing good" (1 Peter 2:15) put criticism to silence.

When we think of Joseph, the descendant of Abraham who brought deliverance from famine and social distress to the greatest nation of the ancient world, we see anticipatory fulfillment of the promise of Abraham's seed blessing the nations (Gen. 12:3). This seems to be symbolized by the account of Joseph bringing his father, Jacob, into the court of Pharaoh that Jacob might twice bless him (47:7, 10). Whereas Joseph recognized that God had sent him to Egypt "to save lives" there (45:5), he told his brothers God's primary purpose was "to preserve for you a remnant on earth and to save your lives by a great deliverance" (v. 7). Indeed, the Israelite people were kept alive because God's worldwide redemptive purpose through them had yet to be fulfilled on behalf of Egypt and all other peoples (Gal. 3:8).

Conclusion

In reviewing the lives of the partriarchs, we should be guided by the writer to the Hebrews. Hebrews commends to us the faith of the patriarchs (Heb. 11:8–22). All the patriarchs were positive and open in their personal response to God's revelation. All guarded their covenant relationship to God and transmitted it to their children. All refused to worship at Canaanite shrines and served God alone (contra Senior and Stuhlmueller 1983: 17–18). All were possessed with the conviction that the God of history had given them a purpose and a destiny. All deliberately sought to remain separate from other peoples so that God's purpose for them and through them would be realized.

The final expression of patriarchal faith was the dramatic way in which Joseph refused to be buried in Egypt. He stipulated that his sealed but not buried coffin be kept in the midst of the Israelite community in Egypt as a physical reminder to the children of Israel that their destiny lay in their own land, the land of promise. "Joseph . . . spoke about the exodus of the Israelites from Egypt and gave directions about his bones" (Heb. 11:22). When the Israelites left Egypt centuries later, they took his coffin with them and buried it in Shechem (Exod. 13:19; Josh. 24:32).

Only the spiritual "children of Abraham" will enter the Kingdom. Jesus stated this most vividly: "I say to you that many will come from the east and the west, and will take their places at the feast with Abraham, Isaac and Jacob in the kingdom of heaven. But the subjects of the kingdom will be thrown outside, into the darkness" (Matt. 8:11–12). To whom was Jesus referring in such dark terms when he used the phrase "the sons of the kingdom"? We believe he was referring specifically to many circumcised Jews of the old covenant as well as to many Jews and Gentiles baptized under the new covenant. Nominal Israelites and merely professing Christians alike were to find their identity with the people of God, not "according to the sinful nature," but "according to the Spirit" (Rom. 8:4). The true "children of Abraham" demonstrate their spirituality by obeying Christ (John 14:21). Among other things, the true "children of Abraham" take the gospel to the nations: north and south, east and west. By faith they look forward to the heavenly banquet with Abraham, the father of all true disciples of the Crucified One. This brings us to the next major stage in God's Kingdom mission: God's direct action to bring Israel out of Egypt at the Exodus.

PART 2

GOD'S
MISSION
THROUGH
ISRAEL

5

God Rules over Egypt
and Covenants
with God's People

Introduction

Genesis ends with a relatively small company of Hebrews in Egypt, living in relative security and possessing two tangible reminders that their destiny lay in another country. First, there is God's promise of coming deliverance (Gen. 15:13, 14; 46:3–4), signaled by Joseph's unburied coffin (50:26). Second, because of Egyptian abhorrence of shepherds, they were forced to live apart in Goshen on the frontier between Egypt and Canaan. There it was possible to maintain their ethnic identity and communal life (Exod. 8:22; 9:26; Acts 7:6). The fact that they were placed in a restricted area for "separate development" (e.g., apartheid) was potentially harmful. Any deliberate segregation of people—even if undertaken for reasons that initially seem to be in their best interests—inevitably proves harmful, since it restricts personal freedom and exposure to other peoples. So it was with the Israelites in Goshen.

As years passed, circumstances changed. When the Hebrews grew in numbers, the Egyptians began to regard them as a security risk. Privileges were withdrawn. Large groups of Israelites were uprooted, scattered throughout the land, and forced into labor camps. The Egyptians even tried genocide by seeking to destroy all male Hebrew infants. Life became increasingly bitter. The Hebrews began to cry to God for deliverance. God graciously raised up Moses to be their liberator, and after a period of ever-heightening confrontation with Pharaoh, God delivered them from slavery in Egypt. We take the record of this historical sequence at face value. Whereas no one is certain as to the number of Hebrews involved or the precise date of the Exodus, we follow Alan Cole, who wisely states:

> It is enough that with later Israel we know and believe that such an event happened, and that we interpret it as a saving act of God. Indeed, to Israel, it was the saving act of God which overshadowed all others, since, in a sense, it was the act of Israel's

creation. All God's subsequent saving acts were measured by this, the heart of Israel's creed. What the cross of Christ is to the Christian, the Exodus was to the Israelite: yet we know neither the exact date nor the exact place of the crucifixion, any more than Israel knew the exact date or location of Sinai. (1973: 16)

The biblical account of the Exodus is vivid. It gives the impression that an overwhelming number of Hebrews left Egypt at that time (Exod. 1:12; Num. 1:46; 26:41; Deut. 10:22; 26:5), even though some scholars seem to delight in contending that only a relatively small company was actually involved (based on Deut. 4:38; 7:7, 17–18; 11:23; 20:1). What is important is that the Hebrews were an enslaved and exploited people, a significant minority presence in Egypt, the most powerful nation of that day. They could do nothing to bring about their own liberation except cry to God for deliverance.

> The Israelites groaned in their slavery and cried out, and their cry for help because of their slavery went up to God. God heard their groaning and he remembered his covenant with Abraham, with Isaac and with Jacob. So God looked on the Israelites and was concerned about them. (Exod. 2:23–25)

As a result, God "came down to deliver" his people (Exod. 3:8) and did so in such a tremendous fashion that all the gods of Egypt, along with Pharaoh, his counselors, and his army, were utterly discredited and finally overcome. The victory is memorialized and celebrated to this day. Significantly, the Hebrews themselves and their leaders did nothing to achieve it. No one could boast of his or her contribution. God alone was the victor. When the Hebrews saw the Egyptians dead on the seashore and began to grasp the magnitude of their deliverance, they could only "put their trust in [the Lord] and in Moses his servant" (14:30–31). It was then that they began to "sing to the Lord" (15:1–18) and confess that he was "a warrior." Surely, they concluded, he would "reign for ever and ever" (vv. 3, 18).

But who was this God? The Hebrews had witnessed his justice (delivering them from their oppressors) and his power (overcoming the Egyptians and parting the sea). But they needed a more comprehensive revelation. Hence, Moses led them to Sinai and "the mountain of God." It was there that the Lord revealed his glory by "coming down" and manifesting himself to them. The Hebrews had to sense the love that made God desire to be near them as well as the holiness that demanded separation and distance from them.

Under Moses' mediation they accepted by acclamation the rule of God over their lives and pledged to keep his covenant (Exod. 19:5–8). In response God greatly amplified his covenantal promises to them and thereby defined in detail the significance of his having taken possession of them. God also gave them his law (Torah) for their sanctity and unity and to promote their well-being. It stipulated in great detail God's concern for all aspects of their individual lives, their families, and their national oneness. This Torah was to serve as their custodian to make them hunger for a personal relationship with God (Gal. 3:24). Most important was their need for some means whereby their sins might be confessed and expiated and their worship conducted in a way that would be fully acceptable in his sight. So then, this chapter will focus on the Exodus deliverance, on Israel coming into national existence as the people of God at Sinai, and on the disclosure of his will for the nation, its individual members, and their worship.

The Exodus

We cannot presume to comprehend the relation between the prayers of God's people and the sovereign decision of God "to come down to rescue them from the hand of the Egyptians and to bring them up out of that land to a good and spacious land" (Exod. 3:8). In the New Testament this linkage is firmly established: God works in answer to prayer. But the steps leading to God's final victory are often surprising and unexpected. So it was with the realities that set the stage for the Exodus. We shall look at the Exodus miracles in five dimensions, each of which has prophetic meaning for mission.

The Conduct of Moses before He Encountered God

The New Testament is quite explicit in its description of the decision that Moses made to identify himself with the ongoing purpose of God.

> By faith Moses, when he had grown up, refused to be known as the son of Pharaoh's daughter. He chose to be mistreated along with the people of God rather than to enjoy the pleasures of sin for a short time. He regarded disgrace for the sake of Christ as of greater value than the treasures of Egypt, because he was looking ahead to his reward. (Heb. 11:24–26)

Actually, before Moses encountered God personally, a measure of ambivalence characterized his attempts to serve his people. When he first identified with the Hebrews in their misery, he killed one of their Egyptian oppressors without attempting first to reason with him. The next day he found one Hebrew oppressing another and sought to intervene. He thereby displayed a passionate nature and an unconditional concern for justice. But his intervention was rejected by his own people. As a result, he became vulnerable to their betrayal and had to flee for his life (Exod. 2:15). Later, while stateless, he again showed his concern for justice and delivered strangers from their oppressors. This resulted in his being befriended by the strangers (2:16–22). These are the first references in the Bible to the use of violence to secure social justice. How are we to interpret these incidents?

The record does not moralize on Moses' acts of violence; it neither praises nor condemns them. By this means Moses did not bring about the deliverance of his oppressed people. His act of violence in killing the Egyptian made it incongruous for him to argue for the genuine reconciliation of his Hebrew brothers and sisters (Exod. 2:14), for he had compromised himself. He had to be removed from the scene lest he be destroyed. Later God would send him back to Egypt with a different authority and a different methodology. In this connection we need to be reminded that Israel was not liberated from Egyptian slavery as a result of Moses' involvement in a divine-human operation. God, and God alone, wrought the deliverance. He used Moses but did not need Moses in order to achieve his victory.

This evaluation emphasizes the urgent need for Christians to think through their penchant for justifying revolutionary solutions. In this connection Brevard Childs adds: "By uncovering the ambiguities in Moses' acts of violence, we are forced to confront rather than evade those basic factors which constituted the moral decision" (1970: 183). Down through church history there have been instances when Christians sought to justify their resort to violence to defend the poor. But this kind of reasoning invariably "crowded out" all other Christian principles. It ended in the total abandonment of the faith, in indifference to the biblical revelation, and "in the atheism that appears to be a normal revolutionary position" (Ellul 1969: 22). Jacques Ellul is very blunt when he states, "Theologians of violence are Pharisees, terrible distorters of Christian truth" (1969: 140).

Suffice it to say that Moses' decision to identify with his people, the promised seed, involved him in personal risk, spiritual conflict, and suffering in the years that followed. In a very real sense he models for all the people of God what effective spiritual service inevitably involves. To the venturesome in every age, Scripture clearly teaches that if they are to amount to anything for God, they must make a similar "faith decision."

True, there will be the "burning bush" of divine encounter, with the assurance of God's faithfulness and of his promise of guidance when needed (Exod. 3:1–6). But there will be the cross too! One thinks of Gideon, David, Elijah, Daniel, and many others. Apparently, if one's generation is to be served in the will of God, there is no alternative to taking the risk of personal and public identification with God, God's people, and God's mission (*missio Dei*) among the nations. Only then will there be personal encounter with God in significant ways. Even in the Old Testament one is confronted with the challenge of losing one's life in the service of God and only then finding it!

The Centrality of God in the Exodus Deliverance

The call of Moses took place in the context of encounter with God at a burning bush. It was there that Moses sensed God's reality and met firsthand Israel's covenant-making God. This God who "causes to be" is eternally unchanging in his glory, wisdom, power, and redemptive purpose. In disclosing his name to Moses, God said in effect: "I am the same God that your fathers and mothers worshiped, but I will give you a new awareness of what I am doing, and also of what I am." No attempt is made to expound what Yahweh means. Moses needed only to know that "God is there"—not what God is. His existence and presence were to be the sufficient guarantee that he would keep his promise and deliver his people from Egypt (Exod. 3:7–12). Although he pledged to be neither absent nor remote from them, he would not be at their disposal to suit their convenience (vv. 13–22).

Consider the controversy with Pharaoh and the gods of Egypt (the plagues challenged their sovereignty): the mounting crises, the final confession of the people of God before the Egyptians with the blood of the Passover lamb staining their doorposts and lintels, the judgment on the firstborn on the "night to be remembered," the "spoiling" of the Egyptians, Pharaoh's pursuit, and Israel's deliverance at the Red Sea. All these events have profound significance. Israelite tradition is unanimous in affirming that Yahweh is the God of Israel. This name came to prominence when the national-religious community called Israel was constituted, that is, beginning with the Exodus from Egypt (Jacob 1958: 53). Only after the Exodus story do we find the Israelites being called "the people of Yahweh" (Exod. 3:7, 10; 6:6–7; etc.).

It was by this liberating deed that Yahweh revealed himself as "the One who takes up the cause of the afflicted and the oppressed, a revelation that was to have a major influence on the way Israel thought about God" (Deist 1977: 60). It significantly shaped their worldview and their self-understanding. If God had been revealed as the One who was primarily concerned for "law and order" in Egypt and would have backed the Egyptian slave masters, it is quite apparent that "a different kind of God would have been revealed" (Deist 1977: 61).

It is inevitable, then, that in the Old Testament the Exodus is more prominent than the Creation, for Israel's history had its actual beginning in this crucial experience. The Hebrew slaves were liberated and transformed into a self-conscious, distinct people. This decisive historical event makes Moses the essential link between Abraham and David. The promises were made to Abraham, but they were not fulfilled in his lifetime. And we cannot say they were fulfilled until Israel was in the land in security under David. For it was David who acquired a place (Jerusalem) that Yahweh would "choose as a dwelling for his Name" (Deut. 12:11; see 2 Sam. 5:6–12; and 1 Kings 8:63).

Later when the psalmists sing of God as Redeemer, they make the Exodus their theme. And when the prophets speak of a new covenant beyond the covenant of Sinai, they expect God to act in an even greater way for the redemption of humankind and yet to be consistent with his actions at the Exodus (Jer. 31:31–34). It is for this reason that God's deliverance during the Exodus, Israel's wandering in the wilderness, and the conquest of the Promised Land are as significant for the New Testament as for the Old. It is in the New Testament that "One greater than Moses" makes possible a liberating and redemptive Exodus, one which leads to a more lasting inheritance (Deut. 18:15–19).

Abraham was called so that through him "all peoples on earth will be blessed" (Gen. 12:3). Mission involves the encounter between the people of God and the nations as God's mission unfolds through human history. The Exodus is a prime example of God's mission working through Israel among the nations. In the case of Egypt, God is working in the midst of the principle political power of the region. Repeatedly God, speaking through Moses, explains God's intention: that Pharaoh (and Egypt and the surrounding nations) "will know that I am the LORD." See Exodus 6:7; 7:5; 7:17; 8:10; 9:14; 9:16; 10:2; 12:12; 14:4; 14:18.

"Yahweh's Passover"

God gave the Hebrews very specific instruction as to the manner in which they were to prepare themselves for the night in which judgment would fall on the firstborn in Egypt. Every household was to select a year-old male lamb, keep it under observation for four days, and then kill it. Its blood was to be sprinkled on the doorposts and lintels of all Hebrew homes to protect their firstborn from the avenging angel of Yahweh. Each Hebrew family was to remain inside its home, fully confident that Yahweh would "pass over that doorway" and not allow the destroyer to gain entrance and kill their firstborn (Exod. 12:23). Within their homes they were to eat the lamb (roasted, with no bones broken) along with unleavened bread and bitter herbs. Following that first Passover observance, by morning all Egypt was so stricken that there was ("not a house without someone dead," 12:30). And Pharaoh drove out the Hebrews in haste (vv. 33–34, 39).

The Hebrews were now free to worship their God in a spontaneous, joyous, and caring fashion because of their unbelievable sense of having been redeemed by him from Egypt. They now belonged uniquely to God and to God alone. And the Passover feast provided them with a divinely authenticated way to celebrate the beginning of their national existence in the years that followed. New significance was also given to the seventh day along with this annual Passover remembrance. This meant that their weekly Sabbaths now had more than reference to God's resting following Creation (12:14–17). From henceforth they also regarded God as the author of freedom and social justice, and this gave them a sense of social responsibility that the Jewish community expresses to this day.

Furthermore, the knowledge of God's covenant-keeping name—YHWH (Exod. 3:14–15)—increasingly took on vibrant significance. He had been with them in their anguish of slavery and bitter oppression in Egypt and "brought them out" of it (this phrase occurs forty-seven times in the Pentateuch). Their Yahweh was "greater than all other gods" (18:10–11). How could they not magnify his name? Yahweh is "Our God since Egypt" (C. Barth 1991: 72). Other biblical titles for God, such as Father, King, Redeemer, Savior, and Shepherd, have significance, but Yahweh embodies the One who was, is, and remains faithful to his covenant with Abraham and with his people.

The Egyptians were cruel to the Israelites. Their nation in Scripture is "the prototype and most representative of foreign nations (*gôyim*) of those that were not God's people" (C. Barth 1991: 74). In this sense when God overcame Egypt and delivered his people completely from its power, God was giving notice to the fact that no power on earth could thwart the ongoing purpose he had intended for them. If Egypt could be utterly humiliated, its military power completely overwhelmed, and its gods totally discredited as unworthy of human worship, then all Egypt and all nations surrounding Egypt would know that the God of Abraham, Isaac, and Jacob was indeed the true God.

We would expect that the Old Testament would include numerous references to the annual celebration of Passover. Actually, they are few and far between. During

Israel's wilderness wanderings only one celebration is noted (Num. 9:1–14). Shortly after entering the Promised Land, the Israelites kept the feast (Josh. 5:10). The revivals under Hezekiah (726 B.C.) and Josiah (621 B.C.) produced Passover celebrations worth noting (2 Chron. 30 and 35), and Ezra records a celebration kept "with joy" by the exiles who returned from the Babylonian captivity and rebuilt the Temple (6:19–22). It is probable that during the days of Samuel, David, and Solomon this annual celebration was not observed. It is worth noting that in the Gospels the Passover was annually observed, as it is by the Jewish community today.

"Yahweh Is a Man of War: He Will Reign Forever"

The utter ruin of the Egyptians led the Hebrews to amazement and worship, more than to exultation over their fallen oppressors (Exod. 12:29; 14:26–31). Indeed, the Exodus was totally the action of God. Deliverance came because Yahweh fought for his people. Pharaoh, wind, and sea stood in the way. But all were overcome, not by human activity but by the power of God. There is no other explanation. God delivered a company of oppressed slaves, who through faith in Moses' prophetic word followed his directions and trusted in Yahweh's pledged victory. They saw him move the forces of nature to destroy the Egyptians and accomplish Israel's own deliverance. He violently judged their enemies and graciously liberated them.

We have already mentioned the ambiguity of Moses' use of violence to achieve social justice. We must also take account of the fact that Yahweh is a "warrior" and that as such God will "reign for ever and ever" (Exod. 15:3, 18). This must be viewed in comparison to the words of Jesus Christ against retaliation in any form (Matt. 5:42–48; 26:52, reinforced by James 1:19–21). One can only resolve the apparent contradiction between the Old and the New Testaments by a straightforward reading of the Bible as it stands. One has to grant that Yahweh is revealed neither as a pacifist nor as an advocate of any form of classical just war. He has never endorsed the sort of patriotic pragmatism that has lured Christians into marching to war whenever their country's drums began to call the people to arms. The God of the Bible is far different. The Exodus account shows God to be the Deliverer and Protector of his people. He is willing to engage in violence to further his redemptive purpose for them. At the Red Sea[1] he encountered the Egyptian chariots and horsemen as a "warrior" (15:3) and forbade his people to get involved. Moses conveyed his word: "The LORD will fight for you; you need only to be still" (14:14). He performed a nature miracle, and the Egyptians were overwhelmed. And he alone received the glory for the victory. Here we are only introducing a theme that will be enlarged as we proceed deeper into the biblical record.

---

1. The place where the Hebrews crossed (and where the waters overcame Pharaoh's army) is called in Hebrew *yām-sûp*, or "Sea of Reeds." Scholars differ on the exact location. The larger sea that lay between Egypt and the Arabian Peninsula (and into which the Nile flows) is known as the Red Sea. The reader may want to consult a Bible atlas or a map in a good study Bible. In this work we will use the more conventional name of Red Sea when referring to the place where the Hebrews crossed and were delivered from the power of Pharaoh.

The Exodus Theme and Political Liberation

During the 1970s and 1980s the Exodus theme was widely utilized as evidence that God desires all peoples to enjoy economic and political freedom and that their struggle for social justice by any and all means is not only pleasing in God's sight but is the primary theological rationale for missions. No one argues with the mandate for justice. But to elevate this theme above all others is to "distort the word of God" (2 Cor. 4:2). Those Hebrews whom Yahweh "brought out" from Egypt were a subdued and enslaved minority who were unable to save themselves. They could only cry out to the God of their fathers and mothers. Yahweh alone liberated them "by testings, by miraculous signs and wonders, by war, by a mighty hand and an outstretched arm, or by great and awesome deeds" (Deut. 4:34). The Hebrews accomplished nothing by themselves. There was no military intervention, no revolution. Indeed, Yahweh saw to it that no one could claim any credit for their liberation except God.

At that juncture in their history the Israelites were not a political entity; they were primarily a religious community. This becomes apparent when we realize that their liberation was primarily to glorify the name of Yahweh and only secondarily to end their slavery (Deist 1977: 61).

This priority follows because redemption is God's central activity. The Exodus account emphasizes the signs, plagues, and victory at the Red Sea as a demonstration to the Egyptians of the power of Yahweh. The phrase "that the Egyptians [and Pharaoh] will know that I am the Lord" and its equivalent (Exod. 7:5; 8:10, 12; 14:17) occurs more frequently than "that Israel may know." On one occasion Moses will later beseech God not to destroy the Israelites because of the negative effect doing so would have on the Egyptians (Num. 14:13–16).

Theologies of liberation have tended to politicize the Exodus motif and remove from it all reference to this confessional dimension. They reconceptualize it as principally a human event. Some regard Moses, the man, as solely responsible: "Every revolution needs a leader." Of course, we grant that the oppressed Hebrews would not have recognized Yahweh as the name of their God apart from Moses revealing this to them and then telling them that Yahweh had sent him to be their liberator (Exod. 6:2–3). In a very real sense, Moses should be regarded as one of God's first cross-cultural missionaries (after Joseph) in that he was called by God to go into Egypt to bring the Israelites out in order that they might worship God. But no missionary should ever claim to be able to redeem a people. Only God can do this. And God alone receives all the glory.

> There was the prophetic personality of the man who appeared in the name of God to promise a deliverance he and the Israelites were helpless to effect; and there was the historic event of the deliverance which responded to his prior promise. . . . Discount the call of Moses, and we are left with no reasonable explanation of his strange errand, or any basis for his confidence of success that no material power was at any point invoked to achieve. (Rowley 1956: 42–43)

Although an Exodus-type theme of deliverance and liberation surfaces repeatedly throughout the Scriptures, at this point we do well to ponder the following evaluation by Ferdinand Deist.

> God is a God who intervenes on behalf of the poor and the needy if they accept their own helplessness and call upon him in the firm belief that he alone is mighty to liberate them. They will not therefore look to an outside power to come to their aid, because God himself will send his servant to act on his behalf. (1977: 69)

Sinai: Covenant, Torah, and Invitation to Worship

Following Yahweh's victory over the Egyptians, Moses led the Israelites to "Horeb, the mountain of God" (Exod. 3:2, 12; called Sinai, 19:1–2). This journey was quite difficult, and Moses found his people openly critical of his leadership because of the scarcity of water and food (15:22–18:8). Furthermore, their progress was hindered for a period by the Amalekites (17:8–16). The Israelites had yet to learn that the service of God would not be easy. Finally, after three months they arrived and encamped at the base of the mountain of God, where Moses "went up to God" and received instruction concerning the Sinai revelation. After he descended, his first task was to ascertain the disposition of the people toward Yahweh. Moses conveyed his will to the people.

> You yourselves have seen what I did to Egypt, and how I carried you on eagles' wings and brought you to myself. Now if you obey me fully and keep my covenant, then out of all nations you will be my treasured possession. Although the whole earth is mine, you will be for me a kingdom of priests and a holy nation. (Exod. 19:4–6)

There are seven aspects of a new relationship centered at Sinai that have bearing on God's purposes for his people as they develop into a faith community.

Covenant Renewal

The response of the people was unconditional: "We will do everything the LORD has said" (Exod. 19:8). The die was cast. Nothing remained but for Moses to consecrate them for two days in anticipation of Yahweh's promise on the morning of the third day to "come down on Mount Sinai in the sight of all the people" (v. 11).

On the morning of the third day, Moses led the people to the foot of the mountain. Most awesome was the scene before them—a thick cloud rested on the mountain, and the great theophany of the Old Testament occurred (Exod. 19:16–19). Yahweh "came down" upon Sinai and "spoke to them from heaven" (Neh. 9:13). His words constituted the central message of the Old Testament. God gave his people "regulations and laws that are just and right, decrees and commands that are good . . . [his] holy Sabbath . . . and commands, decrees and laws through . . . Moses" (Neh. 9:13–14). At Sinai the Israelites entered into a solemn commitment to the God who had delivered them. Election demands response: the response of worship and service. Israel was called to the privilege of responsibility, to accept Yahweh's call to be his people and to accept God's covenant. Hence, at Sinai Israel as a nation became the Lord's people through an extension of the covenant made with Abraham and the patriarchs. Still later, after Israel's conquest of Canaan, the covenant would be reiterated by declaration and acceptance (Josh. 24:1–28).

In a very real sense this pattern of covenant renewal was an obligation put before each succeeding generation. One might wonder why an "everlasting covenant" needs constant renewal. At Sinai God created Israel and made the Israelites his people, a once-for-all birth event. But the witness of Scripture is that "Joshua made a covenant with the people" at Shechem on the occasion of his retirement (Josh. 24:25), and Yahweh confirmed its reinforcement of the full revelation at Sinai. Occasions of covenant renewal are important and need to be celebrated to underscore the continuity of God's people under his rule. New leaders were thereby reminded of Israel's need to pledge unconditional loyalty to Yahweh, reaffirm the obligation to "fill a priestly role as a people in the midst of the peoples," and thereby "represent Yahweh in the world of nations." As Johannes Blauw states: "What priests are for a people, Israel as a people is for the world" (1962: 24). By covenant renewal Israel was reminded of its dual character. It is a religious community—a church under the Abrahamic-Sinaitic covenant—and a nation in the midst of other nations.

In this connection the name Yahweh is important, not as something to be verbalized endlessly in repetitive ritual, but as a pointer to God himself. God liberated his people so that they might voluntarily choose to be a worshiping community in the midst of the nations. This is the significance of Yahweh's word via Moses: "Let my people go, so that they may hold a festival to me in the desert" (Exod. 5:1). Israel was called to the worship of God. This means the focus of all the nation's activities should be God himself and that no activity is to be undertaken that is not in some way related to the nation's divine calling. The Israelites were delivered from slavery that they might become the devoted people of Yahweh. The law of God (Torah) was given to them at Sinai so that their devotion might be directed in ways pleasing to him and their worship in a manner befitting a redeemed people.

Torah—Its Content and Purpose

Once the covenant had been offered and accepted, the people were ready to receive the law of God (Torah). Torah comprises almost half of the content of the Pentateuch. It consists of the "covenant law" (Exod. 20:2–23:19), later called the "Book of the Covenant" (Exod. 24:7). Then follows the law of holiness, or Holiness Code (Lev. 17–26). On the plains of Moab through Moses the "Deuteronomic Law" was given (Deut. 12–26). It was not a "second law" as the name erroneously implies but a contextualized restatement of the basic law for the Israelites as they faced the conquest of Canaan under Joshua. The ritual for covenant renewal is detailed in Deuteronomy 27:15–26. Beyond these major units we find detailed instruction on the regulation of all priestly ministries, Israel's cycle of annual feasts, acceptable worship, sexual prohibitions, stewardship (tithes and offerings), the sale of patrimony land, the Sabbath and the jubilee year, laws of inheritance, and so forth. Biblical scholars generally agree that

> We cannot make clear-cut distinctions or classify the laws according to different degrees of authority or importance. . . . Moral laws and liturgical rules might seem to differ in quality, but in the Old Testament all are equally God's Word. (C. Barth 1991: 133)

We recall that in his condemnation of the scribes and Pharisees on the occasion of his last visit to the Temple, Jesus stated that there were levels of relevance within Torah.

> Woe to you, teachers of the law and Pharisees, you hypocrites! You give a tenth of your spices—mint, dill and cummin. But you have neglected the more important matters of the law—justice, mercy and faithfulness. You should have practiced the latter, without neglecting the former. (Matt. 23:23)

Then again, we recall how Jesus commended the lawyer who, when asked what was written in the law, replied by calling attention to the dual obligation to love God and neighbor (cf. Luke 10:26–28 with Deut. 6:5 and Lev. 19:18). On another occasion a scribe asked Jesus to identify the "first of all the commandments." In response he quoted the Shema of Deuteronomy 6:4 and made the obligation to love God primary (Mark 12:28–31), even above loving one's neighbor.

The Torah constitutes an eternal revelation of God that was given to Israel for its unity, its sanctification, its preservation within the covenant relationship, and its well-being. The details constitute a complete whole, in that no subsequent additions were ever made. God spoke once and for all through his servant Moses. The Torah has permanent authority although "each generation has to hear it afresh and see its application to changing circumstances" (C. Barth 1991: 135).

The prohibition that Israel should worship no gods other than Yahweh (Exod. 20:3; Deut. 5:7) is not an explicit denial of the reality of other gods so much as a demand that Israel not worship them, for "the LORD, whose name is Jealous, is a jealous God" (Exod. 20:5; 34:14). We deduce from this the utter reasonableness of God making "totalitarian claims" upon his covenant people. He has the right to penetrate every facet of their individual and corporate life (Deut. 18:13). The "zeal" of the Lord was his "jealous" love for Israel (both words are the same in Hebrew; see Josh. 24:19). From henceforth the Israelites were to be a "holy" people. Their relationship to God separated them for special service. Through their obedience to the law, their "holy" character was to take on an ethical quality as well, for its primary concerns are ethical. We should not be surprised, therefore, that severe strictures are made against even speaking the names of other gods (Exod. 23:13). Yahweh had a passionate desire to consider Israel as his own. He refused to share Israel with any other deity. "Having bound himself unconditionally and unrestrictedly to Israel, he asked for no less dedication on Israel's part" (C. Barth

1991: 141). From among all the nations God chooses Israel ("nations" in the Old Testament has a religious, nonpolitical meaning) (Deut. 10:15). That Israel was elected by God does not mean that other nations have been rejected by God. The Old Testament never states or even implies that individuals or nations were ever elected unto damnation.

The concrete relation of the nations to Israel is the primary frame of reference by which God regards them. These nations are free to enter into an open-ended relationship with Israel and share in both its blessing and its salvation (Exod. 12:47–49). Since the active presence of God is the central problem and dominant reality in the history of all nations, God may use the nations as his instruments for judgment as well as for blessing (Isa. 10:5–13, 24–27). And yet beyond this, Israel represents the rule of God, his first fruit from among the nations (Deut. 28:10). Hence, the nations are called to recognize God as the God of the whole earth. When they witness Yahweh's deeds in Israel, they are summoned thereby to acknowledge him (Ps. 67:7; Blauw 1962: 25–27). Earlier we stated that Moses was a missionary to the Israelites. We now add that he also was a missionary to the Egyptians. He demonstrated to them the weakness of their gods, with the result that some followed him and joined the Israelites (Exod. 12:38).

The gods of the nations are unimportant and powerless when compared with Yahweh. We tend to be baffled over the Israelite penchant for idolatry. They fashioned and worshiped a golden calf almost immediately after the Exodus and persisted in the worship of idols until the Babylonian Captivity. Just prior to that final catastrophe they introduced the grossest images into the inner precincts of the Temple (Ezek. 8:7–18). In his defense before the Sanhedrin centuries later, Stephen reminded Jewish leaders of this and of the Exile, the judgment of God brought about because of Israel's worship of other gods (cf. Acts 7:40–43 with Amos 5:25–27).

The Sabbath

At Sinai God instructed the Israelites to associate in their minds the implications of the Creation story with their own deliverance from Egypt. As a result, they began to divide time into weekly units. The six days of God's creative work were followed by the Lord's Sabbath rest, when God contemplated with contentment what had been achieved. This reminder was coupled at Sinai with the stipulation that because they had been brought out of Egypt with "his mighty hand and out-stretched arm," henceforth they were to "keep the Sabbath day" (cf. Exod. 20:8–11 with Deut. 5:15). Like their God they were to live by a Sabbath rhythm of time: six days of work followed by a day of rest. This would bring them physical renewal and the opportunity to enjoy the fruit of their labors. Not only would it provide relief from the heavy routine of work, it also would bring them the possibility of psychological and spiritual renewal.

Because the Sabbath was given to a redeemed people who had chosen to live under the rule of God and for his glory, it was also to be a commemoration and a sign of his redemptive acts on their behalf. Hence, the Sabbath was to be "the holy day of the Lord," made honorable by their taking delight in him during its quiet hours. The Sabbath was not to be regarded as a day for doing what the Israelites liked to do (Isa. 58:13). It provided them with the privilege of worship and the opportunity to offer up special sacrifices to him (Isa. 58:14; Num. 28:9–10). In this sense it was a sign between Yahweh and Israel that they had been set apart as his very own (Ezek. 20:12, 20). The Sabbath belonged to the Lord and to God's people, his choice possession. Through faithful observance of the Sabbath, God would be assured of their gratitude. Furthermore, by keeping the Sabbath they proclaimed to the surrounding peoples God's "mighty acts" of Creation and Redemption.

Later the prophets would denounce Israel for profaning the Sabbath (Isa. 56:2, 6; 58:13; Jer. 17:19–27; Ezek. 20:12–13, 24; 22:8, 26; 23:38), thereby marring Israel's witness to the nations. In the early church Jewish believers kept the Sabbath and also gathered to worship the Christ on the first day of each week in joyous commemoration of his resurrection. The apostle Paul kept the Sabbath yet warned against becoming legalistic about Sabbath observance (Col. 2:16, 23). Christians were to remember that "the Sabbath was made for man, not man for the Sabbath" and that "the Son of Man is Lord even of the Sabbath" (Mark 2:27–28). Even so, the church in missionary obedience needs to avoid underestimating the potential for Christian witness contained in observance of the Sabbath. Not only by this celebration is confession made of the God of Creation, it also expresses confidence in Christ's redemptive activity. Christians also bear witness to Christ's triumphant resurrection by setting aside everyday concerns and gathering for worship with God's people. They look forward with joy not only to each new week before them but to their eternal hope and final rest in God (Heb. 4:7, 9).

The Worship of the Redeemed

It was a redeemed people that began to sing to the Lord on the shore of the Red Sea following the destruction of Pharaoh's army (Exod. 15:1–18). At the end of the New Testament, when the final eschatological triumph of God is achieved, the redeemed sing the song of Moses, the servant of God, and the song of the Lamb because the Passover lamb is given Christological significance (cf. Rev. 15:3 and 1 Cor. 5:7). But in the narrative of Exodus the Israelite's understanding of redemption is portrayed as largely confined to an awareness of the deliverance of their firstborn by the protecting blood of the Passover lamb and to the rod of Moses that summoned Yahweh to the rescue of his people and enabled them to escape from the pursuing Egyptians (Exod. 14:16, 21, 26). It was only when Yahweh confronted them at Sinai and proclaimed the essence of their covenantal relation to him that they began to sense themselves as a redeemed people, chosen by him to be his possession forever.

The Book of the Covenant (Exod. 20–23) defined the boundaries of their existence as Yahweh's people. The Ten Commandments (20:2–17) constituted the basis of all the civil and cultic laws that followed. By this intimate association God decreed the complete absence of any false dichotomy between the sacred and the secular. The people of Israel heartily accepted this covenant and promised to be an obedient people (24:3–11).

The stage was set for Yahweh to begin the lengthy disclosure of his will concerning the sort of worship that alone would be acceptable to him. Significantly, God did not begin with any reference to sacrifice or the need for expiation or atonement or forgiveness or reconciliation. First was a call for a freewill offering of gold, silver, precious stones, and other items (Exod. 25:1–7). Yahweh would have his people use these materials to construct a portable sanctuary for God where he might dwell in their midst. They were to begin with his throne (represented by an ark and a mercy seat) and then construct the surrounding structures, furniture, and furnishings as directed. These were all symbols of Yahweh's intent to dwell in the midst of God's people and receive their worship. When all the components of this portable "tent of meeting" were in place, the glory of God flooded the inner sanctuary, the Holy of Holies, and acceptable worship became possible.

The Israelites were also taught that they could not meet with God directly, but only through the mediation of priests whom he had personally chosen. Hence, the Torah devotes considerable space to the special covenants Yahweh made with the Aaronic priests and their subsidiary helpers, the Levites (Num. 25:12–13). Detailed instruction was given for their installation and consecration (Exod. 28–29, 40; Lev. 8). Central to the priestly duties was the annual Day of Atonement, the only day of fasting that was mandatory for all Israel in the Mosaic legislation. On this day the high priest exercised his most solemn and significant mediatorial office. Its purpose was to avert the holy wrath of God on the nation for its sinfulness. Total cleansing was required to remove all defilement from priests and people, from the sanctuary, the land, and the nation. Its objective was to ensure the continued dwelling of God in the midst of God's people. This day of national atonement prefigured the future when all the causes of God's displeasure with his people will be utterly and finally removed.

From the perspective of the New Testament, we see that the Old Testament sacrificial system enabled the remnant to manifest their personal faith so that their sins were "covered," looking forward to the one truly efficacious sacrifice of Jesus the Christ. The older system, demanding the "blood of bulls and goats," could never "take away sins" (Heb. 10:4, 11), but these sacrifices anticipated the final sacrifice once for all of the "Lamb of God, who takes away the sin of the world" (John 1:29). Christ's perfect and final sacrifice marked the end of the old sacrificial system of animal sacrifice (Heb. 9:12–28).

The Challenge of Rabbinic Judaism

We should take note of the fact that contemporary Judaism speaks out against the New Testament thesis that "without the shedding of blood there is no forgiveness" (Heb. 9:22). Rabbis argue that if a Jew sins, Jewish law enables him or her to return to God and right action through repentance—in Hebrew, těšûbâ, from the word for "return."

We should not underestimate the serious nature of this challenge. When the Temple was destroyed by Nebuchadnezzar, it was rationalized that God sanctioned forgiveness and redemption apart from any reference to blood atonement. However, when God made "a lasting ordinance: . . . Atonement is to be made once a year for all the sins of the Israelites" (Lev. 16:34), he called particular attention to the blood of the sacrifice offered upon this solemn occasion. "I have given it to you to make atonement on the altar; it is the blood that makes atonement for one's life" (Lev. 17:11).

Israel abused the sacrificial system prior to the Babylonian Captivity. But this did not cause God to reject what he had instituted (Amos 5:21–22). The prophets saw to this. They stressed that if the penitent offered first the sacrifice of "a broken spirit; a broken and contrite heart," God would then delight in "righteous sacrifices" and "whole burnt offerings" (Ps. 51:16–19). To argue that God changed his mind with respect to his institution of the sacrificial system as normative for Israelite worship is contrary to Scripture. One looks in vain throughout the Old Testament and in Israel's subsequent history for any convocation comparable to Sinai at which by divine command this immensely important sacrificial system was explicitly terminated. We can only conclude that Jewish worship today no longer conforms to the law.

On the contrary, the tabernacle and later the Temple, with its elaborate ritual, enabled the devout to experience the sort of dynamic interaction with Yahweh that brought assurance of forgiveness and acceptance. God's instruction in Torah on sacrifice and atonement gave to the devout a deepening consciousness of their need for purity of heart and absolute sincerity of motivation if their sacrifices were to be acceptable (Isa. 1:10–15; Jer. 7:21–26; Amos 4:4, 5; 5:21–24). This sense of need prepared them for Yahweh's subsequent promise that one of their own kind would effectively provide in himself the perfect sacrifice and acceptable worship, becoming the mediator. Only the Messiah—the Holy One of Israel—could validate the great principles of the Sinaitic sacrificial system and become (1) the priestly instrument through whom the Israelites might approach the living God of fire without being burned; (2) the means of continuing communion between God and the penitent; and (3) the all-sufficient thank-offering offered by the redeemed to God. The Messiah would thereby mediate a total forgiveness for sinners as well as guarantee that the redeemed would continue to stand in the divine presence.

The Land

Of all the promises made to the patriarchs, the one that concerned the land is as prominent and decisive as the promise that all the nations would be blessed through their seed. The land had been unconditionally promised to them, although their retention of it was contingent on their obedience. If Yahweh's commandments were disobeyed, they would be expelled (Lev. 26:32–33; Deut. 28:63–68; 29:28). Their national and cultic life would end. However, when they repented, they would be restored (Lev. 26:40–45; Deut. 30:1–10). Even though they might be scattered among the nations, Yahweh promised that his grace would follow them to bring them to repentance.

The promise of land was so significant that it made the rise of the Israelites as a people appear almost incidental next to the importance of the conquest of the land of Canaan. The land was all-important. The land would come to them as a gift. Because of the wickedness of the Canaanites, God wanted them driven out of the land that he had promised to the patriarchs (Deut. 9:4–5). Yahweh alone, and not the Israelite armies, would give them the land (Ps. 44:3). His redemptive purpose underlay this transaction: "He gave them the lands of the nations, and they fell heir to what others had toiled for—that they might keep his precepts and observe his laws" (Ps. 105:44–45).

The land was subsequently divided by lot for cultivation (Num. 26:55), whether by families or by tribes. The casting of lots involved a process by which God alone decided upon its division. The land was God's to divide, and the produce of the land was also his. As a result he was jealous for his land and decreed that it be respected. The Israelites were obligated to keep regular Sabbaths in order to preserve and renew their land (Lev. 25:2, 4). The Israelites were to present their tithes as representing themselves and all the fruit of the land (Deut. 14:22; 26:9–15). The land was a good land, "flowing with milk and honey," and God wanted its goodness to be enhanced, not marred, by his people.

One stipulation stands out above all others: the covenant obligation that Yahweh's people practice justice and show mercy to the poor and minority groups within the land (Deut. 10:17–19; 16:18–20). The Israelites' oppression at the hands of the Egyptians was to serve as a constant reminder that they were not to be exploiters and dehumanizers of persons in the way Pharaoh's people had treated them. Freedom and justice for all were to be the hallmarks of God's land. Obedience to the covenant would bring "rain on your land in its season" and abundant harvests, but disobedience would cause God to withhold the rain and even cause the Israelites to lose their land (Deut. 11:13–17; 28:63–68).

The Lifestyle of God's People

At Sinai Yahweh gave to the Israelites explicit instruction as to the lifestyle befitting a redeemed people. In doing so, he amplified the cultural mandate and emphasized key concepts inherent in his character and reflective of the Exodus motif. Mission as it develops in the New Testament embraces the holistic principles that are laid out clearly as follows.

Land: tenancy, not ownership. The land promised to Abraham and his posterity through Isaac belongs to Yahweh and not to Israel or to individual Israelites ("The land is mine," Lev. 25:23). It was to be divided equally among all the families. For their tenancy they were to pay to Yahweh a tithe (10 percent) as rent. The rent was not to be paid to some rich landlord living at ease in a nearby castle! The tithe was given to the Levites, who were forbidden to own land. Every seventh year the land was to lie fallow. For the sixth year God promised a larger harvest, after the pattern of his provision of manna in the wilderness (Exod. 23:10–11; Lev. 25:2–7).

Land: redistribution, not accumulation. Every fiftieth year the land was to lie fallow; in addition all peasants who had lost their freedom through insolvency were to be set free, and all lands that had been sold were to be returned to the original owners or their families (Lev. 25:8–17). God thereby showed his hostility toward the emergence of a landowning aristocracy because this inevitably leads to the oppression of the landless (Isa. 5:8). Mutual helpfulness was to characterize the people of God. The perils of both affluence and poverty were to be everyone's concern (Lev. 25:18–55).

Slavery: justice, not exploitation. A slave was the property of his or her master. The slave could have been acquired by purchase (Gen. 17:12; 37:28), by capture in war (Num. 31:9; 2 Kings 5:2), by birth from slaves already owned (Exod. 21:4), in place of a debt owed by the one enslaved (Lev. 25:39, 47), or as a gift (Gen. 29:24). Yet we should not confuse the lot of the slave in Israel with that of slaves in the polytheistic societies surrounding Israel. In Israel the relation between slaves and masters was essentially the same as that between family members and the master. Slaves were not regarded as inferior. Though they had no civil rights, they were regarded as "of the family." In the treatment of their slaves, Hebrew masters were bound by the regulations of the Mosaic law (Deut. 15:15). Slaves were to be protected and not exploited (Exod. 21:2–27; Lev. 25:25–55). The subsequent disregard of these regulations led to numerous abuses (Jer. 34:3–22).

Minority peoples: protection, not denigration. Non-Israelites who placed themselves under Israel's protection (distinct from the foreigner whose stay was temporary) had certain rights, privileges, and responsibilities and were classified with widows, fatherless children, and the needy (Deut. 10:19). One reason given for the observance of the Sabbath is that "sojourners" might rest and be refreshed (Exod. 23:12). The gleanings of the vineyard and the harvest field were left for them (Lev. 19:10; 23:22; Deut. 24:19–21). They were included in the provision made regarding the cities of refuge (Num. 35:15). Because they were defenseless, God promised to be their defense and the judge of those who oppressed them (Jer. 7:6; 22:3). The sojourner, or resident alien, was virtually on a level with the Israelite (Lev. 24:22), and in Ezekiel's vision of the messianic age they are to share the inheritance of Israel (Ezek. 47:22–23; Carson 1962: 1219). The extended emphasis in the Old Testament on the "stranger within the gates" means that the church-in-mission today must give priority to the needs of all minority and immigrant peoples, an issue particularly important today with regard to the millions of displaced and refugee people we find all over the globe. There is a good reason why Jesus included Samaria in his final reference to the missionary task (Acts 1:8). The Samaritans were a despised minority people among the Jews in Jesus' day. It would have been a temptation for those early Jewish believers to withhold the gospel from them. But they did just the opposite (Acts 8:4–25).

Widows. Widows were regarded as helpless, needy persons, unable to protect or provide for themselves. They were to be given special consideration and treated with justice (Exod. 22:22–24; Deut. 10:18; 24:17–21; Mal. 3:5). Since their rights were often overlooked or denied, God made them his particular concern (Ps. 68:5–6;

146:9; Prov. 15:25). In a sense widows represent all the disenfranchised persons in society, those who are deprived of reasonable livelihood and need care by others.

This view of an egalitarian society exalted labor, denounced idleness, expected fathers to train their sons to acquire skills with their hands, furthered human reciprocity and justice, and demonstrated an active concern for one's neighbors. It respected the dignity of both men and women, the bearers of the divine image. In Deuteronomy the Israelites were constantly reminded of their deliverance by God from Egyptian slavery. The gracious God who had liberated them wanted them never to forget that they had been an abused and exploited minority people, totally unable to relieve their misery. Hence, they were urged again and again to be mindful of the poor, the needy, and the politically deprived in their midst (Deut. 8:11–18; 10:17–19; 15:7–15; 16:11–14; 24:17–22; 26:5–12; Deist 1977: 61).

We shall find that many years later when the Israelites established the monarchy and Israel became a political entity in its own right, this original pattern of social egalitarianism was replaced with an unhealthy stratification of the rich and the poor, the powerful and the helpless, the privileged and the exploited. God countered by sending his prophets. In protest the prophets recalled the Egyptian bondage, the Hebrews' undeserved deliverance, the Sinaitic laws, and the alternatives of divine blessing or judgment.

The Relation of Sinai to the Gospel

In our day we increasingly hear that the Jewish people by virtue of the Sinaitic covenant are redemptively related to and hence fully accepted by God. The implication is that this relationship to him is such that Christians have no evangelistic obligation to them. It follows that for a Christian to press the claims of Jesus Christ on them is an affront to their piety, expressed at Sinai: "We will do everything the LORD has said" (Exod. 19:8). Furthermore, such evangelistic effort is unwarranted, since, it is claimed, they already have access to God.

The apostle Paul's arguments in Romans and Galatians presses us not to misunderstand the Old Testament witness. His crucial issue is the relationship of law to gospel. The tragic error is to assume that what was revealed at Sinai in some way supercedes the Abrahamic covenant. One encounters this confusion in contemporary Judaism. All Jews regard Abraham as their father and appropriate tenaciously the promise of "the land" as well as keep the rite of circumcision as the sign of the covenant God made with Abraham. However, when it comes to their obedience to a personal relationship with God, the Sinaitic law is made to be determinative.

We might ask, "Why Sinai, if it was to be subordinate to the Abrahamic covenant?" Paul says it was "added because of transgressions" (Gal. 3:19). "The law was added so that the trespass might increase" (Rom. 5:20), as a sort of afterthought (*pareisēlthen*) to serve the interests of the Abrahamic promise by making people aware of their fallenness and sinfulness. Only thereby would the awareness of their spiritual need press them to seek the same grace that Abraham received because he believed (Gen. 15:6). One has only to ponder the promise of the new covenant (Jer. 31:31–37) to realize that the Sinaitic form of the covenant was to be replaced with the final and full revelation of Jesus Christ and his redemptive cross. When the writer to the Hebrews speaks of the old covenant becoming "obsolete," his reference is not to the Abrahamic covenant but to the Sinaitic administration of it (8:8–13, especially v. 13). When Jesus inaugurated the Eucharist, he explained that the wine represented his "blood of the covenant" (Matt. 26:28) and thereby pointed the way to a new time in which the administration of the covenant of grace would be of the Spirit and inward, written on "the fleshly tables of the heart" rather than on "tables of stone." This matter will be discussed further when we seek to trace the apostle Paul's understanding of the missionary dimension of the Kingdom of God.

Conclusion

In this chapter we have found anticipations of many components of the Kingdom theme that will be developed more fully in the New Testament. First, the sovereign activity of God: He is the God who delivers but particularly who redeems and brings into being a covenant-defined people. Second, the essentialness of personal commitment to God: "Whosoever will may come" is an invitation written large over the whole sacrificial system. God seeks the worship of his people, and it is only when they turn to him personally in repentance and faith that a relationship is established with him. Third, the communal character and societal responsibilities of his people: There are only two essential commandments: to love God and to love one's neighbor (Lev. 19:18; Deut. 6:5). Concerning these commandments, Jesus said, "Do this and you will live" (Luke 10:25–28). The faith that responds in personal commitment conditions the heart to serve God and neighbor. Fourth, organized evil opposing the will of God is a reality. When God acts in human affairs, interfering with the natural sequence of events,

> the forces working against him enter into coalition, for the world revolts against the claim of the divine upon it. In this case, Pharaoh embodied all the demonic forces of resistance. Evil had to display all its power so that the judgment upon it could be more significant and God's glory shine forth to greater effect. (de Dietrich 1960: 66)

Finally, the Exodus event anticipates the Last Judgment. God will not be mocked. Those who revolt against him will perish, that is, they will be excluded "from the presence of the Lord and from the majesty of his power" (2 Thess. 1:9). He will triumph in human history as both Savior and Judge. This means the certainty of a future for the people of God in the coming of God's Kingdom rule that is already a present reality but is not yet fully realized.

6

God Forms a Nation
of People
Belonging to God

Introduction

The period from Sinai to Samuel began with Israel's wilderness wanderings and the final march to the borders of Canaan. The closing discourses of Moses on the eve of entry into the Promised Land set the stage for the conquest of Canaan under Joshua. Then followed more than two hundred years of troubled history, marked by fitful obedience to God, foreign invasions, and occasions of limited deliverance achieved by charismatic leaders called judges. The account of Samuel, the last of the judges, coupled with the flawed attempt of Saul to forge a political unity of the people, provide transition to the beginning of the Israelite monarchy.

Israel was to be a "blessing to the nations." Yet Israel's encounter with other nations involved mostly conflict and conquest rather than showcasing to these nations the covenant relationship to God envisioned in Deuteronomy. Yet throughout Israel's history one concept is central: the God of Abraham, Isaac, and Jacob rules over Israel and over all the nations. Throughout this troubled period Israel was exposed to divine lessons we do well to heed. First, the wilderness wanderings consumed the generation that had experienced liberation from Egyptian bondage. At the outset everything seemed to point toward what would be a quick ten-day march from Sinai to Canaan via Kadesh. But at Kadesh the people willfully rejected God's will, and almost forty years elapsed before they came to the plains of Moab on the eastern border of Canaan. During this period a new generation of Israelites replaced those who had experienced the Egyptian oppression as adults. They were tested in various ways, particularly by hostile Amorites, Moabites, and Midianites (Num. 21, 25, 31). When they finally reached Moab, Moses ordered their last encampment under his leadership. He then gave detailed instruction in the Sinaitic law, particularly in the light of the new situation that would confront the younger generation in the Promised Land. Significantly, he did not attempt to alter in any way the instruction the Aaronic priests and Levites had received while at Sinai. This earlier instruction was quite extensive (Exod. 28, 29, 39, 40; Lev. 1–8, 11–17, 21, 22, 27; Num. 15, 29). The concern of Moses was that God's will be fully understood. He particularly stressed the thesis that obedience to Yahweh brings blessing, but disobedience can lead to disaster. Then he appointed Joshua to be his successor. When this final task was finished, Moses ascended Mount Pisgah, was given sight of the land afar off, and died alone. God buried him.

With Joshua a new, second era began. The Jordan River was crossed, and under his leadership three massive thrusts were made into Canaan: first in the center, then in the south, and finally in the north. Despite the incompleteness of this effort, the land was shortly thereafter apportioned among the tribes of Israel. It is the Book of Joshua that introduces us to the phenomenon of Yahweh's warfare.

In the Old Testament, God intervened in human affairs through electing Israel and choosing this people to constitute a theocracy. This meant that they would live under his direct rule and thus foreshadow the coming of the Kingdom of God. At Sinai God made Israel his people. With the conquest Israel became a nation among the nations of the ancient world. God did not endow the Israelites with superhuman faculties, but because of his theocratic presence in their midst, it was possible for them to function as an incipient Kingdom of God in the midst of the kingdoms of other peoples. Although this unique theocracy failed, the failure reflects less the weakness of ancient Israel than the fallenness of all human beings.

So then, Israel in the land began to take on the aspect of permanent acquisition and geographic space, although its borders would not have precise definition. The sword was to be given to its leaders. By this act God gave legitimacy to the defense of the state against hostile neighboring states. Israel was an altogether human institution, not something miraculous. Its uniqueness was that Yahweh participated in the activities of its members and their societal institutions. It was only because of God's presence in Israel that we can regard the nation as constituting a preview or incipient expression of the rule of the King, the Kingdom of God. Although other nations in the ancient Near East also regarded themselves as theocracies, each with its particular god or gods, Israel's God was unique. Yahweh alone claimed to be the creator of the entire universe, forbade all efforts to image him, and regarded all other gods as nonentities, devoid of all function and power. Furthermore, he was the moral governor who reigned over the universe in righteousness and justice (Isa. 32:1).

We recognize that the political nation of Israel was a failure, for, as we shall see, it did not directly culminate in the redemption of the human race. But its very failure was a necessary demonstration that nothing of human achievement could bring about a world of peace and justice. This failure pointed to the need for a solution outside the human realm. The direct intervention of God is needed to transform human history.

This means that Old Testament instances of Yahweh's warfare, which we are about to review, will not be identical to his Kingdom activity in the New Testament. Indeed, this phenomenon will take on a different significance when Jesus inaugurates the Kingdom of God, not as a nation-state but as a realm within the hearts of God's people among all nations. The Kingdom of God will then have no geographic or racial boundaries but will be found wherever the King is acknowledged in personal faith and obedience. Warfare will then give way to something entirely different, for Jesus will have denied his people the use of the sword to further his mission (Matt. 26:52; John 18:36). Furthermore, by the cross Jesus will have completely undone "the devil's work" (1 John 3:8) and made futile any need to use violence to further the righteousness of God (James 1:20). Through the gift of the Holy Spirit at Pentecost, the key reality of the new covenant, it will be possible for the people of God to enter upon a different kind of warfare: wrestling against principalities and powers and preaching the good news of the Kingdom. We shall discuss all this in due course.

Encountering the Wilderness

We have already referred to the three-month journey of the Hebrews from the Red Sea to Sinai (Exod. 15:22–18:27). This was their first experience with the wilderness, and it provoked much grumbling against Moses. Where was there water to drink and food to eat? In response, God began the pattern of providing these necessities in ways that reflected his faithfulness. Even when they were threatened by the hostile Amalekites, God enabled Joshua to drive them off. At last Sinai was reached, and in the months that followed, memories of this difficult journey faded. However, from this wilderness experience, before and after the Sinai encampment, we note three mission-related lessons: God's provision, Israel's rebellion, and Jethro's conversion.

First, let's consider God's provision. In the second month of their second year at Sinai, the Israelites began their second wilderness experience. At the outset none dared to believe that it would last almost forty years. The full story is found in Numbers 9:15–17:13; 20:1–26:65. The stages in the journey are reviewed in Numbers 33:16–49. The generation that endured these long years in that "terrible place" (Num. 20:5) indelibly planted on the conscience of Israel the fact that it was God who miraculously sustained them, so much so that God's provision in the desert became a foundational element in Israel's faith (C. Barth 1991: 86 and Ps. 78, 105, 106, 136). During this period God demonstrated in many ways his faithfulness to his covenant people, despite the fact that again and again they revealed themselves to be stubborn, rebellious, impatient, unbelieving, and even arrogant.

Strange as it may seem, many subsequent Old Testament references to this transitional period between Egyptian bondage and settlement in Canaan convey the impression that God's election-care was even more vividly demonstrated in the wilderness than at the Exodus or through Joshua's conquest of Canaan (Deut. 32:9–12; Jer. 2:2, 3; 31:2, 3; Hos. 13:4–6; Amos 3:2; etc.). Despite all the negative things that Scripture says about the conduct of Israel in the wilderness, God managed to awaken in his people a willingness to belong to him.

To state this is not to overlook the constant grumbling of the people. When they cried out in pain and sought relief, God heard them and responded. But when they complained by charging God with having overlooked their inherent rights, he regarded them as "rebellious" people (Num. 17:10) who "tested" and "grieved" him to his face (14:22; Ps. 78:40–41).

A second theme coursing through the story has to do with Israel's rebellion. Instances of Israel's rebellion against the God who "carried" them "as a father carries his son" increased in frequency (cf. Deut. 1:31 with Num. 11:11–18 and Isa. 63:9). Even Aaron and Miriam revolted (Num. 12:1–15). But the rebellion reached its climax over the report of the twelve men Moses sent to reconnoiter the land of Canaan and evaluate its peoples, their cities and fortresses, the soil and its produce. When they returned after forty days, they all agreed that the land had tremendous potential. But ten men argued that its inhabitants were so numerous and strong that it would be foolhardy, even disastrous if they were to attempt to occupy it. This "bad report" (Num. 13:32) and the general revolt against God that it precipitated brought the wrath of God upon God's people, and God decreed that the first Israel ("every one of you twenty years old or more," 14:29) would die in the wilderness (vv. 31–35). Only after this first generation of Israelites had totally expired would their children, the second Israel, be allowed to enter the land. Caleb and Joshua would be spared because they alone among the twelve had courageously challenged this majority report (13:30; 14:6–10, 24, 30, 36–38). In arrogant disbelief the Israelites then sought to enter the land, only to be routed at considerable loss (vv. 39–45).

This precipitated a revolt against Moses under the leadership of Korah (Num. 16:1–11). One is amazed at the number of those who aligned themselves against God at this time. One is also sobered by God's anger. The rebel leaders were punished (v. 26), with thousands perishing in the plague that followed (vv. 41–50). Even so, God's anger was restrained: "Yet I looked on them with pity and did not destroy them or put an end to them in the desert" (Ezek. 20:17).

With the passing of time the wanderings of that earlier generation came to the same bitter end—death in the wilderness (Num. 26:63–65). A new generation emerged and developed under the wilderness discipline. It emerged as a new Israel, alongside disobedient Israel. In one sense we might say it was a renewed Israel. By the time its members reached maturity, all had become aware that the older generation had passed away. Leadership was then transferred from Moses to Joshua.

This transfer of leadership reminds us of the heavy judgment brought against Moses. He did not escape God's wrath (Num. 20:2–13) but remained part of that wandering generation who never entered the Promised Land. His brother, Aaron, died soon after this judgment was announced. Moses then sensed that his own death was also at hand (vv. 22–29). At the plains of Moab, he gave his final instructions to Israel, largely a contextualized review of the Sinai legislation. He then publicly designated Joshua as the leader of the new Israel. His lifework finished, Moses withdrew to die alone and be buried by God "in Moab" (Deut. 34:6).

A third significant element of the wilderness narrative concerns the conversion of Jethro, Moses' father-in-law. Exodus 18 tells the story. One can well believe that Jethro went through a succession of experiences before responding positively in commitment to a covenantal relationship with the God of Abraham, Isaac, and Jacob. Jethro had a religious upbringing and was "the priest of Midian" (v. 1). When Moses, the refugee from Egypt, entered his household and later married his daughter Zipporah, his religious horizons must have expanded through Moses' sharing the stories of the patriarchs and describing God's covenant with them. And we can be sure that he was troubled when Moses, while preparing to return to Egypt under God's direction, spurned Zipporah. It was a daring and unwomanly act for her to circumcise their firstborn son and then rebuke Moses for his careless avoidance of performing this covenant rite (Exod. 4:24–26).

The narrative then changes its tone. Almost immediately Moses began to tell Jethro "everything the LORD had done to Pharaoh and to the Egyptians for Israel's sake and about all the hardships they had met along the way and how the LORD had saved them" (Exod. 18:8). Significantly, Moses did not mention himself; he merely related what the Lord had done. As a result, Jethro rejoiced (v. 9) and then wonderfully identified himself with Moses, with the Israelites, and with God's ongoing redemptive purpose.

Most startling is Jethro's public confession: "Praise be to the LORD" (v. 10). He now knew Yahweh as the God of deliverances (Rom. 10:9–10)! Scholars contend that the name Yahweh was probably known to Jethro prior to the Exodus (see Bright 1953: 25 and Albright 1946: 197–98). But the text clearly states that it was only after he had heard what Yahweh had done that he identified himself with Moses' understanding of this name (Exod. 18:12). The story ends with Moses receiving greater personal understanding about his own service through the radical suggestions that Jethro shares from his experience.

Preparations for the Conquest of Canaan

Earlier we noted that in delivering Israel from the Egyptians, God, and God alone, received the glory. He was the victor, not Moses nor Israel. God triumphed over the forces of Egypt and over the forces of nature. Yahweh is "the Lord of Hosts." This title, "the Lord of Hosts," includes both Yahweh's people on earth and his angelic creatures in heaven. This means that he is Lord in heaven and on earth.

God redeemed his elect people from Egypt so that they could be his agents in liberating the nations. As Yahweh fought, so Israel then would fight—but in a manner so strange that the only designation suited to it is "Yahweh's warfare." The Exodus, like the cross, has no religious value apart from the manner in which it is interpreted in Scripture. It was the act of God. When the apostle Paul later sought to understand the meaning of the cross of Jesus Christ, he would fall back on this early major triumph of Yahweh. In fact, Paul made almost forty references to the Exodus in his epistles.

This sequence of thought is important for us to understand how the Bible looks at history, in contrast to the way other polytheistic religions of the ancient world regarded human existence. These religions do not appear to have been interested in uncovering the meaning of history. They were dominated by the rhythm of the nature cycle with its changing seasons and sought to integrate themselves and their societies into this cyclical reality through individual and corporate cultic activities. But for Israel the Exodus marked a radical break with such activity. The Israelites saw themselves as a people with a destiny shaped by God. Their interest in nature was confined to his control of rain, wind, and sea. God was working in space and time to reveal himself to them, the people he had redeemed. The living God was not controlled by the vagaries of nature but was motivated by the determination to realize his purpose for his people and for the nations.

The great confessions of faith imbedded in the hymns and prophetic utterances of Scripture are replete with recitations of God's mighty acts and the responses of God's people. Creation marks the beginning of time. And the last day will mark God's achievement of the goal that has been his from the beginning. To the biblical writer, history is in movement toward a goal, and God has created both the movement and the goal.

Thus the Bible affirms that God does not fight as humans fight. When he reaches out to extend his rule over the world that the enemy has usurped, he invariably uses his people to achieve his victories. But God's people must not forget that they are to fight as God fights. This means God's people are to stand back and see their God deal with whatever opposition stands in the way of his purpose.

The tragedy is that the human race is fallen, knowing only "wars and rumors of wars" because of the constant desire of the strong to dominate and enslave the weak. When people wage war, it is against other human beings. But God's purpose runs counter to all the hateful dreams of humans and their violent efforts to dominate and exploit one another.

Israel's wilderness wanderings ended with the people encamped "east of the Jordan in the territory of Moab" (Deut. 1:5). As earlier intimated, it was there that Moses briefly undertook to explain the Sinaitic law to the new generation of Israelites poised to enter the land of Canaan. He did not merely repeat the law but rather interpreted it to the desert-born and desert-disciplined people who would commit an act of war by crossing the Jordan River. Under Joshua they would then begin the conquest.

It was necessary that the Israelites be reminded of the reasons for the terrible war they were to unleash upon the various nations in Canaan. Concerning this, Moses was explicit:

> When the LORD your God has delivered them over to you and you have defeated them, then you must destroy them totally. Make no treaty with them, and show them no mercy. (Deut. 7:2)

Furthermore, Moses was equally precise as to the divine reason for the merciless extermination of these peoples:

It is not because of your righteousness or your integrity that you are going in to take possession of their land; but on account of the wickedness of these nations, the LORD your God will drive them out before you. (Deut. 9:5)

This instruction troubles many who want to believe that God's love and mercy are such that he would never command the annihilation of a whole cluster of separate peoples. But God must be true to himself. God's love for his moral order and his principles of justice and retribution demand that he hate evil and not protect wickedness.

Other reasons prompted this destruction of the Canaanites and their religious symbols. God knew that if his judgments were not carried out, these pagans would teach Israelites "to follow all the detestable things they do in worshiping their gods, and you will sin against the LORD your God" (Deut. 20:18; also 18:9–13; etc.). We should also recall that these people had descended from a godly line through Noah's sons. They also had the witness of righteous persons such as Melchizedek (Gen. 14) and the patriarchs who had lived among them. And they had been warned by the destruction of Sodom and Gomorrah (Gen. 19:23–25). In addition, they knew of the deliverance of Israel from Egypt and were not unaware of the vicissitudes of the Israelites in their wanderings for almost forty years in a nearby desert. Any right the Canaanites may have had to the land through having dwelt there over the centuries was forfeited through their wickedness (Lev. 18:21–25; Deut. 12:30–32).

The Israelites were later warned that if they likewise sinned and forsook their covenant with Yahweh, they would suffer the same punishment. God has no favorites whom he spares. He judges his people when they sin and deliberately resist his will. When Yahweh through Moses stated that he would drive the peoples of Canaan out before them (Deut. 9:4–5), he was deliberately involving the Israelites in the conquest. They would be active instruments by which God would drive out the Canaanites. This would include breaking down Canaanite altars, dashing into pieces their pillars, hewing down their Asherim, and burning their graven images with fire (Deut. 7:5).

In our day of religious pluralism and widespread emphasis on tolerance, this language seems utterly unreasonable. But God was keeping paramount the satanic power and demonic presence behind the religious rites of Canaan. Moses alluded to them in his denunciation of certain Israelites who "sacrificed to demons, which are not God" (Deut. 32:17). And the apostle Paul centuries later would confirm this reality: "The sacrifices of pagans are offered to demons, not to God" (1 Cor. 10:20). Idols may in themselves be inanimate objects, but the awe with which they are regarded often arises from their being the embodiment or habitation of potent spirits that crave the worship expressed before them.

With the death of Moses, Yahweh gave to Joshua explicit instruction concerning his leadership of the Israelites (Josh. 1:1–9). He is to "be strong and courageous" (v. 6). He is to believe that every place that he treads upon has been given him by divine decree (v. 3). He is to believe that his adversaries will be powerless to prevent his occupation of the land (v. 5). But there is a condition:

> Do not let this Book of the Law depart from your mouth; meditate on it day and night, so that you may be careful to do everything written in it. Then you will be prosperous and successful. (v. 8)

Joshua was called to give the Book of the Law undeviating obedience. No turning from it. No adding to it or taking from it (v. 7). Then followed the ringing promise: "The LORD your God will be with you wherever you go" (v. 9). Joshua must study the Word to understand it. He must fully recognize its authority and seek by it to know the will of God. On that basis Joshua sent two spies across the river Jordan to make a reconnaissance of their first objective: the fortress city of Jericho (chap. 2). When they returned, they reported that the fear of God was already upon the people of Canaan (2:9–11, 24). This news greatly encouraged Joshua. God was already at work on his behalf. What he had begun he would carry to completion. Canaan would be conquered!

Without further delay, the Israelites were told to get ready to cross the Jordan (chap. 3). As they confronted this torrent, they remembered how they were able to cross the Red Sea on dry ground through Yahweh's intervention. Would Yahweh once again exert his power on their behalf? This was a critical, first test of Joshua's leadership. He gave explicit instructions for the marching order of Israel across the Jordan: the Levitical priests in front alone, carrying the ark of the covenant and not protected by any supporting force. Then came a gap of almost half a mile, followed by the various tribes (Josh. 3:1–6). When this procession plunged into the river and reached the middle, the water began to recede, having been blocked upstream through divine activity (vv. 14–17), even as God had promised (vv. 7–13). Joshua now knew that Canaan could be conquered. Furthermore, this miracle confirmed Joshua in the eyes of the people: "They revered him all the days of his life, just as they had revered Moses" (4:14). And a cairn of stones was erected in the riverbed to memorialize this crossing (4:1–10, 19–24).

The Problem of Yahweh's Warfare

What is the Christian to do with the account of the liquidation of Jericho, in which the Israelites "destroyed with the sword every living thing in it—men and women, young and old, cattle, sheep, and donkeys" (Josh. 6:21)? But more, what ethical problem does this pose when the text states that "the LORD was with Joshua" (v. 27), not only supporting this drastic action but fully participating in it? Whereas in the Exodus event the Israelites did nothing to achieve their liberation from Egypt—God alone won the victory—here we find that God was with them, aiding and abetting their total destruction of the people of Jericho. Similar conduct today would result, rightly, in global public denunciation and possibly even a war crimes trial. Is there any possibility of reconciling the Christian claims of love and peace with this account of hate and war?

Sadly, down through church history there has been an all too close identification of Christendom with war, all too often based on a flawed application of Romans 13:1–7. This passage enjoins citizens to "submit . . . to the governing authorities" but does not condone participation in unjust conduct. At the Nuremberg trials (1945–46) of the Nazi war criminals following World War II, the old argument "Ein Befehl ist ein Befehl" (an order is an order) provided no defense for a soldier committing unjust acts. During the centuries of Western colonial expansion, the motif of "Yahweh's warfare" was occasionally used to justify the exploitation or extermination of indigenous peoples.

How easy it has been for the church to justify the most outrageous acts of violence by claiming that such conduct was God's will. Who does not weep over the reminder that the favorite Bible text with which Bernard of Clairvaux (twelfth century) recruited men for the Second Crusade was: "A curse on him who keeps his sword from bloodshed" (Jer. 48:10)? Individual texts torn from their contexts and then misapplied have caused irreparable harm. Although we desire to be vigorous in our defense of Yahweh as the warrior (Jer. 20:11), we need to condemn those who would use the war accounts in the Book of Joshua to justify war today. In this connection G. Ernest Wright comments:

> Israel's holy war—something that looks to us today as a kind of fanaticism—can be conceived as an agency which God made use of at one time for his own purposes and without in any way sanctifying the participants. . . . Each moment is unique. A past pattern of response by an agent can be used as a guide only with great caution in the present. Israel's wars of conquest became no mandate for wars of God's people today. (1969: 130)

Actually, it is rather surprising that the Book of Joshua contains relatively few details of the aggressive warfare by which the land was reduced to Israelite control. One chapter is devoted to the fall of Jericho (chap. 6), two to the complexity of reducing Ai (chaps. 7, 8), and one to the conciliatory treaty made with the Gibeonites (chap. 9). Chapter 10 briefly records the southern campaign: the reduction of six cities in what would later be the region occupied by Judah (vv. 1–39). Chapter 11 records the northern campaign (vv. 1–15). Since the decision to go to war was Yahweh's, the Israelites drew the conclusion that war was a sacred instrument of God. He determined who would win and on occasion did so by miracle.

Because it was by the hand of God alone that the Israelites possessed the land, the conquest is included in the recital of God's mighty acts on behalf of his people (Josh. 24:2–13). Indeed, from this time forward three major emphases dominate the "confessionals" of the people of God: their election via the call of Abraham; their deliverance from Egypt through Moses' instrumentality; and the gift of the land (Deut. 26:5–11). These elements obviously parallel the New Testament gospel with its spiritual triad: the election of a people to belong to God; their deliverance from the guilt and consequence of sin through the cross; and the divine gift of the Holy Spirit, providing eternal linkage with Jesus Christ the Lord. The apostle Paul appealed to these same redemptive acts in his preaching to the Jews. He identified Israel's God with the God and Father of our Lord Jesus Christ (Acts 13:16–41).

When the major battles were over, the land was formally divided among the tribes and their family members (Josh. 13–21). This process took considerable time, for it demanded that all mopping-up operations be carried out beforehand. It was then possible to implement a pattern of assemblies whereby all Israelites might gather at reasonable intervals to affirm their oneness in devotion to Yahweh (Josh. 24:1; Judg. 20:1; 1 Sam. 10:19; etc.).

Toward the end of his service as "war leader," Joshua convened at Shechem a national assembly and issued what might be loosely termed a prophetic oracle (Josh. 24:1–28). The first section of this inspired address was a review of salvation history (vv. 2–13). He began with reference to the Amorite ancestors of Abraham and their service of other gods. Then followed Abraham's election and call, his move to Canaan, and the descent of Jacob and his children into Egypt, there to multiply greatly over the centuries. The Exodus deliverance was stressed, particularly the prophetic and priestly roles of Moses and Aaron. Strangely, Joshua did not mention Sinai. He was more taken with Israel's deliverance from the Amorites, Moabites, and the peoples of Canaan. One significant line is "I sent the hornet ahead of you, which drove them out before you. . . . You did not do it with your own sword and bow" (v. 12). Joshua makes no reference to using human weapons and attaches no significance to human participation in the conquest. The land was Yahweh's gift to his people.

> I gave you a land on which you did not toil and cities you did not build; and you live in them and eat from vineyards and olive groves that you did not plant. (v. 13)

Joshua then shifts his ground and enters into dialogue with the people (vv. 14–27). The issue is their covenant obligation to Yahweh, their need to pledge that they will "serve [him] with all faithfulness," putting away other gods (v. 14). This public affirmation was recorded "in the Book of the Law of God" (v. 26) and memorialized by a massive stone adjacent to an ancient oak where the tabernacle was then located. As the people returned to their varied inheritances scattered throughout the land, all thought was taken with Joshua's challenge to

> choose . . . this day whom you will serve, whether the gods your forefathers served beyond the River, or the gods of the Amorites, in whose land you are living. But as for me and my household, we will serve the Lord. (v. 15)

The Period of the Judges

The generations of Israelites following Joshua, recorded in the Book of Judges, proved largely faithless to Yahweh. Despite his assistance, they were unable either to possess the total land of Canaan or to clear it of the Canaanites. Again and again they resisted the will of God. Even so, in this dreary succession of Israel's infidelities and foreign invasions, followed by times of repentance and divine intervention through unlikely deliverers, the reality of their corporate nationhood began to crystallize in the consciousness of the people.

At the time of the conquest of Canaan, Israel was merely an informal tribal league under the leadership of Joshua. Even so, this loose confederation was conscious of its essential unity through the worship of Yahweh, but it was devoid of statehood or central government. Yahweh did not decree that Joshua appoint a war leader to succeed him. Hence, in the years that followed, Israel was a people with only a religious center. Their theocratic existence was unique in the ancient world. With the coming of Samuel, who combined the functions of judge, prophet, and priest, a new era began to take form. The tribes started to come together, and the monarchy slowly and falteringly emerged.

For a long period, however, the Israelites deliberately rejected the idea of a monarchy and refused to imitate the city-state pattern of old Canaan. They wanted to remain a tribal theocracy. Gideon epitomized this best when he rejected out of hand any idea of kingship: "I will not rule over you, nor will my son rule over you. The LORD will rule over you" (Judg. 8:23).

The focal point of intertribal religious life remained the shrine of the ark (1 Sam. 4:4). It was before this physical symbol that the covenant was reaffirmed whenever the Israelites gathered on feast days to confess their allegiance to Yahweh. In the period of the judges the central reality dominating public consciousness was that Yahweh the warrior would continue to stand between the people and the hostile powers of this world. God would also chasten those of God's people who opposed his will and would be involved in their struggles to possess and develop the land.

Every incident and every expression of God's will in the Book of Judges contain lessons that help us understand the cosmic conflict between God and Satan. These lessons will be heightened and enlarged when we come to the eschatological kingdom to be inaugurated by Jesus Christ. Most solemn is the fact that, whereas God willingly waged war against the enemies of his people, there were times when he poignantly told his people he would fight against the people of God because of their disobedience: "I myself will fight against you with an outstretched hand and a mighty arm in anger and fury and great wrath" (Jer. 21:5). So then, the Book of Judges reveals the patient endurance of God. Although his people are revealed as "stiff-necked," he bore with them, chastening, rebuking, and then delivering them. God did this again and again, for God will not forsake his people. All this stands in sharpest contrast to the impatient "separatist" who would hastily decree a church apostate and seek to form a new church, thereby furthering the fragmentation of the people of God. Under the old covenant God never ordained a "second" Israel.

Samuel, the Last Judge of Israel

The era of the judges was a time of seemingly endless conflict between the people of Israel and the Philistines. The Philistines did not suddenly appear on the scene as Israel's massive, well-organized, predatory neighbor. For centuries prior to Philistine occupation, that area of Canaan had been ruled by the Egyptians. With the decline in Egyptian power, aggressive sea peoples of Aegean origin began to overrun the Hittite Empire and the Syrian Coast and even started south to assault Egypt. One segment of those aggressive peoples attacked Egypt from the west, from present-day Libya. But they were defeated by Rameses III in 1188 B.C. The northern force then proceeded to consolidate what gains they had made earlier and settled on the long Palestinian coastal plain (Bright 1953: 33). Hence, they came to be known as the Philistines. Their growing presence alongside Israel provoked years of border fighting, chronicled in part in the story of Samson (Judg. 14–16).

The opening chapters of 1 Samuel introduce Eli, who served the ark at Shiloh. He was a judge and also functioned as a high priest. Although a man of personal integrity, he refused to restrain his sons, Hophni and Phinehas, from immoral conduct. One infers that during his lifetime a great decline in the worship of Yahweh took place. This led to the consequent disintegration of Israel. Eli was warned of coming judgment by an unnamed prophet (1 Sam. 2:27–36) and by the boy Samuel, who at that time was being reared in the tabernacle (3:10–18). All this was to no avail, and in 1050 B.C. the Philistines utterly defeated Israel. Shiloh and the shrine were razed, the ark was captured, Hophni and Phinehas were slain, and Eli died when he heard the news (4:1–22). This military and spiritual humiliation reduced Israel to a disarmed, subservient people, utterly devoid of hope.

We need to take the full measure of this disaster. Psalm 78 reviews the details:

> [God] rejected Israel completely.
> He abandoned the tabernacle at Shiloh,
>   the tent he had set up among men.
> He sent the ark of his might into captivity,
>   his splendor into the hands of the enemy. (vv. 59–61)

Shiloh was never rebuilt, and its ruins remained a constant warning to subsequent generations of the folly of apostasy. When centuries later a similar crisis confronted Judah (at the hand of the armed might of Babylon), Jeremiah called attention to this historic precedent.

> Go now to the place in Shiloh where I first made a dwelling for my Name, and see what I did to it for the wickedness of my people Israel. . . . what I did to Shiloh I will now do to the house that bears my Name [the Temple in Jerusalem]. (7:12–14, see also 26:6, 9)

Conclusion

While Samuel was the judge in Israel, and prior to the beginnings of the monarchy, Israel largely operated on the basis of deliberately maintaining a position of military weakness. Their confidence was in their united worship and obedient submission to the rule of Yahweh—and thus in Yahweh's provision and care for them—rather than in their own efforts to achieve military superiority over all neighboring powers. Over the years they realized that Yahweh was faithful to God's people and to his covenant commitment to them. God was their king and moral governor, chastening his people when they sinned as well as blessing them when they obeyed his law.

But the idea of human kingship had been long in the thinking of this people (Gen. 36:31; Exod. 19:6; Deut. 17:14–20). Even so, in the providence of God it was kept in abeyance for several hundred troubled years. Was God seeking to give them a lengthy experience of his ability to work mightily on their behalf, even while they were widely scattered throughout "the land" and only linked by their common faith? Did God also desire them to experience fully the fallibility of their faith and the superficiality of their obedience to him? Perhaps this long period was needed to inculcate the desire for an ideal man of God, a victorious Messiah, to be their king.

The advent of recurring Philistine invasions brought matters to a head. The efforts of Samuel to bring the disparate tribes to the place of common and united repentance before Yahweh and the administrative leadership he provided made the people hungry for change. Despite Yahweh's faithfulness, they persisted in seeking a human solution to their corporate life: a king whom they might appoint "for the duration" of the Philistine menace.

When their leaders came to Samuel and asked for a king, he was very displeased. A word of caution is needed here. We should not assume that the premonarchic period with its charismatic judges was theocratic and that in contrast the time of the kings automatically represented something nontheocratic. Whether there were judges or kings in Israel, the theocratic reality would remain operative, as we shall see. Yahweh was both Judge and King. Even so, God's dramatic interventions in the national life of Israel would be much less frequent.

What grieved Samuel was the untheocratic spirit in which the Israelites' request was made. He prayed to God for counsel and was told:

> Listen to all that the people are saying to you; it is not you they have rejected, but they have rejected me as their king. As they have done from the day I brought them up out of Egypt until this day, forsaking me and serving other gods, so they are doing to you. Now listen to them; but warn them solemnly and let them know what the king who will reign over them will do. (1 Sam. 8:7–9)

Samuel then described what would result from their seeking a king "such as all the other nations have" (8:5). This king would burden them with the maintenance of his standing army along with an exploitative bureaucracy. In addition, taxation would be heavy (8:10–18). Samuel also knew that when Israel as a nation joined the political establishment of pagan peoples, its understanding of war as Yahweh's sacred instrument would fade. It would be impossible to keep alive the fact that war was not to be under the control of humans. In other words, the establishment of a state order with a human king would secularize Israel's political order and secularize war as well. The tragedy is that this is what the people wanted:

> We will be like all the other nations, with a king to lead us and to go out before us and fight our battles. (1 Sam. 8:20)

The people rejected Samuel's counsel, and God granted them the freedom to pursue their choice. Because God was gracious to them, he provided Saul as their first king, a provision that gave the people much joy because of his initial success in turning back an Ammonite incursion (1 Sam. 9–10; 11:1–15).

With Saul's enthronement, the period of the judges came to an end. This was marked by a memorable farewell address by Samuel. He took the occasion to remind them that despite their desire for an institutionalized monarchy, the Israelites were still the covenant people of God. Hence, both king and people would still be subservient to Yahweh. Furthermore, his providential care for his people would not diminish.

> If you fear the LORD and serve and obey him and do not rebel against his commands, and if both you and the king who reigns over you follow the LORD your God—good! But if you do not obey the LORD, and if you rebel against his commands, his hand will be against you, as it was against your fathers. (1 Sam. 12:14–15)

Saul eventually proved to be a total failure. Ominously, his reign began with the establishment of a standing army (1 Sam. 13:2–4). Nevertheless, God overruled this independent action, quite possibly so that through Saul's tragic abuse of the royal office, the Israelites might turn to Yahweh and seek a king after his heart. What he also doubtless intended was that by their reflection on "the law of the king" given to them by Moses (Deut. 17:14–20), they would hold this highest standard of kingship before any king who would presume to rule Yahweh's covenant people.

Because of the failure of Saul to live up to this standard, the Philistines eventually dominated the land following his overwhelming defeat on the slopes of Mount Gilboa (1 Sam. 31:1–7). This set the stage for Yahweh eventually to institute the Davidic dynasty, beginning with David, the remarkable person he "took . . . from the pasture and from following the flock" to become "ruler over my people Israel" (2 Sam. 7:8).

We have been quite selective of the material for this chapter because of our central desire to awaken awareness of the phenomenon of Yahweh's warfare. During the conquest Yahweh used his covenant people to wage war against the Canaanite peoples. This pattern was completely reversed during the period of the judges and will continue during the monarchy. Increasingly, during the monarchy the prophets would predict that foreign peoples would be used by Yahweh to chasten his people when they disobey him.

The theological heart of Yahweh's premonarchy warfare finds classical expression in the mouths of two witnesses. Jonathan said: "Nothing can hinder the LORD from saving, whether by many or by few" (1 Sam. 14:6). Furthermore, when David confronted Goliath, we read that Goliath "cursed David by his gods" (1 Sam. 17:43). In response David affirmed:

> I come against you in the name of the LORD Almighty, the God of the armies of Israel, whom you have defied. This day the LORD will hand you over to me. . . . All those gathered here will know that it is not by sword or spear that the LORD saves; for the battle is the LORD's, and he will give all of you into our hands. (vv. 45–47)

These two statements are significant. As we press deeper into the biblical record, we will find their underlying principles confirmed again and again. No weapon forged by the enemies of God can ever ultimately succeed in thwarting the ongoing purpose of Yahweh, who "will reign for ever and ever" (Exod. 15:18). So then, let us enter into the experience of Israel as a monarchy.

7

God's Rule Is Challenged
by the Kings of Israel

Introduction

At this point in the story it is important to remember the overall theme of our study: God's mission of announcing the Kingdom of God among the nations. The Davidic era was the golden age of Israel as a political entity. And during that time there was still an understanding that Israel was to be a showcase to the nations of God's rule through David. Many Psalms emphasize this theme. However, the era of the kings teaches us more about what the Kingdom of God is not rather than about what it is. For the predominant reality was the disobedience of the kings to the God of Abraham, Isaac, and Jacob and consequently their failure to proclaim God's rule among the surrounding nations as well.

David came to prominence at a time when the surrounding nations of the ancient world were in political decline. At first the situation in the land was quite confused. Saul, the first king, dominated all Israel with the exception of Judah. During Saul's time Israel was constantly beset by Philistine incursions. Moreover, Saul was driven by an irrational fear of David that aggravated his hostility toward Judah. His troubled life ended tragically in suicide following the total defeat of his army at the hands of the Philistines (1 Sam. 31).

In the years that followed, David consolidated his rule over Judah and increasingly prevailed over a steadily weakened Israel. After seven and one-half years of pointless struggle, peace was declared, and the Davidic monarchy was enlarged to include all the tribes of Israel (2 Sam. 5:1–6). According to the record, shortly following his consolidation of the kingdom David and his men did something that greatly impressed all Israel. Almost single-handedly they captured the Jebusite fortress of Jerusalem, an outpost of Canaanite power that until that time had been regarded as impregnable. The fact that David achieved this victory without the assistance of the "twelve tribes" meant that it could not be regarded as belonging to any one particular tribe. This made Jerusalem an ideal capital for the kingdom.

This move was accepted by the Israelites but challenged by the Philistines. When they saw David begin to reinforce and enlarge the defenses of Jerusalem, making David "more and more powerful," they resolved to destroy him. (2 Sam. 5:9–10). They mounted two massive attacks, only to be repulsed at great loss, because Yahweh fought for Israel (vv. 17–25). This confirmed to David what he had perceived earlier: "Yahweh had established him king over Israel, and had exalted his kingdom for the sake of his people Israel" (v. 12).

Almost immediately thereafter David took steps to erect a tent in Jerusalem in which the ark of the covenant could be temporarily housed (2 Sam. 6:17). His centralization of political power propelled him to begin to take steps to bring the public worship of Yahweh to Jerusalem. Whether this initial step was taken in the light of Yahweh's desire for a place in the land where his name might dwell, we cannot say (Deut. 12:5–14). In any case, this step marked the beginning of radical changes in Israel's religious life.

During the conquest the ark had been temporarily located in the tabernacle at Gilgal, near Jericho. When the fighting ceased and the land was apportioned among the tribes, the ark and the tabernacle were moved to Shiloh (Josh. 18:1), which provided a central and more accessible location for all the tribes. Actually, the record is a bit obscure, because prior to David there were separate sanctuaries at Shechem, Bethel, and Hebron. Does this mean that the portable tabernacle was moved to places in turn, on a circuit basis? We cannot say, but by Samuel's day the tabernacle while at Shechem gained the aspect of permanence and was even called "the temple of the LORD" (1 Sam. 1:9; 3:3).

After the episode during which Israel lost the ark in a battle to the Philistines (1 Sam. 5–6), the ark was kept for twenty years at Kiriath Jearim (6:19–7:2). The ark was then moved to Nob (21:1–6) and later to Gibeon (1 Chron. 16:39). Apparently, the ark and the tabernacle were not together during this period. Early in the period when David was conquering the remaining Canaanite fortress towns and making all Transjordania his tributary, the ark was moved to Jerusalem. This made Jerusalem the official residence of Yahweh, and its very presence there tended to confirm David as God's anointed. When David extended his power to Syria and began to fashion an Israelite empire of vassal and covenantal states, it must have further confirmed to the populace that God was on their side. The golden age had dawned, and the treasury began to be filled with plunder taken from the nations. Was this a sign that the promise made to Abraham concerning the blessing of the nations through his seed was being fulfilled? Although the populace may have thought otherwise, this conquest model of mission was a far cry from what God had intended when he called Abraham.

David impulsively decided that the time had come to institutionalize the theocracy in accordance with Yahweh's revelation through Moses (Deut. 12). Six times in this chapter there is reference to "the place" that Yahweh would choose for his dwelling (vv. 5, 11, 14, 18, 21, and 26), after God has given rest to his people from all their enemies (12:10). Thus, David felt constrained to initiate steps to build a house for Yahweh in Jerusalem. When David mentioned to Nathan his desire to accomplish this, he received an unguarded, "Whatever you have in mind, go ahead and do it, for the LORD is with you" (2 Sam. 7:3). However, this was not God's will. It was a chastened Nathan who had to convey to David that David was forbidden by God to build the temple. But Nathan's "oracle of prohibition" (2 Sam. 7:5–16) was turned into an oracle of hope. Far from David building Yahweh a house, Yahweh would build the house of David. Although Nathan only spoke of an ongoing succession of Davidic kings, in the years that followed Yahweh's prophets enlarged this promise to embrace a "messianic hope" of covenantal proportions. We will discuss this in more detail later.

When Solomon erected the Temple and made it the seat of an official royal cult, further changes took place. Charisma in leadership gave way to dynasty. Power and wealth increased, culture flourished, the people of Yahweh became the Kingdom of Israel, and the state supported all religious life. An inevitable sacralizing took place. The state became "God's kingdom" composed of "God's chosen people" ruled by "God's anointed son." The purpose of God in history came to be equated with maintaining the existing order. But merely existing as the status quo could hardly be equated with being a blessing to the nations.

The exaltation of the Davidic dynasty increasingly dominated cultic life. Some scholars contend that the older festal rituals were transformed and blended into an enthronement festival that initiated and dominated the religious year. The Psalms provide us with insight into the liturgical forms of this central celebration. First, we find the events of preparation when all Israel made pilgrimage to Jerusalem and when Zion was proclaimed to be the chosen dwelling place for Yahweh, the Creator of heaven and earth. Second, there are the affirmations when Yahweh was recognized as King ruling from Zion, over heaven and earth, and when his eschatological coming to judge the nations was heralded. Finally, we see the benedictions that detail the way in which Yahweh bestowed righteousness and loving kindness on the Davidic king, on Zion, and on Israel. When one reflects on this sequence—the imagined splendor with which this annual festival took place and the vicissitudes of Israel's subsequent history—one begins to realize how inevitable were the distortions that came to Israelite minds, conditioning their resistance to the sort of kingdom that Jesus later proclaimed.

Carroll Stuhlmueller suggests that when foreign peoples marched into Jerusalem to pay tribute, they possibly did obeisance before Yahweh in the Temple. He argues that "one such ceremony seems to be recorded in Psalm 87" and cites pertinent parts of the text:

> On the holy mount stands the city he founded;
> the LORD loves the gates of Zion [the Temple] more than all the dwelling places
>   of Jacob. (vv. 1–2)
> Among those who know me I mention Rahab and Babylon; behold, Philistia and
>   Tyre, with Ethiopia—
> "This one was born there," they say (v. 4).

And of Zion it shall be said,
  "This one and that one were born in her";
  for the Most High himself will establish her (v. 5).
The Lord records as he registers the peoples,
  "This one was born there" (v. 6).
Singers and dancers alike say,
  "All my springs are in you" (v. 7). (Senior and Stuhlmueller 1983: 90, citing
    Ps. 87 RSV)

The activities of Solomon generated the political vision of Israel, reaching out to the nations to incorporate them into a dynamic, conquering kingdom. The enthusiastic populace sacralized all this by boasting that Yahweh would rule the nations through Israel and its Davidic Son. On the surface this was the golden age indeed (1 Kings 4:20–21; 5:13)!

However, the Davidic monarchy eventually collapsed because of its neglect of God and the ethical failure of its rulers, priests, and people. Even Solomon's day was characterized by acute social tension, arising from nepotism and favoritism in the royal court, burdensome taxation, conscription, and religious compromise. In time, most Israelites rejected the Solomonic state as the fulfillment of Israel's destiny. Revolution broke out in 930 B.C. under the leadership of Jeroboam, a labor-gang boss of the hated corvée (forced labor) system. Israel broke away from Judah, and neither nation ever fully recovered from this disaster.

With the disruption also came apostasy. The Northern Kingdom soon set up its own state cult, which in time merged the worship of Yahweh with the worship of Baal. The judgment of God finally fell on Israel with the Assyrian conquest of 722 B.C. and obliterated both nation and people. This demonstrated that its citizens were neither God's people nor did they collectively constitute his Kingdom (Bright 1953: 75).

Only Judah remained. During its final years, spiritual apostasy and moral decay likewise characterized its life despite some godly kings, national reforms, amazing deliverances (e.g., from Sennacherib, Isa. 37:33, 35), prophetic warnings, and the loving concern of Yahweh for Jerusalem and the Temple. Actually, Judah never sank to the depths of Israel in its departure from its covenant relationship with God. There was always a remnant of God's people in its midst whose presence, witness, and social concern served to hold Judah back from total spiritual eclipse. Nonetheless, because of Judah's tributary relationship to Assyria for a hundred years, the worship of Assyrian deities was practiced in Jerusalem, along with divination and magic, sacred prostitution and human sacrifice. When Assyria suddenly collapsed, Judah knew respite from foreign oppression, but only for a brief period.

Spiritual renewal came through Josiah (2 Kings 22–23), though with his tragic death the final period of spiritual decline began. Jeremiah proclaimed God's rejection of Judah as the vehicle of his kingdom; indeed, Jeremiah's total pessimism regarding Judah's moral condition drove him to virtual treason (chaps. 2, 27, 38, 39). In the end Babylonian power under the leadership of Nebuchadnezzar was

God's chastening instrument. By 587 B.C. practically every fortified town, including Jerusalem and the Temple, had been reduced to rubble. Hundreds of thousands perished. Only a relatively small number went into captivity. It was the end of Israel as a political and religious entity. For several centuries the Davidic line virtually disappeared from public knowledge. We sense some of the poignancy of this in the psalmist's lament:

> You said, "I have made a covenant with my chosen one,
>   I have sworn to David my servant:
> 'I will establish your line forever
>   and make your throne firm through all generations.'" (Ps. 89:3–4)

> But you have rejected, you have spurned,
>   you have been very angry with your anointed one.
> You have renounced the covenant with your servant
>   and have defiled his crown in the dust. (vv. 38–39)

> How long, O LORD? Will you hide yourself forever?
> How long will your wrath burn like fire? (v. 46)

> O Lord, where is your former great love,
>   which in your faithfulness you swore to David? (v. 49)

The Prophets as Guardians of the Kingdom

The historical unfolding of the kingdom enthroned Yahweh in the midst of his people and replaced a succession of unrelated charismatic leaders with a formal kingship. This process also called forth prophetism, a phenomenon of far-reaching importance. Actually, there had been an earlier prophetic role. One can detect at least five stages in the prophetic office in the Old Testament. First, there was Moses the prophet, whose comprehensive role embraced such varied functions as kingly authority, priestly intercession, prophetic revelation, and the counsel of the wise man. Hence, he could speak of the messianic prophet who would embody in fullness all that he was and much more (Deut. 18:15–18). Then followed the prophets from the time of the judges through Solomon, both named and unnamed, whose messages are not recorded in the canon. The third phase involved the ministry of Elijah and Elisha, along with their disciples. Again they left us no written records of timeless significance. Then came the great succession of preexilic prophets, inaugurated by Amos. Their messages were recorded and have abiding relevance to every subsequent generation of God's people. Finally, there were the named and anonymous postexilic prophets, whose writings provide wonderful transition to the coming of the Messiah and the messianic era.

Prophets, both true and false, were common throughout the ancient world. Baalam was a Moabite (Num. 22:7), and the prophets of Baal were Canaanites (1 Kings 18:19). In sharp contrast, however, the prophets of Israel saw themselves

as God's gift to God's people (Amos 2:11). As such, they were without real parallel in any of the neighboring nations. Their true function can best be understood
through reflection on the analogy expressed in Exodus 7:1, in which Yahweh says
to Moses: "See, I have made you like God to Pharaoh; and Aaron your brother
will be your prophet" (see also Exod. 4:15–16). Simply put, the prophet was God's
spokesperson, speaking primarily to his own generation. What he said arose from
the immediate circumstances in which he lived. Whereas knowledge of a prophet's
particular background—its historical setting and social realities—helps one understand his message, we must keep in mind that this message was supernatural, not
natural. He was no mere social critic or religious reformer. What he proclaimed
came from direct communication with God via visions and dreams (Exod. 33:11;
Num. 12:6; Jer. 23:18–22; Amos 3:7). There is a depth to what the prophet reveals
concerning God that goes far beyond his own understanding of what he actually
proclaims (1 Peter 1:10–12).

Generally speaking, prophets were forth-tellers, although occasionally they
foretold the future in order to disclose the true nature of God and his purpose
for the nations. Invariably, the predictions of true prophets came to pass (Deut.
18:21–22) and thereby authenticated their technical credentials (13:1–3). Even
so, it was the ethical and spiritual quality of their messages that remained decisive
in demonstrating whether they were true or false prophets (13:2–3).

The people of God can be greatly strengthened by prophetic revelations of what
God will do in the future. For this reason, on occasion a prophet might predict an
improbable event and state that it will be fulfilled in the immediate future. When
this happened, it authenticated a prophet's ethical and spiritual consistency (e.g.,
Zech. 4:9). Furthermore, the people were solemnized by the realization that his
predictions of more remote events should be taken seriously.

Isaiah described the sequence through which he passed in receiving a specific
word from Yahweh for the people (chap. 6). It began quite possibly with the urge
to go to the Temple to worship the Lord, who resided there.[1] Suddenly, a vision
of divine holiness descended and quite overwhelmed him (vv. 1–4). Compunc-
tions of guilt and self-condemnation flooded his heart and mind. Confession and
utter self-abnegation followed (v. 5). This brought Yahweh's gracious cleansing (vv.
6–7) and a growing awareness that a new message was to be revealed. In gratitude
for this privilege Isaiah committed himself anew to his prophetic calling and was
recommissioned by Yahweh (v. 8). Only then did he begin to receive the message
he must deliver (vv. 9–13).

The prophets stressed the significance of the Sinaitic and Deuteronomic revelation. Israel could only be assured of the permanence of its divine election by
teaching the people that the law must be obeyed at all costs (Deut. 4:5–6, 32,

---

1. Care must be exercised in referring to the Temple as the dwelling place of Yahweh. This concept must
be spiritualized. Whereas the prophets agree that Yahweh and the Temple are permanently linked ("The
Lord . . . thunders from Jerusalem," Amos 1:2), they envisage the Temple less as a dwelling place than as
the place where Yahweh meets with his people (Jacob 1958: 260). Actually, the Temple is his particular
possession in the land.

36; 28:63; 30:9, 11–14). They exhorted the leaders to pursue righteousness less as a quality or state than as a means to stress the essentiality of justice in society. By their focus on *ḥesed* (God's strong faithfulness to himself), they underscored the imitation of God as the mainspring of all that related people to him and to the ethical life (Mic. 6:8). They called the people to enter into communion with God. This involved participation in his plan for human history by faith, that is, by sharing in God's perspective with confidence. The greater one's knowledge of his revelation, the deeper one's trust in him and the more actively one obeys his will. Apparently, the prophetic ideal was that the people of God be energetic in their cooperation with him, rather than that they be "beatified enjoyers of God" (Jacob 1958: 176).

So then, we must stress that everything the prophets proclaimed was related to Yahweh's holy rule over Israel and over all creation. The prophets faithfully exposed and condemned all sin and unabashedly spoke again and again of God's wrath against those who committed it. Happily, their messages were also filled with the assurance that Yahweh's purposes would culminate in deliverance and salvation for God's people.

When we think of David as prophet (Acts 2:30) and of the many Psalms in the Psalter ascribed to him, we believe that among the many references to the nations (76) is his prophetic reminder of the universal dimensions of God's mission. George Peters found over 175 references in the Psalms to the world, the nations, peoples, and all the earth. Some are in the context of Israelites bringing the hope of salvation to them (1972: 166).

Whether or not Psalm 67 is Davidic, its opening lines express Israel's role in God's worldwide purpose.

> May God be gracious to us and bless us
> and make his face to shine upon us,
> that your ways may be known on earth,
> Your salvation among all nations. (vv. 1–2)

Walter C. Kaiser comments on this Psalm in the following vein:

The Psalmist longed and deeply desired that God, the King of Israel, might be acknowledged as Lord and Savior of all the families of the earth. [He then added] God's challenge to Israel . . . [was] to have a mediatorial role in proclaiming His name among the nations. (1981: 33)

Johannes Verkuyl emphasized this view of Israel as a people elected for service in God's mission. He stated that "the prophets never tire of reminding Israel that her election is not a privilege which she may selfishly keep for herself; election is a call to service" (1978: 46). Whether this service is to be expressed in a missionary-sending fashion, such as we find explicitly developed in the New Testament, is a matter to which we shall return later. Isaiah struck the highest note in expressing the prophetic concern for the nations in his Servant Songs (chaps. 40–55) (H. H. Rowley 1944: 64).

The true prophets were also constantly beset by false prophets. The unvarying message of those truly called by God was that leaders and people had to heed God's call to repentance before they could expect to hear God's Yes! and know themselves as continuing in the sequence of his "salvation history." In contrast, the false prophets ignored this sequence. They spoke of peace and of God's blessing. But they misconstrued Yahweh's covenant with David, thinking it guaranteed unconditionally the perpetual security of Jerusalem. They spoke of political realism, of alliances with powerful pagan neighbors, and of the legitimate right of the people to resist the enemy that Yahweh had sent against them (Nebuchadnezzar's armies, 2 Chron. 36:15–18). But they were wrong. The nation was doomed, and the monarchy was coming to an end, just as the true prophets had predicted.

When it became increasingly apparent that the Israelites had repeatedly failed to sustain a kingdom characterized by righteousness and justice or to exercise a vital, spiritual influence among the nations, the prophets began to speak of a kingdom not of man but of God. To this kingdom messianic expectations began to attach themselves. With the Babylonian overthrow of Judah, these expectations increasingly pointed in the direction of a people of God that were no longer a mere political entity but rather a religious community with the potential for worldwide outreach and spiritual blessing. And in time there would be a new covenant and a new expression of the Kingdom of God that would not fail (Jer. 31:31–34; 32:38–40; Ezek. 36:26–27). A new Israel by faith would be God's principal means of proclaiming redemption among the nations.

The Institutionalized Theocracy and Spiritual Renewal

In the Sinaitic legislation we find that God anticipated the frequent need of God's people for spiritual renewal and provided varied mechanisms to facilitate this. He knew that, despite their spontaneous acceptance of his offer at Sinai of covenant relationship (Exod. 19:4–8), the Israelites had within themselves the possibility of erosion of commitment and even total apostasy. One of the last communications Moses received from Yahweh contained the dark prediction:

> You are going to rest with your fathers, and these people will soon prostitute themselves to the foreign gods of the land they are entering. They will forsake me and break the covenant I made with them. (Deut. 31:16)

We should not presume to regard ourselves as superior to the Israelites. They reflect the moral and ethical perversity that characterizes all human beings. The most godly among the redeemed will candidly confess to have discovered that abiding in fellowship with Yahweh hangs on the slenderest of threads. Because all people know "the cravings of sinful man, the lust of his eyes and the boasting of what he has and does" (1 John 2:16), all people know themselves as walking on the edge of the abyss. The temptation to court religious disaster is always present. Hence, the Torah contains two basic mechanisms for the avoidance of nominality in an Israelite's relation to Yahweh: the weekly Sabbath and the required attendance of all men at Israel's three annual religious convocations.

First, let us examine the Sabbath. Following his acts of creation, God provided an opportunity to offer special sacrifices of worship to God (Num. 28:9–10). This made attendance possible at local "sacred assemblies" (Lev. 23:3) where the Torah was read and studied. The Sabbath was also recognized as an occasion for visiting spiritual leaders to seek special counsel (2 Kings 4:22–23). The recurring Sabbath provided Israelites with time for private prayer, deliberate reflection on the growing corpus of Scripture, and self-examination of the sort that would enable them to become more faithful in their worship and walk with God. Concerned Israelites and later Christians developed a variety of patterns to intensify and, they hoped, to make more vital this "means of grace" provided by God in authorizing that one day in seven be particularly devoted to his service. Such intensification activities by themselves, however, rarely eventuated in community renewal, although they have on occasion set the stage for such movements.

The second mechanism for spiritual renewal involved the annual religious calendar, filled with special occasions when all would be confronted with the need for personal transformation and covenant reaffirmation. Accordingly, God decreed that three times every year special feasts be convened at Jerusalem (Deut. 16:16) and that all Jewish males attend them: Passover and Unleavened Bread, the Feast of Weeks or Pentecost, and the Feast of Booths (Lev. 23; Deut. 16). This schedule demanded that the nation's routine of life and worship be broken, that its networks of leadership and followership that had developed in all communities be suspended, and that everyone travel together to Jerusalem. En route they would lose all social differentiations, and in Jerusalem as equals they would submit to Levite instruction and devote their time and thought to reflecting on religious matters.

At Passover they would be reminded of their oppression in Egypt and of the haste with which they were enjoined to leave when God made this possible (providing no time for their bread to be leavened). At First Fruits (or Weeks, Lev. 23:15–17; Num. 28:26), the promise of the coming harvest and the ongoing benefits from their Egyptian deliverance (e.g., the covenant and the law) were made the object of grateful praise. At the Feast of Booths they recalled Israel's wilderness wanderings and the blessing of the year's major harvest (Lev. 23:37, 43). Every seven years at this third feast the law was publicly read (Deut. 31:12).

It is significant that today within rabbinic Judaism and most Christian traditions the pattern of convening special occasions for the deepening of religious practice and spiritual renewal is commonplace. Camp experiences for children and youth, student missionary conferences, retreat weekends, and a host of other activities not related to either Sabbath or Lord's Day routines have been significant in bringing participants to various decisions.

But what one must keep in mind is that genuine spiritual renewal cannot be programmed. It is the gift of God to God's people. Although we should never underestimate the possibility of a concern for renewal being conceived in the mind and heart of the respected leader of a believing community, we must always be open to God's surprises. God's key person may be a charismatic person marginal to the community's power structure. Yet it is always strategic to pray: "O God our Savior. . . . Will you not revive us again, that your people may rejoice in you?" (Ps. 85:4–6).

Prophetic Encounter: Yahweh versus Baal

The massive religious encounter of Israel's history was with Baal worship, the religion of the Canaanites. For many years patriarchal Yahwism was steadily undermined by this determined rival. During the reign of Ahab (874–852 B.C.) it gained official sanction (1 Kings 16:30–33), and Elijah was the first prophet to challenge its presence and influence in Israel. A hundred years later, Baalism resurfaced and again virtually eclipsed the worship of Yahweh. The second vigorous confrontation was mounted by Hosea in the Northern Kingdom (c. 743 B.C.) and by Amos in Judah (c. 760 B.C.).

Before we explore the salient elements of this encounter, we must reflect on the issue and peril of syncretism. It needs to be distinguished from contextualization. Contextualization represents the careful and refined use of a people's cultural forms in order that the truth of the gospel can be correctly expressed in their language through a judicious use of their own thought forms. Syncretism, on the other hand, involves mixing elements of other religious thought and practice with the covenantal thought and practice revealed by God to God's people.

The distinction between contextualization and syncretism can be illustrated in the ministry of Moses. Moses as prophet was God's vehicle through whom the Israelites learned that the name of the God whom their fathers worshiped was Yahweh (Exod. 3:15). Previously he had been known as El, Elohim, El Elyon (God Most High) and El Shaddai (God Almighty). Moses' introduction of a new name was carefully protected against any endorsement of syncretism. Hence, he deliberately underscored the fact that Yahweh alone was the sovereign God of Creation, election, covenant, *hesed* (faithfulness), righteousness, compassion, mercy, and love. He alone is to be loved and served, for he alone is the Lord of the *kosmos*. Besides Yahweh there is no other god.

But when Israel came to Canaan and became an agricultural society, taking over the fields and orchards that previously had been worked by the Canaanites, Israel was surrounded by much evidence of their predecessors' religious orientation. Local shrines along with residual patterns of seed sowing, crop cultivation, and harvest must have fascinated people whose skills had been confined to animal husbandry. Their temptation was to reproduce the apparently successful Canaanite methods of farming, including the development of vineyards and orchards. What they failed to do was to disassociate themselves totally from the religious system upon which Canaanite agriculture was based. This provoked a gradual syncretism in that the worship of Yahweh became increasingly debased to the level of Canaanite religion.

Fundamentally, the religious systems of the ancient world were similarly complicated polytheisms. They were designed to bring people and society into harmony with the rhythmic yearly cycle of nature in which life is recreated each spring and the sequence of fertilization, growth, harvest, and death recommenced. People saw themselves as "bound in the bundle of life" with nature, where all sorts of gods and goddesses interacted with one another (harmoniously!) and thereby preserved order against demonic powers that sought to disrupt the beneficent status quo.

The three great cultic festivals of Canaanite religion were (1) the new year's festival, in which the myth of creation was refought and rewon—the outcome of a struggle between the god of order (Marduk) and the demon of chaos (Tiamat)—thereby ensuring the repetition of the nature cycle for the new year; (2) the spring marriage rite, when the rain and vegetation god copulated with the goddess of fertility ensuring the germination of grains, vegetables, and fruits—thus making possible the growing season; and (3) the rite of resurrection, when the god of rain and vegetation was renewed following his death in the heat of summer drought.

This brings us to the issue of Baal. This Hebrew word etymologically conveys a mingling of two correlative notions: ownership and lordship. A wife called her husband her "baal." He was both her owner and her master. The leader of a village was similarly designated. Canaanite religion claimed a supreme Baal (Baal of the Heavens). He was the storm god, having power over rain, wind, clouds, and fire. His authority was regarded as comparable to that of El Elyon (God Most High, Gen. 14:18), so much so that the Israelites at the sanctuary in Shechem referred to God as both El-Berith and Baal-Berith (*bĕrît,* meaning covenant, Judg. 8:33; 9:4, 46). It takes little imagination to see how a syncretistic pattern developed between the religion of Yahweh and that of Baalism. The former focused in popular thought on national and heavenly matters. In contrast, Baal the great Semitic deity, assisted by lesser Baals and goddesses, was able to guarantee the fertility of the people and the land.

In time there was a tendency to downplay the priority of Yahweh, whom the Israelites associated with the wilderness, and give superiority to the deities that dominated their agrarian civilization. Inevitably, the cult of Baal grew in the range of its impact on their lives (McCarthy 1968).

At first the Israelites took a casual approach to Baalism. The Baals were regarded as merely the local fertility gods of Canaan worshiped at every village shrine. They were allegedly the manifestations of Baal, the great sky god of the Canaanites. But this led to asking questions concerning the myths behind the symbolism of these shrines. They soon learned that the "high places" were as nipples on the breasts of mother earth, upraised to meet her "baal" (husband and lord), who came as the rain god to fertilize the earth.

With the growing prosperity of the nation under the monarchy—especially following its division into Israel and Judah—the people increasingly reacted against the ethical and egalitarian demands of the worship of Yahweh as defined in the

Sinaitic covenant. Apparently, their own religious festivals left them hankering for "something else." Baal worship seemed to supply this.

When Ahab came to the throne, he had already capitulated to the worship of Baal under the influence of Jezebel, his non-Israelite wife (1 Kings 16:29–33). In no time at all, the established order of both Tyre and Syria was so admired that political alliances and religious interpenetration became mandatory. This brought about the transformation of Israel: it too became an expression of the outworking of innumerable Baals. By their power and approval, rulers held office, the wealthy lived in luxury and exploitation, slaves worked the fields, and males dominated households. Israelite culture was increasingly shaped by a landowning aristocracy, an oppressive autocracy in which Baal worship buttressed the status quo.

Elijah was the first prophet to challenge the presence and influence of Baalism in Israel. Through the power of Yahweh, Elijah deliberately turned off the rain, stopped the nature cycle, and provoked a showdown with the prophets of Baal (1 Kings 17–18). By his dramatic victory, God endorsed the prophetic ministry that challenged not only the worship of "the Baals" but the whole social structure they represented (1 Kings 18:18–40). The worshipers of Yahweh were not to buttress the status quo but rather to do God's will, to "do justice and to love mercy," and to look for the coming of the Kingdom of God.

The Old Testament has an important function for the church in acting as a warning against idolatry and spiritual experimentation. It delivers Christians from becoming preoccupied with the subjective and the mystical. It fastens their attention on God's "mighty acts" in history. When these are publicly confessed and their implications seriously faced, Christians inevitably look forward with hope to the coming day of Yahweh and to his ultimate triumph in human history.

> Yahweh is a jealous God because he is a living God and a loving God. He is a God of absolute moral and ethical values. He is a holy God whose Kingdom rule over all creation and among God's People has salvific and transformational purpose. In contrast, Baalism had neither moral law nor historical purpose. Baal was a false and powerless god, as Elijah demonstrated. In today's world the God and Father of our Lord Jesus Christ must alone be worshiped.
>
> Unlike Baal, Yahweh has no consort at his side. He is neither sexual in nature, nor is he to be worshiped by sexual rites. Although Yahweh is Lord of fertility, he is not a fertility god subject to the death and resurrection of the natural world. He is the Living God who reveals himself in the arena of men's history—where human life touches life, where injustices oppress and hopes for deliverance are felt, where men are called to make decisions that alter the course of the future. While Baal religion taught men to control the gods, Israel's faith stressed serving God in gratitude for his benevolence and in response to the task which he lays upon his people. Yahweh could not be coerced by magic. He could only be trusted or betrayed, obeyed or disobeyed, but in all things his will was sovereign. (B. Anderson 1957: 102)

Israel's Social Structure

At this point we must take the measure of Israelite "tribal" society as Yahweh intended it to be and its subsequent deterioration during the monarchy, because of the failure of its leaders and the disobedience of God's people. We are particularly concerned to underscore the reaction of the prophets to the abuses this failure and disobedience created, since this is of abiding relevance to the prophetic ministry of the church in our day.

Israelite society was originally conceived as a loose confederation of twelve separate tribes, consciously constituting the entity "Israel." Each tribe was autonomous. Through their united commitment to Yahweh, strengthened by their observance of Torah and their joint worship before the ark three times annually, all Israelites gained a sense of mutual obligation to help one another in times of crisis.

Israelite society was socially decentralized and nonhierarchical. It protected the social health and economic viability of the lowest units, not the wealth, privilege, or power of any structured hierarchy. Its aim was to preserve the broadly based egalitarian self-sufficiency of each family and protect the weakest, poorest, and most threatened persons in the nation. Israel was not a society structured to promote the interests of any wealthy, landowning, elite minority in its midst (C. Wright 1984: 13). Political activity was likewise deliberately diffused and decentralized. The elders—the senior male members of each extended family—were at the heart of all sociopolitical decision making. Norman K. Gottwald summarizes this premonarchial system as a "sociopolitical egalitarianism" in the following fashion:

> A self-governing association of economically self-sufficient free farmers and herds-men constituted a single class of peoples with common ownership of the means of production vested in large families. . . . [This involved a] paradoxical combination of political decentralization, on the one hand, and of socio-cultural cohesiveness, on the other. (1979: 613–14).

When Joshua introduced the land tenure system at the end of the conquest of the Promised Land, he saw to it that the kinship system was dominant insofar as the possession and use of the land were concerned. He sought to prevent the emergence of any absentee landlord system, in which a wealthy landowner could claim a portion of each harvest from those who worked his land. This meant that generally the overall economic viability of all Israelites was guaranteed. In the light of Israel's social structure, Yahweh could promise the ideal: "There should be no poor among you" (Deut. 15:4). Of course, there was a condition: "If only you fully obey the LORD your God and are careful to follow all these commands I am giving you today" (vv. 5–6 and 1–3). Knowing the weakness of his people, however, he also warned: "There will always be poor people in the land" (v. 11). Hence, it is not without reason that he commanded, "Be openhanded toward your brothers and toward the poor and needy in your land" (Deut. 15:11).

The Prophets' Message regarding the Poor

What caused the prophets to become so concerned for the poor? Their writings are replete with this theme. The deterioration of Israelite society began when the people persisted in demanding a monarchy. Samuel spoke prophetically when he announced that their hankering for a monarchy modeled after the surrounding nations would result in economic exploitation (1 Sam. 8:10–17). He warned that the only monarchy pleasing to God must reflect the Sinaitic revelation earlier given to Moses. This contained the dominant requirement that a monarchy reflect the egalitarian reality of God's Exodus deliverance of the Israelites. There must be no exploitation of anyone in God's land. Indeed, Yahweh's "law of the king" (Deut. 17:14–20) is explicit in this regard.

Whereas the Book of Proverbs states that people become poor through laziness, involvement in worthless pursuits, wasting time in idle chatter, and through pre-occupation with the search for pleasure (Prov. 6:6–10; 28:19; 14:23; 23:19–21), Moses constantly reiterated the solemn fact that there are occasions when God punishes with poverty those who transgress his laws (e.g., Deut. 28:15–46). When the prophets speak about poverty, however, they almost invariably relate it to the ways in which rich people contribute to this acute social problem. The two aspects of society are not independent phenomena. They are intimately interrelated. During the period of the monarchy the prophets constantly linked wealth with injustice; the oppressors of the poor were the rich. Furthermore, poverty was rarely portrayed as an accident. More often than not, it is determined by the structure of society. Poverty brings unnecessary misery to people, a misery that is heightened when it is realized that the poor are the victims of the injustice of others (e.g., Isa. 10:1–2; Jer. 5:28; Ezek. 16:49; 18:12–13; Amos 2:6–7).

The prophets denounced the greedy accumulation of goods as both a challenge to the lordship of God and as evidence of lack of faith in him (Isa. 5:8). They called for the pursuit of the knowledge of God that keeps one from the neglect or exploitation of the poor (e.g., Jer. 22:13–16). Furthermore, they contended that authentic, God-pleasing religious devotion will invariably be expressed by involvement in the struggle for social justice as well as by direct ministry to the poor (e.g., Isa. 58:2–7).

Jesus and the apostles later confirmed and amplified in various ways this unas-sailable line of truth. To be a faithful custodian of the good news of the Kingdom of God means that one seeks to be the sort of person who is dominated by a heightened concern for social justice and the poor. And, quite unexpectedly, when we later review these perspectives in the New Testament context, we shall find that certain key elements in Israel's social structure are found in the structure and ethos of the New Testament understanding of the local church. Indeed, one of the notable activities of the Holy Spirit on the day of Pentecost was to remind affluent believers in Jesus the Messiah of their obligation to the needy in their midst (Acts 2:44–45; 4:36–37).

The Prophets as Evangelists

When the Israelites left Egypt under the leadership of Moses, the record states that "many other people went up with them" (Exod. 12:38). This mixed multitude consisted of those who seized the opportunity to leave Egypt by joining the Israelites, but without having rootage in the religious traditions of the larger community. Nor did they share in any real commitment to the God who made the Exodus possible. They subsequently became the occasion for dissension and sin within Israel (e.g., Num. 11:4).

God provided a special means whereby the people of Israel might be helped to resist the temptation to nominality and covenant violation. Beginning with Moses (Deut. 34:10), he brought forth an order of prophets to address the nation while the Hebrew canon was in the process of development. The prophets were men and women whom God called and equipped to make known his true nature and character and to exercise a ministry of spiritual renewal among the people. In a very real sense they were the evangelists/revivalists of Israel. They exposed the sinfulness of nominality and all violations of the covenant.

For years in some circles it was argued that the Old Testament prophets, whose writings make up more than one-third of the Old Testament, were "irregulars" standing in noble isolation from the priesthood, sacrifice, and the Temple. The prophets allegedly were against all institutionalized expressions of the religion of ancient Israel. They contended for a higher level of ethical religiosity and made the concern for societal justice their sole priority. As a result, they were allegedly in almost constant tension with the Levitical priesthood. In contemporary terms the prophets argued that their mission was to deliver the people from traditional religious practices defined by the Temple and to concentrate all "religious" energy on the humanization of society.

Today, however, this portrayal of Old Testament prophetism is regarded as invalid. The prophets castigated the religious practices of the people because these reflected acute abuse and misuse of the temple rituals. The prophets constantly emphasized that an Israelite's relation to God must be personal and that sin is evidence of either a wrong relationship or defective communion with God. If both personal and national life were to be renewed, the only solution was to be found in turning to Yahweh, who graciously promises to the penitent: "I will give you a new heart and put a new spirit in you" (Ezek. 36:26; 11:19; etc.). God issued a strong evangelistic appeal through the prophets: "I have swept away your offenses like a cloud, your sins like the morning mist. Return to me, for I have redeemed you" (Isa. 44:22).

This phrase "return to me" or its equivalent was frequently on the lips of the prophets. The verb šûb (to turn back, to return) occurs over one hundred times and invariably refers to the change in relationship between a person and God.[2]

---

2. For a detailed study of the covenantal use of šûb, consult *The Root sûbh in the Old Testament* by William L. Holladay (Leiden: Brill, 1958). Its key meaning is "a change of loyalty on the part of Israel or God, each for the other" (2). It can also mean "having moved in a particular direction, to move thereupon in the opposite direction, the implication being (unless there is evidence to the contrary) that one will arrive again at the initial point of departure" (53).

The prophets never affirmed that merely because of the Sinaitic covenant, all Israelites were rightly related to God. Rather, within the covenantal context, they challenged the Israelites to turn to Yahweh and thereby affirm the covenant for themselves. Only thereby could they be sure of their personal relationship to him. The account of Joshua calling for this form of commitment is a vivid illustration of what all the prophets contended for (24:14–28).

Indeed, this preaching of the need for "turning" is widespread throughout the historic period covered by the Hebrew Bible. God repeatedly called upon his people to "rend their hearts," to "turn again," to "be converted." Jewish persons today who are familiar with the Bible need not take offense at such language as long as the word *convert* does not imply the total rejection of one's cultural heritage to embrace an entirely new religious allegiance.[3]

Incorporation of Proselytes

There is another factor of Israel's mission that must be taken into consideration: the incorporation of outsiders into the community of Israel. Remember that during the centuries from Moses to the destruction of the First Temple, the Israelites did not occupy the land alone. The Old Testament mentions three distinct types of non-Israelites: natives (*'ezrāḥîm*), foreigners (*nokrîm*), and sojourners (*gērîm*). Most common were the *gērîm*, people without nationality, who placed themselves under the legal protection of the Israelites. They were not fully entitled to become part of the "congregation" or "assembly" of Israel, but were permitted involvement in much of the religious life of the people (Deut. 5:14; 16:11, 14; etc.). In Deuteronomy 31:12, it is explicitly stated that the *gērîm* are to be present for the solemn reading of the law; in other words, they were exposed to its demands and accountable for their response.[4]

Because of this, we conclude that as long as the Israelites remained in the land, their openness to non-Israelites was genuine. The problem of children of mixed marriages was resolved by appealing to the invariable pattern of biblical genealogies: only the names of men are listed, except in cases where the mother was notable in Jewish history. David was definitely Jewish, although two Gentile women (Rahab and Ruth) were among his ancestors. This stress on paternity is reinforced by appealing to the case in Leviticus 24:10–12, in which "the son of an Israelite woman and an Egyptian father" is not identified as an Israelite.[5]

Later Paul deals with the ongoing role of Israel in God's redemptive purpose for Israel itself and the Gentile nations (Rom. 11). His whole argument turns on the

3. When a Jewish person today accepts Jesus as his or her Messiah and Lord, no rejection of Jewish roots in the Law, Prophets, and Writings is involved. Rather, the decision to submit to the authority of Yahweh, the God of Abraham, Isaac, and Jacob brings the Jewish person's essential Jewishness to completeness and fullness.

4. See article by D. Kellerman on the *gēr:* in *Theological Dictionary of the Old Testament*, vol. 2 (Grand Rapids: Eerdmans, 1975), 439–49.

5. Why then does rabbinic Judaism teach just the opposite: that Jewishness is determined by the mother? If the mother is Jewish, then the children are Jewish. There are valid reasons for this, as we shall see.

distinction he made earlier between nominal Israelites and the believing company of Abraham's true descendants in the nation:

> A man is not a Jew if he is only one outwardly, nor is circumcision merely outward and physical. No, a man is a Jew if he is one inwardly; and circumcision is circumcision of the heart, by the Spirit, not by the written code. Such a man's praise is not from men, but from God. (Rom. 2:28–29)

Prophetic Tension: The Covenants and the Land

When God called Abraham out of Ur of the Chaldees, he promised him land, a posterity, personal blessing, and a blessed impact on all peoples of the earth (Gen. 12:1–3). These promises were repeated (18:17–19) and accompanied with a solemn oath to make them a binding covenant (22:15–18). Significantly, they were not made contingent on any conditions that Abraham had to meet. All that he had to do was to trust in the faithfulness of God. The elements of a Promised Land and innumerable progeny particularly constituted the heart of patriarchal religion. It is not difficult to sense the growing optimism of Israel concerning their future following the Exodus, the conquest, and their development of the land. This optimism was buttressed by the sure promises of Yahweh, their long possession of the land, and the unfolding of the monarchy. Their future was secure. Yahweh's unconditional promises to Abraham, Isaac, and Jacob fueled this optimism.

But the Israelites tended to overlook something of tremendous significance in the Sinaitic covenant that had constituted Israel as a nation. Before this covenant was revealed, God had placed God's people under obligation to do his will (Exod. 19:4–6). The promises that God made in covenant with Israel at Sinai were conditioned upon their obedience. The Sinaitic covenant offered no unconditional promises. As John Bright pointedly states:

> The future is not assured by the promises: it may be blessing, or it may be curse. All depends on Israel's faithfulness to the covenant. One might say that the future and the promises are laid under the little word "if." (1976: 44)

But this fact was easily forgotten. We must keep in mind that the Exodus experience indelibly printed on the Israelite consciousness the conviction that Yahweh would reign over them "for ever and ever" (Exod. 15:18). They had many promises of God to support this (e.g., Num. 23:19–24; 24:5–9; Deut. 33).

However, over the years, indeed by the eighth century, great deterioration took place in Israel's religious thought. It was widely rationalized that if one observed cultic ritual and offered the prescribed sacrifices, all would be well. Yahweh would be satisfied. Jerusalem would always be secure. Then Yahweh responded by sending a succession of prophets. They spoke of God's coming interventions in Israel's history. God would come to judge God's people. Unless they repented, God would uproot them from the Promised Land. At a later, more remote time, they said,

God would deliver them from their enemies and restore them to their land. God would bring to glorious consummation his purposes for them.

From Hosea and Amos onward the prophets did not follow any single pattern in speaking of these matters (Bright 1976: 83). Amos first challenged the popular confidence that because the Israelites were God's chosen people, God had no alternative but to protect them. In contrast, Amos charged that because they were divinely chosen, they would be especially judged: "You only have I chosen of all the families of the earth; therefore I will punish you for all your sins" (3:2). Amos called the nation to "hate evil, love good; maintain justice in the courts" (5:15). And then came his rather hesitant and tentative conclusion: "Perhaps the LORD God Almighty will have mercy on the remnant of Joseph" (5:15). Even so, beyond this intimation of hope in the distant future, he could only predict that Yahweh would restore the Davidic kingdom, but in ways not previously imagined (9:11–15).

Hosea was more explicit. Israel was mortally sick, because of the apostasy of the people. The people openly expressed this by flocking to the orgiastic rites of Baal worship (4:11–14). Hosea judged Israel on the basis of the Decalogue and then proclaimed Yahweh's conclusion: the covenant has been broken. Israel has no future as a nation; it is going to be uprooted from the land, sent into exile, and return to wilderness wandering. You are "not my people, and I am not your God" (1:9; see also 7:12, 16; 9:11–12; 12:9). You "will return to Egypt" (8:13; 9:3; 11:5). Even so, in the distant future Yahweh will restore Israel on the basis of a new covenant that will bring blessing to the whole world (2:14–23; 5:15–6:3; 14:4–7).

Isaiah speaks in similar fashion. The two covenant traditions—the Sinaitic and the Davidic—are both upheld, but in tension. The Davidic dynasty will collapse, but the eternal purpose of Yahweh will not thereby be thwarted. There will come a "root of Jesse" who will stand as "an ensign to the nations." But the nation of Israel will be terribly chastened by the Assyrians. Even so, in the distant future the earth will be filled with the knowledge of Yahweh "as the waters cover the sea" (11:9–16).

In the seventh century the growing apostasy of Judah—all that was left of Israel— was checked from time to time by God's grace. He accomplished this by bringing spiritual renewal under the instrumentality of several godly kings. During the reign of Josiah the people were spiritually awakened through the discovery of the Sinaitic covenant. They then became aware that their retention of the land was contingent upon their obedience to Yahweh's law. Unfortunately, this relatively brief period of reform tended to create a false sense of security. Now the people could claim anew God's unconditional promise to David and relax. Because they were becoming religious again, Yahweh would certainly not forsake his king, his city, and his Zion.

Toward the end of Josiah's reign Jeremiah emerged as the prophet of catastrophe. Although we know he admired Josiah and doubtless supported his efforts at reform (11:1–17; 22:11–16), Jeremiah had the premonition that the growing strength of Nebuchadnezzar's Babylonian armies bode ill for Judah (4:5–8, 11–17; 5:15–17; 6:22–26). Furthermore, he knew that no state-ordered reform could provide the nation's radical change in attitude and moral outlook that Yahweh was looking for. It had produced only "a great cloud of incense smoke and throngs of people in the Temple, but no return to a life of righteousness in obedience to God's commands" (Bright 1976: 152). Slavish devotion to religious externals could not save Judah (6:19–21).

Inevitably, Jeremiah would clash with those prophets who could only refer to the unconditional promise of Yahweh to David, that the Davidic dynasty, the royal city of Jerusalem, and the sanctuary on Mount Zion would be eternally secure (7:1–15; 8:8–9; 23:1–40). We can readily imagine the derision with which Jeremiah was regarded when he stated that the then ruling Davidic line would be forever removed from Yahweh's ongoing purpose (22:28–30; 36:29–31). Even so, Jeremiah hinted at the certainty of an ideal Davidic king coming to the fore in the distant future (23:5–6).

But we should never forget the personal anguish that Jeremiah endured. He was hated and ostracized by the leaders of the nation. Plots were made to kill him, and he himself came to utter despair, despising his prophetic role, cursing his enemies, and even charging Yahweh with having abandoned him (9:2; 11:20; 18:19–23; 20:7–9, 14–18). But Jeremiah did not quit. The message Yahweh had given him had to be proclaimed, and he was determined to do this (20:8–9).

In the end Jeremiah was right. Nebuchadnezzar captured, then destroyed Jerusalem. The Temple was reduced to ruins, and the Davidic dynasty ended. Even so, Jeremiah did not despair. He pointed to a distant future and included some details of it in a letter to the exiles in Babylon (29:1–10). True, it was a dark future, but a bright one too, because of the assured faithfulness of God to God's people and covenant. God's mission would continue in a new future, and God would work in new ways to bless the nations of the earth.

> "I know the plans I have for you," declares the LORD, "plans to prosper you and not to harm you, plans to give you hope and a future. Then you will call upon me and come and pray to me, and I will listen to you. You will seek me and find me when you seek me with all your heart. I will be found by you," declares the LORD, "and will bring you back from captivity. I will gather you from all the nations and places where I have banished you," declares the LORD, "and will bring you back to the place from which I carried you into exile." (Jer. 29:11–14)

Conclusion

The story of Israel in the Promised Land during the period of the monarchy has much to teach us about the Kingdom of God. The chosen people enter it and remain in it, but only by the grace of God. Their never-ending struggle finds echo in the struggle of Christians to be faithful to their Lord, whose Kingdom rule is already established and not yet fulfilled. The land is a shadowy representation of a future time when righteousness will truly reign. Over the years the focus of the faith and hope of the believing Israelites was on Jerusalem, the site of David's throne, and on the Temple, where God dwelt in the midst of his people. They could sing, "The LORD loves the gates of Zion more than all the dwellings of Jacob. . . . [And he]

will write in the register of the peoples, 'This one was born in Zion'" (Ps. 87:2–6).
Indeed, citizenship in the holy city was the greatest possible honor given to them.
But they were also aware of the element of mystery in God's earlier dealings with
the Northern Kingdom. They pondered Hosea's record of Yahweh's agony:

> How can I give you up, Ephraim? . . .
> My heart is changed within me;
>   all my compassion is aroused.
> I will not carry out my fierce anger,
>   nor will I turn and devastate Ephraim.
> For I am God, and not man—
>   the Holy One among you.
> I will not come in wrath. (Hos. 11:8–9)

Although they knew that God never gives up on God's people, their sense of
mystery grew with the realization that God did in fact give up on the Northern
Kingdom. Its people were taken into captivity after the destruction of Samaria in
721 B.C., never to be reconstituted a nation under God. A sense of uneasiness overtook them when they reviewed Yahweh's promises to David and his successors:

> I will maintain my love to him forever,
>   and my covenant with him will never fail.
> I will establish his line forever,
>   his throne as long as the heavens endure. . . .
> His line will continue forever. (Ps. 89:28–29, 36)

Even so, the Davidic line was destroyed. We can imagine, then, the despair
that followed the destruction of the first Temple, the note on which this period
of the monarchy ended. Further details of this anguish of heart are expressed in
this Psalm:

> But you have rejected, you have spurned,
>   you have been very angry with your anointed one.
> You have renounced the covenant with your servant
>   and have defiled his crown in the dust. . . .
> How long, O LORD? Will you hide yourself forever? . . .
> O LORD, where is your former great love,
>   which in your faithfulness you swore to David? (89:38–39, 46, 49)

Fortunately, in their despair some Israelites turned toward God and reread the
messages of their preexilic prophets. And there began to grow in the minds of
the devout not hope for Judah and Jerusalem's physical restoration but hope for
the coming of the Messiah, hope for the messianic advent and the Kingdom of
God about which their prophets had also spoken. This leads us to consider the
story of God's mission during the time of Israel's exile among the nations.

PART 3

GOD'S MISSION AMONG THE NATIONS

8

God Sends Israel into Exile among the Nations

Introduction

We have noted that the period prior to the Assyrian and Babylonian captivities was characterized by the growing appeal and power of Baal worship and the steady reduction of the worship of Yahweh to mere formalism. This heightened the concern of the prophets to denounce all external worship and call the people back to the righteousness demanded by the Sinaitic covenant. An unknown chronicler summarized the outcome:

> The LORD, the God of their fathers, sent word to them through his messengers again and again, because he had pity on his people and on his dwelling place. But they mocked God's messengers, despised his words and scoffed at his prophets until the wrath of the LORD was aroused against his people and there was no remedy. (2 Chron. 36:15–16)

In the end the prophets announced that Yahweh was against the state and its profanation of his worship. Because his law was disobeyed and neither righteousness nor justice practiced, he decreed that political Israel (the Northern Kingdom) would no longer be identified as the people of God. "I will destroy it from the face of the earth. . . . I will shake the house of Israel among all the nations" (Amos 9:8–9).

In the middle of the eighth century B.C., a series of disasters began to overtake both kingdoms. Earlier they had known almost constant conflict with the Semitic peoples of greater Palestine, but from this time onward their territories became the center of titanic struggles between great powers from beyond their borders. Actually, the Northern Kingdom attained the zenith of its glory during this period under the leadership of Jeroboam II (786–746 B.C.). But the nation was rotten to the core, and God was determined to reject it totally. His judgment fell when Samaria was captured (721 B.C.) by Shalmaneser, the Assyrian monarch (Bright 1953: 75). Shortly thereafter most survivors were deported to Upper Mesopotamia (2 Kings 17:6) and through assimilation lost forever their identity as Israelites. Those who had remained in the land intermingled with immigrants from Babylon and elsewhere (17:24) and in time emerged as the racially mixed Samaritans.

Only Judah remained, although it was forced to become an Assyrian puppet state. Judah experienced brief periods of relative independence and spiritual renewal, but its final years were also characterized by departure from Yahweh. From time to time it was ruled by godly kings (e.g., Hezekiah, 2 Chron. 29–31, and Josiah, 2 Kings 22–23), but they were unable to reverse the downward trend of the nation. Although God loved Jerusalem and the Temple, the sins of God's people demanded judgment. The final collapse came with the Babylonian invasion (in two successive waves: 598 B.C. and 586 B.C.). Many lost their lives in the hopeless struggle, but a sizable number were taken to Babylon (2 Chron. 36:5–10, 17–21).

The Necessity for Judgment

Why did God allow such massive catastrophes to overtake God's people at the hands of cruel peoples who did not honor God's name? The reasons are many. They were unthankful for the divine love behind all the mercies lavished upon them (1 Kings 16:29–18:46; Hos. 2:1–13; Rom. 1:21). They were unfaithful to the marriage vow that had sealed the covenant God made with them at Sinai (Exod. 32:1; Amos 5:25–27; Acts 7:39–43). This also made them deliberately reject the standards of Sinai in order to give themselves to ease and luxury (Isa. 5:8–24; Amos 2:6–8; 5:10–15; 6:1–7; 8:4–6; Mic. 2:1, 2). Finally, they were unjust in their dealings with one another, especially with the minority peoples and the poor in their midst. They nonetheless assumed that God would somehow be pleased with their formal worship and external piety (Amos 5:4–7, 21–27; Mic. 6:6–8).

Although the prophets identified Assyria (Isa. 10:5–11) and Babylonia (Jer. 25:8–11) as the instruments that God would use to punish Israel and Judah and indicated that their punishment at the hands of those foreign nations would be for the sake of the abused poor, these Gentile powers should not be seen as either "liberators" or "freedom fighters" (Deist 1977: 63). They represented the rod of God's anger. Yahweh fought through them against Israel and Judah. As a result, all efforts of defense, intercessory prayers, and expectations of miraculous intervention (e.g., Jer. 21:2) were of no consequence. The omnipotent God had decreed judgment. Subsequently, judgment fell on these rapacious nations. Whereas they served as the instruments of God's punishment of his people, they too were judged, particularly for the arrogance with which they tormented God's people (Isa. 10:12–19; Jer. 25:11–14).

These judgments of God—taking his people into captivity after destroying their national and religious life—were designed to strip them of all that previously enabled them to live apart from him in indifference to God's will. They had to

lose their riches, their glory as a free and independent people, their land, their king—everything, even up to and including the Holy City, which they had believed could not be destroyed, and the Temple, the visible sign of God's presence. Israel had to go back to the wilderness, into a dreadful solitude, where, no longer having anything of its own, it might learn to look to God alone for everything. (de Dietrich 1960: 109)

God was, is, and always will be in control of history. God's purposes move forward despite the failure of his people. Israel's experience of failure and unrealized hopes could not but motivate devout men to reach out with longing for the new covenant of which Jeremiah spoke (31:31–34; Bright 1953: 126).

We would do well to reflect on the spiritual effects that the Babylonian experience had on the Jewish people. Jeremiah had been so complete in portraying the finality of this judgment that he used the word divorce to describe what had taken place in their relationship to Yahweh. As a result, the conviction increasingly grew among some that Israel could never return to its former standing before God (Jer. 3:8). A divorce is a termination, once and for all. Others may have protested and pointed out that Isaiah seemed to imply that the divorce was only temporary (Isa. 54:4–10).

It is probable that many believed that the destruction of the Temple and the exile to Babylon demonstrated that Yahweh had been defeated by the gods of Babylon. In their despair, having no further possibility of sacrificial worship, they could only echo Ezekiel's lament: "Our offenses and sins weigh us down, and we are wasting away because of them. How then can we live?" (33:10). All that they could hope for was that Yahweh in grace would somehow help them endure the present and give them the faith to believe that he would restore to them all the patterns of the past. But this was hardly God's intention. We find a clue in the way in which Isaiah ties the end of the Babylonian captivity with the Exodus (chaps. 40–55) and states that Yahweh will accomplish a "new thing" in the process (43:16–21). This will be more glorious than anything that had gone before and will demonstrate the power of God in ways beyond imagining.

We cannot forget the larger purpose Isaiah had in mind. At first Babylon was in the foreground along with Cyrus as Yahweh's servant. As the Exodus marked a significant new beginning for Israel—its liberation and nationhood—so the return of the exiles to the Promised Land held promise of something new for Israel. What this "new thing" would be was not immediately apparent. The prophets had spoken of a new Exodus (Jer. 31:2–6, 15–22; Ezek. 20:33–38; Hos. 2:14–20). But Isaiah poured into this concept something that went far beyond any restoration of the old monarchy. The greater Exodus would involve liberation from a greater captivity—and Isaiah alone of the prophets would reveal the exciting details.

The Mission of the Exiles

While in exile in Babylon the Jews were given two collateral tasks to perform apart from being concerned with justice, steadfast love, and walking humbly with their God (Mic. 6:8). They were to survive as a people. This involved building houses, planting gardens, marrying, and bearing children—"increase in number there; do not decrease" (Jer. 29:5–6). Furthermore, they were to serve their captors (Jer. 29:7). If faithful, God promised they would be permitted to return to their land when the seventy-year captivity was at an end (Jer. 25:11–12; 29:8–14).

Particular attention should be called to the second of these two tasks: the mandate that the exiles "seek the peace (šālôm) and prosperity of the city" where they were exiled "and pray to the LORD for [the city]" (Jer. 29:7). This mandate has generated much discussion in our day. The word šālôm is used more than 350 times in the Old Testament. It covers a wide range of meaning: wholeness, without injury, undivided, well-being, a satisfactory condition, bodily health, and all that salvation means in its Old Testament usage. If a person or a nation has šālôm, no lack exists in any direction, whether personal or national. The concept is positive and proactive: šālôm never means "absence of war"; it means "victory in war." It has to do with community (Ps. 29:11) and means total harmony within the community. It is "founded upon order and permeated by God's blessing, and hence makes it possible for men to develop and increase, free and unhindered on every side" (Gross 1970: 648). Šālôm is the gift of Yahweh, and we shall later find that it becomes the dominant characteristic of the promised messianic age (Isa. 9:7). Although in the Old Testament it is not explicitly equated with spiritual peace with God, this eschatological-salvation concept is intimated (Blauw 1962: 53). In the New Testament the equivalent word is eirēnē, or "peace," and is particularly identified with the redemptive work of Christ, bringing the repentant individual into a new relationship with God and neighbors and giving hope for eschatological salvation that will embrace the whole person and the whole kosmos (Rom. 5:1, 10; Eph. 2:14–17; Rom. 8:19–23; Heb. 13:20).

When God told the captives to seek the šālôm of Babylon, he was in effect telling them to carry out all the obligations of the cultural mandate. In obedience, Daniel and his three friends were willing to be trained for the Babylonian civil service (Dan. 1:3–20), and Mordecai was willing to serve Xerxes, the king of Persia, as "second in rank" (Esther 10:3).

The Right Hand of God

One of the surprises of ancient history is the relative ease with which the Persians under Cyrus overcame Babylon—almost without a fight (539 B.C.). Another anomaly was the decree of Cyrus granting the right for politically unimportant Jews to restore their cultural and religious life in Palestine (Ezra 1:1–4; 6:1–5). It is remarkable that when Isaiah refers to Cyrus (e.g., 45:5–7), he uses concepts congenial to Zoroastrianism, a religion built around a thoroughgoing dualism that fostered religious toleration. In the wisdom of God this provided a political climate in the land so that Ezra's reforms could be effectively carried through (Ellison 1976: 6).

Cyrus's personal devotion to Zoroastrianism made him one of the most enlightened rulers of the ancient world. He really believed that his empire would be more tranquil and more durable if all subject peoples within its borders were free to develop their distinct cultural values and enjoy a measure of political independence within the Persian Empire. Behind this we see the hand of Yahweh. All of this is the work of Yahweh even though Cyrus did not know Yahweh (Isa. 45:1–4).

Despite the fact that by this time the great majority of the Jews had become well established in Babylon, a surprising number appeared willing to leave this life behind and deliberately commit themselves to what they perceived to be the ongoing purpose of God.[1] And this despite their awareness of the difficult and dangerous return journey (nine hundred miles!) and the uncertainties awaiting them in their ruined land. We would distinguish their activities as "the right hand" of God in contrast to the activities of those who remained in Babylon or migrated elsewhere. These latter activities reflected "the left hand" of God. Some biblical scholars distinguish these separate activities in terms of the directive will of God and the permissive will of God. Overarching both is the sovereignty of God. He desired his people to be in their own land to set the stage for his Son being "born of a woman, born under law" (Gal. 4:4). And without the Jews in diaspora throughout the Mediterranean world, it would have been impossible for the apostles to plant the church so widely and so rapidly in the first century. The fortunes of both groups of people must be studied simultaneously since their distinct experiences and achievements only gain significance when viewed together.

The first years of the exiles back in the land were disappointing and frustrating. Apparently, they encountered no significant signs of God's favor encouraging their obedience to what they regarded as his specific will. Although they commenced the restoration of the Temple so that they might resume the cultic life of preexilic times, opposition to their obedience mounted, and after a short time they turned from this priority task and became involved in personal concerns. This meant great spiritual loss, for there was no provision for Yahweh to dwell in their midst and no possibility of their performing worship acceptable to him. Tragically, the Temple remained unfinished for almost eighteen years (Ezra 4:1–24).

Then God graciously raised up Haggai and Zechariah, "the prophets of work," to stimulate his people to complete the reconstruction of the Temple (Ezra 5:1–2). Inasmuch as a primary focus of Christian mission today involves laboring with Jesus Christ in the building of his church, one can strike an analogy between the physical labor involved in building the Temple and the spiritual service involved in extending the church. Hence, the seven messages of these prophets are relevant today. The meaning of these messages for mission in Kingdom service is significant for our understanding of a Kingdom-based vision of missionary participation today.

1. From Babylonia there returned about 50,000 together with 7,537 slaves (Ezra 2:64–65). The total given in Ezra 2:2–60 is 29,818, in Neh. 7:6–62, 31,089, but both agree on a grand total of 42,360 (Ezra 2:64, Neh. 7:66); the difference can be explained by the larger figure including the women. The parallel passage in 1 Esdras 5:41 says, probably correctly, that the 42,360 included persons over twelve years of age. If we allow for the children as well, we reach the round figure of 50,000 previously suggested (Ellison 1976: 1).

The Loss of Priorities (Hag. 1)

Haggai found the people virtually blaming God for their spiritual failure (1:2) and not realizing that his withholding of good harvests (1:5–6, 10–11) was his judgment on their preoccupation with their own concerns: "My house . . . remains a ruin, while each of you is busy with his own house" (1:9). When spiritual life is dull and barren, with little evidence of God's blessing, the problem may be the loss of priorities—generally through self-centered preoccupation with personal, family, or material concerns and not with "justice, mercy and faithfulness" (Matt. 23:23; see also Mic. 6:8). Reassurance concerning the presence of God in the midst of his people can be enjoyed when they make God's purpose their priority concern (Hag. 1:13).

The Absence of Faith (Hag. 2:1–9)

Haggai later found the people contrasting unfavorably their reconstruction of the Temple with the glory of the original Solomonic structure, and hence they began to despise their own work: "Does it not seem to you like nothing?" (2:4). In response Haggai encouraged them to persevere and claim God's covenanted promise to "do wonders never before done in any nation" (Exod. 34:10). When discouragement overtakes the servants of God, the problem may be the result of failure to exercise the sort of faith that claims the promise of his involvement in their work—generally through an unwarranted self-confidence.

In order to add significance to their labors, Haggai conveyed an unexpected word from Yahweh:

> "In a little while I will once more shake the heavens and the earth, the sea and the dry land. I will shake all nations, and the desired of all nations will come, and I will fill this house with glory. . . . The glory of this present house will be greater than the glory of the former house. . . . And in this place I will grant peace," declares the LORD Almighty. (2:6–9)

This promise reminds us of Isaiah 60 with its repeated prediction that when Yahweh finally comes to Zion as Redeemer (59:20), all the nations will gather around his transformed people (60:1–4). They will confess to him the righteousness of his people and will know that Israel "will possess the land forever" (60:17–22). Then they will bring their treasures—"the riches of the nations"—and use them to build Jerusalem and adorn his "glorious temple" (60:5–16).

The Curse of Professionalism (Hag. 2:10–19; Zech. 1:1–6)

Haggai referred to Leviticus 5:2 and showed that whereas defilement is transferred by contact, ceremonial holiness is not. To be physically involved in performing "holy tasks" does not mean that one automatically becomes holy in God's sight. When those building the Temple had still another poor harvest (2:16–17) because their work and worship were "defiled" (2:14), Haggai had to call attention to their failure to respond to Zechariah's message from God: "Return to me . . . and I will return to you" (1:3, with Hag. 2:17). When anticipated blessings are unmistakably withheld, the problem may arise from the neglect of direct cultivation of God's presence through confession, worship, and celebration. This neglect is occasioned either through spiritual laziness or excessive activism, which in turn brings defilement to the actual work in which one is involved.

The Paralysis of Fear (Hag. 2:20–23)

When people neglect the worship and enjoyment of God, they inevitably lose their sense of quiet confidence in his providential care. At that time Jerusalem's walls were still in ruins, and the people had no army to defend them. As their enemies grew in number, fears multiplied. One can imagine that they began to call for a halt to the reconstruction of the Temple so they might defend themselves.

Haggai's task was to assure them that Yahweh had promised to bring them safely through whatever crises lay ahead, but they must persevere in the work he had given them to do. He would triumph on their behalf and judge all the kingdoms opposing Israel. The elect, epitomized by Zerubbabel of the Davidic line, would then know that he had not failed them. Hence, the exhortation was to cultivate Yahweh to such an extent that no menacing reality could make them afraid. After all, he will ultimately win in human history.

The Importance of Vision (Zech. 1:7–2:13)

We have in these two chapters a series of visions that speak of God's faithful care for Jerusalem and the Temple, despite appearances to the contrary (1:7–17), of his judging the nations that assaulted Judah (1:18–21), and of the certainty of his presence in the midst of his restored people (2:1–13). The people of God need to be stimulated by frequent reminders of "the big picture." Granting them visions of this sort is essential if they are to persevere in the work set before them. When they lose their forward momentum, it may be because of the lack of vision imparted to them by their local leaders.

Personal Inadequacy (Zech. 3)

Although called by God to leave Babylon and bring to an end the possibility of his life being wasted there (3:2), Joshua, the high priest, fell prey to the subtle insinuations of Satan that he was unworthy, unspiritual, and unholy, and forgot that he had an advocate with God, who had equipped him for acceptable service and whose intercession before God's throne could sustain him (3:4–5). When those doing God's work are tempted to quit, this may be because of their rejection of themselves, arising from a morbid introspection or a failure to distinguish the inward scolding of the enemy from the convicting work of the Holy Spirit.

It is significant that this brief section ends with reference to "my servant, the Branch" (3:8) and his great achievement: "I will remove the sin of this land in a single day" (3:9). This unusual designation gathers messianic implications when we later learn that "the Branch" is the one who not only enables the colonists to complete the Temple, working through Joshua and the rest, but also will become the conquering Priest-King, the final victor in human history (cf. 6:9–15 with 3:10).

Leadership and Complexity (Zech. 4)

By revealing the diversity (trees, lampstand, pipes, and oil) behind the single function—to produce uplifted light—Zechariah emphasized the importance of Zerubbabel, their God-appointed leader. When leaders fail to lead and as a result followers lose both their concord and their buoyancy of spirit, the problem may have arisen because of their neglecting the Holy Spirit or failing to appreciate and support the diversity within the unity of the people of God. Through this vision God affirmed that his purpose for the nations is achieved "not by might nor by power, but by my Spirit" (4:6).

The Rebuke of Exclusivism

Over the centuries Israel had fallen into the trap of believing that its election by God made it his favorite.

> They were convinced that God had chosen them because he needed them. As King he needed Israel as his People, as Husband he needed her as wife, as Father he needed him as son, as Master he needed him as servant. Israel would never have existed but for Yahweh, but Yahweh was incomprehensible without Israel, at least in the popular mind. (Ellison 1976: 4)

Israel reasoned that nothing it might do would jeopardize its standing with God. This conviction arose from what was judged to be an unconditional promise made to David concerning the security of Jerusalem, the inviolability of the Temple, and the permanence of the Davidic line (2 Sam. 7:8–16). As a result, Israel largely forgot that it was chosen by God for service and that this was both a privilege and an obligation. Only a few sensed with Isaiah that God was concerned that his people be "a light for the Gentiles" (42:6; 49:6). Almost none of them translated their calling into dynamic outreach. In the postexilic period this concern of the exiles diminished to the point where they sought to preserve their faith and religious practice by living in complete withdrawal from the nations. "Judaism became exclusive instead of aggressive, a little garden walled around instead of a great missionary force" (Rowley 1939: 48). Jewish exclusiveness steadily gained ground during the postexilic period.

Two Old Testament books (Ruth and Jonah) are introduced at this point since both, in strikingly different ways, underscore Yahweh's universal concern for all peoples and his rebuke of Jewish particularism. The story of Ruth makes it clear that Gentiles are within the circle of God's concern. "Your people will be my people and your God my God" (1:16). This book was undoubtedly written before the postexilic period. Its setting is the period of the judges (1:1), although its explanatory glosses (e.g., 4:1–12) were intended to help readers understand its references to ancient practices. That it traces the ancestry of God but omits any reference to Solomon would seem to indicate that it was written before Israel's golden age. Its purpose was to inculcate "filial piety and unselfish devotion" as well as to remind Israelites that

> a foreigner who exemplified the qualities of piety and fidelity, in conjunction with a sincere trust in the providence of God, was certainly worthy to be reckoned among the Chosen People. In this sense the composition not only presented a case for racial tolerance, but also demonstrated convincingly that true religion transcended the bounds of nationality. (R. Harrison 1969: 1063)

The story of Jonah, an eighth-century prophet with a popular message (2 Kings 14:25), is unique in many ways. We do not know if Jonah finally came out on the side of accepting Yahweh's will for his life. But the message of the book is abundantly clear. Jonah is not portrayed as a missionary of monotheism or of messianism. He merely delivers to Nineveh the sort of oracle of judgment that the prophets frequently gave against the nations. He does not call the people of Nineveh to honor Yahweh or embrace the religion of Israel. He merely exposes their sin of having broken the natural law that "gives light to every man" (John 1:9). The nub of the story is Yahweh's persistent effort to reveal to a stubborn prophet his compassion and mercy for a great heathen city, in those days the byword for cruelty and arrogance. Yahweh cares for the nations and sought through revealing his encounter with Jonah to rebuke Israel's distorted understanding of its status before him. He despised its nationalistic and self-righteous pride as well as its aversion to its neighbors. Yahweh's love embraces alien peoples (Amos 9:7). He does not delight in the death of those whose God is not Yahweh. He is not indifferent to the good or evil that people do. God wants to forgive sin, but people must first repent.

The Concern for Renewal: Ezra, Nehemiah, and Malachi

In the Books of Ezra and Nehemiah we encounter a form of devotion to Yahweh strongly pervaded by a legal spirit—an exclusiveness that characterized post-Babylonian Judaism. Both Ezra (9:1–4; 10:1–5) and Nehemiah (13:23–29) refer to their efforts to enforce the separation of the returned exiles from the pagan peoples in the land. Intermarriage with foreigners was forbidden, and mixed marriages were broken up in what appears at first sight to have been very harsh and inhumane measures. And yet those marriages had caused an increasing number to abandon both Jewish culture and Jewish faith. Drastic action was necessary:

> The hard shell of Judaism which was being here formed, while it limited the life of Judaism, at any rate preserved it as its precious inner kernel, destined to germinate and burst forth into more splendid life in a later age. (Rowley 1939: 48–49)

It was through resolute particularism that the faithful sought to preserve the religious inheritance of Israel. Admittedly, it also inevitably led to the development of a superiority complex and a sense of self-righteousness. The Jewish people carelessly reasoned: "If we are forbidden by God to marry non-Jews, we must be better than they are. They must be lesser breeds, for they are outside the law."

The rebuilding of the Temple and the repair of the walls of Jerusalem (Nehemiah) did not bring about the messianic Kingdom. This must have been a great disappointment to successive generations, even though Daniel had predicted that the long period "from the issuing of the decree to restore and rebuild Jerusalem until the Anointed One, the ruler, comes" would involve almost five hundred years (9:24–27). Deep in the Persian period times became hard. Crops were poor and neighbors bothersome. A disappointed, struggling people eventually became disillusioned about Yahweh. This led to an erosion of their commitment to him. Furthermore, the star of empire was passing from Asia to Europe (the emerging Greeks). Palestine was left alone, far removed from exciting world events. Internal conditions went from bad to worse. The colonists lived unto themselves, absorbed in petty, local problems and plagued with disputes over the troublesome Samaritans. They became a listless, cynical people, hiding their misery behind a careless indifference and frivolous mockery of sacred things. Furthermore, the priests became slovenly in their administration of the Temple ritual and were neglectful of their teaching responsibilities. The Word of God was no longer heard in the land, only the grumbling of the people. A prophet was needed. God's gracious response was Malachi.

Malachi used the device of dialogue: the question and answer method. As he moved among the people, listening to their problems and observing their ways, he sought to remind one and all of Yahweh's unwavering love for them and his just dealings with them. But their response was a shrug of the shoulders and the reply, "How so? Prove it!" They admitted no failure and were aghast that their God, who they felt had treated them shabbily, could think so ill of their "righteous indignation." As a result, Malachi made their "How so?" the key to his discourses (1:2, 6; etc.).

He charged them with doubting the love of God (1:2–5) and despising his service (1:6–2:9). He exposed their violations of God's covenantal stipulations regarding marriage fidelity (2:10–16) and their disputing the justice behind God's dealings with them (2:17–3:5). They defrauded God of his possessions (3:6–12) by withholding their tithes and offerings from him. Furthermore, they tended to discount the benefits God lavished on them for being his people (3:13–18). Finally, they flatly denied the inevitability of his judgment of all people (4:1–3). Malachi concluded with two exhortations. First, remember the Torah of Moses—the record of God's faithfulness to his covenant promises—and their obligation to obey him. This is foundational to all else. Second, look for the coming of Elijah and the dawn of the messianic age (4:4–6). Nothing will prevent God's consummation of salvation history.

Because the problem of nominality is so widespread today, we need to be alert to the obligation to be instruments of renewal in the churches. Malachi addressed a stultified, calloused, and critical people. They possessed a form of devotion but were virtually devoid of any vital experience of God himself. As we reflect on Malachi's ministry, we need to ask ourselves whether we deal forthrightly and biblically with the issues that are uppermost in the minds of God's people today. The major question is, Do we adhere to Malachi's pattern of stressing the certainty of God's ultimate victory in Jesus Christ?

This type of ministry comes under the rubric of intensification activity. It involves the concern that all the religious activities in which people participate are diligently improved—personal worship, private prayer, the reading and study of Scripture, and the careful attention to liturgical worship. All are important. There is also the need to be repentant before God. This demands the courageous removal from one's lifestyle of all elements not worthy of biblical faith.

When the exiles finally completed the rebuilding of the Temple through the encouragement of the prophets Haggai and Zechariah, they celebrated Passover and the Feast of Unleavened Bread. This brought the beginnings of spiritual renewal (Ezra 6:19–22) since "the LORD had filled them with joy" (v. 22). We can well believe that this religious convocation stimulated the intensification of the religious devotion of many.

Then came Nehemiah, their governor, with his burden that they rebuild the walls of Jerusalem (Neh. 2:11–20). Under the impetus of the earlier quickening, the people gave themselves to this task, and they were enabled to complete it "in fifty-two days" (6:15)!

Shortly thereafter the Feast of Booths was celebrated, a convocation that had not been correctly observed since the days of Joshua (Neh. 8:17). Actually, Moses had stipulated that the law be read publicly to the people every seven years on this occasion (Deut. 31:10–12). The impetus for observing this week-long festival came from the people themselves (Neh. 8:13–15). They pressed Ezra into the task, and on the opening day he and other Levites "read from the Book of the Law of God, making it clear and giving the meaning so that the people could understand what was being read" (8:8). This brought a spirit of mourning and weeping upon them, which their leaders sought to alleviate by calling attention to the gracious forgiveness of Yahweh. Joyous worship followed (8:9–9:5).

Then came the climax. Ezra reviewed the history of Israel, from the election of the patriarchs until the present, and spoke most pointedly of Israel's persistent disobedience to Yahweh (Neh. 9:6–37). He called for a formal act of recommitment to the covenant, to the service of the Temple, and to one another as Yahweh's people (9:38–10:39). This was a great awakening. It contributed significantly to the reestablishment of Israel's social, cultural, and religious coherence in the land. It even influenced Jerusalem's demography (chap. 11).

The Left Hand of God: The Jews in Diaspora

The "left hand of God" represents the totality of his activity on behalf of those Jews who declined the opportunity to return to the land following the proclamation of Cyrus (Ezra 1:1–4) and whose descendants permanently settled in other countries beyond its borders. Although our information on them is very limited, sufficient is known of their movements and achievements to enable us to discern that they continued to be the objects of God's love and care. Actually, they made no small contribution to preparing the way for the expansion of the church in the first century.

In the Book of Esther we encounter Mordecai. He may be regarded as typical of many Jewish people throughout this long historic period. His obedience to God, or even his preoccupation with God, is not mentioned. Doubtless it was not particularly significant. However, he sacrificed personal advantage to assist his own people and made every effort to enhance their security. When we first meet him, we find that he deliberately avoided bearing public witness to his faith and seemed somewhat uncertain of God's keeping power. His instruction to Esther not to reveal her Jewishness (2:10, 20) is in sharp contrast with Daniel's public observance of his submission to the Levitical dietary code (Dan. 1:8–16). Mordecai seems to have had a sense of God's providential care for the Jewish people (Esther 4:13–14), and his influence on Esther does appear to have given her robust faith in God (4:16). Yet, he was inclined to put his trust in human solutions to both his own problems and those of his people. He remained a loyal member of the larger Persian community and took no part in subversive political activity (2:21–23). On the whole, he was concerned to exercise a wholesome influence on his generation. He may be typical of those who in jest would say the Song of Solomon was written for the young, the Proverbs for those in middle age, and the Book of Ecclesiastes for the elderly. Nonetheless, as a Jewish person, Mordecai was dominated by a sense of mission: not to share the good news of Yahweh with the Gentiles, but to make sure that he and all other Jewish people retained their Jewish identity.

The "left hand of God" prepared for the missionary outreach of the apostolic church in a variety of ways. So much so that we should guard against making sweeping criticisms of those Jewish people who were unwilling to follow Zerubbabel and Jeshua back to the land (Ezra 1:5–3:13). They contributed in a significant fashion to the growing conviction that a universal faith was about to appear on the world scene.

Conclusion

We have seen that the God who speaks in revelation is the God who acts in history. A significant part of the Old Testament records the great moments in Israel's history when God uniquely acted on Israel's behalf and revealed his will concerning its mission. Although Israel actually first became aware of itself as "the people God calls" during the Exodus event, the prior election and call of Abraham and the other patriarchs marked the beginnings of God's redemptive purpose (Acts 7:2–4; 13:17). Some scholars list five such moments (e.g., Knight 1959: 202–17). Metaphorically, when viewing the nation of Israel in relationship to God, we would contend for at least nine monumental events. We regard each one of them as relevant to the calling of the people of God into his fellowship and purpose. They are as follows:

First, the people of God were *courted* in Ur and Haran and led into "the land of promise," there to become a pilgrim people dwelling in tents—in the world but not of it (Gen. 12:1–3; Isa. 51:1–2). The Abrahamic covenant provided God's gracious basis for this relationship: an election unto divine possession and service.

Second, the people of God were *begotten* out of the anguish of Egyptian oppression. At one point in history they were "a few people" (Deut. 26:5), but Yahweh called them into being as his son and gave them life and liberation (Exod. 4:22; Jer. 31:9; Hos. 11:1).

Third, the people of God were *baptized* immediately thereafter in the sea as a public confession of themselves as the people of God, separated from all other nations (Exod. 20:2; Deut. 7:6; Hos. 11:1; 1 Cor. 10:2).

Fourth, the people of God were *married* to Yahweh at Sinai by a covenant that he defined and they accepted, thus marking the beginning of interaction with him through the revealed instruction of the law and the prophets' corrective ministry (Exod. 19:8; Jer. 7:25; Gal. 3:24).

Fifth, the people of God were *given* the land of promise as a national inheritance. This land was not acquired through Israel's military prowess but by means of the irresistible power of Yahweh's hosts, who triumphed repeatedly over the desperate and massive opposition of the Canaanites.

Sixth, the people of God were *established* as a kingdom under the Davidic dynasty. The Davidic line was promised an eternal place in God's economy (2 Sam. 7) and the focal point in Israel's blessing of the nations (Isa. 11:10; Zech. 8:23).

Seventh, the people of God were *tested* on Mount Carmel to ascertain the genuineness of their professed loyalty to Yahweh and his covenant and to press home to their consciences the irreconcilable antithesis between the worship of Yahweh and the worship of all other gods (1 Kings 17; 18).

Eighth, the people of God were *slain* by Yahweh for their sins; Assyria and Babylonia were his instruments of judgment. This led to their being buried: they "descended into sheol" in heathen lands (Jer. 8:19–22; Lam. 1:12–13; 2:3).

Ninth, the people of God were *resurrected* by Yahweh through the instrumentality of Cyrus the Persian in order that they might reestablish their national, social, and religious life back in their own land (Ezra 1:1–4).

Beyond these events is the "eschatological moment," the day of the Lord. As the Son of David, the Son of Man, and the Suffering Servant (three distinct offices of one Person), the Messiah of Israel will return to restore all wasted and ruined places in the land, delivering it from the curse, in order to remarry his people that they might share in his total reconciliation of the cosmos (Isa. 62:1–4; Ezek. 36:36).

9

God Sets the Stage
for the Messiah's Coming

Introduction

We have traced the central events in God's dealings with his people: the call of Abraham, the establishment of the covenant of grace with Abraham and the patriarchs, their Exodus deliverance, the covenant at Sinai, the wilderness wandering, and their entrance into the Promised Land. We noted their subsequent experience under the judges, then under Samuel and Saul, and finally under the kings of Israel and Judah. However, because of their persistent violation of the Sinaitic covenant and their disobedience to God, all of this came to naught. The Davidic kingdom experienced disruption, division, and civil war. The Northern Kingdom was eliminated, and Judah went into exile in Babylon. Only around fifty thousand colonists returned to the homeland after an absence of seventy years. Although God enabled them to restore in part their civil and religious life, the Davidic monarchy was not reestablished. In this God was setting the stage for the inauguration of the messianic Kingdom and the transformation of his people into a religious community that would become a light to the Gentile nations.

Before we review the basic themes enunciated by the prophets throughout this long history in which the Kingdom purpose of God for the nations began to unfold, we must clarify the meaning of the word *Torah* (the law) as it unfolded especially during the exilic and postexilic periods. Admittedly, this issue is complex. Over the centuries Torah has been identified with a wide range of specifics, ranging from the Ten Commandments, to the Sinaitic law codes, to the entire Pentateuch, to the whole Hebrew Bible, to all the religious literature of postbiblical Judaism. Within the Old Testament it denotes bodies of instructions or teachings of priests, prophets, and sages and even of parental advice to children. Yet it appears that the oldest and most common meaning is something approximate to what we mean by the word *revelation*. Priestly and prophetic oracles are called *torahs*. And in the case of the prophets, whole collections of oracles or systems of thought (as in Isaiah) are called Torah (Sanders 1972: 2–4).

While it is true that in the New Testament the word *law* may refer to the Pentateuch (e.g., Luke 24:44; Gal. 4:21–22), it is also used in the larger sense of the Old Testament revelation. Note the following: "Is it not written in your Law, 'I have said you are gods'?" (John 10:34, quoting Ps. 82:6). "We have heard from the Law that the Christ will remain forever" (John 12:34, quoting Ps. 110:4; see also Isa. 9:7; Ezek. 37:25; and Dan. 7:14). "But this is to fulfill what is written in their Law: 'They hated me without reason'" (John 15:25, quoting Ps. 35:19 and 69:4).

This usage of the term *law* has caused critics to regard the New Testament writers as imprecise! Actually, after the Old Testament era came to an end and during the intertestamental period, the term *Torah* came increasingly to be used in a still wider sense to include Judaism's codification of its authoritative teaching and evolving tradition. This was completed around A.D. 500. When Jesus and the New Testament writers used the word *law* to refer to non-Mosaic portions of the Old Testament, they were merely following the practice of first-century Jewry.

The Torah is the gospel of the Old Testament era since it embraced the saving activity of God on behalf of his people (Mic. 6:5). The prophets' task was to remind the people of this "good news" and exhort them to live out its implications in their individual and corporate life. This led, on occasion, to repentance and faith and direct personal encounter with God. We have already reviewed this sequence of failure, which characterizes much of Old Testament history: Torah; proclamation; the people's pledge of obedience; Torah violation; divine withdrawal; grievous suffering at the hands of their enemies; national repentance; deliverance by God; and, finally, restoration to fellowship with God.

We shall now consider those specific elements in the instruction of the prophets by which they set the stage for the great messianic event in the ongoing sequence of salvation history. Our task is to trace the manner in which God not only aroused anticipation of the coming Kingdom but also provided all that was needed for it to be realized. Although in previous chapters we have discussed a wide range of issues that bear on the mission of the church in our day, our task now will be to call attention to what is more directly related to the coming of Jesus and his inauguration of the Kingdom of God.

The Need for a Believing Community: The Remnant in Israel

The great mystery of the Scriptures is the reality of the Incarnation, when God "became flesh and made his dwelling among us" (John 1:14; see also 1 Tim. 3:16). Strange as it may seem, this could not have taken place without a believing people "under law" (Gal. 4:4), already dwelling in the land in which this wonderful act of God occurred. There had to be a virgin daughter of Abraham willing to be the chosen vehicle for the Incarnation. And there had to be a devout Joseph to be the guardian of her vulnerability. Many others would also be needed, all consciously living under God's control and for his glory. They would be part of the larger context of believing Jews that we encounter when we begin the New Testament.

The messianic hope necessitated a believing remnant throughout the long centuries from Abraham until the birth of Jesus. God's grace made this possible. And it was the prophets who encouraged its emergence and faithfulness despite the waywardness of most Israelites and their leaders. Isaiah spoke for the remnant when he said, "The zeal of the Lord Almighty will accomplish this" (Isa. 9:7). And the New Testament reflects the continuation of this tragic polarization. The apostle Paul described it as follows: "A man is not a Jew if he is only one outwardly, nor is circumcision merely outward and physical. No, a man is a Jew if he is one inwardly; and circumcision is circumcision of the heart, by the Spirit, not by the written code. Such a man's praise is not from men, but from God" (Rom. 2:28–29). Such Jews constitute "a remnant chosen by grace" (11:5).

The people of God—those truly his by faith and obedience—were never free from ethnic admixture. Even Moses' wife Zipporah was not Hebrew by birth (Exod. 18:2). When the Hebrews came out of Egypt, "many other people went up with them" (Exod. 12:38). We conclude from this that not all those who shared the same faith commitment belonged to the same ethnic and racial lines. On the other hand, many years later when Baalism posed such a religio-cultural threat that it challenged the very existence of Israel, Elijah spoke of the fact that not all who ethnically belonged to Israel shared the same Israelite faith in obedience to God's covenant. This distinction between Israel by faith (the remnant) and Israel defined ethnically can be seen in the story of Elijah. When his own life was threatened, in self-pity Elijah complained that he alone was faithful. In response God disclosed to Elijah that despite the widespread worship of Baal in Israel, he had "seven thousand in Israel—all whose knees have not bowed down to Baal and all whose mouths have not kissed him" (1 Kings 19:10, 14, 18).

There are five characteristics of the faithful remnant within Israel that are instructive about the messianic Kingdom that is coming:

The Remnant and the Prophets

At least nine of the "writing" prophets spoke in some way about the continuity, year after year, of the true people of God. But they were not agreed as to who actually comprised these people. In a sense this was not important. Only "the Lord knows those who are his" (2 Tim. 2:19). As Knight states: "What is important is that the fact of a remnant is central to the thoughts of so many of the prophets" (1959: 259). This arises from their shared conviction that the existence of a faithful remnant within Israel was crucial to God's redemptive purpose for Israel and the nations.

Amos was the first prophet to make extensive use of the remnant motif. He attacked the popular notion that the whole of Israel (ethnically defined) constituted the remnant God would preserve when he would judge the nations in the last day. Amos held before Israel no self-confident salvation based on physical descent, no continued boasting of divine election, no assured certainty of a glorious future. Rather, he extended to them the call of God: "Seek me and live" (5:4–6). In other words, this invitation heralded the possibility of a remnant of faithful Israelites, despite the apostasy of the majority. And as far as God was concerned, these faithful people were differentiated from the majority of Israel. In other words, the remnant by itself has eschatological significance. In the last day it will embrace the total people of God from all the nations (cf. 9:11–12 with Acts 15:16–17).

The concept of the remnant was greatly developed during the early ministry of Isaiah, when it became increasingly apparent that Judah must go into captivity for its sin and waywardness. As a true prophet of the Lord, Isaiah built upon the witness of Amos and was greatly concerned for this believing remnant in the Syro-Ephraimitic crisis of his day. He first introduces the remnant as a "holy seed" (6:13). At first one gains the impression that Isaiah uses the term to refer mostly to those who survive a national catastrophe, rather than to a believing minority within the unbelieving majority (10:20–22; 37:3, 32). But then he becomes more specific and follows Amos in connecting the remnant motif with eschatology. Although the house of David was like a tree to be cut down by the Babylonians in judgment, sap would remain in the stump and a "shoot" would one day emerge that would become a fruitful tree (6:13; 11:1). John Bright regards this concept of the "pure remnant of God's People," cleansed in fiery trial and made amenable to his purpose, as "among the great themes of Isaiah" (1953: 89). Isaiah even named one of his sons Shear-Jashub ("A Remnant Shall Return," i.e., repent, 7:3). He distinguished the remnant as a spiritual Israel within political Israel and found in its existence a basis for hope: God will triumph in human history and make possible its consummation when "every knee will bow; . . . every tongue will swear" (45:23).

The Remnant's Corporateness

The remnant represents a narrowing down of the people of God. It is not so much an ill-defined collection of believing individuals as a corporate whole whose devotion to God is expressed in the singular: "You are my God" (Hos. 2:23). The remnant is the whole of the *true* people of God, the heir to the promises, the recipient of the divine oracles, and the responsive vehicle of God's redemptive purpose (Zeph. 3:12–13). It is a continuum not after the flesh, but a continuum of grace alone (Knight 1959: 259). Some of Isaiah's statements narrow the remnant down to Israel as a single representative individual, the Servant of the Lord.

The Remnant's Ethical Character

The remnant is not always righteous: "Who is blind but my servant, and deaf like the messenger I send? . . . You have seen many things, but have paid no attention; your ears are open, but you hear nothing" (Isa. 42:19–20; see also 1:4–9). This unexpected reality complicates our understanding of the remnant and its bearing on the mission of God's people. Sometimes the prophets spoke as though God must spare the people of the remnant, not because of their merit, but because of their role as a transitional link to a yet brighter day ahead, when God is finally married to Israel, his chosen bride, and makes his final covenant with the land (e.g., Hos. 2:18–23). Only the solitary Servant of the Lord is sinless, and it is this distinction that finally separates him from the remnant.

The Remnant's Eschatological Significance

Isaiah regarded the believing Jews of his day as a foreshadowing of the eschatological remnant, a new and redeemed Israel over which the Messiah would reign in the last day. They were not members because they were born Jews but because of their individual surrender to God. This is not the view of Judaism that affirms: "Salvation is assured every Jew on the basis of belonging to the covenant." The rabbis then quote Isaiah 60:21 to establish this universal: "Then will all your people be righteous and they will possess the land forever. They are the shoot I have planted, the work of my hands, for the display of my splendor" (Isa. 60:21; see also Trepp 1982: 49).

The context of this verse is Jerusalem's glorious restoration through the second advent of the Messiah (Isa. 60–61). Furthermore, in this connection the later prophets frequently wrote of a new and eschatological Israel "according to the Spirit." Jeremiah also mentioned that the Messiah would make a new covenant with Israel and Judah quite unlike the covenant made at Sinai. Rather than hold before them another external code, God said:

> "I will put my law in their minds
>   and write it on their hearts.
> I will be their God,
>   and they will be my people.
> No longer will a man teach his neighbor,
>   or a man his brother, saying, 'Know the LORD,'
> because they will all know me,
>   from the least of them to the greatest," declares the LORD.
> "For I will forgive their wickedness
>   and will remember their sins no more." (31:33–34; see also 32:36–41)

Ezekiel was more explicit in calling attention to the coming of the Spirit of God (11:19–20; 36:22–32). He saw a vision of a vast plain covered with the dry bones of a defunct nation (37:1–3). Then he predicted the eschatological coming of the Spirit (37:11–14) and the emergence of a reborn Israel (37:15–28). This sequence of death because of sin and resurrection life through the gracious bestowal of the Spirit must be seen as the end of all human efforts to redeem the human race. "The state and its policies, its wealth and its prosperity, even its religion and its noblest efforts at reform—these cannot produce the Kingdom of God, cannot create a people over which he will rule" (Bright 1953: 126). The new covenant with the Spirit of God writing the Torah on the hearts of his people is God's provision for his new day when his Son will create a new covenant, but not without the shedding of his blood (Matt. 26:26–28; 1 Cor. 11:25).

The Remnant and World Mission

The concept of the remnant was abused by the Jewish people. During the time of Zedekiah, false prophets seized upon it to bolster hopes for an early end to the exile in Babylon (Ezek. 11:13; 33:24–29). During the restoration following the captivity, Zerubbabel was looked upon by some as "the man whose name is the Branch," because of his Davidic ancestry and his role in the building of the Second Temple (Zech. 3:8; 4:9; 6:12–13). In the centuries that followed, segments within Jewry frequently succumbed to the temptation to regard their leader as the Messiah and themselves as the remnant about to participate in his eschatological triumph. Jesus Christ deliberately warned his disciples against being similarly deceived: "Watch out that no one deceives you. Many will come in my name, claiming, 'I am he,' and will deceive many" (Mark 13:5–6).

First-century Christians affirmed that it was the believing remnant within Israel that carried the stock of Israel and the promises and responsibilities of Israel forward in the founding of the church. It had also perceived world mission to be the goal of Israel's election. Because it carried this world mission "forward with it, it became a universal community of faith, mediating the blessings of Israel's heritage to people of all races, and lifting them into the election of Israel. It did precisely what the Bible of the Jewish people had declared it would do" (Rowley 1944: 79).

Many in our day are critical of any attempt to legitimize the idea of "the church within the church" (*ecclesiola in ecclesia*). They regard this as a pietistic aberration devoid of biblical foundation. But is this so? The concept of a faithful remnant in the midst of Israelite nominality is too pervasive throughout the writings of the prophets. Again and again we come upon references to the people over whom God rules and find that this remnant motif coincides in some measure with what we shall later discover to be the Kingdom of God in the New Testament. The very fact that God promised to preserve a believing and obedient people in every generation is exhilarating. Christians today should humbly seek to be within their number. It is personally reassuring and challenging to turn to God and find in him true security, lasting peace, genuine love, and confident hope.

Ideally, we tend to argue that God would like to involve all who profess to be his followers in the worldwide task of mission. In actual practice, however, "the laborers are few," and too often only a minority in the church become vitally involved in bearing witness to the gospel locally and globally. Some utilize the concept of the remnant to explain this. Certainly, without the efforts of members of the remnant, generation after generation, to make Jesus Christ known, there would be no ongoing Christian mission in our day.

The Need for a Savior-King

The theme of the remnant is intimately associated with "the hope of Israel," but the two should not be equated. The prophets never ceased telling the people of God to "stop trusting in man" (e.g., Isa. 2:22). They were to look to God for guidance and solutions to their problems. Inasmuch as God had performed great things for Israel in the past, they could count on his acting on their behalf in the future. Amos introduced the phrase: "the day of the Lord" (5:18). Under this rubric a messianic hope and a portrayal of the eschatological consummation of history took form in the writings of the prophets. As with the doctrine of the remnant, this hope can be traced by inference and intimation from the earliest sections of the Old Testament. Later the prophetic witness became more explicit. The Jewish synagogues and early Christian communities initially agreed on almost a score of narrowly defined messianic passages, most of which are clothed with universal implications. Later, after the messianic movement began to spread throughout the Mediterranean world, Jewish rabbis began to popularize reconceptualizations of these texts to nullify their evangelistic use by the Jewish and Gentile believers in Jesus.

In ancient rabbinic writings more than four hundred Old Testament passages are applied to the Messiah. This does not mean that the Old Testament provides that many distinct "previews" of Jesus of Nazareth. Yet a sufficient number of precise predictions exist to vindicate Jesus' confident postresurrection affirmation: "Everything must be fulfilled that is written about me in the Law of Moses, the Prophets and the Psalms" (Luke 24:44).

Whereas from its earliest days the Christian church has held that many Old Testament passages contain prophecies that were fulfilled in the first coming of Jesus Christ, much critical biblical research has sought to discount their messianic import. In recent decades, however, there is a growing movement to defend the messianic import of these passages. Helmer Ringgren, among others, devoted a significant volume to outline "the principle features of this new understanding and to illustrate with some examples its consequences for exegesis" (1956: 7). He reviewed nine royal psalms, eleven messianic prophecies, five Servant Songs, and eight Servant Psalms. In his conclusion he states:

> There has existed in Israel a pattern of [innocent] suffering, death, and restoration, and the Psalms built on this pattern. On some occasions [these were] laid in the mouth of a king (Ps. 18; Isa. 38). . . . The idea of the king as doing penitence and atoning for the sins of his people leads the thought to one who is to come, in whom this mission of Israel is, so to speak, concentrated, just as the power of the people was concentrated in the king. Thus, at the same time, the idea of a coming Messiah appears, who is to bear the sins of the many. This person is the servant of the Lord, and hence come all the individual traits in the songs that have always puzzled those scholars who have tried to interpret the servant as a collective entity, e.g., the people. . . . The prophet has defined the idea of vicarious suffering so sharply that the New Testament interpretation of the work of Jesus is hardly conceivable without the servant songs as its background. . . . It is of decisive importance to the messianic self-consciousness of Jesus, and to the New Testament idea of Christ. (1956: 64–67)

Quite apart from these specific passages, the Old Testament can be described as "broadly messianic." Since the word *messiah* primarily means "anointed," its application in the Old Testament ranges from priests (1 Sam. 12:3) to kings (1 Sam. 16:6) to a pious believer (Ps. 84:9) to even a pagan king (Isa. 45:1). But it becomes specific when applied to the Davidic line, and we now turn to this and other messianic representations to grasp the varied themes that make up the composite whole: the Messiah. We will not review the total range of messianic prediction, only those passages that focus on three major concepts: his humanity as a Davidic prince, his deity as Son of God, and his redemptive suffering as the Servant of the Lord.

Messiah as Son of David

When David brought about the beginnings of Israel's golden age, it seemed that he was the fulfillment of the promise made to Abraham about his seed becoming a great nation. With the disruption that followed Solomon's death, and the subsequent periods of national decay and apostasy, devout Jews looked back on David's era, doubtless helped by their capacity for retrospective imagination, and "hankered for the good old days." Much was made of what their prophets included under the rubric of "the faithful love promised to David" (Isa. 55:3)—the sum total of the promises made by God to David and made secure by covenant. David's house would hold a unique relationship to God, and his dynasty would remain forever (2 Sam. 7:14–16; 23:5). God used this yearning to kindle the hope of God's people. Eventually, Jeremiah (23:5–6; 30:8–9), Ezekiel (34:24; 37:24–25), and particularly Isaiah translated it into prophetic speech. Because God was concerned to save God's people and bless the nations, a son of David, born of man, would be the deliverer. He would destroy their enemies, transform and rule the faithful remnant, and, in turn, bring blessing to the nations (Isa. 9:1–7; 11:1–5; Mic. 5:2–4). This new Adam would rule in a new Eden over a renewed and enlarged Israel. He would bless all the nations of the world from Jerusalem, God's royal capital (Isa. 2:2–4; 11:6–9; Mic. 4:1–4). The "faithful love promised to David" would always stand, despite the apparent destruction of the royal line in 587 B.C. (Isa. 55:3 and Jer. 22:24–30).

Even so, it should be noted that Isaiah spoke of "a shoot" coming forth from the stump of Jesse and a branch growing out of his roots (11:1, 10; see also 53:2 and Zech. 3:8; 6:12). This introduced a death-and-resurrection motif and underscored as well the fact that the branch emerges from David's roots yet is somewhat independent of David's marred dynastic line. The people's deepest longings would be realized by the messianic Son of David coming in power and glory. Inasmuch as God is the Lord of history, God will consummate history "on the earth" (Rev. 5:10). This final victory of the Davidic King, ruling over a restored Israel and removing all sin and evil so that peace and righteousness might prevail, was the great hope of Israel during the dark days of the Babylonian captivity and the troubled centuries that followed.

Messiah as Son of Man

Following the return from exile, the Jews went through a long period of foreign oppression and exploitation. The house of David languished in mediocrity. Lest the Jews utterly lose heart, the prophetic witness shifted from

the prophetic hope for an earthly kingdom within history to the apocalyptic hope of a kingdom beyond history. The earthly Davidic Messiah was overshadowed by a heavenly transcendental Son of Man who is to come with the clouds to initiate the new order. (Ladd 1964: 50)

This was at the heart of Daniel's vision of the future. The Deliverer (7:13–14) would usher in the everlasting Kingdom.

> He was given authority, glory and sovereign power; all peoples, nations and men of every language worshiped him. His dominion is an everlasting dominion that will not pass away, and his kingdom is one that will never be destroyed. (7:14)

This Kingdom was earlier attributed to the God of heaven (Dan. 2:44, 45), but Daniel went on to say that it "will be handed over to the saints, the people of the Most High" (7:27, see also v. 22). Apparently the designation "Son of Man" implies one in whom Israel is present. He is represented less as a descendant of the house of David than as a person human in form but superhuman in essence. The new idea suggested by this passage is that the Messiah exists before he is manifested to humankind. Although as a Davidic prince he is a shoot from Jesse's stock, he is also the root from which Jesse springs (Isa. 11:1, 10). Also, he can be addressed as "God" and yet receive anointing from "God, your God" (Ps. 45:7). He is born in David's line and yet is referred to as "Mighty God" (Isa. 9:6–7) and "the arm of the Lord" (53:1–3).

During the intertestamental period most Jews became increasingly pessimistic over the movement of history. They saw their own postexilic history as so dominated by evil that it scarcely could be regarded as the center of God's glorious Kingdom. This produced a shift from interest in prophetic eschatology within history to apocalyptic eschatology beyond history. What they began to look for was the catastrophic in-breaking of God—his abrupt irruption into history to bring about the final consummation. They were comforted by the prophetic revelation of the Son of Man motif with its stress on a heavenly being to whom the rule over all nations and kingdoms will be committed in the last day.

Messiah as Suffering Servant

If the coming of the Messiah is the hope of Israel, what does this mean for his mission to the world? And in what manner is this mission to be carried out? These questions drive us to the very heart of the Old Testament revelation, for they are at the heart of the Abrahamic covenant with its promise of blessing for all the nations. It is in the Servant Songs of Isaiah that we find the key (42:1–9; 49:1–6; 50:4–9; 52:13–53:12). It should be noted that the title "Servant of the Lord" is a title of honor; the relation between the true Israelite and God is not to be thought of as identical to the slave-master relation of the ancient world.

The Servant fulfills his mission by death, despite his commission to carry the light of the true religion throughout the world (Isa. 49:6). He dies as a willing sacrifice (53:10), superior to any animal involuntarily slain in the Temple. He is free from the blemishes of sin (53:9). His sacrifice is of widest efficacy: the Gentile nations for whom he would die confess that they deserved what he vicariously endured on their behalf (53:4–12).

When Isaiah summoned Israel to its destiny as the servant of God, he introduced the strangest figure as a model, a figure so unattractive and so laden with offense that he remains a mystery to the Jews and the world to this very day (Bright 1953: 146). The Suffering Servant is absolutely unique. Isaiah said that by means of his suffering the people of God and the Kingdom would come to triumph and eschatological fullness. The "songs" of the Servant speak of election, preservation, divine anointing, universal mission, and certain triumph. In contrast, the Servant is also despised, rejected, and slain by humans. But the Servant's existence extends beyond death, for in his subsequent exaltation he sees his numerous progeny gather into his kingdom (Isa. 53:11–12).

Apocalyptic Literature

The Book of Daniel stimulated an apocalyptic literature that rapidly proliferated in the years that followed. The longing of the people for the coming of "the prophet" of whom Moses spoke (Deut. 18:15) was not satisfied. Decade followed decade with the repeated frustration of the Jews' hopes for God's intervention on their behalf. Deep-seated pessimism regarding God settled on the people. They wanted God to judge their enemies (the Gentiles) and establish his kingdom with the Jews at the center! The conservatives regarded themselves as the "in group, the pure remnant," and sought to function as a restoration community. Judaism proliferated. One of the groups that emerged was characterized by an apocalyptic preoccupation, "scanning the times for signs of the coming end, drawing diagrams, as it were, of how that end should come" (Bright 1953: 168).

However, we should not be too hasty in our condemnation of apocalyptic literature. Despite its pessimism about the ongoing history of the world, it nonetheless helped keep alive the flame of hope in the final triumph of God. And it made God's people strong in their confession of him before a hostile, pagan world. It made them concerned to know and to do the will of God. During this period the Mosaic revelation became normative while the prophetic movement waned, then died altogether. Jewish religious life increasingly reduced itself to an extreme form of legalism.

Messianic Expectations

When we seek to put together the various streams of messianic prediction found in the Old Testament, we experience a certain fluidity of understanding. This is especially true because Isaiah oscillated in his description of the Servant of the Lord, ranging from the corporate group to a representative individual. At first, the Servant is merely Israel, blind and deaf (42:19). Then he is the righteous remnant (44:1; 51:6–7). Finally, he is the new Moses about to lead God's people into a new Exodus from the captivity of sin. He is the Great Servant who will lead a servant people out to the nations in mission. But his greatest mystery is his sinlessness. This qualifies him to take upon himself the sins of God's people and expose himself on their behalf to God's holy wrath against sin. Only thereby could the Servant Messiah fully and finally make possible the victorious rule of the Kingdom of God over their lives.

We should not forget that the wealth of messianic predictions to be found in these three distinct though interrelated figures contain attributes and dimensions common to all three. Whether a Davidic king, a divine Son of Man, or a Suffering Servant, all are the embodiment of wisdom and righteousness; all act in judgment, and all possess the Spirit of God. All three are associated with God's covenants and with God's mission that his people be "a light to the Gentiles." All three receive royal homage and raise the mighty from their seats.

The Old Testament does not attempt to synthesize the prophetic concepts of "Son of David" (what God will do in history) and "Son of Man" (what God will do eschatologically). Neither does it reveal the manner in which these two are related to the Suffering Servant of Isaiah 53. As Ladd states:

> Jews [in Jesus' day] looked for a conquering Davidic Messiah or a heavenly Son of Man, not for a humble Servant of the Lord who would suffer and die. The messianic mystery—the new disclosure of the divine purpose—is that the heavenly Son of Man must first suffer and die in fulfillment of his redemptive mission as the Suffering Servant before he comes in power and glory. (1962: 911b)

Jesus of Nazareth claimed to fulfill all three major images and was totally opposed to the apocalyptics, with their lack of faith in what God was doing or could do in the present in human history.

The conviction of the apostolic church that Jesus of Nazareth was the Messiah of Israel, the Christ of God (Acts 2:36), can be upheld when we consider several additional streams of Old Testament corroborative witness. First, there are the royal psalms (2, 24, 47, 72, 96, 99, etc.), which intimate an eschatological kingship far beyond God's use of kings merely to chasten or serve God's people. The church has found Jesus in these psalms. Second, there are references to the land that God gave to his people. Although it largely consists of barren hills, watered only occasionally by brief seasons of rain, the prophets predicted that the land will be transformed by God on the last day. It will no longer be "desolate" because it will be "married" to its creator (Isa. 62:4). The church has seen in Jesus' nature miracles the certainty that "the wilderness and the dry land" would become glad because of God's "streams in the desert" (Isa. 35:1–10). Third, there is the portrayal of God becoming a priest-king after the unique order of Melchizedek (Ps. 110:4). The church has found in the crucifixion of Jesus such a priestly ministry. Indeed, it forms the heart of the argument of the Epistle to the Hebrews (chaps. 7–10). Finally, there is Moses' prediction of One like himself being raised up to accomplish a greater liberation and more complete redemption than he accomplished at the time of the Exodus (Deut. 18:15). The church has always seen in Jesus one "greater than Moses" (Heb. 3:1–6) and in his exodus (Luke 9:31) a greater victory than that achieved by Moses.

All these images serve to confirm the certainty that in Jesus and his teaching, history and eschatology are held together in dynamic tension. The very coming of the apocalyptic kingdom is made dependent upon what he will accomplish in history through his mission and death. It was therefore inevitable that Jesus should stand with the prophets against the apocalyptists in his regard for God's relationship to history. The optimism of the messianic Kingdom is expressed by Ladd:

> The heart of Jesus' message is that God has once again become redemptively active in history. But this new divine activity takes on an added dimension in comparison with the prophetic view: the eschatological kingdom has itself invaded history in advance, bringing to men in the old age of sin and death the blessings of God's rule. History has not been abandoned to evil; it has become the scene of the cosmic struggle between the Kingdom of God and the powers of evil. In fact, the powers of evil which the apocalyptists felt dominated history have been defeated, and men, while still living in history, may be delivered from these powers by experiencing the life and blessings of God's Kingdom. (1964: 322)

Thus redemption is inherent in the concept of Messiah in the Scriptures: "You are to give him the name Jesus, because he will save his people from their sins" (Matt. 1:21). Messianism divorced from redemption has proved both pernicious and destructive for the Jews from the Maccabean Revolt (167 B.C.) onward.

God's Concern for the Nations

One seldom finds in the Old Testament any expressions of compassion for those whose god is not the God of Abraham, Isaac, and Jacob. True, the Israelites often called upon God to act on their behalf so that the nations might see his works and glorify him. When the Assyrian aggressor Sennacherib was at the gates of Jerusalem, Hezekiah prayed: "Now, O LORD our God, deliver us from his hand, so that all kingdoms on earth may know that you alone, O LORD, are God" (Isa. 37:20). The glory of God, not the spiritual need of the heathen, is the dominant motif. Israel knew of the demonic elements in heathen religion and life, its pride, sinfulness, and ruthlessness. Their prayers to God have this in mind: "Arise, O LORD, let not man triumph; let the nations be judged in your presence. Strike them with terror, O LORD; let the nations know they are but men" (Ps. 9:19–20).

What particularly moved God's people was the desire that the whole world recognize that Israel's God alone is the true God. Beside him there is no God. The Israelites manifested virtually no concern over the world's spiritual darkness but were greatly concerned for God's vindication before the nations. They were possessed by a deep consciousness that God had separated them from these nations to be God's people. Many of the prophets, however, began increasingly to proclaim that the treasure that Israel possessed was not for Israel only, but for the world. Habakkuk prophesied: "The earth will be filled with the knowledge of the glory of the LORD, as the waters cover the sea" (2:14). Zephaniah spoke of God gathering the nations, first to judgment and then to blessing.

> I have decided to assemble the nations,
>   to gather the kingdoms
> and to pour out my wrath on them—
>   all my fierce anger.
> The whole world will be consumed
>   by the fire of my jealous anger.
> Then will I purify the lips of the peoples,
>   that all of them may call on the name of the LORD
>   and serve him shoulder to shoulder. (3:8–9)

After describing the "fishers" and "hunters" God will use to regather God's people through a greater triumph than the Exodus, Jeremiah went on to speak of the nations being drawn by God's power (16:14–21). We affirm with De Ridder that the future golden age of God's people will include the Gentiles (1971: 23). We take note of three Old Testament sources that witness to this fact.

The Contribution of Isaiah

When Isaiah denounced idolatry and affirmed that God is the only God, he stressed that all the gods of the nations are but dead and useless idols, less worthy of respect than those who make them (44:9–20; 46:1–13). He denigrates their worship virtually to mummery and fetishism. From the broad range of his writings, we are able to draw irresistible corollaries. First, God who created all is the God of all. Second, God desires the worship not only by Israel but by all his creatures. Third, God has chosen Israel to be the medium of this revelation to all nations. Fourth, God has decreed that only in his appointed destiny for all nations will Israel find its supreme glory and distinction (45:22–23; 51:4–5; 55:5). It seems clear from these passages that Isaiah conceived of the coming Kingdom of God as all-embracing, including not merely a few choice souls from other ethnic groups but the entire human race. It is equally clear that he yearned that the obedience of Israel would so transform the nation that surrounding nations would be drawn to God. Indeed, he perceived that Israel's central vocation was to be "a light for the Gentiles, that you may bring my salvation to the ends of the earth" (49:6).

Isaiah's Servant Songs amplified these correlations, presenting Israel as a people with a vocation. Israel is charged by God with the sacred task of mediating the divine message to women and men and of leading the whole world into the Kingdom of God. In terms of the nations, "the Servant" is a representative individual and is variously described. First, in 42:1–7 the Servant exercises a gentle, far-reaching ministry that will bring the nations to right religion and to the acceptance of the divine will ("justice") in all relationships of life. Second, in 49:1–6 although his primary mission is to Israel, his wider task extends beyond the borders of Israel and embraces aliens as well as Jews. It is pointedly stated that even a refined and renewed Israel by itself is an insufficient inheritance for the God of all the earth. Its redemption can only be completed and perfected through participation in the larger redemption of all humanity. Third, in 50:4–9, although his sufferings at the hands of all people become prominent and are not identified as redemptive, he gains vindication and deliverance through God's faithfulness. Fourth, in 52:13–53:12 his sufferings have vicarious redemptive power. Various persons of faith exclaim in amazement that he was "pierced for our transgressions, he was crushed for our iniquities" when they realize that "the LORD has laid on him the iniquity of us all" (53:5–6). Specifically, "for the transgression" of Israel "he was stricken" (53:8) but in universal terms, he is portrayed as bearing "the sin of many" (53:12). The passage ends with the servant making "intercession for the transgressors," that is, for those who inflicted this suffering on him (53:12).

Isaiah's universal scope of mission is expressed in chapter 56:

> "And foreigners who bind themselves to the LORD
> to serve him,
> to love the name of the LORD,
> and to worship him,
> all who keep the Sabbath without desecrating it
> and who hold fast to my covenant—
> these I will bring to my holy mountain
> and give them joy in my house of prayer.
> Their burnt offerings and sacrifices
> will be accepted on my altar;
> for my house will be called a house of prayer for all nations."
> The Sovereign LORD declares—
> he who gathers the exiles of Israel:
> "I will gather still others to them
> besides those already gathered." (56:6–8)

Having reviewed this promise of the future ingathering of "all nations" and the prominence of Zion, the Lord's "holy mountain," and joyous throngs at his "house of prayer for all nations," we leap to the end of this section (66:18–24). This closing passage represents the high point in the Old Testament revelation of God with respect to Isaiah and the nations. It begins with the final Epiphany of God, revealing himself as the Deliverer of a beleaguered Israel, surrounded by its foes (66:15–16). Suddenly, the nations are caught up in judgment, and a final end comes to all their religious pluralism (v. 17). God then summons them—"all nations and tongues"—and they respond, only to be confronted by his "glory" (v. 18). Claus Westermann says:

> Here we have in verse 19 the first sure and certain mention of mission as we today employ the term—the sending of individuals to distant peoples in order to proclaim God's glory among them. This completely corresponds to the mission of the apostles when the church first began. One is amazed at it: here, just as the Old Testament is

coming to its end, God's way is already seen as leading from the narrow confines of the chosen people out into the wide, whole world. (1969: 425)

The following verses (20–24) describe the nations, now willing to move toward Jerusalem and upward to Zion, bringing their gifts and becoming so completely identified with Israel that some individuals who had been won from the nations are now enrolled as priests and Levites. They thereby join the innermost circle of the elect of God (v. 21). What follows is "the new heavens and the new earth" (v. 22) along with multiple assurances concerning the permanence of God's salvation and his eternal worship (v. 23). Then, quite surprising, the final statement of this beautiful portrayal of Mount Zion in its eschatological glory is contrasted with the dark valley of God's judgment. Here is the earliest Old Testament intimation of hell as the state of perdition "for those who rebelled against me" (v. 24). One can appreciate why the rabbis reread verse 23 after reading verse 24 "in order that the reading in the synagogue should not end with the awful oracle of doom, but with a promise" (Westermann, quoting Volz, 1969: 429). What impresses us in this closing section, however, is its vivid demonstration of the fulfillment of the promise made to Abraham: "All peoples on earth will be blessed through you" (Gen. 12:3). God has truly kept the Abrahamic covenant!

How are we to bring together the total contribution of Isaiah to our understanding of the relationship between Israel and the nations in the redemptive purpose of God? Let us turn back to the beginning and the lead-off passage in his sequence of references to the ingathering of the nations (25:8; 42:6; 49:6; 60:4–9; 66:16–24). The key passage is Isaiah 2:1–5 (Mic. 4:1–5). Its focus is the Temple in the midst of Judah and Jerusalem. The sequence begins with the Temple being uplifted and exalted. Then follows an eschatological summons to the nations in response to the Torah, the word of the Lord that is sent forth from the Temple. Many respond and express their desire to attach themselves to God and live under God's rule and for his glory. The vision concludes with God's judgment on the nations. Only then is the weaponry of warfare transformed into the instruments of agriculture. In response Isaiah calls the people of God to reaffirm their covenant obligation to him: "Come, O house of Jacob, let us walk in the light of the LORD" (2:5).

This passage becomes clear only when we reflect on the ministry of Jesus. He saw himself as "sent only to the lost sheep of Israel" (Matt. 15:24). Jerusalem and the Temple were the focus of his concern and the locus of his rejection.

But the Gospels do not end with Jesus' crucifixion—the uplifted Temple and its destruction (John 12:32). By his resurrection he is vindicated as the True Israel, the King of a heavenly Zion and the eternal Temple around which the nations will gather. He becomes the center of a gathered community whose members will transform the world (Bosch 1969: 10–11). Hence, it is not without reason that a tradition early developed that the "upper room" where the disciples met in prayerful anticipation of the coming of the Holy Spirit, and where they first experienced his baptism, was in the Temple (Acts 1:13–14; 2:1). From that place they went forth onto Jerusalem's streets to proclaim the new Torah of "the wonders of God"

(Acts 2:11) to the diverse nationalities gathered there for the Feast of Weeks (a harvest occasion). When Peter declared that the last days had begun (v. 17), he was clarifying yet further the prophecy of Isaiah. By itself the Old Testament sees no possibility of the nations coming to Zion and submitting themselves to the Torah within the space/time sequence of their cultural existence. Peter saw the age of the church and its worldwide missionary responsibility as the beginning of the penetration into human history of the eschatological Kingdom of God. Isaiah's vision by itself underscores the incompleteness of the Old Testament revelation of God's redemptive concern for the nations.

The Contribution of Malachi

It is rather significant that during the postexilic period the prophets had almost nothing to say concerning the restoration of the Israelite monarchy. Doubtless their vivid memory of its terrible failure made them desire "a new thing" fashioned and established by God. Hence, they looked to a future that was almost solely religious and not political. They understood that God was not going to reestablish a politically independent people, but rather create a community of faith that would be able to survive, first in the Babylonian empire, then in the Persian empire, and on down through history. They called the people to worship God in the manner he had revealed at Sinai. For this reason the postexilic prophets were primarily concerned with cultic rectitude and obedience to Torah.

Haggai and Zechariah initially focused on the rebuilding of the Temple, the place of worship and revelation. When Malachi appeared, his concern was almost totally in the area of cultic regulations, marriage laws, and priestly instruction (McKenzie 1974: 289). As he peered into the future, Malachi saw proper sacrifice offered to God throughout the world (1:11). He also intimated that the faithless priests of his day in Jerusalem would have no part in bringing about this worldwide adoration of God. For this reason, he turned on the priests and exposed their spiritual laxity. Indeed, the worship of the Jews in Malachi's day reflected widespread contempt for God; the sacrifices they offered were far below the Levitical standard (1:7–9). It was as though they thought: "Anything is good enough for God!" In the midst of his dialogic controversy with them via Malachi we find the Lord saying:

> I am not pleased with you . . . and I will accept no offering from your hands. My name will be great among the nations, from the rising to the setting of the sun. In every place incense and pure offerings will be brought to my name, because my name will be great among the nations. (1:10–11)

The Eschatological Sequence

We now summarize the contribution of the Old Testament to our understanding of the total activity of the Messiah in the eschatological sequence. If we deliberately set aside any New Testament insights, we are confined to certain key events.

When the Messiah comes, he will be the means whereby Israel is converted and transformed by the Holy Spirit in accordance with the new covenant. This will be far more efficacious than the old covenant because God will provide his people with "a heart of flesh." He will place his Spirit within his people, thereby making possible their walking in his statutes and observing his ordinances (Jer. 31:31–33; Ezek. 36:24–27).

Further, when the Messiah comes and "will restore David's fallen tent, . . . repair its broken places, restore its ruins, and build it as it used to be" (Amos 9:11), it is so "that they may possess the remnant of Edom and all the nations that bear my name" (v. 12). The new Israel thus becomes the gathering point around which the nations assemble in order to participate in God's salvation. The key passage again is Isaiah 2:2–4. In one sense this gathering will be in response to God's spontaneous and imperative eschatological summons, through the preaching of the good news of the Kingdom by the church. In another sense it will take place on the last day and will be quite unlike anything related to missionary work as traditionally conceived. Then at long last, it will be said, "Israel will be . . . a blessing on the earth" (Isa. 19:24). The promise made to Abraham will have been finally fulfilled.

Another factor concerns the nations. When the Messiah comes, he will judge the nations for their sins and particularly for their shocking treatment of Israel (Mal. 3:2). According to the Old Testament, the final salvation that the Messiah brings will be all-inclusive. It will embrace the reconciliation of sinners to God, the forgiveness of their sins, the renewal of nature, the removal of the curse of death, and the wiping away of all tears (Isa. 25:6–8; 11:6–9). It will embrace the totality of human existence and will be cosmic in its significance. Even so, we must keep in mind that throughout this sequence the passivity of a restored and renewed Israel will be a dominant motif:

> Israel which had itself undergone the severe judgment of God shall not emit its magnetic light and draw the peoples of the world to itself. Israel's role in this great salvation event will be predominantly passive. Israel shall not so much itself go out to attract the nations, but rather the jealousy of the heathen will be quickened by Israel's spiritual riches in God. The Messiah himself will, however, be revealed to the nations as the great witness. (Bavinck 1960: 23)

When we ponder this vision of a renewed Israel in the midst of the nations and God in the midst of his Israel (Ezek. 36:22–23), a caution needs to be sounded.

Certainly, only God himself can convert the nations. His secret presence in the midst of the church is its glory. But evangelization of the world is a matter of both words and activity. It cannot be reduced to mere presence without dismissing all the valid data in the New Testament about imploring people "on Christ's behalf: Be reconciled to God" (2 Cor. 5:18–21).

Knowing God Involves Social Responsibility

When the apostle Paul commenced his discussion of the sinfulness of the human race, he spoke of men "who suppress the truth by their wickedness"

(Rom. 1:18). His contention was that people know God primarily in the moral imperative of justice, for it is to this reality that the Old Testament speaks and to which the conscience bears witness (Rom. 2:14–15, 29). This is consonant with the earlier witness of the prophets that to know the Lord is to be actively committed to seeking justice for the poor (Miranda 1974: 44; see Jer. 22:13–16; Hos. 4:1–2; 6:4–6; Mic. 6:8). This does not mean that God is known only in the human acts of seeking justice and displaying compassion for the neighbor (contra Miranda 1974: 49), but that God is so identified with the oppressed, the poor, the orphans, and the widows that he bears an intimate relation to them. The apocalyptic vision of Isaiah (11:1–16) depicts the realization of universal justice: "They will neither harm nor destroy on all my holy mountain." Furthermore, he attributes this solely to the achieved reality of the universal knowledge of God, which "the earth will be full of . . . as the waters cover the sea." Habakkuk's apocalyptic picture ends with virtually the same correlation (2:12–14). This must be the reason behind the remarks of the prophets. Why did the God of Amos denounce Israel's feasts, festivals, oblations, and religious activity? Not because he regretted having instituted them but because of the absence of an accompanying practice of justice (5:21–25). Isaiah also underscored the sequence: first justice, then sacrifice and worship (1:11–17).

There is a regrettable tendency in our day to endorse the sort of involvement in devotional exercises (prayer, Bible study, fasting, etc.) and even in evangelism that makes such religious activities ends in themselves. Isaiah denounced such formal religious activity when it was not accompanied with social service (58:3, 6–7). Christians are told to "remember the poor" in the course of their missionary obedience (Gal. 2:10). Never has this injunction been so needed as in our day, when the current population explosion coupled with widespread economic exploitation keeps compounding the plight of the poor.

Wisdom Literature and God's Kingdom Mission

The patterns of life and the rules of conduct to which individuals and peoples adhere are derived from their past experience. This gathered "wisdom" enables them to come to terms with their environment and with one another. They thereby discern good from evil, truth from error, virtue from vice, and duty from self-indulgence. More, this wisdom stresses the importance of industry over laziness, prudence over presumption, honesty over all forms of deception, and a pattern of adhering to values that have long-range validity rather than pursuing the attractions of the moment.

Within the canonical Scriptures of ancient Israel, several books—some of the Psalms and the Proverbs—are devoted to "wisdom." They do not deal with God's redemptive purpose in history but with the basic issues of life that together give order and system to human existence in this world. Concerning this part of the canon, Von Rad has written:

This experiential knowledge is not only a very complex entity, but also a very vulnerable one. It renders man an invaluable service in enabling him to function in his sphere of life other than as a complete stranger and puts him in the position of understanding [it], at least to a certain extent, as an ordered system. (1972: 3)

Whereas this ordered system of moral maxims is strengthened by the experiences of individuals and nations, it is terribly threatened by each contrary experience for which the system has no explanation. It is at this point that the Book of Job and Ecclesiastes have their role, almost as "antiwisdom." They encourage faith when bad things happen to good people, that is, when a godly person keeps all the rules and yet experiences catastrophe. But they also cast light on positive ways to face the imponderables in daily life. Although the tendency within any society is to resist change and preserve its accepted norms, there are times when revision and addition are necessary. While it is then that such changes become invaluable to us, making them is always traumatic. There are four dimensions of wisdom literature that bear on Israel's relations with the peoples outside of Israel.

Wisdom's Development

Israel gathered into literary form its experiential knowledge, generally in the form of sentence-type proverbs, and these precepts were often similar to those of its neighbors. Israel's wisdom literature was no isolated literary phenomenon, but part of the larger cultural heritage common to the ancient world. A case in point would be sections in Proverbs 22 and 23 in which Israel's formulation of certain maxims apparently developed analogously to the Egyptian wisdom of Amenemope. This confirmed to the Israelites the universality of such perspectives. It reminded them of the unity of the human race, a factor they had to take into consideration when they reflected on their unique relation to the nations through their election by God.

Even so, Israel's growing deposit of wisdom literature contained perspectives that went beyond those of its neighbors. Strange as it may seem, although wisdom literature is one of the oldest literary forms known, it is surprisingly "one of the most secular forms of ancient literature; references to the gods and to religion are rare" (McKenzie 1974: 203). In sharpest contrast, the Israelites attributed their wisdom literature not to any insightful discernment or linguistic ingenuity they possessed, but to God and to his moral governance of all peoples: "The fear of the Lord—that is wisdom, and to shun evil is understanding" (Job 28:28). Wisdom is derived from God and should be attributed to God alone (Job 12:13; Prov. 3:19–20; 8:22–31; Isa. 31:2; etc.). Although wisdom is one and the same, whether worldly or divine, Israel's sages continually argued that apart from the conscious application of this religious principle, sound morality—whether personal or social—required a theistic basis. These two aspects of wisdom—the secular and the religious—differ in degree rather than in kind. Whereas Israel would grant that victories were achieved through heeding good counsel (Prov. 24:6), it was always quick to recognize that any and all victories were ultimately attributable to God alone (Prov. 21:31).

The highest point in Israel's reflection on wisdom is Proverbs 1–9. Here one encounters the sudden personification of wisdom—a female figure set in contrast to Dame Folly. The climax is its direct equation with deity. Wisdom "calls aloud in the streets" (1:20–33) and "blessed is the man who finds wisdom" (3:13). More, wisdom was the first component in the drama of Creation (8:22–26) and became God's "assistant" in its subsequent development (8:27–31; see R. Harrison 1969: 1008).

Wisdom's Limitations

The existence of wisdom literature in the Old Testament raises two sets of basic questions. There are the questions regarding personal salvation. In one sense the nations possess the same wisdom that Israel possesses. "By me kings reign and rulers make laws that are just; by me princes govern, and all nobles who rule on earth" (Prov. 8:15–16). In 8:35–36 we read that to find this wisdom is to find life and favor with God. Does this mean that where wisdom is present among all nations, God is there also? Is God savingly available through positive response to this experiential wisdom? Should one argue that when it is heeded, salvation is attained? Would this line of thought not challenge Isaiah's view that the idols of nations are vain, nonentities, the creation of fallen humanity, and that only through Israel's God is salvation to be found (44:9–20)? Should we infer that "the salvation of the world lies in the wisdom that was already present when the world began," as Johannes Blauw asks (1962: 62)? Or should we merely state that all human wisdom reflects the reality that humanity is the bearer of the divine image and accordingly must engage in this fundamental activity of the human mind?

Besides the issue of salvation there are the questions regarding divine revelation. What is the relation between wisdom literature in the Old Testament and special revelation? The key to the apostle Paul's polemic against human wisdom is that "the world through its wisdom did not know" God (1 Cor. 1:18–31, esp. v. 21). Should one argue from this and similar passages (e.g., 1 Tim. 6:20–21) that the New Testament retreats from the lofty concepts contained in the wisdom literature of the Old Testament? Or should we say that the call of Jesus to all who are weary and burdened to learn from him, represents his deliberate use of the wisdom motif to describe himself (cf. Matt. 11:28–30 with Prov. 1:20–23; 3:13–18; etc.)? If the New Testament does indeed downgrade wisdom, would the apostle Paul have quoted a Greek poet in his gospel address to the Athenian intellectuals (Acts 17:28)?

This brings us to the antiwisdom literature of Job and Ecclesiastes, referred to earlier. Conventional human wisdom would suggest to the victims of such divine judgments as the Flood and the destruction of Sodom and Gomorrah that they deserved it. As if to say, "You had it coming." On this basis Job's friends sought to justify the calamities that overwhelmed Job. They argued that God always punishes the wicked and delivers the righteous. Elihu advanced an alternative view: the sufferings of the righteous have disciplinary value. Divine punishment beforehand may keep a person from faults not yet committed (33:14–30). However, when God entered the debate, he brushed aside these human rationalizations and spoke of the wisdom of God, not only attested in creation but also in its paradoxes that defy explanation. If God is wise, not only is his wisdom beyond human comprehension, but his actions will also be past understanding. "Job must believe that the power and wisdom which produced the world are able to sustain it in wisdom, even though God's wisdom is impenetrable to [human beings]" (McKenzie 1974: 225). After all, God is not human.

Ecclesiastes contains some conventional wisdom, but its dominant support is in the direction of antiwisdom. It was written "to convince men of the uselessness of any world view which does not rise above the horizon of man himself" (Archer 1964: 459). The writer tried all the options open to the person who regards personal happiness as the highest good. In the end he was totally frustrated over his efforts at self-deification. Life is uncertain; death is inevitable. People are not always rewarded for their righteousness nor punished for their wickedness. Indeed, wisdom is no better than folly. Compared to Job, the writer of this book appears almost an atheist. He saw the human enterprise as largely characterized by pain and vanity. The wise people of this earth know nothing of God. Indeed, a common judgment is that Ecclesiastes is the last sour apple on the tree of wisdom. Even so, it ends with the exhortation: "Fear God and keep his commandments, for this is the whole duty of man. For God will bring every deed into judgment, including every hidden thing, whether it is good or evil" (12:13–14). But is this call to remain within the guidelines of the Torah really satisfying to the human heart, with its longings for eternity (Eccles. 3:11)? Does God have nothing more to offer?

Wisdom's Decline

In the intertestamental period this personification of wisdom was lost, and wisdom came to be equated with Torah, largely defined in legal terms. This tended to elevate human reason. Jesus Ben Sira, the author of the very popular apocryphal book commonly called Ecclesiasticus (180 B.C.), is held responsible in large part for diverting the attention of Jewry away from the Hebrew Bible and to the rabbinic perspectives in the Talmud. He made the authority of learning and human reflection more attractive than the authority of divine inspiration (Ellison 1976: 73). On this basis the Torah as God's revelation was handed over to the interpretations of the rabbis. God became remote, and legalism became central. Ecclesiasticus does not mention belief in either a resurrection or a future life and holds essentially to a rationalistic, antisupernatural perspective. Its concern is with great men and their deeds rather than with God and his purpose in history (Von Rad 1972: 258; R. Harrison 1969: 1231–37). It was doubtless inevitable that Israel's growing convictions of the contingency of all historical events should divert it from an abiding faith in God's irreversible decrees and involve it in feverish preoccupation with searching out a rational rule for life.

Wisdom's Missiological Implications

We grant that the wisdom literature does not directly concern itself with the ongoing redemptive purpose of God, even though some might argue that Job intimated otherwise when he said: "The fear of the Lord—that is wisdom, and to shun evil is understanding" (28:28). But missionaries have on occasion used these Old Testament books to prepare the way for the gospel. Proverbs 1–8 can be used to provide linkage with the universal history of Genesis 1–11, since these chapters speak of the wisdom that all peoples have because of their common human ancestry. We should encourage cross-cultural missionaries to gather and collate the wisdom literature of the people they serve, even if it only exists in oral form. They should then utilize it to construct bridges to make more natural and effective their transmission of the message of Jesus Christ.

Conclusion

The dominant personal application that emerges from this review of the Old Testament revelation of the purpose of God concerning the nations involves servanthood. If Israel is to serve in the Messiah's universal mission, Israel must be willing to become the servant of others for his sake. Unfortunately, this role was not attractive to most Jewish people. We rejoice that during the latter part of their history, especially during the intertestamental period, individual Jews here and there began to reach out and serve the peoples of the Gentile world. Daniel and Mordecai are cases in point.

Furthermore, we know that many non-Jews eventually became proselytes. Apparently, before anything more substantial was to occur among the nations, the Messiah had first to come, take the road of missionary obedience (John 12:31–33), and demonstrate true servanthood. The tragedy is that the Judaism that had begun to develop after the end of the Old Testament had no place for this kind of service.

The indebtedness of the Christian mission today to the Jewish people and their Scriptures remains enormous. Israel's prophets, with their sense of God's universal mission to the nations, are a constant rebuke to all narrowly conceived visions of what the churches should be doing in the world today. Isaiah's portrayal of the Suffering Servant of the Lord provides an abiding protest against all triumphalism in carrying out the Christian mission. Valid proclamation of the gospel reflects the Servant's patient and humble persuasion and is permeated by his willingness to suffer for the sake of its truths. And when Jeremiah spoke of a day coming when most external worship forms would be replaced by the law of God being engraved on human hearts by the Holy Spirit, he gave the church confidence in the irresistible power of the Pentecostal gift to carry the life-transforming gospel to the very ends of the earth.

Because Passover and baptism had been prominent in celebrating Israel's deliverance from Egypt and its birth as a nation, the church finds linkage thereby with its sacraments. The Eucharist celebrates Christ, the church's Passover Lamb, and baptism marks its death and resurrection to new life under the new covenant.

Furthermore, the rich ethical heritage of the Sinaitic law codes and their reiteration and contextualization in Deuteronomy are another vital link between ancient Israel and the church. Moses' exaltation of sympathy and kindness as well as his concern for righteousness and justice provide a fundamental model for all types of Christian service. Wherever the church has gone, its philanthropy and selfless service have reflected this linkage, and this has both humanized and ameliorated the raw nerves of every society in which the church has gained permanent foothold.

The Jewish people were taught to reject all vehicles of alleged revelation, such as nature, mythology, and human speculation. They believed that God reveals himself through his acts of mercy and judgment in history, supplemented by God's disclosure via his prophets of the significance of these acts. Whereas he faithfully dealt with the nation of Israel down through its long history, God also graciously spoke through individuals from time to time at critical junctures in that history. The Christian church has similarly known God's grace in providing apostles and prophets, as well as his acts on its behalf through physical deliverances and visitations of spiritual renewal. Human history remains the sphere of God's activity. In its midst God hears and answers the prayers of his people.

Finally, and most important of all, the Old Testament does not lead us astray when it speaks of God: his unity and his holiness; his wisdom, power, and love; his faithfulness to his people; his grace in providing them with an inspired and utterly trustworthy Scripture; his inclusion of varied patterns of spiritual worship in the psalter; and his endorsement of their local worship through synagogue-type gatherings. Christians are indebted to God for all these mercies and benefits. Christians and Christian churches need to acknowledge gratefully their Jewish spiritual heritage and express their indebtedness to the Jewish people for having preserved it at great personal cost over the centuries.

10

God Works through the Jewish Diaspora

Introduction

The four centuries between the cessation of Old Testament prophecy and the sudden appearance of John the Baptist in the wilderness of Judea were most significant for their impact on the life and culture of Israel. The narratives surrounding the birth of John and Jesus (Luke 1–2) give one the impression that little had changed since the time of Malachi, the last of the postexilic prophets. And yet profound changes had, in fact, taken place. During this period Israel developed from a small city-state of agrarian orientation to an urbanized, populous people that had known benevolent Persian rule, then oppression by the Greeks, the ups and downs of a precarious independence, and finally iron subjugation by Roman power. In Jesus' day the Jews had among them a significant number of Roman and Greek proselytes. Moreover, the sequence of political upheavals they experienced, particularly their encounter with Greek thought and culture, made a massive impact on their religious consciousness. Even so, many Jews in the Diaspora were caught up in a growing movement to convert the peoples of the Gentile world to Judaism. The stage was now set: "the fullness of time" had come. God sent forth his Son, born in the land and under the law (Gal. 4:4), and salvation history would now turn from the particular to the universal.

Historical Overview: Israel and the Nations

During this period Egypt continued to deteriorate as a major power. Although it had earlier been recognized as the most highly developed civilization of antiquity, Egypt was unable to withstand the successive invasions of younger, more vigorous peoples seeking to incorporate it into their imperialistic dreams. This meant that Jewish history was no longer influenced by Egypt, but rather by Egypt's assailants. To these we now turn.

The Jews under Persian Rule (539–332 B.C.)

During the more than two hundred years that the Persians ruled over Palestine, the Jews enjoyed almost unbroken peace, and their institutions developed significantly. The Davidic line earlier represented by Zerubbabel had dwindled in importance. The heir to the throne when the New Testament narrative begins was a village carpenter in Galilee named Joseph. In contrast the priestly line steadily gained power and influence. This meant that political as well as religious authority slowly gravitated to the increasingly secularized office of the high priest. This shifting of power, however, provoked a rivalry between Judeans and Samaritans that in the end resulted in two competing centers of worship, sacrifice, and pilgrimage in the land: one at Jerusalem and one on Mount Gerizim in Shechem.

Inevitably, the strengthening of priestly power led to a growing preoccupation with the law and the development of an oral tradition to ensure its faithful observance. Old Testament regulations were greatly amplified with the drafting of precise rules that could be applied to every conceivable situation. By thus "fencing the law"—adding other laws to protect and perfect the Torah—a burdensome legalism developed that increasingly removed God from the central focus of the religious consciousness.

The Jews under Greek Rule (323–167 B.C.)

Then came the dramatic cultural shift known as the Hellenistic Age. Alexander, the youthful king of Macedonia (334–323 B.C.), led an army to liberate the Greeks of Asia Minor. In no time the momentum of his successes resulted in the wholly unexpected obliteration of the Persian Empire and its replacement with Greek language and culture as the new international norm for all its diverse peoples. The conquests of Alexander and the incorporation of these diverse peoples into his realm brought a growing sense of unity throughout the eastern Mediterranean world. As the power of his centralized government was extended and road systems were established, people began to migrate toward the emerging commercial and political centers, thus disrupting the rhythm of indigenous religious life. Some sought to take their cults with them. Others became disoriented from their former loyalties and joined in the widespread search for spiritual identity and personal satisfaction that increasingly characterized urban religious life. Syncretism was in the air. The Christian church later would be significantly helped in its missionary outreach by this religious huckstering that dominated the non-Jewish world of the first century.

During his Syrian campaign, Alexander came into contact with the Jews. Because of a dream he spared Jerusalem and then met with a delegation of its religious leaders. Flavius Josephus describes the encounter. Apparently, Alexander was quite impressed when the delegation shared with him the prophecies of Daniel concerning his conquests. In response he sacrificed to God in the Temple and began to draw able Jewish men into his army. In time many diasporal Jews began to imitate the Greeks and came to be known as Hellenists. The Pentateuch was translated into

Greek for their use, to be followed by the rest of the Old Testament. This version came to be known as the Septuagint. Its obvious superiority to all other religious literature was a major factor in the success of Jewish proselytizing activity.

After Alexander's death (323 B.C.) his four generals divided the empire among themselves into separate Hellenistic kingdoms. Because two of these kingdoms, the Ptolemaic (over Egypt) and the Seleucid (over Syria), had Palestine as a common though disputed frontier, the Jews experienced much distress as these two antagonists struggled to possess it. It remained under Ptolemaic control until 198 B.C., when the Seleucids came to power in the land. Fortunately, during this period the Ptolemies were cosmopolitan moderates and opposed any radical Hellenization of the Jewish people and their unique religious culture. As a result upper-class Jews in the land were increasingly drawn to liberalize their institutions and social life. These Hellenists became a significant influence in Judea.

The first thirty years following the Seleucid seizure of Palestine were reasonably tranquil. Jews continued to be attracted to Grecian philosophy and its concomitant sophisticated urbanism. But some of their number became restive and sought to accelerate the Hellenizing process, even to the point of repudiating both the Abrahamic covenant and circumcision. Inevitably, this precipitated an open struggle with more traditional Jews, and at this time the Hasidim, or "pious" Jews, emerged, determined to resist this secular drift. In 167 B.C. King Antiochus Epiphanes IV of Syria, a violent fanatic for Hellenism, led a struggle among the Jews against those who opposed Hellenistic influences. He deposed the existing high priest and sold the office to the highest bidder. When his nominee was rejected, he declared outright war against the non-Hellenistic Jews. In his subsequent capture and reduction of Jerusalem, many of these traditionalists were slaughtered. By desecrating the Temple and rededicating it to Olympian Zeus, "the abomination that causes desolation" of which Daniel had written (11:20–35) appeared to be taking place. This precipitated the Maccabean Revolt of 167 B.C., and a pattern emerged that was to become characteristic of subsequent Jewish history. Menahem Stern describes this phenomenon in the following fashion:

> As was to happen so often in the future, martyrdom was accompanied by heightened eschatological yearnings. There was a growing belief that a time of divine retribution, which would bring with it the downfall of the kingdom of evil, was approaching and so would fulfill the prophecy of the "end of days." In the face of attempts to Hellenize them forcibly, there arose among the faithful a renewed and strengthened loyalty to the religion of Israel. (1976: 205)

The Maccabean Revolt (167–142 B.C.) and the Hasmonean State (142–63 B.C.)

During the ensuing period of suffering, oppression, and war, Judas the Maccabee and his brothers led a guerrilla movement against Antiochus's attempts to defile the Temple through prostituting it to offensive pagan rites involving Grecian gods and goddesses. One of their first achievements was to regain control of the Temple and purge it of all Grecian defilement. Actually, three years to the day after Antiochus had profaned the Temple and offered pagan sacrifice on the altar, the Temple was rededicated to the God of Israel. This was memorialized by the Feast of Hanukkah, or Dedication, and has been celebrated annually ever since (1 Macc. 4:59; John 10:22).

We should not minimize the achievements of the earlier Maccabees. They were persons of stature and of faith. They had a zeal for God and a love for their people. Initially they were few in number, and their resources were limited. Even so, they defied the oppressive Greeks, engaged them in open combat, and succeeded in winning battle after battle. After years of heroic warfare, they were finally able to break Grecian power and become a free people. Admittedly, their recourse to violence later proved their undoing, for those who reach for the sword to advance the cause of God are invariably destroyed by it (Matt. 26:52). Even so, they gave their people a pattern of Messianic consciousness of which we find many signs when we examine carefully the New Testament record of the fullness of time when Jesus "came to that which was his own" (John 1:11).

War ended in 142 B.C., and in the years that followed, the Jews under the Maccabees were able increasingly to extend their borders until they virtually repossessed the area ruled by David and Solomon. Since the revolt of these remarkable brothers had been initially sparked by the inspiration of their father, an obscure priest named Mattathias, two of his sons, first Jonathan, then Simon, came to the office of high priest. Inevitably, not all Jews were happy about this because the old Zadokite line of legitimate priests was thereby deliberately bypassed. Simon's son John Hyrcanus became the most successful political leader during the eighty-year period the descendants of Mattathias (called Hasmoneans) ruled over this independent state.

With the passage of time, however, the quality of Hasmonean leadership disintegrated as family jealousies, patricide, and moral corruption made the Jewish state easy prey to the rising power of Rome. Civil war broke out, and this virtually invited the Romans to invade and bring peace to Palestine's war-weary people. The Romans captured Jerusalem in 63 B.C., and after a rather lengthy period of turbulence, the Herodian dynasty was appointed to serve under their direction. This proved to be very satisfactory as a political arrangement, but to the Jews the Herodians were nothing more than Arab intruders. In the time of Christ the land knew Herodian rule, propped up by Roman procurators and the Roman military presence. The Jewish people were very restless under this double yoke.

The Antecedents of Rabbinic Judaism

The expulsion of the Jewish people from the Promised Land to exile in Babylon was a profoundly traumatic experience. Some contended that because they had broken the covenant, the exile was God's just punishment. They should accept their corporate guilt, confess it, and beseech God to look again with favor on the restoration of the Temple in Jerusalem. Daniel's prayer was their model (9:3–19). Even so, they should not forget Jeremiah's counsel that they "increase in number

. . . and not decrease" while in Babylon—not merely mark time there. They should "seek the peace and prosperity of the city . . . and pray to the LORD for it" (29:4–7). They were to be a socially responsible people among the Babylonians. Intimations of change came from four developments.

The Exile as Challenge

As the captivity lengthened, a radically different inference came to be drawn from Jeremiah's counsel, especially from the promise that if Babylon prospered, they also would prosper (29:7). The new inference was that they were not to regard themselves as a people God was punishing, but rather as a people to whom he was giving a challenging mission. Leo Trepp summarizes:

> The Babylonian Jewish community and all their descendants were advised that they dwelt among people of other religious convictions because God had willed that they creatively participate in the upbuilding of a good society. Not sinfulness but a divine challenge had caused their dispersion. (1982: 25)

No longer were Jews to form encapsulated societies living in withdrawal from other peoples and cultivating homesickness for the Promised Land. But not all agreed. Those who returned to the land in response to the challenge of Cyrus (Ezra 1:3) sought to restore the past. Along with rebuilding the Temple and Jerusalem's walls, they reproduced a pattern of life that reflected continuity with the past. The early reform of Ezra (7:6–10; Neh. 8:1–10:39) confirmed to them the primacy of the Pentateuch. They made it the divinely appointed basis for a distinct style of life and thought that has shaped Orthodox Judaism ever since.

Behind all this was the desire to look at their history and derive salutary benefit from the failure of their fathers to take the demands of the covenant to heart. At the same time there was the natural desire to free themselves from the burden of past guilt. Attention increasingly focused on an oracle from Ezekiel (18:3–17) that Jeremiah seemed to support (31:29–30). Ezekiel was very explicit: "The son will not share the guilt of the father" (18:19–20). Whereas they had earlier questioned God's justice in punishing the children (themselves!) for the failure of their fathers, they now began to contend that a key line from the Decalogue no longer had validity: "God punishing the children for the sin of the fathers" (Exod. 20:5). In time this became a rabbinic principle, summarized by Leo Trepp in the following fashion:

> There is no inherited guilt, there is but personal responsibility of every individual for himself and for those he may influence. (1982: 25)

The Torah as Priority

On this basis it is not difficult to see why Ezekiel is commonly called the father of Judaism. It follows then that the exile did not merely mark a great divide in Jewish history. It was also notable in marking the beginning of rabbinic Judaism in the sense that a shift began to take place away from the authority of inspiration.

Of course, Scripture, especially the Torah, would continue to be treated with the greatest of respect as God's revelation. But the final authority increasingly resided in those who interpreted it. This perspective crystallized into rabbinic dicta years later when Greek culture pervaded the Middle East.

We have little reliable data on the development of this principle during the Persian period. Bright says that following the return of the exiles to Jerusalem, "we know very, very little" of what they experienced under Persian rule until the empire came to an end—332 B.C. (1972: 374). What is known is that during the early part of this period Nehemiah the governor and Ezra the scribe struggled to prevent their total assimilation into the Gentile world. They partially succeeded by strengthening the wall of particularism around Jewry through promoting a way of life that involved punctilious observance of the minutiae of the law. They denounced and forcibly dissolved mixed marriages and thereby sought to purge the Jewish communities of all pagan influence (Ezra 10:3, 44; Neh. 13:3).

An illustration of the pattern of placing scholarly authority over Scripture surfaced when the rabbis sought to resolve the issue of the status of the offspring of these marital tangles. A realistic and reasonable answer had to be given to the question, Who is a Jew? The leaders called attention to Deuteronomy 7:3–4 and decreed that the Jewish status of a child depends upon that of its mother. Actually, this text merely contains a divine prohibition against Israelites making marriage arrangements with the Canaanites. Even though all Old Testament genealogies define status by the father, the rabbis recognized that since mothers tend to shape the spiritual development of children more than do fathers, and since a child's maternity is more easily traced than its paternity, the decision was made that only those whose mothers were Jews were certified as Jews by descent.

Understandably, those Jews who lived outside Judea, whether in Babylon, in surrounding districts, or in other lands, became increasingly concerned with rectitude in these matters. Not only did genealogies become important, but they were increasingly concerned with formalizing and normalizing the procedures whereby Gentile converts would be admitted to the community.

This concern came to focus on the issue of circumcision. All male children of Jewish parents, despite the blood ties that destined them for admission to Jewry, had to be circumcised. All agreed that this alone separated them unto God and his service and made them members of the covenant. Circumcision likewise was essential to the transformation of even the most zealous converts into what their conversion experience apparently could not make them: real Jews. It is not surprising that the rabbis referred to circumcision as "being born again" (Cullmann 1950: 57, 60–61). This stress on circumcision was fundamental to all the various forms of Judaism existing during the time of Jesus. Only by ritual circumcision could one enter the redeemed community.

The term *Jew* gained precise definition: Every Jewish child is a Jew by birth. The yoke of the law was accepted by one and all as the sign of personal commitment. All sought to affirm their Jewishness by obeying and fulfilling the Sinaitic law, since this was regarded as the only way to win the divine favor.

Inevitably, human limitations prevented even the most zealous from achieving this goal. On the face of it, Scripture gave them little comfort: "There is not a righteous man on earth who does what is right and never sins" (Eccles. 7:20). The people could only presume that God's compassion for human weakness had provided in the law the way of repentance. This heightened their preoccupation with legal rectitude.

The Synagogue as Focus

Midway in the Second Temple period—we do not know precisely when, how, or by whom—the synagogue came into existence in order to keep alive Jewish tradition and practice. Its emphases were on worship and education, although it also served to stimulate social and cultural life. Few would challenge the claim that the creation of the synagogue precipitated nothing less than "one of the greatest revolutions in the history of religion and society" (Ben-Sasson 1976: 285). It became the prototype of Christian churches and Muslim mosques. The synagogue radically changed Jewish religious thought, particularly in the Diaspora. The mediating priesthood of the Temple tended to be eclipsed by the scribe or scholar, the rabbi, the rule of wisdom, and the study of Torah. The growing focus was on the informed individual who needed neither priesthood nor mediation but addressed God with boldness, having achieved an ever-growing sense of self-worth through legal rectitude. Needless to say, the synagogue greatly shaped the Jewish sense of call to the academic tradition. One's life should be devoted to study, particularly to the study of the Torah.

This accelerated the development of a tradition of additional rules—the oral law—whereby obedience to the law would be fully secured. National pride was promoted, non-Jews were regarded with contempt, and all Jewish communities tended to draw ever more tightly within themselves. Increasingly, it became apparent that the Jewish nation was undergoing transformation from a people whose identity was linked to the Promised Land to a religious community scattered widely. Hence the stress on physical descent to legitimize Jewishness and provide clear demarcation from all outsiders.

Problems arose, however, when the non-Jews (*gērîm*) in the midst of whom they dwelt increasingly began to seek varying relationships with this strange though attractive people and their singularly different faith. These Gentiles naturally envied those who were Jews by birth and were free to become involved in synagogue study and worship. Was there not some way whereby they might also be accepted? They could point to Israel's past history when non-Jews were welcomed (e.g., the Book of Ruth).

Although the Jewish people regarded these *gērîm* as potential proselytes, the whole matter of their entering synagogue life in the Diaspora necessitated the development of a careful pattern for incorporating them into their communities. The absence of the prophetic call "to turn" meant that the issue of inward spiritual transformation was not in their consciousness, hence was not raised. Conditions for admission focused on external compliance.

Admittedly, not many became proselytes and formally converted to Judaism. The majority of those attracted were content to develop only a loose attachment to the Jewish people. They came to be known as "God-fearers" but were never regarded as real Jews. Naturally, those who persevered in their efforts to convert to Judaism had to submit to circumcision and accept a rigorous regimen of submission to the law before they were accorded full Jewish status. One gains the impression that proselytes were welcomed but not always sought.

Hellenism and Religious Authority

Under Greek rule the Israelites found themselves confronted by a people who were convinced that they alone were civilized and that Greek culture and religion were needed to unite the diverse peoples of the Middle East. It was inevitable that despite their best efforts to the contrary, Jewish leaders were not totally successful in protecting their people from the blandishments of Hellenism. This brings us to Jesus Ben Sira, the author of the apocryphal book popularly known as Ecclesiasticus. He was a scribe who almost unconsciously imbibed the Greek ideal of the autonomous man, unfettered by any external authority. Those whom he influenced acquired with him a distinct form of self-complacency, an uncritical confidence in human reason. One has only to compare Ecclesiasticus with the Book of Proverbs and Ecclesiastes to sense the marked change in mood and perspective it reflects. Ellison judges rightly when he refers to the way in which Jesus Ben Sira gave classical "rabbinic" significance to the statement, "The law was given us from Sinai. We pay no attention to a heavenly voice. For already from Sinai the law said, 'By a majority you are to decide'" (Exod. 23:2). Ellison states:

> This means quite simply that the rabbis believed that God so delivered himself into the hands of men by the revelation of the Torah, that it was for them to decide how he was to be served, provided that the decision was consistent with the Torah, or could be made to appear so. (1976: 71–74)

Despite our awareness that the Jewish people vigorously opposed the Greeks for desecrating their institutions and mocking their monotheism (the Maccabean Revolt 167–142 B.C.), this legacy of Hellenism's impact on Jesus Ben Sira remained: the right to elevate human reason and scholarly study over the authority of Scripture. Inevitably, this meant the slow transition in Jewry from the Bible to the Talmud, from divine revelation to an alleged "oral" Torah—a growing tradition of human impulse and creation that would dominate the thought and practice of Judaism from that time onward.

Emergence of Jewish Parties

In general terms Judaism represents the dynamic reconceptualization of the religion of ancient Israel into forms that were regarded as congenial to the varied diasporal experiences of the Jewish people. On the one hand, there were rabbis who were most eager to fence the law by adding all sorts of commandments to make every aspect of daily life immune to assimilation into the Gentile world in which their people were forced to live. On the other hand, rabbis serving upper-class Jewry were drawn to elements in Greek rationalism that they regarded as potentially liberating for the human mind. They were mesmerized by the seemingly irresistible march of Hellenism that followed Alexander the Great after his destruction of the Persian Empire (331 B.C.).

Inevitably, among the common people an ultraorthodox, lay, protest movement began to emerge. Its leaders were known as the Hasidim—"God's loyal ones." They sought to structure this resistance, but a splintering took place; moderates were soon pitted against radicals, and both were against the Hellenists. The result was that by the first century homogeneity was largely lacking in Jewish thought and practice. In the midst of this diversity, several significant parties are identifiable. Each represented a distinct response to the older traditions and the newer political and religious realities within their troubled land.

The Pharisees

This essentially lay group regarded themselves as the legitimate successors to the patterns developed years before by Ezra. They reflected the fierce pietism of the early Hasidic purists who had been in the vanguard of the Maccabean revolt. Because they were convinced that the Babylonian Exile was God's judgment on Israel for failing to keep the Mosaic law, they stressed the importance of observing every least detail, whether individual or national, written or oral. Their relatively small numbers came initially from the lower-middle and artisan classes; hence, they were respected by the common people. As a result their beliefs and practices came to represent the majority population in first-century Israel. The Pharisees were the sole party to survive the revolt against Rome (A.D. 66–70), and their influence was so all-pervasive that by A.D. 200 Judaism and Pharisaism had become virtually synonymous.

Pharisees only bought and sold from one another. They refused to eat in the homes of non-Pharisees, lest they become defiled. They were "separatists" in their self-righteousness and in their unwillingness to make concessions. Because of their conviction that the will of God could be known for every circumstance of life through the careful study of the Torah, Pharisees were very close to the scribes, the professional students of Torah, and were its most loyal defenders. This meant that upper-class scribes were often their leaders, although as a body the scribes were distinct from the Pharisees. Because this preoccupation with the law tended to reduce religion to an external formalism, the Pharisees caused Jesus great inward pain. Although they subscribed to the unity and holiness of God, the unique calling of Israel, and the authority of the law of Moses, their stress was on ethics and not theology, with the result that they were often lacking in compassion. Furthermore, they refused to acknowledge the validity of any interpretation of the law other than their own.

The Sadducees

The Sadducees were the rich and aristocratic priestly party. Sadducees were rather remote from the people although they controlled the Temple. Patrician families were among their number, and along with the Pharisees they composed the Sanhedrin, the highest tribunal in Jerusalem. In general they were less strict than the Pharisees in religious observance; they differed from them in that they regarded the Torah as more binding than the oral law. They rejected such post-Torah doctrines as the afterlife of the soul, the resurrection of the body, the final judgment, and the existence of angels and demons. Sadducees were regarded by Josephus as boorish, even disagreeable in spirit toward one another (*Wars* II, viii:14). Their doctrines were not popular among the masses, and their positive cooperation with Rome made them politically suspect. It was their negotiations with Rome that resulted in the Temple area being decreed out of bounds to Gentiles. When they transformed the former Court of the Gentiles into the place where animals were kept and money exchangers served, Jesus protested (Mark 11:15–18). He reaffirmed God's original intention that the Temple be a house of prayer for all peoples (Isa. 56:6–7).

The Herodians

Little is known of this nationalistic party other than that they favored the Herodian dynasty. They drifted into quasi-association with the Pharisees on the issue of paying taxes to Caesar but allegedly were not as strict in religious observance. Their relentless hostility toward Jesus both in Galilee and in Judea attests to their conviction that his message had too many universal implications; it was a threat to their narrow nationalism (Mark 3:6; 12:13).

The Zealots

This ardent group represented the revolutionary option. They were convinced that the Romans had to be driven out by force of arms. Only then could the Jews gain control over their own destiny. Oscar Cullmann asserts that at least five of Jesus' disciples were from this "desperate class." He identifies one particular guerrilla group as "sons of thunder" and suggests that "Iscariot" in Judas's name could mean "a man or member of the Sicarii (Long Knives)," another terrorist organization (1957: 8–23). The Zealots precipitated the revolt against Rome in A.D. 67. This revolutionary option has always appealed to a segment of Jewry—then and now—but Jewish believers in Jesus repudiated all recourse to nonredemptive violence to achieve spiritual goals. His disciples took seriously Jesus' word, "My kingship is not of this world. If it were, my servants would fight" (John 18:36).

The Essenes

The Essenes represented the strictest of the strict. They avoided pleasure, wealth, and to some extent marriage. They created their own way of showing devotion to God, namely, that of withdrawal. Today, whenever the Essenes are mentioned, the popular reaction is to conjure up the image of the austere community at Qumran near the Dead Sea. But they were more than an "isolated pocket or resistance group" within Judaism. According to Josephus, they were a sect that "existed in different and diverse but related splinter-groups throughout Palestine." He adds that they were found in every town of Palestine: "They have no certain city, but many of them dwell in every city" (*Wars* II, iii:4). Since their primary objective was purity, they sought to be scrupulously clean. They were a quasi-monastic order that excluded women. They regarded themselves as the only true Israel and were dedicated to learning. They supported a different line of priests from the Sadducees, so there was tension between the two groups. The Essenes said the world was in such a mess, they must go to the wilderness to wait for the Messiah to come, and then "true priests" would take over the Temple.

The presence of the Essenes in Jewish life throughout a major part of the inter-testamental period had both positive and negative influence on Judaism's outreach to the Gentiles. Their positive influence was chiefly in diminishing the importance of the religious symbols of land, city, and temple. They were so opposed to the Hasmonean-defiled Temple in Jerusalem that they widely broadcast the idea that what was really important was "the condition of the heart," wherein devout Jews, then and now, whether in exile or diaspora, could be priests, worshiping God and bringing him delight. The Essenes looked for the Messiah to come, cleanse the Temple, and then install them as its future priests. Their deliberate injecting of the primacy of the heart into the stream of Jewish thought and their concept of the priesthood of all believers could not but strengthen Judaism's self-identity as a universal faith. If Jerusalem and the Temple are unimportant, why not accept this evolution of Judaism from a national religion to a universal faith?

On the other hand, the Essenes exercised a negative influence on Judaism largely because they saw themselves as a "saved" community, but not a "saving" community. Indeed, they were quite hostile to those Jews in the Diaspora who sought to gain proselytes from among the Gentiles. Some of their more zealous members were particularly intolerant of all Gentile "God-fearers," who took God's name on their lips but refused to be circumcised. When coupled with the Essene practice of a more rigorous and burdensome legalism than that of the Pharisees, the hostility of the Essenes repelled many Gentile inquirers. They regarded truth in an esoteric fashion, all doctrines and revelations being reserved for "the man of understanding." The Essene movement resembled a perfectionist mystery cult; it was a priestly legalism dominated by a priestly hierarchy. In his ministry Jesus significantly rejected the Essene pattern of deliberately withholding "the knowledge" from the common people. Rather, he rejoiced in the privilege of sharing the good news of the Kingdom with "the poor, the maimed, the lame, the blind" and manifested nothing of Qumran's gloomy exclusiveness when he prayed:

I praise you, Father, Lord of heaven and earth, because you have hidden these things from the wise and learned, and revealed them to little children. Yes, Father, for this was your good pleasure. (Matt. 11:25–26)

Because the Essenes never engaged in public preaching, it is pure speculation to contend that John the Baptist was brought up an Essene. Both he and Jesus were preachers, heralding the beginning of an entirely new dispensation when they proclaimed throughout the land of Palestine, "Repent, for the kingdom of heaven is near" (Matt. 3:2; Mark 1:15).

Jewish Proselytism as a Movement

In years past much attention has been given to identifying the characteristics and extent of the Jewish proselytizing movement that slowly gained momentum and significance throughout the latter half of the Second Temple era (Bamberger 1939; De Ridder 1971: 58–120). Suffice it to say, during this period the Jewish faith expanded as it never had before and never has since. This was not because of the impulse of any central authority in Jerusalem, training and sending out missionaries. It was largely the outcome of local and lay initiative, with the result that most Jews rejoiced over the conversion of Gentiles to their monotheistic faith and took pride in the fact that Jewish customs were being observed in large sections of the Roman Empire. Josephus expresses their boasting:

> There is not any city of the Grecians, nor any of the barbarians, nor any nation whatsoever, whither our custom of resting on the seventh day has not come, and by which our fasts and lighting up lamps, and many of our prohibitions as to our food are not observed. . . . And as God himself pervades all the world, so has our law passed through all the world also. So that if anyone will but reflect on his own country, and his own family, he will have reason to give credit to what I say. (*Against Apion* 11, 40:899)

Actually, Jewish proselytism during this period poses a controversial subject for the scholarly community. Jewish scholars today tend to downplay its extent. In contrast, Christian scholars such as Johannes Blauw admire its vigor and consequent impact on the missionary consciousness of the church (1962: 55–58, 63, 64). On the other hand, Edward Gibbon almost dismisses its relevance and contends that the success of the apostles was more the result of the restlessness and inadequacy of Gentile polytheism.

> The obligation of preaching to the Gentiles the faith of Moses had never been inculcated as a precept of the law, nor were the Jews inclined to impose it on themselves as a voluntary duty. . . . They were apprehensive of diminishing the value of their inheritance by sharing it too easily with the strangers of the earth. . . . Whenever the God of Israel acquired new votaries, he was much more indebted to the inconstant humor of polytheisms than to the active zeal of his own missionaries. (1952, vol. 1: 179, 180)

No one knows precisely the size of the Jewish community during this period. Josephus seems to have believed that every community in the entire Mediterranean world had within it a portion of the Jewish community as a result of their proselytizing activity. Frederick Derwacter is somewhat more cautious, although his final conclusion of the matter is more positive than negative.

> We cannot give even an approximate count of the proselytes to Judaism in the Mediterranean world of the New Testament period. They were numerous enough to claim the attention of Philo and Josephus, conspicuous enough for pagan writers such as Tacitus and Horace and Juvenal to see them as a part of the Judaism of their time. They are looked upon as a factor in the great growth of the Jewish population following the exile. The rapid development of Christianity into a Gentile religion seems inexplicable without a large proselyte constituency. More than this can hardly be said. (1930: 119)

Despite this cautionary word, Adolf von Harnack estimates that there were 3 million Jews divided equally between Palestine, Syria, and Egypt, and that 1.5 million more were scattered throughout Asia Minor, Europe, and Asia (Blauw 1962: 57). When one recalls the relatively small number that returned from Babylon to reconstitute the Jewish community in Palestine (Ezra 2:64 gives 42,360) and their size at the time of the Maccabean Wars (second century B.C.) of 180,000, one is pressed to conclude that this substantial growth must have been the result of intensive proselytizing activity.

When Paul wrote to the Christians in Rome (where there was a Jewish colony of at least ten thousand), he described the Jews as "convinced that [they] are a guide for the blind, a light for those who are in the dark, an instructor of the foolish, a teacher of infants, because [they] have in the law the embodiment of knowledge and truth" (2:19–20). Apparently, the Hellenized Jews of the Diaspora were not so introverted that they were unaware of the superiority of their faith to the Gentile mystery religions. Indeed, the very corruption of the nation in Palestine, first under Hasmonean and later under Herodian leadership, diminished Judaism as a national faith and transformed it into something universal, for monotheism is implicitly a universal and missionary faith.

Harnack lists the reasons why the Christian mission was indebted to the Jewish mission that preceded it. He states:

> It provided in the first place, . . . a field tilled all over the empire; in the second place, . . . religious communities already formed everywhere in the towns; thirdly, . . . what Axenfeld calls "the help of materials" furnished by the preliminary knowledge of the Old Testament, in addition to catechetical and liturgical materials which could be employed without much alteration; fourthly, . . . the habit of regular worship and control of private life; fifthly, . . . an impressive apologetic on behalf of monotheism, historical teleology, and ethics; and finally, . . . the feeling that self-diffusion was a duty. The amount of this debt is so large that one might venture to claim the Christian mission as a continuation of Jewish propaganda. (1972: 15)

In expanding these points, Harnack describes extensively the tensions within the Jewish community. One segment under the inspiration of the Books of Isaiah and Jonah, along with the wisdom literature, was "fully conscious" that God ruled over their nation and all of humankind. They hoped for the ultimate conversion of all the heathen. They were the "progressives," committed to proselytism. Another segment was dominated by the Maccabean experience. They desired the downfall of the heathen that Judaism might emerge in full exclusiveness. They were the "nationalists," committed to particularism. Even the Pharisees were torn between these two polarizations. The schools of Hillel and Gamaliel were propagandistic; that of Shammai was reactionary, laying down eighteen rules to control the confession of God before the Gentiles. Scholars have spoken of the constant strain that existed between the demand that the heathen be included and the dread that this excited. It is the common testimony of Hellenistic, Roman, and rabbinic sources that in the main Jews were not only eager to make converts but successful as well. When Jesus spoke of their traveling "over land and sea to win a single convert," he was not condemning per se this missionary outreach but was denouncing Pharisaism, for the Gentile converts were thereby transformed by Pharisaism into "twice as much" the children of hell that they themselves were (Matt. 23:15).

Diasporal Judaism appealed to certain segments of the Gentile world. It represented moral strength, the intellectual vigor of a consistent monotheism, the attractiveness of disciplined living, and the martyr tradition of a persecuted minority. The question of Jewish religious identity was constantly raised by their Gentile neighbors: Who were these people? To whom did they belong? What was their God like? This brought forth the recital of their Torah: the story of God's mighty acts on their behalf and his interpretation of these acts. Religious encounter eventually developed into a lay form of missionary activity. The Jewish apologetic generally included confessing the one true God: the invisible Creator of heaven and earth, who cannot be represented by images. He is the moral Governor of humankind, who blesses those who deliberately live under his rule and for his glory. This message was so strikingly different from the mythology of polytheism that many Gentiles found it appealing and wanted to hear more. The universals of Jewish wisdom literature provided the added attraction of identifying wisdom with God and thereby bridging the gulf between Israel's history and the best signs of the oneness of the human race within the religious and philosophical thought of the Greco-Roman world. With the Greek Scriptures (the Septuagint) diasporal Judaism laid the foundation for the spread of the gospel in the Western world.

Throughout the intertestamental period those aliens who resided contiguous to Jewish communities were encouraged to assimilate. In Esther 8:17 we encounter the phrase "became Jews." This is its only appearance in the Old Testament, but it represents a reality that became increasingly common. Indeed, in later Judaism it was natural to equate the foreigner who resided temporarily or permanently in the land of Israel with "proselyte." Actually, the Greek word *prosēlytos* was used only to describe Gentiles who became Jews, not Gentiles who shifted from one mystery cult to another ("one who has left country, friends, and relatives, also patriarchal customs, and set himself under the Jewish constitution," Philo). Circumcision was not readily accepted by most Gentile "inquirers," much less the binding cultic commandments of rabbinic Judaism. They remained "worshipers" or "God-fearers." Palestinian Judaism, however, placed far more emphasis on conversion through circumcision. The closer to Jerusalem, the more intensely Jewish its communities became. They regarded the importance of observing all the laws of the Old Testament, as detailed by the Hasidim and which were being incorporated into what eventually became the Talmud. This complicated proselytism. To join the Jewish community, Gentiles had to submit to circumcision and baptism as well as perform sacrifice in the Temple. This made them "in every respect" a Jew and placed them under the continuing obligation to keep the whole law (as Paul later confirmed, Gal. 5:3).

Legalism, Pessimism, and Apocalypticism

It has often been said that the Babylonian captivity cured Israel of its idolatry. This is true. Most of the prophets inveighed against the Israelites for their worship of images, and some even announced that as a result they would be taken into "exile beyond Damascus" (Amos 5:25–27). It was in Babylon that the Israelites finally and for all time renounced all idolatry and resolved to become a people completely devoted to the law. Under the influence of such men as Ezra and Nehemiah, they were transformed into a people who both loved the law and were willing to die rather than violate it. Their devotion to God made the difference.

Despite the passage of time, they did not waver in this resolve. They instituted "correct" worship in the Second Temple, developed their synagogues into training centers for the reverent study of the law, and fully expected that God would reward them for their devotion. When the Seleucids tried to force them to adopt Greek ways, they resisted. Many embraced martyrdom rather than compromise their submission to the law. This only heightened their expectation that God would reward them for their transformed national character.

But God did not seem to take notice of anything they did. It was his silence, his unwillingness to intervene on their behalf that caused them increasingly to despair. However, they did not turn away from the law and become apostate. They sought to become—if anything—more determined than ever to make sure that they were obeying all its stipulations to the letter. At the same time their leaders began to play down the prophetic sections of Scripture and play up an entirely new genre of literature based on dreams, visions, and oracular revelations. This literature pointed to God's ultimate triumph: the Israelites would possess the world as their inheritance, and he would bring it about through his sudden irruption into history on the last day. The literature on this massive shift from the historical to the eschatological is designated as "apocalyptic." It flourished during the period 200 B.C. to A.D. 100, although in Isaiah 24–27, Daniel 7–12, and Zechariah 9–14, we find one of the themes of this literature—the cataclysmic dimension of God's activity on the last day. At the same time we must add that these three prophets also included the historical dimension—something totally absent from the writings of the apocalyptists.

The big problem facing the apocalyptists—who were authors, not preachers—was to establish credibility and gain a hearing for their writings. This was achieved through the deliberate pseudonymity they chose to hide their own identity. The age of prophecy was over; God no longer spoke through the living, human voice. Hence, the apocalyptist could not speak as a prophet with the ringing conviction: "Thus saith the Lord." As a result he would borrow an Old Testament saint and attribute the visions to him, that the writing might receive authority from the prophetic name (Ladd 1964: 80).

The result was something both artificial and imitative. What the apocalyptists called "visions" were fictional, quite removed from the transcendent nature of the subjective insights that came to the prophets and which caused them to know and proclaim what they affirmed was the Word of God. No Israelite could be sure that the apocalyptist was proclaiming the living Word of the Lord. All that was heard was hopeful human speculation, usually in the form of colorful and radical reinterpretations of Israel's history. Not that the apocalyptists were not sincere in their desire to explain why the promises of the prophets had not been fulfilled, why evil still ruled the world despite the alleged obedience of Israel, and why the Kingdom of God was being postponed. Their motifs had dualistic overtones: "this age" was characterized by evil, but "the age to come" would see the glorious manifestation of the Kingdom of God. No interrelation or tension existed between them. God's ways are inscrutable. Hope lay in the future, not in the present. But how God would come, no one knew. What would be, would be. A fatalism coupled with pessimism dominated all speculation on the present. This led to ethical passivity, despite the fierce obedience the Israelites gave to the law. And yet within the nation a believing remnant kept "waiting for the consolation of Israel" (Luke 2:25). They resisted the pessimism of the apocalyptists and remained convinced that the earlier prophetic promises of God were true. He was working within history, and his faithfulness to his people should not be forgotten. The messianic age would come within the continuum of history. His eternal, redemptive purpose for his creation would be realized.

Conclusion

It is rather significant that a generation before Christ, Judas the Galilean (Acts 5:37) appeared on the scene. Josephus describes how he "prevailed with his countrymen to revolt, and said they were cowards if they continued to pay a tax to the Romans" (*Wars* II, viii:1). Judas's followers had "an inviolable attachment to liberty and [contended] that God is to be their only Ruler and Lord" (*Ant.* XVIII, i:6). Judas virtually claimed that a new order was about to be introduced that would be marked in a special and unprecedented manner by "the kingship of God." In the light of this, Bruce wonders whether Judas felt that the time had come, as foretold in Daniel, for the God of heaven to "set up a kingdom that will never be destroyed . . . an everlasting dominion that will not pass away" (Dan. 2:44; 7:14, 27)? Had Judas been impressed by the oracle of Balaam, with its prophecy that "a star will come out of Jacob; a scepter will rise out of Israel" (Num. 24:17)? Years later in the Bar-Kokhba revolt of A.D. 132–35 the leader, a certain Simeon ben Kosebah, was renamed Bar-Kokhba ("Son of the Star") by the great Rabbi Aqiba, who hailed him as the promised "Star out of Jacob" (Bruce 1978: 16–19).

Furthermore, Daniel had not only predicted the coming of the Kingdom of God but had also stated the time when it would be manifested (9:24–27, "seventy weeks" from the decree of Cyrus to "rebuild the temple" and until the "Anointed One will be cut off"). Since Josephus tells us that these predictions were known to the Jews of Judas's day, should we conclude that in the public mind Judas's revolt set the stage for God's apocalyptic conquest of their enemies (*Ant.* X, i:6)? At any event, the mood of those days was one of expectation. And when Jesus finally appeared and said, "The time has come. . . . The kingdom of God is near" (Mark 1:15), the probability is that some were reminded of Daniel's prediction of the time when "the sovereignty, power and greatness of the kingdoms under the whole heaven will be handed over to the saints, the people of the Most High" (7:22, 27).

So then, just prior to the coming of Jesus, the Jewish people were fragmented into a variety of contending schools of thought. Some nonestablishment Jews were actively engaged in reaching into the Gentile world for converts. In their own eyes, they were a "saved remnant" that had a "saving" mission to perform. Although all Jews believed in the sovereignty of God, many were doubtless troubled by the fact that his rule appeared to be confined to heaven. It was not apparent on earth. The only power they knew and bitterly resented was the power of imperial Rome. They could not understand why Israel, God's chosen people, confident in their obedience to God had to experience such national oppression and individual misery. Even so, there were those far more humble people who eagerly looked for "the consolation of Israel" (Luke 2:25). They believed that somehow and in some fashion the new age would soon come.

> The new age to which they looked forward was a revival of the best ideals of the old age. They looked forward to a new Temple, a pure sacrificial worship and the reinstatement of a worthy priesthood; but the Temple would still be a building made with hands, the sacrificial worship would still involve the slaughter of bulls and goats, the priesthood would still be confined to the sons of Aaron. (Bruce 1956: 147)

There is a terrible incompleteness to the Old Testament. The history of Israel is inconclusive. Its great period receded deeper and deeper into the past. Revelatory words from God through his prophets had become fewer and fewer and finally with Malachi ceased altogether. The excitement aroused by the proliferation of apocalyptic literature made it increasingly difficult for the people of God to live by means of the old faith. In the end the various parties within Judaism, although often at loggerheads with one another, united to participate in the final tragedy of standing against Jesus Christ when he came as the self-confessed "son of man" of Daniel, the "Suffering Servant" of Isaiah, and the "smitten shepherd king" of Zechariah.

PART 4

GOD'S
MISSION
THROUGH
JESUS
THE
CHRIST

11

Jesus Inaugurates
the Kingdom

Introduction

"When the time had fully come, God sent his Son" (Gal. 4:4). The sending of Jesus into the world was in keeping with the Old Testament pattern of God's sending mission. We cannot forget that Jeremiah said, "From the time your forefathers left Egypt until now, day after day, again and again I sent you my servants the prophets" (7:25). And yet this "sending" of Jesus was unique. The fallen condition of humanity was so acute and the need for redemption so great that only the incarnation of God and the atonement of the cross could provide for the salvation of God's people.

The New Testament begins with careful attention to genealogies. By beginning the Jesus story in this way, Matthew establishes continuity with all that has gone before. Jesus is "the son of David, the son of Abraham" (Matt. 1:1). He comes as "the Christ of God, the foretold and expected Messiah, the true heir of the throne of David and the heir to all the promises made to Abraham" (de Dietrich 1960: 156). As Immanuel, "God with us" (Matt. 1:23), he came to liberate his people and establish an eternal kingdom that would fulfill Israel's messianic hope (Luke 1:32–33, 51–55, 68–79; 2:29–32). At the same time his earthly life and ministry would be challenged by fallen humans, by religious and political leaders, and particularly by the demonic powers.

A striking new element is introduced when the New Testament begins with intimations of a heightened renewal of the cosmic struggle between God and "the rule of this world" (Matt. 2:13–18; Luke 2:34–35; John 12:31). But with the coming of the Wise Men, it also suggests that the Gentile nations will be drawn to the grace that God will provide (cf. Matt. 2:1–12 with Isa. 2:2–4).

Jesus and John the Baptist

The ministry of John the Baptizer marks the dividing point between two epochs. John was the final prophet of the older dispensation (Matt. 11:12–13; Luke 16:16). He called for national repentance and adopted the stance of radical condemnation of the established order: "The ax is already at the root of the trees" (Matt. 3:10). He denounced the religious leaders as vipers and pointedly affirmed that reliance on one's physical descent from Abraham was of no value (Matt. 3:7–9). But what drew immediate attention was his announcement, "The kingdom of heaven is near" (Matt. 3:2). His message brought to mind the "smashing stone" that, as Daniel had prophesied, would destroy Gentile world power and become a kingdom that would itself never be destroyed (Dan. 2:25–35). The long awaited eschatological event, the day of the Lord, was about to dawn!

Although John's witness to the appointed one was not uniquely messianic, his forthright message brought renewal to all those who believed his word. It was apparent to many that God was speaking once again to God's people in the prophetic tradition of earlier periods in their history. John's message of the intimate coming of the Kingdom and his call to the people to prepare themselves by returning to the standards of Sinai took on the dimensions of a renewal movement.

Early in his ministry John baptized Jesus, and the two of them engaged in similar activity for almost a year, preparing the nation for its rendezvous with destiny. When Jesus asked for baptism, John drew back. He recognized the stark contrast between the condition of the people to whom he was ministering and the sinlessness of Jesus. Here was One who had no sins to confess (Matt. 3:13–15). But Jesus insisted, and Luke states that "as he was praying, heaven was opened and the Holy Spirit descended on him in bodily form like a dove" (3:21–22a). God responded to Jesus' prayer with approbation and with the anointing of the Holy Spirit. From that time onward Jesus fully represented all that Isaiah had foretold as characterizing the Messiah: the righteous, Spirit-anointed, and Suffering Servant of the Lord. It is significant that only when the Father spoke and the Spirit descended did John realize who Jesus truly was (John 1:31–36).

In the temptation that immediately followed his baptism, Jesus chose to place himself "on exactly the same footing as any other Jew who undertook to live by the words of God revealed through Moses, or any sinner who had come to John for baptism" (Michaels 1981: 56). In this way Jesus provided his followers with insight into the values of the Kingdom of God. First, life is not sustained by bread alone, but by the Word of God (Luke 4:4). Second, the priority of the Kingdom is to give God, not people, the preeminent place in all worship and service (Luke 4:8). Third, believers must never put God to the test (Luke 4:12).

Jesus then returned to Judea and became involved in a renewal ministry similar to John's, yet possessing a distinctive and arresting newness (John 1:29–4:2). He began to gather his disciples, and, accompanied by them, he went among the people, speaking of God and his righteousness, of sin and the necessity of repentance. Both Jesus and John called the people to prepare themselves against the imminent coming of the Kingdom. Both baptized the repentant (John 3:22–23). Both called for spiritual reformation as well as social responsibility.

Although the ministries of Jesus and John were similar in many respects, there was a difference between them. Whereas on the surface it might appear that both spoke of the imminence of divine visitation, it was Jesus who added the assertion that this visitation was "in actual progress, that God was already visiting his people" (Ladd 1964: 109). It is equally significant that in Jesus' subsequent preaching we find frequent references to John's basic themes, although John's fierce style differed markedly from the "gracious words" of Jesus (cf. Luke 4:22 with Michaels 1981: 14–24). Therefore, a mood of expectation grew and spread throughout the land. Its focus was Israel's long deferred hope: the Kingdom of God! To the believing remnant, this could only mean that God was about to intervene and act redemptively on behalf of God's people. In the popular mind the expectation grew that the time had come for the deliverance of the Jews from the oppressive rule of Imperial Rome.

Soon, however, a crisis arose, and the renewal movement was suddenly checked when Herod seized and imprisoned John. In the weeks immediately following this event, Jesus did nothing to effect John's release. We can well imagine the consternation that overtook John's followers. Their champion was silenced. He had spoken of the coming judge, but there was no "smashing stone," no evidence of judgment. Was Jesus just going to keep on preaching and healing the sick? Had John not said that Jesus would display his messiahship and dismantle the edifice of society? Would he not purge the threshing floor, gather grain into the barn, and destroy the chaff with unquenchable fire (Matt. 3:12)?

The Beginning of Jesus' Kingdom Ministry

Something of tremendous significance did happen. Mark tells us that when Jesus heard of John's arrest, he abruptly terminated his renewal ministry, withdrew from Judea and the Jordan Valley, and hastened to Galilee (1:14). He went to Nazareth, "where he had been brought up," and "on the Sabbath day he went into the synagogue, as his custom was" (Luke 4:16). On that occasion he inaugurated a new era in the ongoing development of salvation history. At this point his preaching lost much of its earlier continuity with John's call for renewal. Jesus introduced an entirely new theme: the gospel was no longer a future hope but a present reality full of eschatological significance. This served to heighten the expectations of the people.

The Announcement in Nazareth

Jesus' messianic identity began to display itself in the synagogue in Nazareth. Earlier John had spoken of the coming of the Kingdom in apocalyptic terms: One was coming whom God would enable suddenly to intervene in human affairs, separate the righteous from the wicked, and establish a Kingdom that would stand forever. But Jesus now spoke differently. The earlier theme, "Repent, for the kingdom of heaven is near" (Matt. 3:2), was now prefaced with a pointed reference to the immediate present, "The time has come. . . . The kingdom of God is near" (Mark 1:15). By these and many other words, he specified that in his own person the Kingdom was "near." Jesus now boldly projected himself into the role of the Servant of the Lord and began to carry out its predicted ministries (cf. Luke 4:18–21 with Isa. 35:1–10; 61:1–4). He announced that the Kingdom was no longer solely a future hope but a present reality. While John's disciples mourned and fasted, Jesus' disciples did not (Mark 2:18–19). His "kingly rule" with its concepts of community and fellowship was essentially a power at work in the present, exercising its force. It also concerned a community, a house, an area "where the goods of salvation are available and received" (Aalen 1961: 223). It made the people crowd around Jesus and his disciples (Matt. 11:12). It "came upon" people (Matt. 12:28) and was a veritable Presence "within you" (Luke 17:20–21).

Opposition to Jesus was immediate (Luke 4:24–29). His words offended the great majority of the people, particularly when he stressed the spiritual and the ethical dimensions, focusing on the salvific activity of God rather than on the overthrow of Rome. True, he spoke of the coming of the Kingdom of God in power and glory and told the Twelve that they would then "sit on thrones, judging the twelve tribes of Israel" (Luke 22:30). By stating this, he was promising their participation in the future joy of the consummation of God's redemptive purpose. Jesus also thereby confirmed that the Kingdom was "not yet" as well as "already" present. There will indeed be an eschatological end. Because of this, it will not do to state that Jesus came merely to contribute a new ethic, to teach a loftier theism, or to provide the basis for a new religious/theological system. In him the old order of forward-looking hope yielded to a new order reflecting "redemption accomplished" and guaranteeing the final triumph of God in history.

The Summons

The Kingdom of God entered the human scene in ways unprecedented and altogether new. In his preaching and teaching Jesus sought to awaken interest in its dominant characteristics by making the sort of aphoristic statements that provoked and elicited response. He fully expected that his hearers would later formulate from his teaching a corpus of truth that would clearly enunciate who he was and what his Father had sent him into the world to accomplish. On one point he was decisive and authoritative. Those who heard the good news of the Kingdom and who became concerned to receive the forgiveness God offered to its sons and daughters were pressed to make an immediate decision of repentance and faith. "If anyone would come after me, he must deny himself and take up his cross daily and follow me" (Luke 9:23). This involved the renunciation of all other loyalties, the unconditional acceptance of the will of God (Matt. 16:24–26), and active participation in the task of recruiting others (Matt. 4:19).

Features of Jesus' Kingdom Ministry

There is a startling distinctive to the messianic age. No longer are the people of God to be an encapsulated, worshiping community in the midst of the nations. They are to face outward to the nations, proclaim the presence of the Kingdom by word and deed, and issue the call to conversion. Prior to the cross, they were to concentrate on the house of Israel (Matt. 10:5–6; 15:24). Even then there were intimations that the compassion and electing grace of God would reach beyond Jewry to the Gentile world (Matt. 8:5–13; Mark 7:24–30; etc.). The universal faith that would emerge after the resurrection would be proclaimed to all peoples everywhere and would demand that all repent of their self-centeredness and sinfulness and submit to the King, to Jesus Christ the Lord. His messianic community was to avoid the tragic preoccupation of Israel, constantly self-absorbed with its own national survival. Rather, this new community of disciples of the risen Messiah was to become "a light for the Gentiles," that it might bring the salvation of God "to the ends of the earth" (Isa. 49:6).

Jesus as Servant of the Lord

The aura of messiahship suffused all that Jesus said and did. His Davidic descent was not unnoticed (Mark 10:47–48). Although reluctant to announce his messiahship openly (Matt. 16:16–20), Jesus' confession before the Sanhedrin was clear and unambiguous (Mark 14:61–62). He sought in every way to portray a messianic Kingdom that came by God's power and not by political or military action. He had no intention of setting up an earthly kingdom. He specifically told Pilate that his kingship was "not of this world" (John 18:36). As a result he was in constant tension with the leaders of the Jews, whose dominant concern was political liberation from Rome. His demeanor, his teachings, his service, and his death clearly reflected the Servant of the Lord described by Isaiah. The New Testament is full of references to this messianic Servant portrayal of Jesus the Christ: "nothing else, nothing less" (Bright 1953: 208–14). As Reginald Fuller states,

> The figure of the Servant gives a unity to all that Jesus said and did from the moment of his baptism to the moment of his death upon the cross. Remove that background, and his life breaks up into a series of unrelated fragments. (1960: 277)

Jesus as Worker of Miracles

Jesus did not work miracles to "prove" his messiahship or to vindicate his personal authority. Nor should his miracles be regarded as simply humanitarian acts of compassion. Actually, the emphasis on his compassion is surprisingly minimal throughout the Gospels. In contrast, his various miracles pointed to the reality of the Kingdom as "already" present in the midst of Israel. They were messianic "signs." When the disciples of John confronted Jesus with their question as to whether he was the Messiah, his reply was that they should ponder the import of his miracles of healing and his preaching of the gospel to the poor. His quotations from Isaiah 35 and 61 showed that these were the messianic signs that Isaiah had predicted would precede the decisive act of God in redeeming God's people. They marked the dawning reign of God.

There is a second aspect of Jesus' healings and exorcisms. On one occasion he said, "If I drive out demons by the finger of God ["the Spirit of God," Matt. 12:28], then the Kingdom of God has come to you" (Luke 11:20). This phrase "the finger of God" was what the Egyptian magicians said when they could not account for the disasters that fell on Egypt through Moses' confrontation of Pharaoh (Exod. 8:19). Those signs achieved then "by the finger of God" were preliminary demonstrations of the power of God that eventuated in the Exodus of the Jews from Egypt. Here Jesus saw his works of exorcism as the Kingdom's preliminary assault on the power of evil in the land. At the cross he would fight these powers to the finish and thereby pave the way for the final exodus: eschatological redemption. In this vein Hoskyns and Davey state:

> The physical miracles are external signs of the supreme miracle, the rescue of [people] from the grip of the powers of evil—from sin. The supreme messianic miracle to which the miracles point is the salvation of [people] by the power of the living God exercised through the agency of the Messiah. (1947: 120)

What then were the distinctions of the Kingdom Jesus had announced as already present? First, the Kingdom is devoid of all dimensions of outward glory. It is a buried treasure, and its acquisition merits any cost or sacrifice (Matt. 13:44–46). Second, its form is hidden. It represents the hiddenness of God, working in the hearts of God's people scattered throughout the world of time and space. Jesus used the phrase "the secret of the kingdom" to represent God's present invasion of Satan's kingdom to release people from Satan's bondage (Mark 4:11; Luke 11:14–22). He added that those who entered the Kingdom that Jesus announced enjoyed in part a foretaste of the age to come. They enter into life (John 3:3). This means they receive both the forgiveness of their sins (Mark 2:5) and God's righteousness (Matt. 5:20). Third, the only acceptable response that can be made to God's gracious gift of the Kingdom is to put oneself consciously under Christ's rule by repentance, faith, and submission.

Jesus Teaches about the Kingdom through Parables

A central objective of Jesus' mission was to announce the glad tidings of the Kingdom of God (Luke 4:43). Scholars are agreed on this. But they differ regarding what he meant by the Kingdom. Jesus stressed its God-centeredness but left unanswered his precise relation to it. Was he its King? He did not directly claim this. Furthermore, he never defined explicitly the term *Kingdom of God*. Even so, it seems legitimate to conclude that when he spoke of the Kingdom as having "drawn near" or "come," he was affirming that "the realm in which God's rule is to be exercised is here in our world and in our history" (Michaels 1981: 75). This would seem to imply that the Kingdom is something more than God's kingship or reign. Hence, it should not be conceived merely as the epiphany or revelation of God. When Jesus stated that the Kingdom is dynamically moving into human history and is sweeping over people "violently" (Matt. 11:12), he was referring to a new world, a new state of affairs, a new community, "the good realm where the realities of redemption are granted and received, where the conditions of fulfillment are realized and evil is no more at work" (Aalen 1961: 232). Michaels adds: "It finds concrete expression in the world. Though transcendent and spiritual, it is also political. . . . Its path toward realization lies on a collision course with all human rule or authority" (1981: 80). We must not lose sight of this note of conflict. Satan is determined to thwart the progress of the Kingdom. Jesus calmly asserts, however, that divine authority and rule have been given to him by the Father (Matt. 11:27; 28:18; Luke 10:22). Furthermore, he will exercise this rule until the dominion of Satan, sin, and death are not only challenged but also brought to a complete end (cf. Mark 9:1; 13:26; 14:62 with Luke 11:20–22). Paul will later add that this authority and rule will then be returned to the Father (1 Cor. 15:24–28).

The Parabolic Method

On one occasion Jesus' disciples asked him why he used parables in his ministry to the "large crowds" (Matt. 13:2, 10). He replied: "The knowledge of the secrets of the kingdom of heaven has been given to you, but not to them. Whoever has will be given more, and he will have an abundance. Whoever does not have, even what he has will be taken from him" (Matt. 13:11–12). He then went on to say that when the heart of a people grows dull—that is, unreceptive—direct presentations of truth evoke little or no positive response (cf. Isa. 6:9–10 and Zech. 7:11 with Matt. 13:13–17). The only alternative then is to use the language of metaphor, narrative, and parable. Furthermore, the mystery of Jesus' person and the spiritual nature of his Kingdom were so new and revolutionary that he could only disclose these realities gradually. Hence, he deliberately hid his "messianic secret" (Mark 1:34, 44; 3:12; 5:43; etc.) and spoke in parables. These tantalized his hearers and compelled them to come to a full stop to reflect and then ask questions. The more his open-hearted disciples began to discern who he was, the more they began to understand his teaching. Conversely, the more people resisted him, the more his teaching reduced itself in their minds to a "hard teaching" that some thought to be utterly devoid of significance (John 6:60).

To the ignorant, the undiscerning, and the willfully obstinate, what Jesus was saying remained a mystery. All they heard were stories, riddles, and paradoxes (Mark 4:11–12). Blindness of mind and hardness of heart prevented their turning to him in repentance and faith (John 12:40). Jesus increasingly used parables as the opposition mounted. The parabolic form then seemed most suited to reaching the hostile, for it involved a kind of delayed action. He knew that his parables would surface in their memories after their emotional bigotry had begun to wane. They would then start wondering just what it was that he was seeking to say to them with those fascinating stories.

Jesus' use of the parabolic form in his Kingdom teaching was unique. Even the most critical scholars agree that his parables represent a particularly trustworthy tradition: "We are standing right before Jesus when reading his parables" (Jeremias 1968: 10). And yet there is little agreement among them as to what truths these parables were intended to convey. Georgia Harkness states rather unequivocally that they "reflect the bearing of the Kingdom on the conditions of everyday living in human relations" (1974: 93). But this perspective is too removed from the broad context of salvation history. Because the Kingdom of God and the mission of God's people are interrelated, the parables may possibly be seen as providing variegated insight into God's mission. This would suit both messianic prediction and Jesus' disclosure that God is a seeking God. Indeed, if the Kingdom means anything, it is that God is visiting his people to invite them to its eschatological feast (Ladd 1964: 168–74).

If this reasonable assumption is adopted, it follows that the parables speak of the nature, growth, and value of the Kingdom, largely under the theme of mission. Some parables specify the sphere in which the Kingdom operates as well as the cost involved in its service. Each parable was essentially an event drawn from human experience and was intended to convey a single truth. Occasionally, however, parables were offered as extended similes in narrative form. Jesus would then expound the meaning of each detail. This transference from parable to allegory was to provide his hearers with the sort of orientation needed to discern the overall thrust of his concern: Kingdom truth must be translated into missionary obedience. If this allegorical teaching is kept in mind, the parables can then be understood as both complementary and supplementary.

The Growth Parables

The parable of the sower comes first and is central to all the parables (Matt. 13:1–9; Mark 4:1–9; Luke 8:4–8). Jesus was explicit about this: "Don't you understand this parable? How then will you understand any parable?" (Mark 4:13). The parable speaks of an unidentified sower who sows "The Word of God" ("the message about the kingdom," Matt. 13:19). The good news is that it is now possible for one and all to come within the realm and under the transforming rule of the King. Much of this good seed is wasted, for the soil represents wide variation in the human response to the Word, ranging from the highly resistant to the genuinely receptive. The parable labors the point that there are unprofitable ways of hearing the Word of God. The Word is only heard aright when it produces tangible and measurable fruit. Hence, its conclusion is most solemn: "He who has ears to hear, let him hear" (Mark 4:9). Its echo is found in James's exhortation: "Do not merely listen to the word, and so deceive yourselves. Do what it says" (1:22). And yet the major thrust of the parable is that although human beings can sow the seed, the seed mysteriously grows and eventuates in God's supernatural reality: the Kingdom.

No parable is more crucial to our understanding of the missionary task. There is a gracious King who desires to invest all individuals and peoples with his life and declare his control. He has ordained that those who have responded and entered his Kingdom and who have begun to manifest the fruit of the Spirit in their lives will be God's agents in sharing the Kingdom's good news with others. They are to proclaim the gospel with every expectation that although many will not respond, there will be true and lasting conversions and transformed lives. These alone will be acceptable to God. They are the ones who "with a noble and good heart . . . hear the word, retain it, and by persevering produce a crop" (Luke 8:15).

Jesus then followed this parable with one that described the growth process, the inworking of the Holy Spirit in the hearts of those who respond to the gospel (Mark 4:26–30). His focus was on the dimension of mystery following a person's conversion. The sower sleeps and rises, day after day, and the seed sprouts and grows, "he does not know how" (4:27). Obviously, it takes time for the convert to "grow in the grace and knowledge" of the Lord (2 Peter 3:18). Much about this process eludes understanding and external control because genuine spiritual growth comes from the inworking of the Spirit of God. This is not to deny the importance of diligent human effort (through worship, Bible study, obedience, and witness). Furthermore, as with individuals, so with the Kingdom: there is the certainty of the final consummation. The quiet and hidden growth of the Kingdom throughout the world today will finally eventuate in a great harvest of peoples from every tribe and nation. Jesus was particularly concerned to stress this consummation: "As soon as the grain is ripe, [God] puts the sickle to it, because the harvest has come" (Mark 4:29).

But are Christians to be primarily preoccupied with their personal growth and communal fellowship, focused largely on heavenly prospects? This is not enough. The next phase is described in the parable of the wheat and the weeds (Matt. 13:24–30). Not all ripened grain is to be immediately and permanently gathered into God's heavenly barn. In his exposition (13:36–43) Jesus speaks of a second sowing. Only this time the details are strikingly different. The good seed represents sons and daughters of the Kingdom, mature in their spiritual lives, whom God would separate from their spiritual rootage. The sowing now represents their being planted in God's field ("the world"). They are to be scattered widely and in many places where the children of the evil one are numerous and powerful. Their presence interjects into the parable the dimension of isolation, conflict, and suffering, implying that a price must be paid if one is to participate in the ongoing of the Christian mission. Throughout the Kingdom age this cosmic conflict will continue. But in the end the good grain will be finally and totally separated from the evil weeds.

We would particularly underscore the central truth that the allegory conveys—that the sowing of sons and daughters of the Kingdom worldwide is so important that the Lord of the harvest does not entrust it to anyone. This crucial sending is uniquely his task. He is the "Lord of the harvest" (Matt. 9:38). Therefore, his abiding concern is to send forth laborers to gather a harvest from the midst of all peoples.

From the sequence described in the preceding discussion we should rightly conclude that the Kingdom advances in history and to all parts of the world through the sovereign and creative activity of God. He accomplishes this as God's people devote their time, hearts, strength, and resources to proclaim the good news of Jesus Christ. God bears witness to the exciting possibilities latent in those persons who open their hearts to his lordship. And it should be noted that these growth parables come to a climax with Jesus speaking of all valid service as intimately associated with his own. He was the unique "grain of wheat" that fell into the ground at a place called Calvary and there entered into death (John 12:24–26). And if any would serve him, they must follow in his steps. His willingness to be lifted up on a cross that he might draw all humanity to himself is the model for all human service in his name. As Bonhoeffer rightly said, "When Christ calls a man, he bids him come and die" (1953: 8).

Note that two other parables, those of the mustard seed and the yeast hidden in the flour, both serve to underscore the Kingdom's insignificant beginnings. The mustard seed becomes a tree incredibly large and useful, and the yeast manages to permeate the totality of the flour to which it has been added (Matt. 13:31–33). Indeed, all the parables of growth unitedly combine to make the point that

> the Kingdom of heaven is breaking in upon the hearers, and that it will come in spite of many things: small and unnoticed beginnings, a mixed response to the message of its coming, acceptance by only a few, and the continuing presence of evil in God's world. There is nothing we can do to hasten or control the Kingdom's coming; we cannot observe it and time its growth. It is God's Kingdom, not ours. But we can take comfort in knowing that even now he is bringing it to realization, and that when this Kingdom comes it will be worth all the waiting, all the frustration, for the sake of those who accept its gifts and obey its demands. (Michaels 1981: 129)

The Banquet Parables

Joachim Jeremias has pointed out that "the parables are full of the recognition of an eschatology that is in the process of realization" (1968: 230). By this he meant the possibility of Christians attaining in their present experience a foretaste of tomorrow's Kingdom realities. They begin to enjoy tomorrow today. In this connection we should note that several of the Gospels record an incident in which Jesus was confronted by the faith of a Gentile. The quality of this faith so surpassed that of the Jews that he used it as an occasion to speak of a future day when "many will come from the east and the west, and will take their places at the feast with Abraham, Isaac and Jacob in the kingdom of heaven," while the ostensible Jewish "sons of the Kingdom of heaven" are excluded (Matt. 8:11–12). This reference to the "eschatological banquet" occurs frequently in Scripture. The language is rich and diverse. For example, Jesus speaks about a great banquet, the marriage supper of the Lamb, the marriage feast for the king's son, and about the man who had no wedding garment. These all refer in one way or other to the same apocalyptic event (Luke 14:16; Rev. 19:9; Matt. 22:2, 11). And yet the impression is given that the festive spirit of that future banquet can be enjoyed even now, as it is connected with the mission of the church.

This dimension of mission is brought out clearly in the cluster of parables in Luke 14 that conclude with the summarizing admonition, "He who has ears to hear, let him hear" (v. 35). The use of this stark and pointed exhortation encourages us to regard this cluster of parables as possessing a coherent togetherness.

The account is straightforward. Jesus has been entertained on the Sabbath "in the house of a prominent Pharisee" (14:1). The atmosphere was tense and critical. Jesus, contending that it is always lawful to do good, especially on the Sabbath, healed a man who had dropsy. He thereby violated the unnecessarily strict Pharisaic interpretation of the fourth commandment about remembering the Sabbath day, to keep it holy. Hostility intensified when Jesus, noting the guests striving for places of honor at the table, extolled the virtue of humility (vv. 7–11). At this point he addressed the banquet's host and spoke of the privilege of extending hospitality to those who would be unable to repay the kindness. He ended by reminding one and all of the last day, when the just will be rewarded.

This provoked a safe theological remark on the part of one of the guests, "Blessed is the man who will eat at the feast in the kingdom of God" (14:15). Jesus took this vague generalization as a starting point and gave his memorable parable of the generous host who at considerable personal expense prepared a sumptuous feast and then invited many to enjoy it with him. Again and again, and in various ways, he pressed the invitation, "Come, for everything is now ready" (v. 17); come, "there is still room" (v. 22); and come, "so that my house may be filled" (v. 23). But those who were invited treated lightly his bounty and replied with irrelevant excuses. In the end he turned to the socially despised, and invited them. The thrust of the parable would appear to be that the good news of the Kingdom is often dismissed by the privileged for trivial reasons, but there are always those humble ones on the edges of society who have the faith to respond.

This parable can be easily abused by removing it from its context and making it representative of the personal and redemptive component of the gospel of the Kingdom. The question is posed: What are the good things Jesus provides for those who receive him (John 1:11–12)? Answers readily given are sonship, personal identity, the forgiveness of sins, peace of mind, a righteousness that alone provides access to God and his friendship, the indwelling Spirit, purpose in life, victory over sin, resurrection hope, eternal life. All these are included with the gift of the One who came that his people "may have life, and have it to the full" (John 10:10). Although now available "without money and without cost" (Isa. 55:1), it cost Jesus everything to provide these gifts. This parable illustrates the "gospel of God's grace" (Acts 20:24). It shows, among other things, that there is more willingness on God's part to save sinners than there is on the part of sinners to be saved. And there is more grace to be given than there are hearts willing to receive it.

In the context of Luke 14 what follows involves Jesus' most searching statements on the conditions for discipleship. To follow him means bearing the cross. Jesus Christ must be preeminent in one's life, before one's nearest and dearest, before one's own life, and before the pull of things, whatever they may be (14:26–27, 33). Then, without the least break, Jesus added three parables in quick succession, all stressing the necessity of counting the cost: a building to be built, a warfare to be waged, and salt that must retain its saltiness. These point up the images of workmen, of soldiers, and of socially responsible citizens. To feast at Jesus' table is without price, but becoming his disciple costs everything. Is this not the total Christian experience? Conversion does open the way to feasting. This is true. But conversion also involves the possibility of taking up the cross daily (Luke 9:23). This leads to participation with Christ in a dynamic movement: the Kingdom of God (Col. 1:24). As Paul Loffler notes,

> The beginning of the Kingdom through Christ's entry into the human history is the main context of conversion in the New Testament. . . . His criteria are not the saving of one's soul nor the increase of church membership *as such*, but rather the mission and ministry of the Church in the world." (1965: 257–60)

Jim Wallis adds insightfully:

> The goal of biblical conversion is not to save souls apart from history but to bring the Kingdom of God into the world with explosive force. It begins with individuals but is for the sake of the world. . . . Churches today are tragically split between those who stress conversion but have forgotten its goal, and those who emphasize Christian social action but have forgotten the necessity for conversion. . . . Both need to recover the original meaning of conversion to Jesus Christ and to his Kingdom. (Quoted by Howell 1983: 366)

Admittedly, one can regard each parable as a stand-alone story: the feast is a representation of the eschatological banquet; counting the cost before one builds or before one wages war are somewhat similar lessons in prudence; and salt that loses its taste is a warning against losing one's pungency. But has one thereby obtained better insight into Luke's having brought these four parables together? Hardly! How much more meaningful to regard Luke 14 as a unit that describes Christian experience as always feasting, always reaching for the joys of the Kingdom-in-consummation today. This involves always passing back and forth daily through the cross-marked door that stands between refreshing communion with Christ and fruitful service with him for the Kingdom. It includes always discovering anew that Kingdom service inescapably involves collaboration with Jesus in building the church through proclaiming the gospel to the whole world. This also involves always fighting the fight of faith and resisting all forces, human and demonic, that would resist the advance of his Kingdom. It means always manifesting Kingdom holiness and social responsibility by prophetic words and loving deeds. And as salt is a covenant sign (Lev. 2:13), so the people of God are to display a lifestyle that is a visible sign of Christ's new covenant and the Kingdom presence. They are to exercise a wholesome influence in society because of their relationship to God. As Jesus said in another place, they are to be as a city set on a hill that cannot be hid (Matt. 5:14).

This cluster of parables, when illumined by the parables of growth mentioned earlier, further develops our understanding of the task of mission. Further, they prepare us to appreciate the significance of another series of parables related to stewardship.

The Stewardship Parables

We noted earlier that the miracles of Jesus awakened messianic expectations in the hearts of many. In response Jesus gave a series of parables on stewardship and implied thereby that the advent of the Kingdom in power and glory was to occur at the end of the age. Luke tells us that Jesus' parable of "the ten minas" was given because his followers "thought that the kingdom of God was going to appear at once" (19:11).

Jesus' intention was to teach his disciples that he would be away for a period of time and that during this period his disciples should concern themselves with being faithful stewards. The parable is straightforward. A nobleman, prior to leaving home on a distant journey, entrusts to each of his servants the same amount ("the ten minas") and gives them the same instruction: "Put this money to work . . . until I come back" (19:13). He then departs, expecting each servant to exercise initiative, persistence, and diligence in putting his or her mina to work. Some responded to the challenge and soon discovered that the mina has an innate ability to multiply itself: "Your mina has earned . . . more" (19:16–18). One servant, however, so restricted his mina, wrapping it in a napkin, that it was unable to multiply itself. Upon his return the master was displeased: "I will judge you . . . you wicked servant" (19:22). Here is the climax of the parable.

The emphasis of the parable is on personal responsibility and personal accountability. All the servants of God have been given the same "mina." Can this "mina" be seen as the good news of Jesus Christ and the Kingdom? One is reminded of the parable of the sower and the life-giving seed: the good news of the Kingdom. As then, so now, all Christians have the same responsibility to trade with their mina; they can thereby participate in the ongoing movement of the Christian mission. They can confess him by word and deed, believing that the Spirit of God will be pleased to use their confession to achieve his own work in the hearts and minds of their hearers.

Some might contend that to view the parable in this fashion is to create an insurmountable problem. How can the mina be equated with the good news of the Kingdom when the nobleman commends his servant for being faithful in a very little matter? When we realize that Jesus stressed continually the Kingdom as God's activity, all human involvement ("Put this money to work . . . until I come back") is truly incidental, even though human faithfulness is highly commended. This parable needs to be pondered alongside its parallel, the parable of the talents (Matt. 25:14–30). There the thrust is also on personal responsibility and personal accountability. But the striking difference is that no two servants are treated alike by their master: "To one he gave five talents of money, to another two talents, . . . to each according to his ability" (v. 15). The expectation, however, is that all are to be diligent and all are to render the service for which they have been equipped. All are to serve up to capacity. The master then departs, with the promise of his return and a future day of accounting. When that day comes, the refrain is "I have gained . . . more" (vv. 20, 22), in contrast to the earlier parable: "Sir, your mina has earned . . . more" (Luke 19:16, 18). The impression is that the right use of one's talents and creativity can be pleasing to God. The refusal to exercise one's God-given gifts can incur his displeasure. One can either grow or diminish in usefulness and productivity. Furthermore, the parable implies that one should neither envy the gifts of others nor be resentful toward God for one's limitations. Everyone should be grateful for what he or she has received on loan from God and should seek to live up to capacity in expectation that God will not only make possible but also enlarge his or her personal usefulness in the service of God.

These two parables, then, contribute another dimension to our understanding of the mission of the church under the rubric of the Kingdom. All the people of God can be fruitfully involved in the ongoing mission of the church. All are called to the ministry.

But something is missing, and this is supplied by two other parables that complete this cluster. In the story of the householder seeking to hire laborers for his vineyard (Matt. 20:1–16), the dimension of grace is introduced, and what relief it brings! The story is simple: a householder needs workers and keeps hiring them throughout a long and busy day to gather his harvest. At the end he pays them off, and all receive the same wage, even those hired at the end of the day. This provokes grumbling among those who had "borne the burden of the work and the heat of the day" (v. 12). But the householder is adamant:

> I want to give the man who was hired last the same as I gave you. Don't I have the right to do what I want with my own money? Or are you envious because I am generous? So the last will be first, and the first will be last. (Matt. 20:14–16)

What a surprising word this is to those who may have neglected putting either God's mina or their talents to work throughout a major segment of their lives! God does not lay guilt trips on God's people. Rather, he encourages them to get to work, even though they may be reaching the end of all natural opportunities for service. God graciously rewards even the least that God's people do to further his mission.

Finally, because one can abuse the grace of God, Jesus added the parable about the ten virgins (Matt. 25:1–13). Five were wise and five were foolish. The difference stemmed from the fact that the wise were prepared against the coming of the bridegroom but the foolish were negligent and failed to prepare. It should be the concern of all God's servants to be vigilant in the light of the certain promise of Christ's return. No one knows when the cry will be heard to go out to meet him. No one can be sure what a day will bring forth (James 4:13–17). We cannot enlist others to serve on our behalf. One dare not presume that second chances will be given to enable involvement in the mission of the church. One cannot be sure that the great opportunity will fall at one's feet at the eleventh hour. Suddenly, the summons will come, and all doors will abruptly close to further service. And no one will be able to make amends at that late hour for previous negligence. There will be no participation in God's reconciling, redemptive mission after his great day. In fact, this so dominated the thought of our Lord that he gave several additional parables to drive these truths home (Matt. 24:43–44, 45–51; Luke 12:39–40, 41–48).

The Seeking Parables

Jesus was most explicit as to the worth of the Kingdom of God. Material matters should never be the primary concern of those who have heard the good news of the Kingdom (Matt. 6:25–33). Indeed, one's pursuit of material things can stand in the way of one's entering the Kingdom: "It is easier for a camel to go through the eye of a needle than for a rich man to enter the kingdom of God" (Matt. 19:24).

The Kingdom is like "a treasure hidden in a field. When a man found it, he hid it again, and then in his joy went and sold all he had and bought that field" (Matt. 13:44). Literally, he suddenly stumbled upon the reality of the Kingdom and sensed the supreme worth of his life being oriented to its purposes. He must devote all that he has to this Kingdom. This parable is followed by the contrasting story of a merchant who searched long and diligently for fine pearls. When he found "one of great value," he abruptly sold all that he had to acquire it (Matt. 13:45–46).

These parables prepare us for the cluster of seeking parables found in Luke 15. Jesus was severely criticized for the company he kept: the tax collectors and sinners. These members of Jewish society were considered outside the law and were largely excluded from participation in its religious and social life. In response Jesus offered three parables about seeking lost things. Actually, the Kingdom is not specifically mentioned in connection with these parables. But they vividly portray the "yearning love of God for every person, whatever one's moral status or station in life" (Harkness 1974: 98). They so relentlessly reiterate God's delight in the repentance with which sinners turn to him that we regard them as mission parables. True, neither the lost sheep nor the lost coin can repent, but the importance of repentance is stressed after both of these parables (vv. 7, 10). When our Lord speaks of the son lost in a far country (vv. 11–24), the seeking love of God is paramount. And nothing delights the waiting father more than when his son turns from a "give me" (v. 12) to a "make me" (v. 19) attitude toward the father.

This cluster ends with a surprising mission note. The final parable closes with the tragic story of the elder son, portrayed as "lost in his father's house" (Luke 15:25–32). One's initial impression is that he is a dutiful member of the household, busy and loyal. But in the crisis of his brother's return, his true character surfaces. He repudiates the bonds of brotherhood ("this son of yours," 15:30), finds his father's love incomprehensible, and does not seek reconciliation.

In one sense, this older brother represents the Pharisees and scribes to whom these parables were primarily addressed (Luke 15:2). Their relationship with God was largely impersonal, confined to a preoccupation with legal rectitude. Their service to others was minimal, and they remained bitterly hostile toward Jesus and his message of grace and forgiveness.

But there is a missionary dimension just below the surface of this parable. One might hoist the sails of one's imagination and speculate in the following fashion. The elder brother had been enjoying abundance in his father's house when his younger brother was in a far country in great need. And the question arises: Did he ever make any correlation between the abundance he enjoyed and the lack his brother knew? The father was deeply burdened over the absence of his son. But was the elder brother moved by his sorrow? Did he ever speak to his father of the one missing from the table? Did he ever open his heart to his father and seek deliberately to enter into his father's sorrow and burden? Had he done so, would he not have offered to seek out his brother and bring him home? And now that the younger brother has returned, how painful must be his realization that he has contributed nothing to make his father's joy complete.

On this basis one might argue that this parable sheds light on the possibility of Christians refusing to participate in the worldwide task of mission. They refuse to be their brother's keeper; they sense no indebtedness to the unevangelized. They give God little opportunity to place his burden for the lost on their hearts. And they make no offer of themselves to do what they can to bring the lost home. Their very self-centeredness makes them impervious to the lesson on compassion for the needy that Jesus taught in the parable of the Good Samaritan (Luke 10:29–37). Though it might be presumptuous to assume that this sequence of thought was Jesus' precise intention in giving this parable, the implications seem appropriate.

The Parables and the Cross

Significantly, in the parables we have reviewed Jesus was virtually silent as to the manner in which the Kingdom will be realized. He made no explicit statements about his coming death and resurrection apart from one of his earliest parables: the story of the happy wedding guests (Mark 2:18–20). It contains reference to the bridegroom being abruptly "taken from them"—something one would least expect at a wedding celebration. Only at the very end of his ministry, when he had already announced on three separate occasions his coming crucifixion, did Jesus introduce a parable about the slaying of a "beloved son," but even this parable says nothing of the resurrection (Mark 12:1–12).

Prior to these predictions of his death, Jesus must demonstrate the Kingdom by a ministry so unique and so significant that his disciples would become completely convinced he truly is "the Christ, the Son of the living God" (Matt. 16:16). This ministry was dominated by acts of deliverance of the demon-possessed, by the healing of all forms of sickness and infirmity, and by proclaiming the forgiveness of sins to the penitent and believing. It was a ministry that included a wide range of demonstrations of his power: feeding the hungry, triumphing over wind and wave, controlling the fish of the sea, multiplying joy at weddings ("the best wine!"), and demonstrating an outgoing love for the marginalized and rejected of society. Seen as a whole, Jesus' ministry set the stage for preparing the disciples for his terribly discordant note: the announcement of his crucifixion. It was in the gathering darkness of the last weeks of his ministry that Jesus gave the parable of the Good

Shepherd (John 10:1–18) to remind the disciples that the crucifixion must take place before mission to the nations could begin. Jesus must first lay down his life for the sheep (vv. 11, 15, 17). Only then could there be the bringing-in of those "other sheep" that are not of the Jewish fold (v. 16). This sequence, first the cross, then the ingathering, is repeated in the account of some Greeks who came to worship at the feast in Jerusalem and who wanted to see Jesus (John 12:20–26). Their inquiry reminded Jesus of the redemptive sacrifice he was about to make. Should he ask to be delivered from its agony, or should he resolutely embrace it? When the latter alternative was freely chosen, he then could confidently affirm: "Now is the time for judgment on this world; now the prince of this world will be driven out. But I, when I am lifted up from the earth [on the cross], will draw all men to myself" (John 12:31–32).

Conclusion

The Kingdom was inaugurated by the very special relationship between John the Baptist and Jesus. John was the veritable bridge connecting the old covenant with the new. John's declaration was that his own popularity and the charisma of his own person must decrease so that Jesus could open the way for entering into the Kingdom that was now present. Jesus spoke about the Kingdom through parables that reveal what the Kingdom of God means. It is a present though ongoing reality to be entered through the new birth (John 3:5), necessitating the conscious acceptance of God's sovereign rule over one's life. The parables point in various ways to the mission of the church and look forward to the final victory of God in history. "The Kingdom is both presence and promise; both within and beyond history; both God's gift and [the believer's] task; we work for it even as we wait for it" (Harkness 1974: 115).

12

Jesus' Ministry Demonstrates the Kingdom

Introduction

The ministry of Jesus is a vivid demonstration of the dynamic character of the Kingdom of God. In this chapter we will examine his ministry in detail, as it sets the parameters and possibilities of the post-Pentecost mission of the church among the nations. Jesus' Kingdom ministry is to be continued and extended as the church moves out in mission to the nations. Throughout the long history of the Christian movement, however, the utilization of Christ's ministry model has often been forgotten. The result has been a static church, concerned only with its own internal life and institutional maintenance. This inevitably happens when Christians lose sight of their calling to "seek first [God's] kingdom and his righteousness" (Matt. 6:33) and let themselves become preoccupied with material things: food, shelter, clothing (6:19–34). To make Jesus' model of Kingdom ministry the object of one's reflection and action means focusing on God's concern for God's world and the physical, social, and spiritual needs of others. Only by pursuing a Kingdom ministry can one keep "churchly" activities in rightful subordination to the will of God. Whenever the church has seen itself as truly the body of Christ and has deliberately sought to exemplify all that this means, it has "turned the world upside down" (Acts 17:6). The difference between these two perspectives is described by Howard A. Snyder.

> The church gets in trouble whenever it thinks it is in the church business rather than the Kingdom business. In the church business, people are concerned with church activities, religious behavior and spiritual things. In the Kingdom business, people are concerned with Kingdom activities, all human behavior and everything God has made, visible and invisible. Kingdom people see human affairs as saturated with spiritual meaning and Kingdom significance. Kingdom people seek first the Kingdom of God and its justice; church people often put church work above concerns of justice, mercy and truth. Church people think about how to get people into the church; Kingdom people think about how to get the church into the world. Church

people worry that the world might change the church; Kingdom people work to see the church change the world. . . . If the church has one great need, it is this: To be set free for the Kingdom of God, to be liberated from itself as it has become in order to be itself as God intends. The church must be freed to participate fully in the economy of God. (1983: 11)

There is something strikingly familiar about the church after Pentecost. The church's loving, self-forgetful, outgoing concern for individuals displayed in the desire to proclaim the gospel is reminiscent of Jesus' unique ministry. No previous era in the long unfolding of salvation history demonstrated a concept of ministry that even began to resemble this. As Walter C. Mavis observes, Jesus' personal ministry provided a "unique model of service, motivated by a new impulse, that of serving others, which represented an emergent idea in the field of religious ministration" (1947: 357).

In order to understand the nature of Jesus' ministry, it is necessary to remember his incarnation. Although he was the eternal Word of God, he nonetheless was born a Jew of the first century, confined himself to Aramaic, and in every way spoke and acted from within the culture of his own people. He used a well-known rabbi-with-disciples form of ministry and was an effective indigenous communicator. He adapted his message to the people he met so that it became both understandable and "good news" to them, regardless of their station in life. His ministry reflects the absolute essentiality of contextualizing both the messenger and the message if the Word of the Lord is truly to be heard in concrete historical situations.

The incarnational model Jesus gave his disciples (that of serving others) inevitably flowed from the messianic role he sought to fulfill. His ministry (*diakonia*) reflected the central elements of the Old Testament prophet, priest, king, and servant. In addition, so that his followers might be effective in their proclamation of the good news of the Kingdom, he also assumed the roles of evangelist and apostle. The One who is sent is also the One who sends. So then, in this section we will review both these earlier Old Testament roles and those that are particularly related to the Kingdom mission to the nations.

Old Testament Roles of Jesus' Kingdom Ministry

Jesus' ministry followed the well-defined Old Testament roles of those who have been called and sent by God for ministry among God's people. In addition to Christ's three-faceted ministry derived from the Old Testament (Christ's *munus triplex:* prophet, priest, and king), we will add a fourth, that of servant.

Prophet

The prophetic voice had been silent in Israel for many years, ever since the time of Malachi (c. 450 B.C.). As a result, the people in Jesus' day had almost forgotten those unconventional individualists who had sought again and again in the past to exercise a corrective ministry in Israel. Because of their absence, the people were "harassed and helpless, like sheep without a shepherd" (Matt. 9:36). They did not know how to apply the truth of God to themselves and to the situations in which they found themselves. But when Jesus assumed the prophetic role in their midst, everything changed. He faithfully proclaimed the Word of God in a very personal way. He spoke to people's hearts and to their condition. He made his hearers aware of what they truly were before God.

Though he was a prophet, Jesus was not interested in visiting royal courts to give counsel or warning to kings and princes, as were the Old Testament prophets such as Elijah, Elisha, Isaiah, or Jeremiah. Unlike them, Jesus said little about pressing national problems and had no word of warning for the Gentile nations. He refused to protest the crass materialism and widespread corruption of Rome. Instead, he called the professing people of God to practice kindness and brotherhood. He said nothing about slavery and did not publicly denounce the graft of the publicans. While he advocated sharing with the poor, he did not condemn the economic system that helped make some people rich. Although he exposed the peril of riches, he particularly warned against covetousness. He mingled with common people, interpreting the will of God to them by stressing personal values such as love, sincerity, truthfulness, humble service, and prudence. Furthermore, he aroused incentives for doing God's will. He was a prophet whose primary concern was to deal with men and women as persons standing before God. Only secondarily did he become involved in what some might erroneously call the larger concerns.

All four Gospels speak of Jesus as a prophet. Certainly, his disciples so regarded him (Luke 24:19), and this was the judgment of the crowds: "A great prophet has appeared among us" (7:16, 39). This follows from Jesus' own self-identification: "No prophet can die outside Jerusalem" (13:33). After Pentecost both Peter and Stephen identified Jesus as the fulfillment of Moses' prediction that God would raise up a prophet for Israel from among their own people just as Moses had been raised up (Deut. 18:15–16; Acts 3:18–23; 7:37). Furthermore, they stressed Moses' warning that those who failed to listen to him would be destroyed by the people (Acts 3:23).

Paul S. Minear confirms this by reminding us that the post-Easter preaching of the apostles reflects the church's deep conviction as to the importance of Jesus' prophetic role. They saw in Abraham, Moses, and Jesus the three prophets without whom Israel would lose its identity, mission, and destiny (e.g., Acts 3:13, 22, 25; 17:3; 26:22–23). Indeed, without these three, particularly Jesus, "all the families of the earth" would be without hope. In short, given the context of their sermons, no Christological confession could be more decisive or more exalted than this: Jesus was a prophet like Moses (Minear 1976: 106).

The significance of Jesus' prophetic role is also seen when one contrasts his ministry with that of John the Baptist, whom Jesus described as not only a prophet but also "more than a prophet" (Luke 7:26). Jesus saw in John's and his ministries two distinct epochs (16:16). To summarize Minear's observations (1976: 112–17), until John, baptism was with water; since John, baptism was with the Holy Spirit. Until John, people were captive to demons and sickness; since John, they have been freed. Until John, the baptism of repentance was in anticipation of the forgiveness of sins; since John, Jesus' baptism by the Spirit enabled him to forgive sins. Until John, disciples shared in the baptism of repentance; since John, disciples were called to "fish" for people. Until John, the summons was to repentance; since John, the call was to unconditional fellowship with forgiven sinners. Until John, sorrow; since John, dancing. Until John, the Law and the Prophets; since John, the Kingdom of God is preached, involving a radical reinterpretation of the Scriptures. And since those who respond to this preaching "force" their way into the Kingdom (v. 16), it is apparent that the prophetic ministry of Jesus marked the beginning of a new era in salvation history. The contrast between John and Jesus was between the old era of conformity to the law and the new messianic era. Paul Minear contrasts the two ministries in the following fashion:

> These two prophets had by their suffering testified to the power of the gospel both to free men from the Law and to fulfill the Law. To the degree that Jesus was empowered to mediate the gifts of the new age (forgiveness, healing, liberation from demons, freedom from the Law, victory over death), to that degree the violence of His enemies would become the greater, but this, in turn would make the benefits of his passion the more redemptive. . . . Among those who prepared the way for the Kingdom, none would be greater than John. But in fulfillment of Jesus' prophecy (Luke 7:28), the Kingdom of God has dawned and Satan has been beaten. The emancipation declaration has been signed. "Greater than John" are the poor, the captives, the blind, the oppressed, the impotent who, baptized by the Spirit, have received forgiveness of sins, together with the other gifts of God in this new age. (1976: 118–19)

Jesus' prophetic ministry and the many signs of the Kingdom that accompanied it demonstrated that the advent of the Kingdom completely altered all previously held criteria of greatness. The humble are exalted, and the least become the greatest. Like Moses, the great prophet before him, Jesus came to inaugurate a new era in which the people of God would be constituted on the basis of a new covenant. And the mission of this new people would demand the exercise of the prophetic gift wonderfully demonstrated by Jesus himself.

Priest

It is rather strange that the Old Testament portrayal of the coming Messiah does not contain the priestly rubric. The Messiah is not represented as One who enters into the presence of God on behalf of the people, providing them with access to God and acceptance with God. And yet the letter to the Hebrews is largely devoted to showing that only Jesus could qualify as the perfect bridge between humanity and God. Jesus Christ was fully divine and fully human. Furthermore, Hebrews also shows that Jesus, being sinless, could and did offer himself as an acceptable sin offering to God (9:11–14). Moreover, even now he continues to exercise a priestly function on behalf of his people: "Therefore he is able to save completely those who come to God through him, because he always lives to intercede for them" (7:25). He continually appears in the presence of God on their behalf (9:24).

In the Gospels we encounter a certain hiddenness to Jesus' manifestation of himself as the High Priest of his people. Perhaps this arose from the distorted image conveyed by the priests of his day. Although meticulous in the discharge of all duties pertaining to sacrifice and worship, they were not particularly concerned about the personal welfare of the people they served. They believed they had fulfilled their responsibilities when all formal duties were discharged, whether or not the worshipers derived personal benefit from them. They believed it was God's responsibility—not theirs—to meet the individual needs of the people.

In his ministry Jesus sought none of the prerogatives of the priests who had exclusive control of the sacrificial system. He neither demonstrated nor authorized formal priestly mediation. In his actual contact with people, however, he maintained the heart of the priestly role—approaching God on behalf of others—and, by precept and example, the idea of a ministering priesthood. He demonstrated that Kingdom ministry meant personal interest in others, expressed by intercessory prayer and spontaneous thanksgiving. He prayed that Peter's faith might not fail (Luke 22:31–32). He prayed for his disciples on the night of his crucifixion (22:40). He prayed for his crucifiers while he hung on the cross (23:34). By his example and teaching "official religious status was succeeded by a personal interest and concern for others. In the example of Jesus the priestly function was person-motivated and person-centered" (Mavis 1947: 365). And in his high-priestly prayer on the eve of his passion and death, Jesus prayed for the disciples and for all those who in later centuries would become his disciples (John 17).

King

It was inevitable that Jesus in the Gospels should be presented as the King. Indeed, how could one whose constant preoccupation was the Kingdom of God not be given this Old Testament title of God? The details of his birth are replete with kingly implication (Matt. 2:2; Luke 1:32–33). Some of his parables concerned the relationship between a king and his citizens: the unforgiving servant (Matt. 18:23–35), the marriage feast (22:2–14), and the great judgment (25:31–46). The last time he entered Jerusalem he rode in like a king (cf. Zech. 9:9 with Matt. 21:5). The crowds greeted him as such (Luke 19:38), and the Jews used his claim to kingship to bring him before Pilate (23:1–2).

It is significant that Pilate's first question to Jesus was, "Are you the king of the Jews?" and Jesus replied, "It is as you say" (Matt. 27:11). Some might comment that Jesus' reply was not satisfactory. Actually, it was very astute. Jesus was stating that the question could not be answered with either a yes or a no. William Barclay comments: "It is as if Jesus said that it was verbally correct to call him a king, but that at the same time neither Pilate nor the Jews had even begun to understand what his kingship meant" (1962: 241).

Jesus' trial was followed with an outburst of crude Gentile anti-Semitism. The Roman soldiers abused him, crowned him mockingly, and derided him as "king of the Jews." Pilate's superscription on the cross underscored this hostility (John 19:19–22). And yet Jesus was truly the King of Israel. Nathanael so confessed him (John 1:49). James and John were so convinced of this, they sought his promise of key positions in the coming Kingdom (Matt. 20:21). And in the last day Jesus will be universally acknowledged as King of kings and Lord of lords (Rev. 19:16).

Throughout the popular first year of Jesus' ministry, there were occasions when the crowds wanted to make him their king (John 6:15). This impulse arose when they found he could supply their physical needs (e.g., his miraculous feeding of the five thousand). They reasoned: "Perhaps he can also deliver us from Roman bondage and help us conquer all our enemies." But he refused to found any kingdom on such an understanding of power. His Kingdom was to be founded on love, on reconciliation with God, and on the liberation that only he and not the world could provide (John 8:36).

We might add that Jesus did not teach his disciples to pray that *his* Kingdom come but rather for the Kingdom of his Father (Matt. 6:10). In this connection William Barclay writes:

> Jesus was never the rival to God, but always the servant of God. Though it was his task to announce the Kingdom, in the end the Kingdom is the Kingdom of God. It was the one aim of Jesus to persuade [people] to respond to the love of God, incarnate in Himself, and to enthrone God as King within their hearts and over all the earth. (1962: 244)

Servant

Just before Jesus gave his final upper room instruction to his disciples and instituted the Eucharist, he washed their feet (John 13:1–11). By this act of lowly service he dramatized his role as the unique Servant of God and called his disciples to put servanthood at the heart of their understanding of the ministry (John 13:12–17). In so doing, he underscored the role of the servant as preeminent within the Kingdom of God. He thereby confirmed an Old Testament model. In support of this interpretation, one may review the uniqueness of those under the old covenant who were designated the servants of God: Abraham (Ps. 105:42), Moses (Exod. 14:31), Caleb (Num. 14:24), Joshua (Judg. 2:8), David (2 Sam. 7:5–8), Elijah (2 Kings 10:10), Job (1:8); Isaiah (20:3), and the prophets (2 Kings 21:10). Actually, Israel had been collectively called to become the servant of God on behalf of the nations (Isa. 41:8–10; 42:1–9). Israel's failure to do so remains the great tragedy of the Old Testament.

Since the great essential of all service is obedience, it is not surprising to find Jesus often saying: "My food . . . is to do the will of him who sent me" (John 4:34); "I have come down from heaven not to do my will but to do the will of him who sent me" (John 6:38). By his conduct he exemplified all that Israel should have done under the old covenant and demonstrated all that the church must do under the rubric of the Kingdom of God. Furthermore, he fleshed out in his life and ministry all that Isaiah had prophesied of the coming Messiah (e.g., 52:13–53:12). This means that he not only gladly served people but embraced and carried out the awesome task of reconciling them to God through his life of obedience and his submission to death. For this he was vindicated by God through being raised from the dead (Rom. 4:25).

The uniqueness of Jesus' ministry as the Servant of the Lord is found in his concern for persons. He truly loved people and esteemed them worthy of respect and appreciation because of what they were: bearers of the divine image. He was not "passively intellectual" about this, as many have been down through history. He was outgoing in his serving love toward one and all. As we intimated earlier (chap. 1), Jesus' messianic ministry involved demonstrating the nature of the Kingdom of God by many and varied acts of healing and exorcism. He gave sight to the blind (Mark 8:22–26); restored paralyzed and withered limbs (Mark 3:1–6); cleansed the leprous (Luke 5:12–16); and healed "all who were ill with various diseases, those suffering severe pain, the demon-possessed, those having seizures, and the paralyzed" (Matt. 4:24). Mark's Gospel particularly records his exorcisms: "liberating people from the mysterious grip of evil spirits" (Senior and Stuhlmueller 1983: 149). Accompanied by these acts, the Kingdom Jesus was announcing pointed toward the ultimate end of all evil, sickness, and death. Hence, all his healings and exorcisms have eschatological significance. In a subsequent chapter we will examine the relevance of these signs of the Kingdom to the mission of the church in our day.

Jesus had a capacity for friendship because of his awareness of the solidarity of all people. He did not avoid the touch of sinners; indeed, his contacts with them were so frequent that he was accused of being "a friend of tax collectors and 'sinners'" (Matt. 11:19). Because he knew that most people do not cry out for spiritual help, and because he was convinced that friendship was the best way to gain their confidence, he sought to love and befriend them in order to win them. He never omitted the least act of kindness; he was always alert to human need and aggressive in his response to it. Of the sixty-four recorded instances of his contact with individuals, we find no instance of his sending a person away without giving personal attention to his or her problem and need. The sick, the sinful, the handicapped, the erring, the spiritually needy—all found in him a helpful, loving friend who was primarily concerned that they understand the moral reasons behind their problems.

Jesus inaugurated a new era when he said that his concern was to "seek and to save" people and to work for their moral and spiritual redemption. When he made this normative in the service of God, he was interjecting something new into the history of Israel. Prior to his day there were those, of course, who were motivated by noble concepts of service for the worthy few. But Jesus made his ministry of personal service as broad as human need. He took the best religious practices of the day and reconstructed them to fit his pattern, no longer passivity in the face of suffering, but eager outgoing love. His unique pattern for ministry in the Kingdom age is seen in the fact that he found no "religious" word capable of expressing his idea of service. As a result, he invested a nonreligious term with new meaning. He called his work a *diakonia* (Mark 10:43–45) from the Greco-Roman word for those whose primary duty was "waiting at tables." This term he made central to the total mission of his disciples in the world.

Jesus' Distinctly Mission Roles

In addition to the traditional Old Testament roles that Jesus adopted and modified in his ministry, he also took on himself three new missional roles: evangelist, apostle, and mentor of missionary leaders.

Evangelist

Evangelism is usually defined as all that is involved in bringing men and women into personal encounter with God through faith in Jesus Christ so that he is received as Lord and Savior. This holistic conversion should lead to a movement on the part of the new Christian into the life and worship of the local congregation through the confession of faith in Christ and by submission to baptism. Because we are concerned to keep the dimension of the Kingdom clearly in view, we would underscore the significance of the transfer of authority involved in receiving Jesus Christ (John 1:12–13; 20:31), for this was at the heart of the gospel that Jesus preached.

Consider Jesus' encounter with Saul of Tarsus on the road to Damascus (Acts 26:12–18). On that occasion he commissioned him for apostolic service: to preach the gospel to the Gentiles (Gal. 1:16). Included in this commission was an evangelistic mandate that is most explicit (Acts 26:18). Upon examination we find that it reflects the sequence Jesus himself followed during his earthly ministry in dealing with a wide range of different individuals. All told, this pattern involved the following five successive steps.

"OPEN THEIR EYES."

Because people are blind to the good news of the Kingdom and its King and are only vaguely aware of their true spiritual state, they must first be made conscious of their need. This is illustrated by Jesus' approach to the woman at the well at Sychar (John 4:7–42). In true Kingdom fashion he ignored the racial and religious issues that kept Jews and Samaritans apart and built a bridge of love and understanding to her. His aim was to accept her as one deserving acceptance. He then aroused her interest and created a hunger for his solution to her problem of social and spiritual need. He did this by speaking of living water and then intimated that this living water was a gift of God. This opened her eyes to her need, something of which she had not been previously aware. Inevitably, she desired that he speak further to her heart.

"TURN THEM FROM DARKNESS TO LIGHT."

Jesus then revealed himself as the great, indispensable solution, the true Savior, the all-sufficient God. An examination of the "I am" claims of Jesus in the Gospels show him to be, for example, Power against temptation (John 8:34–36), Peace to the troubled heart (John 14:27), Purpose in life (Matt. 4:19), Presence to the lonely (John 14:18; 16:7), Light to those in darkness (John 8:12), Provision to the needy (Luke 22:35), and Eternal Life to those fearing sickness and death (John

11:25–26). He pardons sin and encourages the weak, but not without first saying: "Follow me." With this invitation, the battle is joined! Note what comes next.

"Turn them from the power of Satan to God."

The good news of the Kingdom has at its heart the offer of newness of life. But there is a condition that must be met before Jesus provides himself as the link to everlasting life. In his evangelistic ministry Jesus called for those who would be his disciples to confess themselves to be sinners before God. Indeed, the first word of his gospel is "Repent!" (Mark 1:15; Acts 20:21). There has to be that judgment of oneself as the sinner expressed by a deliberate dislodging of oneself from the solitary throne in the heart. The woman of Samaria had to be confronted with what she was and confess her sin before she could become the happy recipient of his forgiving mercy (John 4:16–18). There must be a conscious transfer of authority from self to God, or Jesus has no grace to extend. Was this not the problem facing the rich young ruler? He refused to accept Jesus' lordship and was unwilling to share his abundance with the poor. This kept him from entering the Kingdom of God (Luke 18:18–25).

"Receive the forgiveness of sins."

After repentance comes faith. Jesus delighted to pronounce the words of forgiveness to the penitent (cf. Mark 2:5, 9 with Luke 15:7, 10). And yet this great gift had to be appropriated by faith before one could truly enter into the joy of the moral cleansing and personal renewal that he was ready to provide. Indeed, without this faith-wrought experience of having been forgiven and the subsequent experience of peace with God, there will never be the accompanying joy of offering oneself freely in service to God and to one's neighbor.

"Receive a place [inheritance] among those who are sanctified."

A further step of faith is to accept one's relationship to the family of God and enter upon its privileges and responsibilities. Jesus accomplished this by drawing people to himself and making them the members of his new community, the "little flock" to whom he was giving the Kingdom (Luke 12:32). After his resurrection Jesus greatly enlarged this dimension by including in it the missionary mandate. Initially, he called for baptism as the essential initiatory rite into the church. By his grace he also qualified members to begin to appropriate the fullness of each one's "inheritance of the saints in the kingdom of light" (Col. 1:12). It is significant that there is no account of conversion of any individual in Acts in which baptism is not mentioned (8:38; 9:18; 10:48; 16:15, 33).

Apostle

It is rather surprising that in the Gospels Jesus is not designated as "Apostle" (lit., "one who is sent"), although again and again he speaks of himself as the One whom God uniquely sent into the world (twenty-seven times: e.g., Matt. 10:40; Mark 9:37; Luke 10:16; John 3:17). Only the writer to the Hebrews actually uses this designation for Jesus (3:1), even though this title was rather popular in the first century. An *apostolos* (Grk.) was merely a messenger delegated to exercise the power and authority of the body or person who had sent him. In this sense Jesus' role was apostolic and ambassadorial. He had a commission from his Father. He was authorized to speak for God and to act for God, demonstrating his love, mercy, and grace.

Since the Kingdom of God is not solely to be equated with kingly rule or royal power but rather with "a community, a house, an area where the goods of salvation are available and received" (Aalen 1961: 223), we would expect Jesus to give particular attention to the task of training those he would specifically call to serve this Kingdom as keepers of its keys (Matt. 16:19; 18:18; John 20:23). But first he would have to select from his many followers those whom he had equipped to serve in the apostolate with him. These apostles were designated to spearhead the advance of the church into the world after his ascension. Hence, they had to be spiritually equipped, well trained, and willing to submit to Jesus' authority.

The methods Jesus used to produce disciples (that is, those who would accept his teachings) were quite different from the leadership training methods he used to train the apostles. His initial approach was largely personal. But he quickly brought them into the growing circle of those who made up the true Israel of God. He did not smother them with continuous attention. They would be with him for short periods and would then return to their secular employment (John 2:12–13; Luke 5:1–12). Later, as convictions crystallized and an inner group began to consolidate and seek longer periods with him, it became apparent that a selection process for the apostolate had to be implemented. It was roughly toward the end of the second year of his ministry that Jesus designated some followers as apostles and gave them that memorable ordination address (the Sermon on the Mount: cf. Matt. 5:1–7:29 with Luke 6:12–49). Shortly thereafter he began the pattern of withdrawing with the Twelve for periods of extended leadership training. This pattern was more common in his third year, when the crowds began to dwindle despite some of his greatest miracles. A major crisis developed following his feeding the five thousand. As a result many turned back and no longer followed him (John 6:66–71). From then on Jesus became a wanderer and took his disciples to rather remote areas such as the Decapolis, Tyre, Sidon, and then on to Perea, back to Judea, and finally to Jerusalem.

This chronological sequence must be taken seriously, for there were many reasons why Jesus changed both the training methods he used and the content of his instruction. One should draw from this the profound awareness that no one methodology for follow-up ministry or leadership training is normative for all situations. Methods must change because situations change and because spiritual growth itself makes new demands.

Teacher-Trainer

Jesus' overall training method had three basic components: prayer, example, and instruction. Prayer was primary and fundamental. We have hints of the content of his prayers, particularly of his prayers for and with his disciples. Specific details are largely hidden from us, although his intercession on behalf of Peter (Luke 22:31–32) gives us a glimpse into its nature and extent. More apparent was the constant pressure of his consistent example. He was always the embodiment of what he sought to impart. For example, it was the reality of his prayer life that prompted his disciples to ask that he also teach them to pray (Luke 11:1). Their request confirmed to him that they were ready to receive his instruction. Needless to say, he never created artificial situations in order to precipitate periods of instruction. One has but to trace chronologically all the references to prayer in the Gospels, and Jesus' training method will become readily apparent. One will then discover that there is an underlying relation between Jesus' own prayers and his instruction on prayer.

The teachers in Jesus' day taught great truths in a formal fashion and often added so many petty and peripheral rules that basic truths were obscured. Jesus rebuked the rabbis for zealously focusing on unimportant additions to the law of God while overlooking matters of ethical and moral significance. He alluded to Micah 6:8 in his final confrontation with the Jewish leaders and thereby reinforced the Old Testament priorities of doing justice, showing mercy, and walking humbly with God (Matt. 23:23). He was grieved that their concern was with people repeating hallowed formulas and pronouncing sacred shibboleths. In his judgment they were spiritually empty, blind guides of the blind, and hypocrites as well (Matt. 15:14; 23:15–16).

Finally, Jesus called for personal response to truth. There must be action on the part of those who hear. The knowledge of God's will is conditioned upon one's personal obedience (John 7:17). True love for him can only be demonstrated by obedience to his words (Luke 6:46; John 14:21).

We will now review the primary principles Jesus followed in his initial contacts with several who became his disciples. These principles are universally applicable to the training of new converts. They are found in his early Judean ministry (John 1–4).

THE PRIMACY OF RELATIONSHIP (JOHN 1:37–39)

Jesus was willing to adjust his personal schedule to give time to anyone who began to follow him. He was accessible, adaptable, and capable of showing love and attention. He called pliable Peter "a rock," thereby awakening in Peter the expectation of change and transformation in the days ahead. He created this same expectation in Nathanael (vv. 47–49) when he intimated to him that there would be enlargement in his understanding and vision in the days ahead. This pattern of building a relationship through deliberately heightening anticipation is crucial to preparing new Christians to face the future with hope and eagerness. Early in their experience they need to realize that Kingdom service is something dynamic because the Kingdom itself is nothing less than the power of God (1 Cor. 4:20).

THE PROBLEM OF EXPRESSION (JOHN 1:41, 45)

Andrew found Peter and brought him to Jesus. However, when Philip found Nathanael, he ran into trouble. A desire to witness is the inevitable result of personal encounter with Jesus. Andrew's witness was successful because its content was simply, "We have found the Messiah" (v. 41). Philip encountered difficulty because he added that Jesus was the One "Moses wrote about in the law, and about whom the prophets also wrote—Jesus of Nazareth, the son of Joseph" (v. 45). He then found that by identifying the Messiah with Nazareth, he could not answer the question that then rose up in Nathanael's mind. All who encounter Jesus in a vital fashion want to broadcast the news, but most converts soon stop witnessing because they begin to add their own preaching, which frequently takes them beyond their depth. When they cannot answer their questioners, they sometimes lose the initial desire to share their newfound faith. Once a person is clear as to the precise details of his or her new experience and is able to articulate them in a winsome fashion, no one will be able to deny their validity, for their experience will be firmly centered in Jesus Christ, not in any limited understanding of everything that is implied through belonging to Jesus.

THE CONSOLIDATION OF FAITH (JOHN 2:1–11)

The very next day Jesus performed a striking miracle at a marriage feast and thereby consolidated the faith of his disciples (v. 11). We should similarly expect him to do unexpected and surprising deeds (modern equivalents of acts such as changing water into wine) to establish new Christians in our day. Paul spoke of signs and miracles accompanying his ministry (Rom. 15:19). But to minister in this way will take a willingness to explore and risk on the part of the mature Christian. The pattern may be described as follows: as one shares life and experience with a new convert and confidence grows as a result, the convert will begin to disclose the residual problems of his or her former life. In discussing these, encouragement should be given to trust God implicitly for his specific deliverance and victory. In response to the prayer of faith, God often answers in dramatic ways and thereby increases the new convert's faith.

THE COST OF DISCIPLESHIP (JOHN 2:13–17)

How did Jesus begin to reveal to these new disciples what it would cost to follow him? In the incident of the cleansing of the Temple, they were given a vivid picture of what they might expect if they continued their association with him. On this occasion they witnessed Jesus' dramatic action and gained new insight into his indifference to public opinion, his loyalty to Scripture, and his forthrightness in seeking to uphold the unique purpose God had set for his Temple, not a "market" (2:16) but "a house of prayer for all nations" (Mark 11:17). They began to perceive, however dimly, that to continue to follow Jesus could conceivably mean opposition from the religious establishment, exposure to public criticism, and possible suffering. In this particular instance they were more observers than participants. It was Jesus who experienced the hostility of the hierarchy because of his deliberate public confrontation of evil (John 2:18). Older Christians should learn from this example that serious involvement in "making disciples" may often bring them to the place where they become public demonstrations of the truths they are seeking to impart. Paul later observed: "For it has been granted to you on behalf of Christ not only to believe on him, but also to suffer for him" (Phil. 1:29).

The Importance of Evangelism (John 3:1–21; 4:1–26)

The record of Jesus dealing with Nicodemus by night and with the Samaritan woman at the well gives us insight into his indefatigable evangelistic activity. These encounters also provided salutary instruction for the disciples. They observed how he varied his approach, reaching one of Israel's most religious people (Nicodemus in John 3) in contrast with the way he disarmed the prejudices and won a person whom all Jews would automatically regard as an outcast (the woman of Sychar in John 4). His constant faithfulness to the evangelistic task is noteworthy. Indeed, the importance of evangelism needs to be constantly stressed, particularly in our day when it is being downplayed. Only as new converts see older Christians remaining faithful to this task will they themselves gain the poise and confidence they need to share with others their experience of Christ and participate with Jesus in announcing the good news of the Kingdom.

Conclusion

In the weeks and months that followed, Jesus continued to stress these fundamentals. His teaching had an authority, a newness, and a uniqueness that must have fascinated the apostles. Increasingly, he disclosed himself as the Son of God and the Savior of the world. There came a time when he elicited from them the confession that he was the Christ, the Son of the living God (Matt. 16:16). Then he began increasingly to speak of his coming crucifixion in Jerusalem (Matt. 16:21–23). By prayer, example, and instruction he relentlessly pressed upon them the need for living by the confession of sin and by the cross (Matt. 16:24–27). That his teaching was not in vain is demonstrated by the Twelve after Pentecost. From that day onward they moved forward in their missionary discipleship, as the apostle Paul himself confessed: "Thanks be to God, who always leads us in triumphal procession in Christ and through us spreads everywhere the fragrance of the knowledge of him" (2 Cor. 2:14).

The ministry of Jesus was admittedly complex, since he had been sent into the world to accomplish a variety of separate goals. But we would underscore the importance of his preparation of the Twelve for leadership in the missionary community of the Kingdom—the church. True, he had many followers beyond the Twelve, but it is significant that the apostles took hold of this community at Pentecost and provided it with significant direction for the future. The apostles led the community to confess that they no longer belonged to official Judaism. Under the leading of the Holy Spirit and motivated by an entirely new set of principles, they began a ministry among Jews with the deliberate intent of calling them to cease being what they were, to submit to Christ's rule, and to join a new religious reality to which Jews as Jews did not automatically belong. The official religiosity of the Jewish community was wrong and stood condemned by God for having failed to recognize the Messiah when he was in their midst. The apostles never wavered in this conviction. And although total separation eventually took place between those Jews who received him and those who did not, the purpose of God moved forward under his blessing through the apostles whom he had chosen and trained.

13

Jesus Announces the Kingdom among the Nations

Introduction

To appreciate Jesus' didactic instruction regarding the Kingdom, we need to understand the profound pessimism with which postexilic Jews regarded the phenomenon of ongoing history. They were painfully aware that the prophetic voice had long been silent. Perhaps for this reason they saw little significance in the hard and evil times through which they were passing. They only knew the growing hostility and burdensome taxation of the Roman occupation. Even though God seemed remote, they persisted in their conviction that they were a people separate from all other peoples. They doggedly retained the comforting vision of a future day of the Lord when God would vindicate them and punish their enemies. So the present had to be endured, though it was apparently devoid of redemptive significance. But that day was sure to come when God would rise up on their behalf. When that happened, there would be nothing lacking in the completeness of God's victory.

There is a sense in which this Jewish mood of apocalyptic eschatology was in sharp contrast to that generated by the Old Testament prophets. The prophets were always deeply rooted in history and invariably contended that God was at work within the historical processes. They held the present and the future together in eschatological tension (Ladd 1964: 187). Despite their shared pessimism about history, the Jews were anything but united religiously. Four major parties dominated the scene. There were the Zealots, who felt their task was to achieve Israel's political independence through armed struggle. In contrast, the Pharisees saw their task as "making actual the ideal of the Holy People of God through strict observance of the Law," believing that this would prompt God to send the Messiah (Bright 1953: 191). The Essenes withdrew from all others and looked for the abrupt cataclysmic appearance of the Son of Man in clouds and glory to receive his eternal Kingdom (Daniel 7:13–14). Because of the widespread popularity of this apocalyptic yearning, Jesus frequently rebuked those preoccupied with a kingdom about which "people will say, 'Here it is,' or 'There it is'" (Luke 17:21)! Finally, there were the rationalistic Sadducees, who saw Israel's only hope through playing the political game with Rome. They had long since lost interest in any hope of divine deliverance.

All these viewpoints were in sharpest contrast to what the Old Testament actually predicted. They represented a misunderstanding of what the Old Testament so clearly stated: that when the longed-for Hope of Israel would come, he would come as a Suffering Servant who would fulfill the righteousness demanded by the law through his sacrificial obedience. Beyond this, his Kingdom would be markedly different from all popular expectations.

It is rather significant that the proselytizing activity of the Jews among the Gentiles during the first century was devoid of any expression of eschatological significance, even though the summons of the Gentiles to God and their conversion to him is portrayed in the Old Testament in the context of the last day (Isa. 2:2–4; 25:6–8). This dichotomy between the biblical witness and Jewish practice helps us evaluate Jesus' one reference to this outreach: "Woe to you, teachers of the law and Pharisees, you hypocrites! You travel over land and sea to win a single convert, and when he becomes one, you make him twice as much a son of hell as you are" (Matt. 23:15).

Jesus' criticism was focused more on what their proselytizing activity produced rather than on the rightness or wrongness of sharing one's faith with Gentiles. At any event, we know from Jeremias that (1) Jewish missionary zeal was intense (e.g., Rom. 2:17–23); (2) Judaism offered an attractive form of divine worship "towering far above all contemporary cults and systems of religion"; (3) those involved made every possible effort to facilitate the incorporation of Gentiles into Judaism, requiring only circumcision and the observation of the Sabbath and the food laws; and (4) their success was extraordinary, despite the absence of support by the Jewish authorities. Actually, it was carried out solely on the personal initiative of individual Jews in the Diaspora (1982: 12–19).

The Diaspora synagogues granted affiliation to the proselytes who embraced Judaism and were then permitted to marry within the community. The synagogues also allowed the "God-fearers" to join the Jews in worship. These latter were Gentiles who had forsaken their idols, embraced the God of Abraham, submitted to the major commandments of the Old Testament, but stopped short of submitting to circumcision (Goppelt 1970: 81–82). It was these "God-fearers" whom the apostles later found most receptive to the gospel of Jesus Christ (e.g., Acts 10:2; 13:16).

Tomorrow's Kingdom Today

The New Testament uses the language of "the present time," "this [present] world" (Rom. 8:18; 11:5; 2 Tim. 4:10; etc.), and "the coming ages" (Eph. 2:7) to distinguish two separate and distinct periods in its overview of human history. With the coming of Jesus into the world and the accomplishment of his redemptive work, we might say that eschatology invaded history. As a result Christians look back to Christ's inauguration of the Kingdom and realize that it has come quietly, unobtrusively, and secretly. They see in the cross and resurrection Jesus' conquest of Satan and the powers. They are persuaded that through the coming of the Holy Spirit at Pentecost it is possible for them to enter into this spiritual order where Jesus reigns and rules over his people. Theirs is the privilege of enjoying God's tomorrow in the world of today. This is the distinctive component of New Testament eschatology. As Rene Padilla states:

> The Messiah *has* come. The curtain has risen, the last act has begun; all that remains to be fulfilled is the climax of the redemptive drama. Eschatology is not limited to the "end things" of a distant future, the study of which is to be reserved for the final chapter of a theology textbook. The incarnation marks the insertion of a new world into the flow of history; consequently, the "end things" have been made present and there is no longer any chapter of theology lacking an eschatological dimension. (1982: 2)

In this connection it is appropriate to remember Oscar Cullmann's widely used illustration of the present experience of the Kingdom in history with its future realization when every knee will bow and every tongue will confess that Jesus is Lord.

> The decisive battle has already been won. But the war continues until a certain, though not as yet definite, Victory Day when the weapons will at last be still. The decisive battle would be Christ's death and resurrection, and Victory Day his parousia. Between the two lies a short but important span of time already indicating a fulfillment and an anticipation of peace, in which, however, the greatest watchfulness is demanded. Yet it is from the decisive battle now won and the Victory Day yet to be achieved that this span of time gets its meaning and its demands. If this interval of time is given greater and greater extension there will, of course, be consequences that must be described in detail. But the constant factor is from the outset the presence of this tension. This means that I see the general foundation for the whole New Testament in a salvation-historical orientation. This is all the more true as the victory achieved in that decisive battle is understood in retrospect as the obvious consequence and crowning of the preceding events. (1950: 44–45)

Jesus and the Poor

What this means in terms of Jesus' relation to various segments of society will now be explored. We turn first to God's priority: the poor. In our references to the poor in the Old Testament, we stated that the "poor of the Lord" were those who submitted meekly to him and waited faithfully for the saving justice of God. They were not like the rich, living lives of self-indulgence and regarding themselves as self-sufficient. In contrast, the poor knew that justice could only come from God; hence, the messianic hope was vital to them. They awaited "the consolation of Israel" (Luke 1:51–53; 2:8–14, 25–38). They were the true remnant within the nation.

When Jesus formally inaugurated his Kingdom ministry in the synagogue in Galilee by identifying his ministry with the messianic prediction of Isaiah 61, he said that he would preach good news to the poor. This was to be their special privilege (Luke 4:17–19) for "theirs is the kingdom of heaven" (Matt. 5:3). The poor, whether materially deprived or spiritually humble, are hereby regarded as most open to the saving action of Jesus. When he said that the poor were "blessed" or "happy," however, he exposed himself to obvious criticism. Did he mean that the poor should forget their misery? Did he imply that one could only be a true disciple by becoming poor and adopting the lifestyle of the most unfortunate and least successful members of society? Julio de Santa Ana cautions us against canonizing any particular sociological component in society by placing it in a privileged relationship within the Kingdom (1977: 15). However, when he reviews the context of Luke 4 and notes that Isaiah's concern (chap. 61) was for the prisoners, the blind, and the oppressed, he finds Gutierrez particularly helpful. In his judgment Gutierrez perceived most insightfully what was involved in Jesus' inauguration of the Kingdom:

> If we believe that the Kingdom of God is a gift which is received in history, and if we believe . . . that the Kingdom of God necessarily implies the reestablishment of justice in this world, then we must believe that the poor are blessed because the Kingdom of God has begun ("is upon you" Mark 1:15). In other words, the elimination of the exploitation and poverty that prevent the poor from being fully human has begun; a Kingdom of justice which goes even beyond what they could have hoped for has begun. They are blessed because the coming of the Kingdom will put an end to their poverty by creating a world of brotherhood. They are blessed because the Messiah will open the eyes of the blind and will give bread to the hungry. . . . Poverty is an evil and therefore incompatible with the Kingdom of God, which has come in its fulness into history and embraces the totality of human existence. (Gutierrez 1973: 298–99)

In other words, the coming of the Kingdom is to provide a tangible manifestation of God's attitude toward poverty and injustice. His people will grapple with the injustice that brings exploitation and poverty and will be particularly concerned to help the poor and the suffering. It is on this basis that the poor can rejoice.

Only in this light can we adequately understand Jesus' radical demand to the rich young ruler who wanted to follow him. This person could not enjoy the privilege of religious fellowship with Jesus without first taking upon himself the yoke of the Kingdom. He had to sell his possessions, distribute them to the poor (Matt. 19:16–22; etc.), and only then follow Jesus.

Behind this mandate is the fundamental principle of Jesus that "No servant can serve two masters. Either he will hate the one and love the other, or he will be devoted to the one and despise the other. You cannot serve both God and Money" (Luke 16:13). Jesus requires that his disciples be "indifferent to material happiness and to money, to practice self-restraint, to have a mind that values the unseen and eternal more than the seen and temporal, and finally to develop a personality which in its central aim is thoroughly harmonious and unified" (de Santa Ana, quoting Troeltsch 1977: 25). By deliberately rejecting the accumulation of wealth and utilizing what one has to help the poor, one is giving tangible expression to the new orientation that the good news of the Kingdom has demanded. The apostle Paul did not use Kingdom language when he expressed this, but what he said in this connection is transparently clear: "Therefore, if anyone is in Christ, he is a new creation; the old has gone, the new has come!" (2 Cor. 5:17). This is the new order of selflessness and sacrificial concern for the underprivileged. Because of this, the poor can rejoice. Their lot will be changed. It is tragic that this element of Kingdom obligation and expectation has been so neglected by the church. We are grateful to liberation theologians who call upon the church to face this neglect as the gulf steadily widens in our day between the rich and the poor.

Jesus and the Gentiles

There is every possibility that Jesus was in frequent contact with non-Jews during his earthly ministry. In Jerusalem, Judea, and the countryside surrounding the Sea of Galilee, it would have been almost impossible for him to avoid them. And yet he deliberately confined his mission to "the lost sheep of Israel" and asserted that this limitation had been defined for him by his Father (Matt. 15:24). As the messianic Son of David, his primary task was to serve his own people (Ezek. 34:23–24). And yet the Gospels occasionally record his ministering to Gentiles (e.g., the Syrophoenician woman of Mark 7:24–30, the Roman centurion of John 4:46–53, and the Gadarene demoniacs of Matt. 8:28–34). Because these encounters involved healings, Jeremias sees them as foreshadowing the day of the Lord: "When Jesus heals, his act has eschatological significance and is always the sign and pledge of the breaking in of the Messianic Age, an anticipatory participation in its blessings" (1982: 28).

During the third year of his ministry when the tragedy of being rejected by his own people was becoming more acute, Jesus left Galilee and entered the region of Tyre (Mark 7:24, 31). Was he withdrawing from their hostility in order that he might devote more time to teaching the Twelve? Or was he returning to areas where earlier his ministry had been eagerly received (Mark 3:7–8)? We cannot be sure what motivated him. It appears that even in those Gentile areas Jesus still focused his ministry particularly on the Jews. We have no evidence that Jesus ever deliberately turned away from his own people to minister to the Gentiles. The apostle Paul confirmed this, for he explicitly stated that Jesus "has become a servant of the Jews on behalf of God's truth, to confirm the promises made to the patriarchs" (Rom. 15:8). He never was a servant to the uncircumcised during his earthly ministry.

Furthermore, Jesus forbade his disciples prior to Easter to minister to non-Jews. "Do not go among the Gentiles or enter any town of the Samaritans. Go rather to the lost sheep of Israel" (Matt. 10:5–6). This instruction was subsequently underscored when he pointed to the possibility of their being persecuted by other Jews. When this occurred, they were not to go to the Gentiles but to other Jewish villages: "You will not finish going through the cities of Israel before the Son of Man comes" (Matt. 10:23).

However, in the Olivet Discourse (Matt. 24–25 and Mark 13) Jesus envisages his disciples bearing witness worldwide to the good news of the Kingdom and predicts that the completion of this task will make possible the coming of the Messiah "with great power and glory." Admittedly, this discourse is tremendously complex, for in it Jesus spoke of first-century events: the destruction of the Temple and the scattering of the Jewish people. He also gave specific details of the last day, when his people would be gathered from the four corners of the earth and when the Kingdom of God would finally come to full manifestation (Mark 13:14–31). In addition, he warned of the problems his people would face during the long interval prior to that glorious return. Efforts would be made to deceive and defile them, to divide and destroy them. And yet they were never to forget the primary task: "the gospel must first be preached to all nations" (13:10).

Furthermore, the Holy Spirit would be given to them to provide utterance and wisdom, that their witness might make an effective contribution to the ongoing redemptive purpose of God (13:9–13). Jesus concluded by stating that to each one of his people specific tasks would be given along with the spiritual authority (*exousia*) that they would need in the inevitable cosmic struggle this worldwide task would involve (13:34).

Matthew gives the same sequence of events (24:3–14, 29–31, 46–51) in response to the request of the disciples for "the sign" of Jesus' coming and of the close of the age. From this we may conclude that visible signs of the Kingdom in the world today will primarily include those efforts by Christians to proclaim the gospel to this generation, to persuade people everywhere to be reconciled to God, and to accompany this message with victories over demonic power. Indeed, their witness may even be accompanied by the sort of "signs and miracles" (Rom. 15:19) that accompanied the witness of the apostles in the first century.

With the death and resurrection of Jesus, the day of the Lord began to dawn as a historic period (Martens 1981: 125–30). Following his ascension and the sending of the Holy Spirit on the day of Pentecost, his people began to proclaim his resurrection triumph and confess his lordship in Jerusalem. But they did not confine their witness to Jerusalem. They went to Judea, then Samaria, and on to the Gentile world. All this marked the beginning of the Christian mission: the confrontation of the nations with the final manifestation of God's free grace.

This thesis is further strengthened by noting that Jesus deliberately removed any reference to the day of judgment (the divine vengeance) from his inaugura-tion of the Kingdom message in the synagogue in Nazareth (Luke 4:18–19). It is true that when he pointedly told the Syrophoenician woman that it was "not right to take the children's bread and toss it to their dogs" (Mark 7:27), he was putting considerable distance between Israel and the Gentile nations. And yet even at that juncture in his ministry he was devoid of any feelings of superiority or hatred toward the Gentiles. By contrast, he treated both Samaritans and Gentiles with courtesy and grace. In this he was the antithesis of the Messiah of Jewish expectation. Jesus' deliberate silence about God's vengeance on the Gentiles is what infuriated the Jews and made them seek to destroy him (Luke 4:24–30; see also Jeremias 1982: 44–46).

We need to keep in mind that Jesus never deviated from this position throughout the remainder of his earthly ministry. Rather, he assigned the Gentiles a place in the Kingdom of God and kept calling the Jews to repentance lest they be excluded from it (Matt. 11:22–24; 12:41–42; 25:31–46; etc.). God's redemptive purpose was not irrevocably tied to Israel. Jesus is the Son of Man, not just a son of Israel. He is the Prince of Peace for all peoples (Zech. 9:9–10). He is the Servant of the Lord, who brings light to all nations (Isa. 31:6; 49:6; Luke 2:31–32).

So then, many of Jesus' sayings about the Gentiles can and should primarily be seen in the light of the Old Testament prophetic witness. He emphasized the thesis that there will be an eschatological banquet in which the Gentiles will be prominent, coming from all corners of the globe and sitting down with the patriarchs in the Kingdom (Matt. 8:11–12). The goal of their pilgrimage will be God, and a heavenly Zion will be the appointed place where they finally encounter him. Then it will be revealed that there is only one inheritance and only one people of God, whether called from Israel or from the Gentiles. And there will be but one banquet: one representation of the universal character of the Kingdom of God. Jeremias rightly concludes:

> The reason why Jesus came to Israel was precisely because his mission concerned the whole world. That is to say, his announcement of salvation to Israel, just as much as His vicarious death, was at the same time an act of service to the Gentiles. Both took place in order that the incorporation of the Gentiles into the Kingdom of God might be possible. (1982: 73)

But we would add that Jesus' offering of the Kingdom to Israel was the precondition of his death for God's people, whether Jews or Gentiles. Moreover, his death rendered the eschatological ingathering certain. Even so, it was necessary that the Holy Spirit come upon the believing disciples at Pentecost. Only then could the people of the new age be brought into being and the "already" of the Kingdom of God begin its movement toward the nations.

Jesus and the Church

Jesus' ministry was not exhausted in his obedience to the law, his parables, his acts of kindness, his exorcisms and healings, and his instruction on the Kingdom of God. In a message sent to Herod ("that fox"), he explicitly stated: "I will drive out demons and heal people today and tomorrow, and on the third day I will reach my goal. . . . For surely no prophet can die outside Jerusalem" (Luke 13:32–33). By this statement Jesus identified his coming death with his prophetic proclamation that the Kingdom of God had come through his person and ministry. It was by statements such as these that Jesus understood his ministry as fulfilling the Servant of the Lord motif (Isa. 61:1). Furthermore, his identification of Jerusalem as the place of his death would seem to indicate his awareness that his crucifixion would be the decisive event in human history. As Reginald Fuller states: "Jerusalem is the place of revelation, the center from which the redemptive activity of God is to go forth to the world, and therefore the death of Jesus is to be the culmination of the sacred history of God's dealings with his people" (1954: 64). Apparently, only by the cross could the coming of the Kingdom be fully realized.

With the confession of Peter at Caesarea Philippi, a significant shift took place in the ministry of Jesus. Mark records five separate statements thereafter in which Jesus predicted his coming death (8:31; 9:12, 31; 10:33–34). The prospect filled his mind. But rather than draw back he resolutely "set out for Jerusalem" that there he might fulfill the role of the Suffering Servant (Isa. 53; Luke 9:51, 53). He allowed nothing to deter him, for he was convinced that his coming death would be the means whereby his Father would inaugurate in power the reign of God among his people.

Naturally, this brings us to the Last Supper and the institution of the Eucharist. When Jesus picked up the bread, blessed it, and broke it, his interpretation was: "This is my body." When he took up the cup, his interpretation was: "This is my blood of the covenant, which is poured out for many." He then concluded with an eschatological prospect: "I tell you the truth, I will not drink again of the fruit of the vine until that day when I drink it anew in the kingdom of God" (Mark 14:22–25). His body broken and his blood poured out spoke of his impending death. His reference to a covenant awakened memories of the Servant of the Lord, given as a "covenant for the people" (Isa. 42:6; 49:8). In fact, in two of the Servant Songs of Isaiah where this phrase appears, the context is that the Servant is "a light for the Gentiles" (42:6). He will gather his own "from afar . . . from the north, some from the west," for it is God's intention that his salvation might reach to "the ends of the earth" (49:6, 12). Once again, we are face-to-face with the universal and redemptive concern of God for a redeemed people drawn from all the nations. In the Gospels no other explanation for the cross is given (R. Fuller 1954: 67). And by these symbolic actions at the Last Supper, Jesus instituted a new covenant with his disciples as representative of the true Israel, the ongoing people of God.

What was to follow the crucifixion and resurrection would be a new community, the church. Some scholars challenge the thesis that it was Jesus' plan to create a new faith community, the church, to function in the interval between his resurrection and the final consummation of the Kingdom. However, we are deeply persuaded that the canonical text speaks otherwise. And the data is extensive. Jesus intended to form "a new religious community, with a new way of life, a fresh and startling message, and an unparalleled consciousness of inheriting the divine promises made to Israel of old" (Flew 1960: 18).

In his precrucifixion instruction on the church, Jesus had to counter the revolution-minded Zealots. They were drawn to him because they too looked for the coming rule of God. But he was repelled by their conviction that only by taking the initiative and precipitating a violent break with Rome could liberation come to Israel. Jesus rejected violent resistance activity as contravening the absolute justice and love that were the main pillars of his Kingdom. As Cullmann remarks: "Jesus was concerned only with the conversion of the individual and was not interested in a reform of social structures" (1970: 55). Of course, this does not mean that he would not have his people concerned with improving all social structures. He is burdened for the humanization of society. We will return to this subject later.

What concerns us here is the relation between the church—this interim community—and the Kingdom of God. Jesus never equated them. When he used the term *basileia*, the dominant meaning he poured into it was of the order of "kingly rule" or "sovereignty" or "kingship." In this he went beyond the rabbinic literature of his day that equated "taking the yoke of the Kingdom of God on oneself" with acknowledging God as King and Lord. Whereas only 15 percent of Jesus' usages of the term *kingdom* have any reference to a domain or community over which the rule of God is exercised, we should not downplay this fact. He speaks of receiving the Kingdom, entering it, belonging to it, shutting the Kingdom against people, and even using keys to open it (Matt. 23:13; 16:19; Mark 10:14–15; Luke 11:52). We should also consider Jesus' much-debated statement about John the Baptist: "Among those born of women there has not risen anyone greater than John the Baptist; yet he who is least in the kingdom of heaven is greater than he" (Matt. 11:11). This statement did not mean that Jesus was excluding John from the final glorious consummation of the Kingdom and the eschatological banquet when the people of God are gathered from the nations (Luke 13:24). It seems, rather, to refer to the present expression of the Kingdom in Jesus Christ.

On the basis of Jesus' explicit teaching, there is not a great deal of evidence that he had the church in mind. But when we examine the things that he did, it appears clear that he was laying the groundwork for a mission-oriented community that would deliberately penetrate society after his pattern of seeking and saving the lost (Luke 19:10). He impressed on this community the priority of consciously responding to his kingly rule so that by proclamation and persuasion its members might increasingly draw others into their life and service (1 John 1:3). He provided for the community's structure and for its worship. Never did he suggest that this community not be a witnessing, serving, and growing presence among the nations.

The primary task of Jesus in the midst of a largely defiled and unbelieving Israel was to call out the remnant that had a heart for God and his righteousness. Those who responded were brought under the kingly rule of God. That he chose twelve of his disciples to become apostles strengthens the impression that they were indeed the beginning of a true Israel. To them he said: "Do not be afraid, little flock, for your Father has been pleased to give you the kingdom" (Luke 12:32). To them he also gave the rudiments of a corporate structure and a pattern of spiritual worship.

Old Israel was facing judgment, and its temple would soon be destroyed. The new Israel was emerging, and a "new building was being erected through his own work, with living men and women as its stones" (Flew 1960: 38–42; see Mark 14:58; 1 Peter 2:4–5).

A secondary task facing Jesus was the need to teach his growing band of disciples the manner in which they were to conduct themselves in the world. They would represent "the upside-down Kingdom." That is, their lifestyle would be just the opposite of "the conventionally accepted values, norms and relationships of ancient Palestinian society and of modern culture today" (Kraybill 1978: 24). And because of the variety of subjects Jesus included in his teaching, we must conclude that he was interested in all aspects of human civilization. Furthermore, because Jesus spoke of future judgment and other eschatological matters, we must likewise conclude that he was providing a basis for the ethical conduct of his disciples in the interim period before the last day. He made full provision for holy and victorious living. When his disciples found that even the demons were "to submit" to them "in [his] name," Jesus rejoiced (Luke 10:17, 21). It was he who had given them "authority to trample on snakes and scorpions and to overcome all the power of the enemy," and that nothing should hurt them (Luke 10:19).

Further support for the thesis that Jesus deliberately intended to build his church during the long interval between his first and second advent is to be found in the disclosure of himself as the Messiah of God's people. This meant that

> a new allegiance was entering the world, disturbing all traditions, transcending the former familial loyalties of kindred and home, and destined to outlive all other totalitarian claims, whether those of Caesar in the early centuries, or those of caste and nationality and Communism in the twentieth. (Flew 1960: 56–57)

This implies Jesus' awareness of a lengthy period prior to the coming of the Kingdom. How else can one understand his explicit statement about leaving house, family, children, or lands for his sake and the gospel's and securing a hundredfold "in this present age" with persecutions and in the world to come "eternal life" (Mark 10:29–30)? The establishment of a missionary community committed to the task of proclaiming worldwide the good news of the Kingdom was not an imaginary alternative that suggested itself to some disappointed followers of Jesus when they realized that the fullness of the Kingdom was not likely to come in their lifetime.

We must also take into consideration the specific dimensions of the Old Testament portrayal of the messianic reign in which peace and salvation will be published (Isa. 52:7), glad tidings will be preached to the poor (Isa. 61:1), and God's glory will be declared among the nations (Isa. 66:19). When Jesus referred to his preaching and that of his disciples, he made it constitutive of his messianic community. His gospel was the Word of God. It had inherent power. It created faith. No one should be ashamed of either Jesus or his Word. After all, his gospel was the announcement of the Kingdom of God. All those resistant to his will would incur divine judgment in the last day (Mark 8:38). But those who receive him and submit to his kingly rule are promised participation in his eternal salvation, whether they are Jews or Gentiles (Matt. 18:1–13; John 1:12–13; 10:16, 27–30).

In this connection the fact that Jesus twice cleansed the Temple, both at the outset of his ministry and at the beginning of the Passion Week, likewise bears on the establishment of an interim community (Mark 11:15–17; John 2:13–22). This was a messianic act in that Jesus' objective was to purify Israel's worship. However, we would underscore the fact that it was the Court of the Gentiles that the Jews had transformed into a barnyard and a place of merchandise. Furthermore, they rigorously excluded Gentiles from this area. In his denunciation of Jewish parochialism, Jesus reminded the people that the divine intention was that the Temple be "a house of prayer for all nations" (Isa. 56:7; Mark 11:17). Since some have argued convincingly that this messianic act marked "the beginning of the eschatological renewal of the world" (Hahn 1965: 28), it is reasonable to conclude that the stage was being set for an age in which Gentiles would pray to the God of Abraham, Isaac, and Jacob. This conclusion is strengthened when one realizes that Jesus' acts of cleansing were rejected by the religious establishment. The leaders regarded his challenge as the act of a rustic upstart. They did not see any need either for religious renewal or for their acceptance of his assertion that the reign of God was present. Obviously, old Israel was proving faithless, and the true Israel was emerging, based on the Messiah, not on the Temple, and confirmed by a new covenant represented by the cross.

There is another group of activities of Jesus that contribute to the idea that an extended church age was in his mind. It concerns the missionary stance he gave to his little flock. When Jesus called people to himself his words were: "Follow me . . . and I will make you fishers of men" (Matt. 4:19). With this he called individuals into vital relationship with himself. He also imparted to them a concept of evangelistic outreach largely foreign to their mandated service under the old covenant. The record states that "calling the Twelve to him, he sent them out two by two and gave them authority over evil spirits" (Mark 6:7). He even organized evangelistic campaigns (the mission of the Twelve in Matt. 10:1–23 and of the Seventy in Luke 10:1–20). Furthermore, he gave them his own credentials: "He who receives you receives me, and he who receives me receives the one who sent me" (Matt. 10:40). Obviously, relationship to Jesus meant involvement in his mission. The empowering of his disciples to exorcise demons and heal the sick, as well as to preach the gospel of the Kingdom, gave eschatological overtones to their mission (Isa. 35:3–10). This authority marked the dawning of a new age: "Lord, even the demons submit to us in your name" (Luke 10:17)! A new community was truly coming into being, and there can be no doubt that it was to be a missionary community.

In his extensive development of the idea of the church in the mind of our Lord, Flew deliberately leaves to the end any discussion of the two passages in the Gospels where the word ekklēsia is found (1960: 35–38). We heartily concur with this approach. It enables us to keep central Jesus' teaching of the Kingdom.

Furthermore, it strengthens the need for keeping the Kingdom separate from the church. As Flew observes:

> The Basileia creates a community, and uses a community as an instrument. Those who enter the Basileia are in the Ecclesia; the Ecclesia lives beneath the kingly rule of God, acknowledges it, proclaims it, and looks for its final manifestation, but the Ecclesia is not itself the Basileia. Since the church is gathered under God's rule, death will have no power over it. (1960: 91)

The word *ekklēsia* is used twice by Matthew. Inasmuch as the context of 18:17 concerns the disciplinary process that is to be followed within the community (18:15–35), it substantiates what we have said earlier about Jesus' provision of the interim community. Of greater interest to us is the missionary dimension arising from Peter's witness to the messiahship of Jesus (16:13–20). Jesus responded to this spontaneous confession with joy, for he could perceive that God had granted this insight into the mystery of the hiddenness of the reign of God. More importantly, he went on to state that on Peter he would build his church and that it would be an irresistible and dynamic presence in the world over which death would not prevail.

Dismiss all efforts to regard "the rock" as something separate from Peter (e.g., his confession), for this cannot be linguistically sustained. True, the church is built upon the apostles and prophets (Eph. 2:20), and Jesus is its essential foundation (1 Cor. 3:11). Peter is but one of many "living stones" that make up the growing edifice (1 Peter 2:4–6). And yet Peter is singled out to occupy the primary position of authority in the new community. True, Acts does not indicate that his leadership was of long duration. Although Peter was prominent in the community prior to Pentecost (1:15) and its spokesman to the Jews (2:14) and to the Gentiles (10:1–11:18) afterward, as well as active in disciplinary matters (5:3–6), it was James who eventually became its chief administrator (15:7, 13–21).

Jesus granted Peter the keys of the Kingdom (Matt. 16:19). This does not mean that Peter thereby gained the exclusive right to admit persons into the church and to excommunicate any from its fellowship. The metaphor of "keys" was used elsewhere by Jesus to represent the sort of knowledge that makes entrance into the Kingdom possible. One recalls how he rebuked the lawyers for taking away "the key to knowledge" and preventing people from entering into the blessing of God (Luke 11:52).

When we recall the authority Jesus granted the Twelve and the Seventy prior to sending them forth on evangelistic tours, we have something comparable to Peter's being given the keys. He opened the door of revelation to the Jews at Pentecost (Acts 2) and to the Gentiles in Caesarea (Acts 10). Those who accepted Peter's message and submitted to Peter's Lord, whether Jew or Gentile, entered thereby the Kingdom. His authority was of the "binding" or "loosing" sort and was intimately related to his preaching, far more than to any disciplinary authority he may have exercised during the course of his ministry, such as his encounter with Ananias and Sapphira (Acts 5:3–11). So then, a good case can be made for affirming that the keys of the Kingdom are not the exclusive possession of Peter, but belong to all Christians who faithfully confess Jesus as Lord (see also John 20:23). The mission given to Peter and to the other apostles is nothing less than "the age-long mission of the church of God, to carry the divine revelation to [humankind]" (Flew 1960: 97).

The Kingdom and the Church

It may seem paradoxical that whereas Jesus summoned men and women to receive the Kingdom, the apostles regarded those who responded as members of the church and heirs of the promises made to Israel (Rom. 4:13–15; Titus 3:7; James 2:5; etc.). This fact raises the issue of the relationship of the Kingdom to the church. Actually, when Jesus called people to repent and follow him (Luke 9:23), he provided the normative witness for the church for all time. This essential call to conversion meant that God's reign (the new age) could be accepted inwardly by simple childlike obedience. Since the Kingdom of God had entered the human situation through Jesus and brought people into direct confrontation with him, to open one's heart to Jesus' person and mission means that the Kingdom of God becomes dynamically active in one's life. Although the one responding is not automatically transformed and translated into the future age of consummation when God makes all things new (Rev. 21:5), this encounter does involve upheaval. "The Kingdom of God acts powerfully and requires a powerful reaction" (paraphrase of Matt. 11:12).

This means that the church is nothing less than the missionary people of the Kingdom of God. The church does not establish the Kingdom. It is rather the custodian of the good news of the Kingdom. It bears witness to the fact that the Kingdom has already been set up by its King. In all the New Testament there is "no brave talk of . . . ushering in His Kingdom—not so much as a syllable" (Bright 1953: 234). Nor does the New Testament encourage Christians to identify their ecclesiastical structures with the Kingdom. They dare not fall prey to the temptation to mark the advance of the Kingdom merely in terms of institutional growth. Actually, only "the church which is his body" (Eph. 1:22–23) constitutes the people of the Kingdom, but local congregations and denominations, still in this world, are not the Kingdom. They are but mixtures of the true and the false, always under the judgment of God, always in need of spiritual renewal and the deepening of commitment to the missionary priority. This age is not for ecclesiastical self-deification but for the proclamation of the gospel of the Kingdom. And it is the age in which Christians should never cease to pray: "Thy Kingdom come!"

What then is the specific relationship between the church and the Kingdom? We have stated that the church is the true Israel, God's covenant and servant people, called to be a sign of the many-faceted righteousness/justice of the Kingdom before the world and seeking through the gospel to draw people into its covenant fellowship. And we have argued that the Kingdom, in contrast, represents the dynamic activity of God and the sphere in which his rule is experienced. K. E. Skydsgaard summarizes their interrelation in the following fashion:

> The Kingdom of God is the conception placed above that of the church; the church is not the Kingdom of God, but the church owes her existence to the Kingdom of God. She exists for the sake of the Kingdom; she represents the Kingdom of God on earth in the present age till through the coming of Christ in power God will grant full and final victory. In the Kingdom of God the church has her ultimate frontiers; from the Kingdom she receives all her substance, her power and hope. (1951: 386)

So then, we should regard the Kingdom of God as God's history in the midst of the ongoing record of the history of the human race. It is woven into it but remains clearly separate from it. The biblical conception of history presupposes a deep gulf between God and Satan, between Christ and Antichrist (Skydsgaard 1951: 388). Since the church is never the ultimate end of history but is always oriented to the Kingdom of God, which is the ultimate end, its interim character is clearly evident. Indeed, the church draws its significance from the Kingdom. Furthermore, the ongoing of the Kingdom in history gives purpose and meaning to history itself. It is this dynamic historical-prophetic-eschatological character of the Kingdom that should make us impatient with a static church preoccupied with its own piety and salvation.

Conclusion

Ladd concludes his discussion of the Kingdom and the church by stating five postulates: (1) The church is not the Kingdom; it is only the people of the Kingdom; (2) The Kingdom creates the church; had it not come into the world by the mission of Jesus, there would never have been the church; (3) The church witnesses to the Kingdom through proclaiming God's redeeming acts in Christ, both past and future; (4) The church is the instrument of the Kingdom in that the works of the Kingdom are performed through its members as through Jesus himself; and (5) The church is the custodian of the Kingdom; through its proclamation of the gospel throughout the world, God will decide who will enter the eschatological Kingdom and who will be excluded (1964: 111–19).

We conclude by affirming what the New Testament teaches everywhere: It is not in the power of persons themselves to effect their own salvation or to perfect human society. History cannot save itself. This is written large over the biblical view of humanity in this world. But in Jesus Christ, God has so decisively acted in history that "the consummation of the Kingdom, although breaking into history, will itself be beyond history, for it will introduce a redeemed order whose actual character transcends both historical experience and realistic imagination" (Ladd 1964: 333). As Bright has summarized:

[The church] is a missionary people—if she is not that, she is not the church. Her gospel declares that the salvation of man lies only in the Kingdom of God, and that salvation she announces to the world . . . and summons men to it. . . . The redemption of man awaits precisely the birth of a new and redeemed race of men. And the Kingdom of God is the new race of men, God's living church. In her is that ever-coming Kingdom. (1953: 217–18)

Inasmuch as this picture of future triumph is related to the witness of the church among the nations today, biblically oriented Christians must jealously guard the primary essentialness of this task. Salvation today means preaching the good news of the Kingdom. Nothing can have higher priority for the "eschatological community" caught in the tension between proclaiming that the Kingdom of God has come and simultaneously looking for the Kingdom that is yet to come. This community understands itself to be caught in the midst of a cosmic struggle. Whenever it contends for the truth committed to its keeping, whenever it performs Christlike deeds among people, whenever it witnesses to the gospel, it is participating in the ongoing of the Kingdom of God among women and men. This is its mission. And this understanding of God's mission leads us to examine more thoroughly Jesus' teaching about Kingdom mission, the subject of the next chapter.

14

Jesus Proclaims
God's Kingdom Mission

Introduction

Luke tells us that in the interval between the resurrection and the ascension, Jesus both confirmed the reality of his victory over death ("gave many convincing proofs") and gave "instructions through the Holy Spirit." But he adds that all this was under the rubric of speaking "about the kingdom of God" (Acts 1:2–3). We should underscore this orientation when we ponder the mandate for mission that Jesus gave "to the apostles he had chosen," for it dominates his postresurrection ministry. The apostles were given this mandate particularly because the leaders of the Christian movement were responsible for mobilizing the church members to this priority task.

What an epochal event the resurrection was. Jesus had predicted that some of his disciples would not taste death until they had seen the Kingdom come with power (Mark 9:1). The resurrection was certainly the central demonstration of that power. In fact, Paul would later affirm that the full significance of Jesus' lordship and his sonship was only realized as a direct result of this mighty victory (Rom. 1:4). According to Karl Barth, the empty tomb along with the "visible, audible and touchable body of Jesus constitutes an absolutely unique event . . . the presence of the eschaton . . . which has laid the foundation of and given shape to the faith of the emerging Christian community" (1961: 56–57).

In the postresurrection appearances of our Lord, the focus is not on the disciples' reflection on this new situation. Their growing awareness of the salvific significance of Jesus' victory doubtless began to increase their assurance of personal salvation. But Jesus quickly moved beyond this to call their attention to what the resurrection made possible: mission to the nations.

Karl Barth emphasized the intimate and unvarying correlation in Scripture between calling and commissioning; divine election invariably entails specific service (1962: 577–92). "The calling of [people] by God and to God [involves] the commissioning and sending of the called [ones], and sees [them] set in a function to be exercised between God and [others], . . . between God and the world" (1962: 593). Those who witnessed the resurrection triumph and who heard Jesus describe his crucifixion as crucial to the redemptive work of God were called to participate with God in the task of making this resurrection message known throughout the world. Everyone who has been called by the good news of the Kingdom must make the task of proclaiming its message and demonstrating its reality his or her primary concern. This involves establishing the lordship of God in the world and serving the righteousness of his Kingdom, or what Karl Barth calls "establishing what is right" in the light of the Kingdom's coming (1962: 593; see also Scott 1978: 19; Matt. 6:33).

Any study of the Great Commission should be related to, but kept distinct from, the lesser commissions Jesus earlier issued (to the Twelve and the Seventy: Matt. 10:1, 5–42; Luke 9:1–6; 10:1–20). In these commissions Jesus spoke of the duties and trials that all who are involved in any missionary movement inevitably have to embrace. We can well imagine that during his postresurrection ministry Jesus restated some of these basic elements. Perhaps this accounts in part for the various ways in which he pressed home the comprehensive nature of this vast and complicated task. In any event, the evangelists vary considerably in their articulation of its details. In this connection Karl Barth wisely affirms:

> These narratives are recounted not in the style of history, but, like the story of creation, in the style of historical saga. Their content bars any attempt at harmonizing. All these narratives deal no doubt with a common subject and are in basic agreement. Yet each one of them needs to be read independently, as a unique testimony of God's decisive word and intervention at the turning point of the eons. Quite obviously each narrative needs to be consulted to clarify the others. (1961: 57)

Thus although the Great Commission is the climax of the earthly instruction of Jesus, this in itself does not make the Christian movement a missionary faith. This movement has its source in God, whose gracious redemptive purpose through Christ was "to reconcile to himself all things, whether things on earth or things in heaven, by making peace through his blood, shed on the cross" (Col. 1:20). It is entirely because of the dynamic leading and empowering of the Holy Spirit that what might be called the "true" Israel became a missionary presence reaching out to the nations. But the Great Commission was needed to remove all doubt, to end all disputation, and to bring into clear focus what the mission of the church really is. So that we might grasp it more fully, we will follow a probable chronological sequence of Jesus' separate statements.

John 20:19–23: The Awesome Analogy

To the sorrowing disciples, the events of Calvary provoked the darkest thoughts. Were their lives also in danger? Their first intimations of the resurrection did not automatically remove all fear. It should not surprise us that on that first Easter we would find them behind barred doors in an upper room in Jerusalem. But suddenly, Jesus stood in their midst and allayed their fears with the words: "Peace be with you!" Although startled at first, they soon awakened to the full realization of his victory over death. In joyous response to his invitation they began to examine the marks of his crucifixion: "his hands and side." The atmosphere became relaxed. Then, as if Jesus anticipated a change in their demeanor, he repeated: "Peace be with you!" and followed with the staggering analogy: "As the Father has sent me, I am sending you."

We can imagine that the disciples were taken by surprise and by sudden apprehension: "Do you mean that we too are to be crucified? Is that horrible death for us also?" Jesus gave them no explanation. Rather, he breathed on them in a fashion reminiscent of the climax of God's creative action in Genesis 2:7 and then said: "Receive the Holy Spirit."

Jesus was issuing a renewed call to cross-bearing discipleship. He was saying that such discipleship is impossible without the aid of the Holy Spirit (even Jesus needed the Spirit when he faced Calvary, Heb. 9:14). His "sending" analogy lifted the missionary mandate to the level of the sublime. They were being sent forth into the world in mission in a fashion analogous to his being sent by his Father into the world to redeem it. Forty-four times in the Gospel of John Jesus alluded to his being sent by the Father, and he intimately identified himself with the Father in all that he said and did (John 8:29, etc.). It now becomes apparent that his presiding presence will be integral to the worldwide mission of the church. Ferdinand Hahn observes that this first statement of the Great Commission is linked with the "sending" dimension of the Spirit. This means that

> the work of the disciples is to be joined even more directly to that of the exalted Lord himself, so that both are seen as one. It is the eschatological harvest, in which the sower and reaper rejoice together, although they are separated. (1965: 159; see also John 4:35–38)

The primary concern of this mission is the sins of people. "If you forgive anyone his sins, they are forgiven; if you do not forgive them, they are not forgiven" (John 20:23). The disciples are herewith empowered in Jesus' name to be the agents of the remission or retention of sin. They will have the intrinsic authority to declare that forgiveness is available to sinners on the basis of his sin-bearing death. And since the Holy Spirit indwells all the people of God in the true Israel, we should conclude that this authority is not confined to the ordained clergy. Rather, all those who have experienced the new birth and possess the Holy Spirit have that same authority on the basis of this commission (John 3:5; Acts 13:38–39; Rom. 8:9–10).

Luke 24:44–49: The Crucial Message

Luke provides us with vivid accounts of two appearances of the resurrected Christ: on the road to Emmaus (24:13–35) and in Jerusalem (24:36–44). On these two occasions Jesus sought to reverse the momentum of their unbelief (24:25, 38) by appealing to the testimony of their senses ("touch . . . see"), their reason ("a ghost does not have flesh and bones"), their common sense (he "took . . . and ate"), and their memory ("what I told you while I was still with you"). Furthermore, by offering himself as a hermeneutical key to the Old Testament (24:25–27) and by focusing deliberately on its predictions of the Messiah's death, he set the pattern and framework for the persistent and original use of the Old Testament that one encounters throughout the New Testament.

Jesus deliberately underscored the importance of the missionary task by deliberately relating it to his death. Although Luke frequently uses the verb "must" in relation to the divine necessity that dominated the life of Jesus (e.g., 2:49; 4:43; 9:22; 13:33), its most notable use is in the pericope concerning the Great Commission. Was it necessary for the Messiah to be crucified? Yes, Scripture predicted it. Was it necessary for him to rise from the dead? Yes, for this was also specifically predicted. And then, without descending from the high level of importance assigned these two essentials, Jesus added that Scripture also predicted the necessity of preaching "repentance and forgiveness of sins" in his name to all nations (24:46–47). It speaks volumes about the importance of the church's mission to the nations that these three themes—his cross, his resurrection, and worldwide gospel proclamation—are linked together so intimately and given equal scriptural endorsement. Marshall states that Luke's use of "must" drives one to the conclusion that within the course of divine history the events that God has decreed become something that "must" happen and are "a result of his decision" (1971: 111). The evangelization of the world is so preordained and determined by the purpose of God that it is of the order of "divine necessity," equal in importance to the cross and the resurrection. In this connection Hendrikus Berkhof states:

> We no longer can conceive of the mission as a mere instrument in Christ's saving work, as the way by which the mighty acts of incarnation, atonement, and resurrection are transmitted to the next generation and the remote nations. Of course, all that is also fine. But as the transmission of the mighty acts, the mission is itself a mighty act, as well as atonement and resurrection. All those other acts would never be known as mighty acts of God without this last one. (1964: 35)

Jesus began this narrative by "opening the minds" of his disciples that they might understand this particular threefold witness of the Old Testament (24:25). We conclude that the redemptive work of Christ and the worldwide mission of his people are understood only by those who are in subjection to him (John 7:16–17). And we likewise conclude that for any person or church to downplay the primary importance of preaching "repentance and forgiveness of sins" is to demonstrate failure to follow the explicit directives of Jesus himself. The worldwide Christian movement needs to be renewed in its commitment to the necessity of the cross, the reality of the resurrection, and the urgency of the missionary task (see Barclay 1975: 298).

Two other details should be noted. The disciples were told that their proclamation of this message was to begin in Jerusalem (24:47). This had also been foretold in the Old Testament: "The law will go out from Zion, the word of the LORD from Jerusalem" (Isa. 2:3; Mic. 4:2). Furthermore, they were told to "stay in the city" until they were "clothed with power from on high" (Luke 24:49). This second reference to the coming of the Holy Spirit (John 20:22–23) was to remind them again of their need for supernatural power before they could presume to become "fellow workers for the kingdom of God" (Col. 4:11). They understood their message: the gospel of the Kingdom. They were well versed in the methodology they should use; and they had seen in Jesus the model for the Spirit-directed life. But they needed more: "what my Father has promised" (Luke 24:49), the anointing of the Spirit of God, "the last mighty act" of God. When the Spirit finally came on the day of Pentecost, they would find him to be "the gate through which the people of God enter all the preceding acts (incarnation, atonement and resurrection). This last act still goes on. Of its ongoing accomplishment we are witnesses" (H. Berkhof 1964: 35).

Mark 16:15–20: The Divine Authority

Most scholars agree that the original ending of Mark either has been lost or perhaps never was written. Verses 9 to 20 represent the oldest attempt to remedy this lack. However, these verses do present certain problems, particularly where the promise of miraculous gifts and signs is made (16:17–18). In this connection the question has often been raised: Why have the other evangelists failed to mention so great an endowment? It was more than passing interest that motivated Calvin to defend the historicity of these verses on a priori grounds. He argued that "the power of working miracles was essential to the establishment of the disciples themselves, as well as necessary for proving the doctrine of the gospel at its commencement, that the power was possessed by only a very few persons—those who believe—for the confirmation of all and granted only for a time" (quoted by Mackinnon 1906: 348).

Until quite recently the tendency among scholars has been to downplay the validity of "signs" (16:17–18) as normative for the church-in-mission throughout this age. Some have even denigrated the references to serpents and poison as "thaumaturgic and fantastic" and have warned against any physical charisma taking the place of the spiritual presence of the exalted Lord. Others, such as Samuel M. Zwemer, have zealously sought to defend every detail of the "long ending" of Mark, knowing that in many parts of the world if missionaries are going to be effective, they must be able consciously to count on "the Lord working with them and confirming the message" by appropriate signs (1943: 69–86, with reference to 16:20). One might likewise contend that the inclusion of the phrase "in my name" is in such harmony with all other expressions of the Great Commission that it needs to be underscored. Indeed, in his sending forth of the Seventy, Jesus said: "I have given you authority (*exousia*) to trample on snakes and scorpions and to overcome all the power (*dynamis*) of the enemy; nothing will harm you" (Luke 10:19).

So then, even in this much debated "long ending" we find that in carrying out the Great Commission, Christians are truly colaborers with Jesus Christ and invested with his authority over all their adversaries.

It is tragic that in Bishop J. Waskom Pickett's monumental study, *Christian Mass Movements in India* (Abingdon Press, 1933), one finds no reference to "signs and miracles," even though he confided to Donald A. McGavran that these movements invariably began when healings and other demonstrations of God's power were present. During the 1930s his book would not have been taken seriously had he made any reference to "signs and miracles." Today, evidence of these phenomena is widespread, and negative attitudes about the supernatural have largely evaporated! Our only fear is that the growing sensational and extravagant claims being made in our day by those preoccupied with "signs and miracles" may cause the pendulum to swing back to the skepticism of the 1930s. This would be a tragedy.

Matthew 28:16–20: The Specific Task

We now come to the most comprehensive statement of the Great Commission. The Gospel of Matthew begins with the royal genealogy of the true Messiah of Israel and ends with the universal Lord and Savior issuing a mandate for mission that is worldwide in scope. But we are surprised when we note the brief pericope immediately preceding Jesus' Great Commission. It records the bribing of the soldiers who had been guarding Jesus' tomb (28:11–15). Here we have all the components of what might be called "the devil's great commission."

Review the details. When the soldiers recovered from the earthquake and the appearance of the angel who had rolled back the stone and reported what had happened, the religious establishment immediately took action. Jesus must be proclaimed as dead, his body merely stolen. Behind this huge lie was a "large sum of money," for money talks. The money itch is such that people "can be bribed to hide the truth and spread an untruth, as modern propaganda well proves" (Buttrick 1951: 621). The good offices of the political establishment were also approached to promote this deliberate deception. In the end the soldiers proved obedient, and among the Jews this explanation of the empty tomb was widely accepted. And still is today.

Then follows the contrast. Jesus has "all authority in heaven and on earth," but is frequently opposed by the religious and political establishments of this world. The message he would have proclaimed is the good news of the Kingdom, including its present hiddenness and the possibilities latent in men and women coming under Jesus' ongoing, kingly rule. The transformation that the resurrected Jesus Christ will effect will refute all talk of his having remained under the thralldom of death. Moreover, although he makes no reference to the vast sums of money needed, generation by generation, to evangelize the world, he says in effect: "I am your pay" ("And surely I am with you always, to the very end of the age"). The apostles in that first century, along with countless others ever since, have found that they often had to confess with Peter, "Silver or gold I do not have." Peter made this response to a man lame from his birth who was begging at a gate of the Temple. But they were able at the same time to say through their identification with the risen Christ, "But what I have I give you. In the name of Jesus Christ of Nazareth, walk" (Acts 3:6). Wherever the true gospel is preached, one invariably finds evidence of the vigorous promotion of ideas that oppose it. Our task now is to ascertain the substance of the Matthean version of the Great Commission.

First, we should note that the grammatical structure of the original contains but one imperative. The task is to "make disciples." This imperative is supported by three modal participles: "(as you are) going," "baptizing," and "teaching." Hence, one should avoid the simplistic sequence: Go! Make disciples! Baptize! Teach! They are not to be separated from one another. Since "going" is in the aorist tense and precedes the imperative "make disciples," also in the aorist tense, to be followed by "baptizing" and "teaching" in the present tense, the best translation is "As you go! Make disciples! (Do this) by baptizing and teaching." Some have seen in the initial aorist participle "going" ("having gone") an oblique reference to the dynamic of the Holy Spirit, who constrains the Christian to move out beyond the frontiers of faith to make Jesus Christ known. This theme is stated more explicitly in Jesus' final statement on the mission of the church (Acts 1:8), hence will be treated later.

Second, the task of making disciples involves three separate yet intimately interrelated dimensions, if one is to take into full consideration the grammatical complexity of Matthew's record of the Great Commission. Jesus stated that making disciples demands not only evangelism but also incorporation into the life of the church (baptism) and the sort of instruction that leads to active participation in the Kingdom of God. Hence, it is altogether correct to state that the main factors in the mission of the church are *kērygma* (the gospel), *koinōnia* (the community), and *diakonia* (the service and obedience of the people of God whereby the one hope of humanity—the rule of God—is demonstrated). Alexander McLeish has well stated:

> It has often been said that "the sowing of the seed" is the main task and that the rest will follow. That this is not so is attested both by experience and by the correlation of these imperatives in the command emphasizing the planting of the church as central . . . . The community is born in witness, exists for witness, and is only successful in doing this effectively so far as it is fully instructed "to observe" all things commanded. (1952: 105–8)

This poses the question whether one can be a disciple in the biblical sense apart from involvement in both church and Kingdom. Admittedly, the word *disciple* is used in a variety of ways in the New Testament. It may refer to a person who has sought to follow Christ for what later proved to have been an unworthy reason. One recalls Judas Iscariot or the disciple whose flawed sense of spiritual priorities made him want first to bury his father (and get his part of the inheritance) and then follow Jesus (Matt. 8:21). The term *disciple* is also used to describe any follower of Jesus. In this sense "making disciples" may be a general term to be equated with evangelism—the initial task of leading people to faith in Christ (e.g., Acts 14:21). Some, however, argue that Jesus' use of the term (e.g., Luke 14:26–27, 33) limits its use to the Christian who has fully met all the demands of mature discipleship. They would make a sharp distinction between mere believers and true disciples. Others would question this narrow perspective.

If one takes all usages of the term into consideration, there is little doubt that becoming a disciple represents both an event and a process. Ideally, it involves yielding oneself wholeheartedly to Jesus Christ as Lord, and this often takes place in a moment of time. But anyone who has been active in evangelistic work knows that it is not wise to take anything for granted. No one can be sure that a person has truly become a regenerated Christian just because he or she made a decision for Christ. And little is to be gained by testing and retesting the validity of one's initial decision. There is every possibility that it may have been made for selfish reasons, as many first decisions are. Hence, both time and active participation in church life are needed, preferably including an apprentice relationship with an older Christian. This will reveal whether or not a new pattern of decision making has truly begun to emerge. In this connection the apostle Paul described the evangelistic sequence he followed as "admonishing and teaching everyone" that he might "present everyone perfect in Christ" (Col. 1:28). Does this mean that Paul was more concerned with the ongoing process than with the initial decision? Not quite, for he went on to state that the components of the initial decision (repentance and faith) were essential to a viable pattern of Christian living (Col. 2:6).

Third, the task of making disciples must include baptism and all that it signifies. The reasons for this are multiple. We begin with several demonstrable affirmations. There were no unbaptized Christians in the apostolic church: all of the five recorded conversions in Acts include baptism: the Ethiopian eunuch (8:36, 38); Saul of Tarsus (9:18; 22:16); Cornelius the centurion (10:47–48); Lydia of Thyatira (16:15); and the Roman jailer (16:33). The form of baptism was directly related to that of John the Baptist, to which many, including Jesus, had submitted. The formula "in the name of the Father and of the Son and of the Holy Spirit" (Matt. 28:19) was not rigidly used, so it may be of only secondary importance (Acts 2:38; 10:48; etc.).

The significance of baptism becomes clear when we take the full measure of the references to it in Scripture. They are varied. First and foremost, it demonstrated the public confession of a person's repentance and faith. As such, it involved what Dunn calls, "The Rubicon step of commitment for the would-be Christian" (1977: 155). There was no going back afterward. Indeed, without taking this forward step one remained uncommitted. The fact that baptism was administered in the name of Jesus or of the triune God indicated God's ownership of the baptized person. And since baptism served as the initiatory rite whereby professing Christians gained admission into the local Christian community, it expressed through the baptizer the community's acceptance as well.

Baptism inevitably has kingdom implications because of its eschatological orientation. When a person is baptized, confession is thereby made of union with Christ in Christ's death; it marks deliverance from the old world order that is passing away. And baptism also marks union with Christ in his resurrection victory. The Kingdom of God, the new world order, is present and operative in the lives of the baptized, although for the present it is hidden from the eyes of the unbelieving.

Baptism is also related to the gift of the Holy Spirit, although it is not to be equated with the baptism of the Spirit. In the Book of Acts we shall see that the gift of the Holy Spirit was "the most important, the decisive element in conversion-initiation . . . the mark of God's acceptance . . . and baptism served as man's acknowledgement of the divine acceptance" (Dunn 1977:154–57, with reference to 10:44–48). Once this decisive step of faith and obedience had been taken, the newly baptized person was free to participate in the dynamic, ongoing life of the local congregation. Here, as nowhere else, one could grow in grace and in the knowledge of Jesus Christ. Indeed, the professing Christian who does not seek baptism is likely to be most casual in his or her regard for the church and most irregular in response to the church's instruction and service.

Fourth, the role of teaching in the formation of disciples is also important. The Great Commission is clear about this. Its focus is on the sort of teaching that "trains," not on the wholesale imparting of religious information. To teach a person to observe the truth of God may call for gradual discipling of the new convert.

Furthermore, Jesus specified that the areas to be covered in this teaching training concerned "all" that he had previously taught his disciples. This corpus takes specific form when we relate it to the structure of Matthew's Gospel. Actually, the Great Commission can be seen as bringing the entire Gospel to a fitting climax. Within Matthew are five major messages that constitute the dominant thrust of Jesus' instruction on discipleship in relation to the Kingdom of God. Each of these concludes with a characteristic phrase that marks off the successive sections of the book (7:28; 11:1; 13:53; 19:1; 26:1).

- **Ethics:** *The Sermon on the Mount* (chaps. 5–7). Jesus was most forthright in describing the attitudes and actions that should mark all those who have come under his control. Neutrality, or uninvolvement in the struggle for justice, is not acceptable. Conduct not motivated by love is equally unacceptable.
- **Mission:** *The Sending of the Twelve* (chap. 10). The task is complex: service must be rendered, reconciliation must be promoted, and evangelistic outreach must characterize all involvement with non-Christians.
- **Commitment:** *The Parables of the Kingdom* (chap. 13). The dimensions of public obedience, verbal confession, wholehearted devotion, and venturesome faith are among the indispensable signs of the Kingdom.
- **Community:** *Discipline in the Church* (chap. 18). The reality of sharing a common life in Christ involves accepting all who receive his message and

holding one another accountable to the highest expectations. This is the complete antithesis of the "solitary" Christian.

- **Stewardship:** *The Olivet Discourse* (chaps. 24, 25). The constant awareness that there is coming a day when each disciple will render account of his or her faithfulness as a custodian of the gospel and of the use made of spiritual gifts and natural talents.

From the preceding discussion it is apparent why a measure of instruction in these matters is essential to preparing would-be followers of Jesus to count the cost before encouraging them to submit to his lordship. Only thereby can one repudiate the charge of preaching a gospel of cheap grace. Furthermore, the postconversion teaching of all converts to "observe" these several commandments is essential if there is to be any movement toward maturity in their pursuit of God (Phil. 3:12–16).

Fifth, we should realize that no small debate has raged in the church over the meaning of "all nations." Taken at face value, the meaning is that individual disciples are to be made within all segments of the human family. Jesus can hardly have been referring to nations as collective entities in themselves, for then there would not have been the shift to the masculine "them" when referring to baptism and instruction because the word for "nation" is neuter. It is argued that the God who formerly "let all the nations go their own way" (Acts 14:16) and who "overlooked such ignorance" (Acts 17:30) now offers the gospel of reconciliation to one and all—Jews as well as Gentiles.

But at this point scholars divide. Some argue that the Great Commission is directed toward the whole world minus Israel, for the Jewish rejection of Jesus marked God's abandonment of the mission to Israel. Others with equal insistence include Israel. One major though not decisive fact is that in Jesus' previous sending of the Twelve only to "the lost sheep of Israel," the *ethnē* are deliberately excluded (Matt. 10:5–6), whereas in 28:18–20 they are mentioned with emphasis. The best way to resolve this is to recall that "all the nations" is the term used in the parable of the Last Judgment (Matt. 25:32). In this parable the only distinctions drawn are between the righteous and the guilty, between those who inherit the Kingdom and those who do not. In this regard Jews are not distinguished from Gentiles (see also the people of God "hated by all" in Matt. 24:9 and Mark 13:13). And we must not forget that the Septuagint translation of the covenant promise to Abraham uses this same phrase: "In thee [Abram] shall all the tribes of the earth be blessed" (Bagster edition, Gen. 12:3). *Ethnē* is an imprecise term that should not be pressed too hard. It means "people" and does not necessarily involve a "unity of common descent, or a political unity or a linguistic unity." However, the obvious scope of the Great Commission embraces every cultural unit within the human family (Schmidt 1964: 369–72).

We may conclude that the gospel is the gracious provision of God's covenant with his people through Jesus Christ, whether they be culturally Jews or Gentiles. It is significant that Josephus in his *History of the Jewish Wars* regularly uses *ethnos* in reference to the Jewish people (Neill 1964: 332).

In our day there is great resistance in the churches to include the Jewish people within the scope of the Great Commission (G. Anderson 1974: 279–93). A variety of arguments are advanced to justify this. For some, a particular reading of the Jewish religious heritage leads them to say that Jews do not need Jesus Christ. They confidently affirm that God "did not reject his people, whom he foreknew" (Rom. 11:2), and they interpret this to mean that all Jews are either included in the new covenant or that the old covenant remains valid for Jews. Others argue that inasmuch as so few Jews down through the centuries have responded to the gospel, the church should admit its failure and cease this activity altogether. Still others feel that almost two thousand years of Christian anti-Semitism have demonstrated the spiritual bankruptcy of Christianity vis-à-vis the Jews. In their eyes, only the most ignorant and insensitive of Christians persist in this unwarranted activity.

Furthermore, within the Jewish community one finds many who accept the basic postulates of the Jewish existentialist philosopher Franz Rosenzweig (1886–1929). Although he called himself an "anti-Christian," he enthusiastically endorsed the Great Commission. "Go, by all means, go into all the world and preach the gospel! Don't let anybody or anything stop you from going! And your hearers, they should come! There is no other way for them but to come." Rosenzweig then went on to say:

> We wholly agree as to what Christ and his church mean to the world; no one can reach the Father save through him. . . . But the situation is quite different for one who does not have to reach the Father because he is already with him. And this is true of the people of Israel (though not of individual Jews). (quoted by Bowler 1973: 12)

This position is called the "Two Covenant Theory," for it is based on the thesis that God made a covenant with the Jewish people through membership in Israel and with all Gentile peoples through Christ. The obvious effect of this theory is to divert Christian attention away from the Jews and, in part, to exalt the principle that race and religion can be the grounds for exemption from the need for Jesus Christ. However, we would contend that no thorough theological investigation of redemption in the Scripture will support the thesis that Israelites can be saved apart from the vicarious suffering of Christ. The Kingdom of God is universal in its scope. The Jewish people should not be denied the message of forgiveness. Some Christians have said, in essence, "If I do not share Christ with the Jews, I either regard Christ as unworthy of them or regard Jews as unworthy of Christ." The biblical portrayal of Jesus Christ underscores the fact that all people, whether Jews or Gentiles, are called to repent and believe because all are under the judgment of God, and he alone is God's provision of a Savior. We will return to this subject later when we examine the apostle Paul's references to it.

Sixth, we also need to remember a significant emphasis not found in any statement of the missionary mandate, but one that particularly surfaces when we reflect on what Jesus said about wealth and poverty recorded in Luke. At the very heart and center of this Gospel is the theme: "good news to the poor" (4:18). Indeed, the gospel is to be directed specifically to the poor. By this is not meant "a collective term for the captives, blind and oppressed" (Pilgrim 1981: 64–69). The poor are too specifically identified in Luke to make this facile judgment (6:20–23; 7:18–23; 14:13, 21; etc.). Luke is particularly concerned with economically deprived people. He faithfully portrays God's bias for the poor and lowly (1:48, 52–53; 4:18). He dwells on Jesus' friendship with tax collectors and sinners (7:31–35; 15:2). Indeed, Luke emphasizes that the ministry of Jesus "is identified inseparably with the poor and the hungry, the sick and the afflicted, the captives and the oppressed, the outcasts and the sinners. . . . [They represent] hard social realities, as well as deep spiritual needs" (Pilgrim 1981: 83).

The fact that Luke's key verse (4:18) was a quotation from Isaiah 61:1–2 brings this theme to a climax. The vision of the jubilee year, with its promise of justice and liberation, means that the good news of the Kingdom involves a radical restructuring of society shaped by this promise. This theme demands extensive and urgent development as Orlando Costas suggests.

> For a long time theology has been done from the perspective of the powerful and mighty; it is time that it be done from the side of the weak and downtrodden. For far too long the poor have been hidden from the eyes of theology; it is time that they be rescued as a fundamental category of the gospel and as a place from which to reflect on the faith. (1982: 127)

Seventh, Matthew's statement of the Great Commission concludes with the same sublime dimensions with which it began. Jesus as King had made the royal claim that all authority had been given him in heaven and on earth (28:18). He thereby revealed himself as far more than the King of the Jews; he is King of kings and Lord of lords of all peoples everywhere. His royal command was that his followers make disciples of all nations. They have a universal faith to proclaim. Never again will God confine his messengers to the house of Israel (Matt. 10:5–6). And he concludes with a royal promise: "Surely I am with you always, to the very end of the age." In other words, this promise of the abiding presence of the King was to provide more than personal comfort to all those engaged in the task of making Jesus Christ known, loved, and served throughout the nations. This underscored the priority of this task until the establishment of the Kingdom in power and glory at the end of the age. And woe to those who would contend that in our day radically different tasks should replace the one the King has commanded. It is not without significance that Basil F. C. Atkinson concludes his commentary on Matthew with the words: "The existence of millions in the world today who have never heard the Savior's name is a disgrace to us all" (1953: 805).

Acts 1:8: The Great Prophecy

The context of the final reference to the Great Commission in the postresurrection ministry of Jesus is portrayed in Acts 1 as the culmination of his instruction in "about the kingdom of God" (1:3). From the rest of Acts we will see that the Kingdom of God was perceived by the apostles as coming in the events of the life, death, and resurrection of Jesus. For them to proclaim these events and demonstrate their kingdom significance was to proclaim fully the "good news of the Kingdom." And yet verses 6 and 7 reveal that our Lord still encountered in his apostles the limited horizon of a stubborn hope: the restoration of an earthly kingdom to Israel. Luke deliberately underscores their flawed understanding at the outset of Acts and records that Jesus brushed it aside as irrelevant. This follows from Luke's dominant objective in this book: to provide a theological-historical explanation of the emergence of a religious movement reflecting the universal dimensions of the Kingdom of God.

In one brief statement Jesus shows that the coming baptism of the Holy Spirit (Acts 1:5, 8) would so empower his disciples that they would individually and collectively become his bold witnesses. They would begin their witness in Jerusalem and eventually reach outward "to the ends of the earth." Down through the centuries concerned Christians have seen that God's redemptive purpose must not be thwarted by contentment with past successes. The gospel must go outward and onward in ever widening circles from Jerusalem. To them mission meant both plan and progress. The singling out of Samaria can only mean God's peculiar concern for minority peoples, the sort that majority peoples tend to despise. Mission history shows us that over the years God has singularly blessed those who have reminded the church of the world's "forgotten peoples" (1 Cor. 1:26–29).

This final reference to world mission stresses the empowering of the Holy Spirit, the priority that all Samaritans represent, and the obligation of the church to extend the frontiers of faith to "earth's remotest bounds." However, to do so would be to overlook the fact that this is a prophecy. Actually, Jesus did not use the didactic form in these final words to his disciples. In a very real sense he was not making another statement of the Great Commission. Rather, he was bringing his earthly ministry to an end by predicting that his people would indeed carry to completion their missionary task. This task would be fully accomplished because of the working of the Holy Spirit. "You shall receive power . . . you shall be my witnesses . . . to the end of the earth." God knows that one day "all human history shall be consummated in Christ" (Eph. 1:9 PHILLIPS).

Conclusion

In this chapter we have examined five different ways in which the Gospel writers recorded Jesus' announcement of God's Kingdom mission. Each of these commissions contains a slightly different emphasis regarding God's Kingdom mission. Yet all five demonstrate a common perspective and a shared commitment: the disciples of Jesus in every age are to announce the coming of the Kingdom of God in Jesus Christ by participating in Jesus' mission of calling women and men to become disciples of Jesus Christ and responsible members of Christ's church.

The announcement of the coming of God's Kingdom, with its accompanying invitation to follow Jesus Christ the Messiah King, is fundamentally an eschatological proclamation in word and deed. It is a declaration that a new future has already begun and is offered to all humanity, Jew and Gentile alike. This eschatological dimension in the present and the future is drawn out most forcefully in the Gospel of John. Thus, in the next chapter we will explore how John's Gospel portrays Jesus' mission of announcing the coming of the Kingdom of God.

15

Jesus Anticipates the Coming of God's Kingdom

Introduction

Over the years considerable scholarly attention has been given to the uniqueness of the Gospel of John in contrast to the Synoptic Gospels. Some scholars have speculated that this Gospel had its origin in a community of Hellenists in serious tension with other segments of the early church. Their distinct theology was allegedly Johannine and not in accord with that of the Synoptics. Others dispute this and argue quite plausibly that we must expect complementary variations in these separate portraits of Jesus Christ. Although this debate as such does not concern us here, we must take the measure of this Gospel's distinctives and relate them to our theme: Kingdom and mission.

The Gospel of John does not mention prominent Synoptic events such as Jesus' birth, baptism, temptation, and transfiguration. John's Gospel contains no call for repentance, no parables, no prominence to the kingdom theme, no Sermon on the Mount, no institution of the Lord's Supper, and only alludes to Jesus' agony in the garden of Gethsemane. In contrast to Jesus' aphoristic statements in the Synoptics on a wide range of subjects, in John's Gospel we find him giving long discourses about himself and God's gifts through him: eternal life, knowledge, light, and truth (Barker 1969: 386). In this connection Ladd observes:

> The structure of John's thought seems to move in a different world. Gone is the idiom of this age and the age to come. Missing is the Olivet Discourse with its eschatological expectation of the end of the age and the coming of the Son of Man in glory to establish the Kingdom of God. . . . Instead of the tension between the present and the future is the tension between the above and the below, heaven and earth, the sphere of God and the world. (1974: 216)

The unique character of this Gospel calls for it to be fully explored and comprehensively related to the Synoptics. No fundamental difference exists between

242

its teaching and that of the Synoptics. Nothing has been distorted or falsified. It does no more than

> make even more explicit what was always implicit in the Synoptics. John chose to formulate his entire Gospel in language used by our Lord only in intimate dialogue with his disciples or in theological argument with learned scribes in order to bring out the full meaning of the eternal Word that became flesh (1:14) in the historical event of Jesus Christ. (Ladd 1974: 221–22)

Missio Dei: A Trinitarian Perspective

The fourth Gospel is uniquely concerned with God as Sender. In the final analysis it is a theological treatise in which the objective is to establish who Jesus is and then to show that those who believe in him "have life in his name" (20:30–31). John the Baptist was "sent" to bear witness to Jesus (1:6–8; 3:28). Jesus was "sent" to make the Father known and to do his work (1:18; 4:34; 5:23; 6:38–39; etc.). The Holy Spirit was "sent" by both the Father and the Son to continue Jesus' witness and work in the world (15:26; 16:7–11). Finally, the disciples were "sent" by Jesus to accomplish Jesus' mission in the world as colaborers with the Holy Spirit (17:18; 20:21). In his summary of the import of these interrelated missions, Donald Senior states:

> All four are accomplished in the arena of the "world" and, ultimately, have the salvation of the world as their goal. All involve a personal relationship between the sender and the sent, between the agent and the one who invests the agent with authority. This is true in all cases, even for the Son (8:28, 29) and the Paraclete (16:13). They do not speak on their own behalf but on behalf of the one who sends them. All of these missions revolve around Jesus: John announces his coming, the Paraclete reinforces his presence and the disciples declare his word to the world. But this constellation of mission around Jesus does not end here. Just as John's Christology is not the final word of the Gospel but is ultimately related to the deeper quest for the face of God, so, too, the end point of this Gospel's missiology is not Jesus but the Father. The Father, alone, is not sent. He is the origin and the goal of all the testimony of the Gospel. (1983: 222)

With this in mind we can appreciate the pathos in Jesus' prayer: "Righteous Father, though the world does not know you, I know you" (17:25a). And then referring to his disciples, he added: "They know that you have sent me. I have made you known to them, and will continue to make you known in order that the love you have for me may be in them and that I myself may be in them (vv. 25b–26)." God is not only Sender; he is Lover as well. It is for this reason that he "gave" his Son (3:16) and "gave" the Holy Spirit (14:16) for the life and mission of his people. The age of the church is preeminently the age of the Holy Spirit, the age of world mission.

The full Godhead is thereby involved in the mission of the church. The Father decreed and sent the Son. The Son redeemed and with the Father and in resurrection power sent the Spirit to quicken the people of God and send them forth into the world on their mission (20:22). John 16:8–11 is definitive in this connection: "When [the Holy Spirit] comes, he will convict the world of guilt in regard to sin," that is, the sin of its unbelief in Jesus Christ; "[in regard to] righteousness," that is, the world's flawed understanding of justice; "and [in regard to] judgment," for judgment is operating already in society-in-history as well as coming to fullness in the last day. Concerning this, Albert C. Winn states:

> According to the Johannine missionary theology, if the church is to be spiritual, that is, filled and led by the Holy Spirit, it will find itself in confrontation with the world regarding sin, justice and judgment. And if it is not in such confrontation, it is not obedient to the Spirit, not carrying out its mission; and its peace and unity, its regeneration and sanctification, its plethora of gifts and graces, are all going to waste. (1981: 101)

John's Trinitarian perspective means that the rule of God extends to all areas of life. When Jesus called people to accept this rule, he was saying in effect: "As ruler of the universe, I desire to establish My control over your life. Turn away from all other demands for its ownership and enter into My reign. Let me rule in the life of the world through My rule in you" (Webber 1978: 159).

The Holy Spirit is invariably described as participating in the mission of the post-Easter believers (e.g., John 3:5–8; 6:63; 7:37–39; 14:16–26; 15:26–27; 16:7–15; 20:22). In John no mention is made of the Spirit bringing any ecstatic, joyous, or overmastering feelings. Rather, the Spirit is described as being with them, teaching and guiding them, and bearing witness alongside them in much the same way that Jesus himself served his disciples—and yet with greater intensity ("greater things" 14:12). Best of all, he will enter with them into "prophetic confrontation with the non-believing world" (Senior and Stuhlmueller 1983: 218).

From John's Gospel, it would appear that a preoccupation with the experiential dimensions of one's encounter with the Holy Spirit might divert one from the demands of citizenship in the Kingdom of God. Instead of filling the role of an abiding presence with each and every believer as a sort of successor to Jesus Christ, the Spirit can become the displacer of our Lord (e.g., the second-century heresy of Montanism). By contrast, in the fourth Gospel, he is clearly the subordinate Remembrancer of Jesus, as Winn recalls:

> He will bring to the disciples' remembrance all that Jesus has said to them (14:26). He will bear witness to Jesus (15:26). He will not speak on his own authority, but whatever he hears from Jesus he will speak (16:13), just as Jesus did not speak on his own authority, but spoke only what he heard from the Father (7:16; 8:26, 28; 12:49; 14:24; 17:8). He will glorify Jesus (16:14), just as Jesus glorified the Father (17:4). As Jesus was utterly transparent, claiming nothing for himself so that the Father's glory might shine through, so the Paraclete is utterly transparent, claiming

nothing for himself so that the glory of Jesus may shine through. The Paraclete no more displaces Jesus than Jesus displaces the Father. (1981: 93–94)

All of which brings us to the term *Missio Dei*. The Fifth International Missionary Council conference, held in Willingen, Germany, July 1952, used this term to underscore the fact that the missionary movement has its source in the triune God. "God is the Lord, the One who gives the orders, the Owner, the One Who takes care of things. He is the Protagonist in the mission" (Vicedom 1965: 5). In this sense the whole of redemptive history (*Heilsgeschichte*) is a history of *Missio Dei*—God's redemptive purpose for the nations. It follows then that the goal of *Missio Dei* is to incorporate people into the Kingdom of God and to involve them in his mission. Because the Father is the Sender, Jesus Christ the One who is sent, and the Holy Spirit the Revealer, it follows that noninvolvement in mission on the part of the church is to be deplored. As was stated in the "Interim Report" at Willingen: "The Church is like an army living in tents. God calls his church to strike their tents and move onward; and God goes with his people until the purpose of his sending his Son, and the Holy Spirit, and the Church is fulfilled" (Goodall 1953: 243). Or as H. H. Rosin states: "He who seeks first the Kingdom must place first God's love for others; he must accept responsibility for advancing God's mission to others" (1972: 17).

The Trinitarian approach to mission theology was well summarized by the Willingen IMC conference.

> God sent forth his Son, Jesus Christ, to seek out, and gather together, and transform, all men who are alienated by sin from God and their fellows. This is and always has been the will of God. It was embodied in Christ and will be completed in Christ. God also sends forth the Holy Spirit. By the Holy Spirit the Church, experiencing God's active love, is assured that God will complete what he has set his hand to in the sending of his Son. (Goodall 1953: 241)

The Kingdom of God and Eternal Life

In 1522 Martin Luther wrote in his preface to the New Testament something that has become almost axiomatic, but that unfortunately has contributed to a distorted understanding of the biblical character of the Christian mission. Luther unwittingly encouraged Christians to settle for a "canon within the canon" when he said, describing the books of the New Testament:

> From all of these books, you can, in a flash, correctly discriminate between all of them and distinguish which are the best. John's Gospel and St. Paul's Epistles, especially the one to the Romans, and St. Peter's first epistle contain the true kernel and marrow among all the books, for in these you do not find Christ's deeds and miracles described very much but you find emphasized in a most masterful way how faith in Christ overcomes sin, death, and hell, and gives life, justification and blessing—which is the true nature of the Gospel. . . . Therefore, John's Gospel is the

only Gospel which is delicately sensitive to what is the essence of the gospel, and is to be widely preferred to the other three and placed on a higher level. (quoted in D. Fuller 1969, vol. 9:9–10)

It is widely recognized that Luther was rather arbitrary when he made this claim that the Gospel of John is superior to the Synoptics. Of course, Luther himself would have denied the accusation, saying that he was guided by "the rule of faith." By this he meant Jesus Christ and the truth of justification by faith, or as he specifically stated: "Scripture contains nothing but Christ and the Christian faith" (quoted in D. Fuller 1969, vol. 9:9). But the result of Luther's view was a "canon within the canon," based on what he thought the normative Word of God should be. Whereas it is true that many of the statements in John are unambiguously clear and of immediate relevance—coming as they do directly from the lips of Jesus Christ himself—this does not mean that the Synoptics are less inspired and hence less authoritative. On the other hand, distortion arises also when one unconsciously makes the fourth Gospel's relative silence on the Kingdom of God normative and downplays the Synoptic contribution to a comprehensive understanding of this theme.

The central focus of John's Gospel is its stress on eternal life. John's dominant concern was that Christians be confirmed in their knowledge of Christ's full deity and in their certainty of eternal life through faith in him (10:10; 20:31). What is significant, however, is that eternal life is not introduced until after Jesus has stated that apart from the new birth one cannot see, much less enter, the Kingdom of God (3:3, 5). From this point onward Jesus makes no further reference in John's Gospel to the Kingdom, although he subsequently mentions eternal life more than thirty times. In fact, no mention is made of the Kingdom until Jesus' trial before Pilate. When asked about his kingship, Jesus states that it is "not of this world" nor is it to be promoted or defended by worldly power (18:33–38).

This stress on eternal life has missiological significance. In the Synoptics Jesus says that salvation is available in the eschatological Kingdom of God that has invaded history in his person and mission. In the fourth Gospel, however, Jesus states that salvation is presently available in his person and mission. Even so, John does not overlook its eschatological consummation. What all this means is that Christians, as signs of the Kingdom, can and should reflect in their lives and express with their lips God's "tomorrow" in the midst of the world "today." As George Ladd observes:

If eternal life is indeed the life of the eschatological Kingdom of God, and if the Kingdom is present, it follows that we might expect the Kingdom to bring to men a foretaste of the life of the future age. (1974: 259)

This has tremendous practical ramifications for ministry and mission today. If God's future is to be characterized by peace and justice, Christians today must see themselves as peacemakers and reconcilers and as defenders of the poor, the marginalized, the exploited. The obligations of the Old Testament's cultural mandate remain their high priority since they constitute in part the demands of the Kingdom. In his extended study *A Biblical Theology of Missions,* George W. Peters recognizes the cultural mandate as embracing "the basic concepts and directives for an ordered and progressive society based on principles of sound morality and ethical monotheism" (1972: 166–67).

The Great Commission includes the obligation to teach converts "to observe all things" that Jesus had taught his disciples. This means that the demonstration of Kingdom values and concerns comes within the circle of the mission obligation, for this was the central theme of Jesus' ministry. Thus, Harvie Conn rightly defines evangelism as "doing justice and preaching grace" (1982).

One corollary of this is John's emphasis on the knowledge of God. Again and again the world is represented as not knowing God (1:10; 8:55; 16:3; 17:25). But in the last day "the earth will be filled with the knowledge of the glory of the LORD, as the waters cover the sea" (Hab. 2:14). Because Christians already know God, they have no alternative but to proclaim that knowledge today. In this connection it is their mission to display such mutual acceptance and love among themselves that the world will draw near, ask questions, and listen and thereby come to know that Jesus is the One whom God has sent to be its Savior (John 4:42; 17:8, 20–26).

The Gospel of John also relates the knowledge of God to the subject of truth. This does not mean that truth in John is presented in propositional form. The thrust is more Hebraic than Greek. "Knowing God" means "experiencing fellowship with God" and not merely knowing about God. John is concerned with a person's direct interaction with the person of Christ and with orthopraxis. For instance, when Jesus stated that true disciples are those who continue in the pattern of subjecting themselves to his word, the stress is on his promise: "You will know the truth, and the truth will set you free" (8:31–32). Jesus' identification of himself as "the truth" means that he is what he says. Furthermore, he does not lead people astray. On the contrary, he is "the full revelation and embodiment of the redemptive purpose of God . . . the disclosure of the faithfulness of God to his own character" . . . [and] of his continuing purpose to make his saving will known" (Ladd 1974: 266).

As the "true light" (1:9), Jesus stands in contrast to the feeble and often false lights in pagan religions and to the gods of the nations. Within the stream of God's revelation there have only been partial lights such as Moses (1:17) and John the Baptist (5:35). But Jesus is the effulgence of God's glory (1:16–18) and "the light of the world" (8:12). Furthermore, as the Creator of the world and the Redeemer of humankind, he alone sustains a determinative relationship with this fallen world (3:33; 7:28; 8:26). Because he is the saving presence of God in the world, all who follow him must "do the truth," which means giving full and unconditional response to the truth that he represents. Not only does he send his disciples into the world to continue his witness (17:18), but he prays that they be sanctified by the truth (17:17, 19). This means that all the dimensions of their lives are to reflect God's character, for "whoever claims to live in him must walk as Jesus did" (1 John 2:6).

Election and Mission

In the apostle Paul's writings there are occasional references to election and predestination (e.g., Rom. 8:29; 9:11; Eph. 1:4–5; Col. 3:12; 2 Thess. 2:13). However, it is largely in John's Gospel that one repeatedly encounters statements that confirm the thesis that faith is a gift granted to some but not to others. Certain people are "born of God" (1:13). Indeed, people are either "of God" ("of the truth," 18:37) or "do not belong to God" (8:47); are given (6:37), drawn (6:44), or granted (6:65) by the Father to the Son; or deliberately chosen by Christ (6:70; 13:18; 15:16, 19). Although scholars today tend to overlook the implications of these texts, this cannot be said of earlier generations (see Alf Corell's brief survey of the exegetical investigation of election in John [1958: 166–86] and D. A. Carson's development of this theme [1981: 125–200]). Indeed, down through church history monumental efforts have been made to explain away these texts, to confine them to the Twelve, or to use them to bolster the dogma of reprobation, an accentuated doctrine of predestination.

Election in this Gospel should be related to the Old Testament teaching of a believing remnant within Israel to serve as God's instrument for the salvation of the whole nation. Later prophets took this theme and concentrated it in a single person: the Suffering Servant of the Lord, the Davidic King Messiah (Isa. 42:1–12; 49:1–13; 50:4–9; 52:13–53:12). The coming Messiah was to include within himself that which he redeemed and perfected: the eschatological people of God. But the Jews of Jesus' day saw things differently. Many claimed to be spiritually secure because of their physical descent from Abraham and their external conformity to the Sinaitic law. They were infuriated when they heard that their attitude toward Jesus was alone determinative. Being blind to who he was, they failed to see his significance. In their unbelief and rage they sought to kill him (John 8:31–59) and clearly demonstrated themselves to be the children of the devil. In contrast, John seeks to show that God's election has come to its "complete realization and assumed its final character through Jesus and the Church founded by him" (Corell 1958: 188).

Jesus as the Chosen One is assigned by his Father the task of bringing those whom he has chosen into the eschatological context of the Kingdom of God (John 15:16, 19). He does this while simultaneously realizing the eschatological Kingdom in his own person. So then, his electing grace is represented as the activity of a shepherd gathering the sheep—"the scattered children of God" (11:52; cf. with 10:16, 26–30). But since they are devoid of that which will alone make them fit for his presence, he must die for them. Only in their being a "redeemed people" will they be given the grace of faith to discern who he is and to respond to his voice. It is their election that gives them security within Jesus' keeping power (6:37, 44,

65; 10:29). For them alone he prays (17:9). As a result they experience peace in the present and have hope for the future (14:1–3, 27; 15:4–5; 17:24–26).

When John the Baptist stated, "A man can receive only what is given him from heaven" (John 3:27), he was affirming the sovereign and unconditional grace of God in his dealings with his people. Even so, John went on to say that those who believed in him were under obligation to bear witness to this grace. And their hearers were morally accountable to God to "believe" (obey) the witness (3:31–36). All this despite the selectivity of God. The fourth Gospel is deliberate in its affirmations that if people are saved, God gets all the credit, but if many are lost, they have only themselves to blame. Those who choose to be unbelievers love "darkness instead of light" because their deeds are evil (3:19). They are variously described as preoccupied with receiving glory from one another, as those who "make no effort to obtain the praise that comes from the only God" (5:44) and as deliberately blinding themselves to the truth (9:39–41). In contrast, believers are challenged to live as becomes their election: loving one another (13:34–35) and bearing the sort of spiritual fruit that passes the test of time (15:16).

The missiological implications of election are intensely practical. Christians must resist the temptation to be passive about issuing the call to conversion following their proclamation of the gospel. If it is the duty of all persons to repent and believe the gospel, then it is the duty of those entrusted with the gospel to endeavor to make it known to all. Furthermore, Christians who are persuaded that God alone makes people responsive to the gospel should seek to bear witness to Jesus where God has already begun his work. There are times and places when and where his Spirit is peculiarly active in the hearts of people. They become "ripe unto harvest." When people begin to respond to the message of Jesus Christ, this empirical factor should influence the allocation of mission resources. Christians thereby learn new ways to be colaborers with God in the building of Christ's church.

But there is a problem inherent in election. Jesus referred to it when he stated, "I have chosen you out of the world. That is why the world hates you" (John 15:19). This scandal of particularity brings offense to those who refuse to accept God's call. Thus, John's Gospel is filled with controversy. Jesus' authority was challenged (2:18); his conduct on the Sabbath was criticized (5:16–18); his healing of the man born blind (9:22, 34–35) and his raising of Lazarus provoked intense reactions (11:50–53, 57; 18:14). All of his good works were met with increasing hostility, and the Gospel climaxed with

> the great drama of the Cross, the biggest "stumbling block" of all. . . . To be offended at Jesus, that is the way of the world—the mark of unbelief. In contrast to the election and the life of the elect in union with Christ in the Church of the redeemed, the scandal is part of a demonic situation marked by enmity to Christ and finally leading to condemnation and eternal death. (Corell 1958: 199–200)

So then, John's Gospel attempts, as no other Gospel does, to confront us with the inscrutable mystery of God's sovereign will and human unbelief. Because there are sheep who respond, come forward, receive Christ, and "despise the shame," a church is formed that becomes increasingly convinced that it is the true Israel. And this tension between light and darkness, faith and unbelief, election and "offense" will continue "until the end of time when God will gather together all his elect in the world of fulfillment" (Corell 1958: 200).

The Passion, Death, and Resurrection of the King of Kings

The passion and death of the Messiah particularly offended many Jews. They could not see how the messianic age could come in mystery form. They brushed aside as mere verbiage Jesus' affirmation that the Kingdom was already present in his own mission before its final apocalyptic consummation. They had been taught that the Kingdom of God, when it came, would require no human involvement. It would be an abrupt, divine invasion of the human scene on the last day. Hence, when this Galilean rabbi preached the necessity of repentance and faith before the Kingdom rule could become operative in their lives, they drew back. Even Nicodemus—that most open-minded "teacher in Israel"—was completely mystified when Jesus told him that he needed the regenerating work of the Holy Spirit in his heart, or he would not even "see," much less "enter," the Kingdom of God (John 3:3, 5).

Jesus also intimated that the Kingdom would be consummated in power and glory. He deliberately instructed his disciples to pray for that day when the will of God would be carried out on earth even as it is in heaven (Matt. 6:10). Nonetheless, this prospect did not evoke positive response. Actually, Jesus did not dwell on the eschatological dimensions of the Kingdom. Perhaps he feared that it would engender the sort of apocalyptic preoccupation that encapsulates one into a dream world of momentary expectations, constant revisions of one's "prophetic" charts, and growing impatience—"How long, O God?" Jesus wanted his disciples to realize that the Kingdom of God had truly come and that his disciples should manifest the "signs" that confirm its presence. This ministry in the present was every bit as urgent as the final apocalyptic display of power that would compel every knee to bow and every tongue to confess that Jesus is Lord (Phil. 2:10–11).

The Crucifixion

It was not enough that Jesus should proclaim the reign of God and perform works that attested to its reality, not enough that he recruit and train people to follow him in his messianic community. There was a deliberate sequence and a climax to his ministry. Concerning this he said:

> "I will drive out demons and heal people today and tomorrow, and on the third day I will reach my goal." In any case, I must keep going today and tomorrow and the next day—for surely no prophet can die outside Jerusalem. (Luke 13:32–33)

His ministry must culminate in his death. Indeed, we are forced to conclude that an intimate connection exists between his proclamation of the presence and future of the Kingdom and his death. The Servant of the Lord had to perform the decisive event by which the Kingdom of God might be fully inaugurated. So then, there was this discordant note in Jesus' instruction to his disciples: "The Son of Man must suffer many things . . . and be killed" (Mark 8:31). The necessity for this arose from the terrible alienation of the human race from its Creator. Nothing is so intolerable to fallen humanity as God's holiness, and nothing is so intolerable to God as human sinfulness. Jesus knew that he would be deliberately destroyed ("Take him away! Take him away! Crucify him!" John 19:15). But he also knew that if human folly put the best of their children to death, God would turn the tables and use this same folly to achieve his greatest victory: the salvation of the world.

Each intimation Jesus made of his death reflects some detail of the Servant of the Lord as the atoning sacrifice, portrayed in Isaiah 53. The cross is the culmination of salvation history: God's redemptive dealings with God's people. His institution of the Eucharist, with its "cup of the new covenant," reminds us of God's "new covenant" promise through Jeremiah (31:31; see also Ezek. 36:24–28). His allusions to drinking wine with his people at the eschatological feast in the Kingdom of God likewise stamp him as the Suffering Servant (Mark 14:22–25; Luke 22:18).

The tempo of the Gospel narratives quickens when Jesus goes up to Jerusalem. He went to die, but his disciples assumed that the time had finally come for him to produce the mighty sign that would establish the Kingdom in power and glory. They saw his "triumphal entry" into Jerusalem as confirmation of their best hopes. It was so messianic! And his subsequent cleansing of the Temple spoke to them of its imminent messianic purging. However, when they saw him betrayed by Judas, forsaken by the rest, condemned by Jews and Gentiles alike, then crucified, their consternation and grief knew no bounds. This was total catastrophe. Their faith failed, and none of the disciples could rise beyond the mournful lament, "We had hoped that he was the one who was going to redeem Israel" (Luke 24:21).

And as for the Kingdom, Jesus' enemies must have been particularly incensed that the Romans by calculated insult deliberately identified Jesus as "King of the Jews" (Mark 15:26). True, Jesus had disassociated himself from Pilate's understanding of the word *king* and had witnessed to his kingship as something of which Roman law took no cognizance (John 18:33–38). The church would understand later that "as sacrificed Lamb he established his claim to universal dominion" (F. F. Bruce 1968: 31; see Rev. 5:5–12), but at the time of his crucifixion there was nothing to suggest that as the dying Messiah he was actually "reigning from the tree." To the disciples all was lost, but from the heavenly perspective, all was victory. As Suzanne de Dietrich pointedly summarizes:

Let it be granted that Satan gathers all the powers of this world together against the Lord's Anointed. Let it be granted that when these hostile forces are mobilized the leaders of Israel, the inheritors of all God's promises, will be in the front ranks. Let it be granted once again that Roman law and order will become the cowardly and obliging accomplices of Jewish intrigue. And let it be granted that Satan will persuade the frightened disciples to renounce their Master, or else will reduce them to silence, and that one of the Twelve will turn traitor. Let all that be granted. Nevertheless, in the midst of all these apparent victories, won by the prince of this world, his ultimate defeat is hidden. He is merely the instrument of a higher purpose . . . and the victory of Jesus becomes . . . his giving his life as a ransom for many. (1960: 183–88)

The Resurrection

The bodily resurrection of Jesus is more than a confession of faith or a proclamation of the victory of good over evil. Taken at face value, the Gospels portray the inescapable fact that the belief of the disciples in the resurrection rested on the empirical experience of their encounters with the risen Jesus. Whereas no one saw him actually rise from the dead, many saw the effects left by the explosion. The visible signs were multiple: the empty tomb, the missing body, the grave clothes, and the actual resurrection appearances. The disciples concluded that Jesus had achieved the central triumph in redemption history (Luke 24:25–46), having been "through the Spirit of holiness . . . declared with power to be the Son of God by his resurrection from the dead" (Rom. 1:4).

Not that they came to this conclusion immediately. In fact, they were "slow to believe" the evidence of his victory: that God had thereby reconciled the world to himself (2 Cor. 5:19), that all powers and authorities had been disarmed (Col. 2:15), that the works of the devil had been destroyed (1 John 3:8), and that he had overcome the world (John 16:33). Was he indeed the Lord of history? Many were more ready to believe that his body had been stolen from the tomb than that a resurrection had taken place (Matt. 28:13, 18). But in time, through much irresistible evidence, they came to faith (Luke 24:36–43; Acts 1:3). And then their joy knew no bounds!

Jesus' Postresurrection Ministry

In the forty-day interval between his resurrection and ascension, Jesus sought to confirm the faith of his disciples and bring to a climax his instruction concerning the Kingdom of God (Acts 1:3). He did this by bringing together three great streams of truth.

First, Jesus "opened to them" the Old Testament through providing his person and work as an authoritative hermeneutical key (Luke 24:25–27). This supplemented the earlier encouragement they had received to count on the continuing illumination of the Holy Spirit to guide them into its truths and into other matters yet to be revealed to chosen apostles (John 16:12–15). He established the indissoluble unity between the older revelation and the things to be revealed in the days ahead, as well as the obligation to condition all thought and practice by submission to its total witness (Eph. 2:20).

Second, he issued the Great Commission. Luke states that Jesus gave them "instructions through the Holy Spirit" and "spoke about the kingdom of God" (Acts 1:2–3). The missionary mandate has three major components:

1. the obligation to proclaim the good news of the Kingdom and persuade people everywhere to respond by repentance and faith;
2. the establishment of a baptized and worshiping community whose focus is Jesus Christ, enthroned in the midst; and
3. the essentiality of obedience: "teaching them to obey everything I have commanded you" (Matt. 28:18–20).

These three components—evangelism, community, and obedience—are all interrelated. "Evangelism is merely beating the air if it does not result in a baptized community capable of growing in witnessing power and obedience" (McLeish 1952: 104). And the obedience of the community must be so comprehensive that each separate congregation is a sign of hope, embodying today all the dimensions of the Kingdom of God that will be manifested tomorrow "in power and glory." So then, Christ's lordship in the church must manifest the Kingdom's universal dimensions: "He must reign until he has put all his enemies under his feet" (1 Cor. 15:25). No longer would their witness to the Kingdom be confined to the house of Israel (Matt. 10:5–6). The resurrection made all the difference. This universal gospel is intended for all peoples. It was not enough that Jesus' universal lordship be assured by his resurrection triumph. This universal reality must now be proclaimed throughout the world; the disciples were obligated to "make disciples of all nations" (Matt. 28:19).

Third, Jesus told them that they were incapable of carrying out the Great Commission on their own. They must wait for the outpouring of the Holy Spirit. After Jesus had stated this, his earthly ministry was finished (Luke 24:49–53).

The Ascension

The ascension of Jesus was the final witness to his divine sonship and the climax of his resurrection appearances. By such a dramatic departure Jesus indicated decisively that there would be no further resurrection appearances. His being raised by God the Father and exalted to his right hand marked the end of an era. Henceforth he is described as "seated" at the right hand of the Father. This seems to indicate that his atoning work was complete and final. The reign of the risen Christ had now begun. He will be bodily absent until he returns in power and glory. By virtue of his being highly exalted, the time had come for the exaltation of his name and the worldwide confession of his lordship. Having earlier been lifted up on the cross, he now was lifted up in glory and began the work of drawing people to himself (John 12:32). By the cross he overcame death. He would now deliver his people from the dominion of darkness and transfer them into the Kingdom of God (Col. 1:13). True, his sovereignty is hidden from the world and known only to his people.

But he awaits that day known only to his Father when he will return to the human scene "in the same way" that he departed "into heaven" (Acts 1:11). Then every eye will see him (Rev. 1:4–7). His enemies will be fully and finally subdued. On that day he will consummate his messianic service by establishing in fullness the Kingdom of God (1 Cor. 15:24–26).

The World, the Powers, and the Last Day

Although the fourth Gospel contains few direct statements about mission, its dominant themes strongly anticipate the Great Commission: "As the Father has sent me, I am sending you" (John 20:21). By this powerful analogy Jesus joined his mission to that of the church. This means that the massive and universal concern that launched Christ's coming into the world was to become the concern of his people. Consider the following: God loves the world (3:16); he desires its salvation (3:17); he sent his Son to take away its sin (1:29) and particularly to overcome its ruler (12:31; 16:11). Jesus, as the light of the world (8:12; 9:5; 12:46), indeed, of every person (1:9), seeks to deliver the world from its darkness, its falsehood, and its bondage to death. Inevitably, his evangelistic invitation is extended to all (3:16; 5:24; etc.). Since the church is unique by virtue of being sent by Christ into the world, its self-understanding matures as it hears and proclaims his words. In this connection it must be able continuously to say: "My teaching is not my own. It comes from him who sent me" (7:16). And this is no small task. The attentive hearing of Jesus' word can illuminate with freshness and relevancy the truths that become overfamiliar with the passage of time. But the cultivation of the attentive ear takes time and single-mindedness. The knowledge of Jesus Christ must be cultivated, or no confessional theology will result.

All of this brings us to the complicated Johannine theme of "world." We have earlier referred to the dualism that characterizes the Gospel of John: "You are from below; I am from above. You are of this world; I am not of this world" (8:23). And yet John's Gospel also speaks of God loving the world (3:16). After all, he created it (1:3), and it continues to be his world. On occasion, the term *kosmos* refers to humankind in general: "The whole world has gone after him" (12:19) in the sense that Jesus had many followers. Although we find no Johannine statement that the created world is intrinsically evil, the Johannine distinctive is that *kosmos* is often used to characterize humankind as evil, rebellious, alienated from God, and spiritually lost. In this sense the world neither knows the Christ (1:10) nor the God who sent him (17:25). Indeed, it hates the One who seeks its salvation (15:18). Behind all this stands an evil personage who has enslaved the world in his opposition to God (12:31; 14:30; 16:11). He is a supernatural intelligence called the devil (8:44; 13:2) and Satan (13:27). His purpose is to frustrate God's redemptive purpose.

What we might call the kingdom of the world always seeks to hide its true face. It conveys the idea that it knows what is best or proper for people; more often than not, its goals seem worthwhile. Hence, its boundary with the Kingdom of God is rarely clearly drawn. One often observes that unredeemed people with good intentions can be easily manipulated by the adversary, with tragic results. Concerning this, Karl Heim writes:

> Nothing that God has created is protected from this demonization. Everything can be seized by it. Therefore there is a demonic self-adulation of the ego, the image of God; a demonic sexuality of which man is no longer the master; the demonism of technology; the demonism of power; the demonic degeneration of nationalism. There is a demonism of piety, and prayer itself can get lost in demonic convulsion. . . . Even the gift of the Holy Spirit can be demonized. The satanic element in the matter lies in this: the demonic power depends entirely on God and what he has created. It possesses nothing that does not come from God. Whatever is demonized and turned against God is always but a distorted image of the glory of God. (quoted in Vicedom 1965: 19)

This antagonism between the kingdom of the world and the Kingdom of God is relentless, with the issue of truth precipitating tension and division again and again (John 5:18; 6:66; 7:12; 7:43; 8:59; 9:16; etc.). Tension is unavoidable because the mission of Jesus was not one of withdrawal from the world but one of being sent into it to confront the world in its totality. In the world he demonstrated by signs that he was the revealed "Word" from God and the redeeming Son of God. The signs authenticated his person and mission and spoke prophetically to his generation. His new wine of the dawning messianic era was in sharp contrast to the sterility of Judaism (the empty water jars, John 2:1–12). He was himself the sign of the messianic banquet, where all are fed the bread of life (6:1–14, 22–59); the light of the world resolving the world's blindness (9:1–7); and the eschatological resurrection to eternal life foreshadowed by the raising of Lazarus (11:1–44) (Ladd 1974: 274).

Jesus' disciples were to do "greater things" after they were sent into the world (John 14:12). This speaks again of the obligation to confront the world, to serve it faithfully, and to resist every temptation to abdicate from the responsibilities it rightfully expects God's people to bear in his world. Even as the climax of Jesus' servant instruction to his disciples was to provide them with the model of washing their feet (13:1–20), so they were to serve the world to which he came to bring life (6:33). Eschatology has been defined as "a dimension of belief . . . that history moves in a direction, and that this direction is set by God, and that God acts within history to ensure this direction" (Hubbard 1983: 34, quoting P. R. Davies). Since the fourth Gospel equates the Kingdom of God with eternal life, its essential perspective is eschatological. This follows because the possession of eternal life implies that one has moved beyond death and hence already enjoys unbroken fellowship with God through his abiding presence and the blessings that his presence implies. In this sense it is an individualized "realized eschatology." This means that on the practical level in the present age, through bestowing eternal life to individuals, Jesus has made possible their experiencing in the here and now the life of the age to come.

Because of this possibility, we might get the initial impression that in the fourth Gospel eschatology, as such, is not very important. Instead of the Olivet Discourse in the Synoptics climaxing with the coming of the Son of Man with the clouds of heaven, one finds the upper room discourse, with its focus on the coming of the Holy Spirit (John 13–16), an event between the first and second comings of Jesus. Not that John is silent about the Parousia. We recall his word to Peter with reference to "the disciple whom Jesus loved": "If I want him to remain alive until I return, what is that to you?" (21:22). Moreover, there will be a future eschatological judgment in which the standard will be the words of Jesus (12:48). Even so, Jesus stated that those who have received him as Lord and Savior have passed from death to life (5:24) and will not experience that future judgment. The only implication one can draw from this is that "judgment is also a present spiritual reality as men respond favorably or unfavorably in faith or in unbelief, to the person and ministry of Jesus" (Ladd 1974: 308).

Conclusion

The fourth Gospel is a profound theological statement that is multifaceted in its references to mission. Winn concludes his stimulating study on mission in this Gospel by calling attention to the man born blind, whose eyes Jesus opened (9:1–7). He is directed to "wash in the Pool of Siloam (this word means Sent)" ("Having-been-sent," 9:7). Winn encourages us to pray that through this Gospel, Christians will be better informed on what mission is all about, that they too will deal with their blindness to the world around them as it really is, and "let a sense of mission be the center of their lives, the center of their identity as Christians." The need is for all Christians to wash in the pool of "Having-been-sent" (1981: 114). This total immersion in God's mission is what it means for Christians to seek first the Kingdom of God and his justice (Matt. 6:33).

PART 5

GOD'S MISSION THROUGH THE HOLY SPIRIT BY THE CHURCH

16

The Holy Spirit Inaugurates
the Missionary Church

Introduction

With the advent of the Holy Spirit on the day of Pentecost, God's redemptive activity shifted from working through a particular people (the descendants of Abraham via Isaac and Jacob and Israel) to working in the midst of all peoples. On that day the New Testament expression of the people of God, the church, was formed and empowered for its worldwide mission. This marks the resumption of universal history with which the Bible begins (Gen. 1–11). As such, its significance is of primary importance to all concerned with the nature and purpose of the church, particularly its mandate to preach the gospel of the Kingdom throughout the world as a witness to all nations (Matt. 24:14).

Pentecost marks the completion of the initial phase of Christ's redemptive work. When he ascended into heaven and presented himself as the firstfruits of the coming worldwide harvest, he could look back with joy on having endured the cross (Heb. 12:2). As the triumphant High Priest, he now "entered the Most Holy Place once for all by his own blood, having obtained eternal redemption" for his people (Heb. 9:12). The church has always believed that when his Father accepted this sacrifice "for the sins of the whole world" (1 John 2:2) and exalted him on high (Phil. 2:9–11), the Father and the Son together sent forth the Spirit. The coming of the Spirit doubtless tended to confirm to the people of God the satisfaction of the Father with the sacrifice. But more, the sending forth of the Spirit was to enable the church to carry out its primary task to "bring [the scattered children of God] together and make them one" (John 11:52).

So then, Pentecost both consummates Easter and represents its fullness. It marks a watershed in salvation history, the beginning of a new age under a new covenant. In fact, an analogy can be drawn between Jesus' baptism and anointing at the Jordan River and what the disciples experienced on this memorable day (Dunn 1970: 40).

Pentecost and Jesus Christ

Prior to Pentecost the Gospels make much of Jesus Christ in his relation to the Holy Spirit. He was conceived by the Holy Spirit (Matt. 1:20), anointed by the Spirit at his baptism (Matt. 3:16–17; Acts 10:38), "led of the Spirit into the desert to be tempted by the devil" (Matt. 4:1), and following this victory "returned to Galilee in the power of the Spirit" (Luke 4:14) to begin his ministry. The evangelists on occasion refer to the Spirit in connection with Jesus' messianic acts of mercy and exorcism (e.g., Matt. 12:28).

In the Gospel of John, Jesus is described as the bearer of the Spirit (given to him fully, 3:34–35) and as the One in whose name the Father will send the Spirit (14:26). Furthermore, Jesus speaks of himself as sending the Spirit (15:26). Directly after his resurrection he enacted the manner in which the Spirit would proceed from him to his disciples ("he breathed on them," 20:22). The One on whom the Spirit descended and remained (at his baptism) becomes the One who baptizes with the Spirit (1:33).

This has tremendous implications when we seek to understand the universalization of the gospel of the Kingdom of God on the day of Pentecost. One recalls Jesus' pre-Pentecost words to the Samaritan woman at the well. She wanted to know where to worship God, whether in Jerusalem or on Mount Gerizim (John 4:20). In response, Jesus affirmed what Pentecost provided: "A time is coming when you will worship the Father neither on this mountain nor in Jerusalem. . . . when the true worshipers will worship the Father in spirit and truth, for they are the kind of worshipers the Father seeks. God is spirit, and his worshipers must worship in spirit and in truth" (4:21–24). How did the woman understand these words? Was Jesus only saying that a new day was coming when geography would be of no significance? We do not think so. Jesus' use of the word *spirit* spoke to her concerning more than only the Messiah and his representation of the vital nature of God: the God of creation and re-creation. She was not uninformed. She knew that the Messiah at his coming would bring newness of life to his disobedient people. The prophets had taught that the long-awaited Messiah would pour out his Spirit on all flesh (Joel 2:28) and would come upon the remnant of his people, the dry bones, restoring them to life once again (Ezek. 37:5, 14). This was "the hope of Israel" (Acts 28:20).

God is Spirit, and the Messiah is God's agent in breathing the breath of life into his people. Furthermore, those who worship him must worship him in Spirit and in truth. This would mean their submission to God's active presence in their hearts in a way that is consistent with God's covenant. Worship must come from the heart. All formal worship, if devoid of heart involvement, is never acceptable. Moreover, when Jesus said to the Samaritan woman the time for such worship "is now," he was saying that God could now be worshiped in Spirit and truth. This means "in his promised verifying presence" (H. Berkhof 1964: 16). Jesus' words probably brought this hope to the woman's mind. Her response was: "I know that Messiah . . . is coming" (John

4:25). This elicited Jesus' most unambiguous confession concerning himself: "I who speak to you am he" (4:26).

This analysis is supported by Karl Barth. Barth repudiated the liberal interpretation that God is to be found in every person's heart and conscience and worshiped there, with revelation considered unnecessary. Barth did not see biblical support for the thesis that the devotees of other religious traditions are in vital contact with the One who is the God and Father of our Lord and Savior, Jesus Christ. Rather, he stressed

> the worship of God mediated through Jesus—the One who makes everything known to us. Salvation is really of the Jews. . . . When it has actually come from the Jews and been rejected by the Jews, as such it is no more simply for the Jews, but from the Jews for all, Jews and Gentiles who are ready to be worshipers of this kind in Spirit and in truth, as the Father wishes them to be. (1957: 481)

God is now to be worshiped in the place where he is present, that is, in the One who is truth incarnate. Jesus Christ means "the real presence of God as Spirit in his indwelling and recreating activity" (Hendry 1956: 32, quoted by H. Berkhof 1964: 17). So then, we should underscore the uniqueness of the person and work of Jesus Christ. In the power of the Holy Spirit, Jesus is the center of God's life-giving presence among all people.

This does not mean, however, that we should then conceive of the Holy Spirit as significantly subordinate to Christ, to be largely occupied from Pentecost onward with awakening faith in him. We put it this way for in our day there is a tendency to forget the full implications of John 16:8–11—"When he comes, he will convict the world of guilt in regard to sin, . . . in regard to righteousness, . . . and in regard to judgment." Actually, the coming of the Holy Spirit at Pentecost marked the great new event in the sequence of God's mighty acts of redemption. To quote Louis Berkhof:

> [The Holy Spirit] creates a world of his own, a world of conversion, experience, sanctification; of tongues, prophecy, and miracles; of upbuilding and guiding the church, etc. He appoints ministers; he organizes; he illumines, inspires, and sustains; he intercedes for the saints and helps them in their weaknesses; he searches everything, even the depths of God; he guides into all truth; he grants a variety of gifts; he convinces the world; he declares the things that are to come. In short, as the Johannine Jesus says: "He who believes in me will also do the works that I do; and greater works than these will he do, because I go to the Father." (1946: 23, with reference to John 14:12)

This statement underscores what charismatic groups are seeking to say to the church at large in our day. The Holy Spirit is not only in the service of Christ as his instrument for worldwide evangelization. He is the actual center of a great variety of "Kingdom actions." True, Jesus Christ remains the sole center and object of faith, and the Spirit always remains intimately connected with him as the Spirit of

Christ. This is what the lordship of Christ really means and is the thrust of Paul's confession in 2 Corinthians 3:17: "Now the Lord is the Spirit." Hence, to be "in Christ" is to be "in the Spirit" for "the Spirit is Christ in action" (H. Berkhof 1964: 24–26). In the same vein Paul states that "the last Adam [became] a life-giving spirit" (1 Cor. 15:45). In the Holy Spirit the resurrected Christ manifests his resurrection power. By the Spirit he seeks to interject himself into the human race as a new stream of life. Hence, we should not confine the Spirit's work to the inner world of the human heart. This perspective should not lessen in our minds the other reality, namely, that the risen Lord Jesus is presently exalted at the Father's right hand. In that glory he is the firstfruits of the people of God (1 Cor. 15:23). His presence there gives assurance of the ultimate victory of God on their behalf. Indeed, his pledged intercession is his guarantee that the people of God will persevere in history until the last day (Rom. 8:34).

The pressure of Jesus' teaching and the events of Pentecost demand that we give priority to a central theme: not the church but the Kingdom. Further, it is not the Kingdom in general terms but Kingdom and mission. The various statements of the Great Commission underscore in a dynamic way the massive priority that mission has over all other activities of the Spirit, even the formation of the church.

Pentecost and Mission

Peter's proclamation when he "stood up with the eleven" (Acts 2:14) was the first expression of Christian obedience to the task of mission. Indeed, "The first cry of life from the newborn Church was the proclamation that Jesus is the Lord of heaven and earth, as well as the Messiah of the Jews" (Kraus 1974: 26; with reference to Acts 2:36). By his identification of the Pentecostal signs as setting the stage for the day of the Lord prophesied by Joel (2:28–32), Peter used the keys of the Kingdom to inaugurate the beginning of a new day of salvation. Men and women, young and old, could now become new creatures in Christ (Jer. 31:33; Ezek. 36:27; 2 Cor. 5:17) and could participate in the worldwide mission of the church. So then, Pentecost marked the initial fulfillment of the prophetic vision of the uplifted Temple in Zion. This is the good news of God's mighty redemptive acts, now culminating in Jesus Christ, by which he has completely reconciled the world to himself (Isa. 2:2–4; Mic. 4:1–3; John 2:19–21; 12:32; 2 Cor. 5:19; etc.). In response, many Jews and later varied Gentile peoples began to turn to God in repentance and faith. A new Israel was being formed consisting of Messianic Jews and "all who are far off . . . all whom the Lord our God will call" (Acts 2:39).

In recent years much debate has swirled around the issue of missionary motivation. Why were the apostles so eager to bear witness to the resurrected Christ? Was it because of his resurrection appearances and the good news they represented? Was it because of the Great Commission and the obligation this mandate represented? Or was it their Pentecostal experience? Actually, all three factors contributed, but the coming of the Spirit must be identified as the central dynamic. As Harry Boer states:

The descent of the Spirit at Pentecost made the disciples apostles, i.e., missionaries. One might say it branded them as apostles. The world-embracing missionary vision is expressed in prophetic reality in the speaking with tongues. At Pentecost, the whole of God's redemptive purpose for the world was for a moment set off in bold relief. (1961: 62)

So then, we do not want to limit the Holy Spirit only to the work of awakening faith (justification) and to the work of perfecting faith (sanctification). The Spirit must primarily be seen as the driving force behind any and all movements of the people of God outward, beyond the frontiers of faith, to share the gospel with those who have not yet heard it. Mission means movement from Christ by his Spirit to the world he reconciled. As such, it stands in sharpest contrast to the individualistic or ecclesiastical introversion so common in large segments of the contemporary Christian scene.

The missionary movement stands uniquely within an eschatological context. With Pentecost the last days have dawned, and they will not be finished until the gospel of the Kingdom is preached throughout the whole world as a testimony to all nations (Matt. 24:14). This means that Jesus Christ has inaugurated this age of the Spirit and will consummate it. The Spirit-in-mission

forms the unity of the Christological and the eschatological poles of God's saving work. He is the expansion of the divine saving presence over the earth. He is the way from the One to the many, from the middle to the end of the times, from the center to the ends of the earth. (H. Berkhof 1964: 35)

When we consider the many texts that refer to the work of the Holy Spirit-in-mission, we see that this Spirit is the primary agent of mission, and human beings are secondary. "The Spirit of truth," Jesus said, "will testify about me. And you also must testify" (John 15:26–27). So then, Christians are to sense their God-given responsibility to put heart, soul, conscience, and resources to the task of proclaiming the gospel; but to one and all, Jesus says, "Do not worry about what to say or how to say it. At that time you will be given what to say, for it will not be you speaking, but the Spirit of your Father speaking through you" (Matt. 10:19–20).

This is in contrast to the tendency to become preoccupied solely with a person's inner spiritual life. In Acts, whenever mention is made of believers being filled with the Holy Spirit, the account always goes on to mention speech (2:2; 4:8, 31; 7:55–56; 9:17–20; 10:44–46; 13:9–10; 13:52–14:1; 19:6; etc.). Whereas it is true that the fruit of the Spirit described in Galatians 5:22–23 is largely his provision of inward graces, Acts would have us understand that a primary work of the Spirit is to open people's mouths and get them to bear witness to Jesus Christ. Indeed, "the higher gifts" of the Spirit are those that make possible the oral ministry of God's Word (1 Cor. 12:31; 14:1–3). When the Spirit opened the heart of Lydia in Acts 16:14, it was by means of the Word of the Lord being spoken by Paul, and it moved her to hear and receive that Word. As Hendrikus Berkhof stated:

If the Lord opens the heart, he does it in such a way that we give heed to the Word. The testimony of the Spirit in our hearts is not heard in our hearts but in the recognition of the testimony of one Spirit in the Word. The Spirit moves through the world in the shape of the Word in its various forms. The Word is the instrument of the Spirit; but the Spirit is not the prisoner of the Word, nor does the Word work automatically. The Word brings the Spirit to the heart, and the Spirit brings the Word within the heart. (1964: 38)

The phenomenon of tongues, equally intelligible to people of diverse languages, underscores the fact that it is of the essence of the church to bear witness "by [what] is said and done" (Rom. 15:18). Deeds need words of explanation, and words need deeds of confirmation (John 5:36). The gospel is for the devout "from every nation under heaven" (Acts 2:5, 39). Therefore, the manifestation of tongues was a confirmation of God's intention to reverse the scattering and hostility of the nations that followed the judgment at Babel (Gen. 11:1–9) and unite in Christ his people from all nations. When the many pilgrims in Jerusalem at that time heard the disciples' witness, "each one . . . in his own language" (Acts 2:6), this underscored God's desire that all persons hear the good news in their mother tongue. Actually, no linguistic miracle was really needed for interpersonal communication on that occasion, for the probability is that the pilgrims and residents in Jerusalem were already able to communicate with one another in either Aramaic or Greek. But hearing in the vernacular brought power and precision to the message. A person's heart language is always the best vehicle for gospel communication.

Pentecost also marked the beginning of the bestowal of spiritual gifts on all the redeemed. Through this provision each and every one, in his or her place, was able to experience joint participation with Christ in the local assembly and to witness through him to the unbelieving world. In this sense Pentecost represented something unheard of under the old covenant, apart from Moses' wistful prayer: "I wish that all the LORD's people were prophets and that the LORD would put his Spirit on them" (Num. 11:26–29). From Pentecost onward all Christians are to regard themselves as called to full-time involvement in the task of making Jesus Christ known, loved, and served throughout the world. All have been given spiritual gifts to make this service possible (1 Cor. 12:4–11). We shall speak more of this when we consider the radically new approach to the ministry that soon developed in the apostolic church.

Pentecost and the Church

Immediately following the passage from Joel that Peter used to interpret the eschatological significance of Pentecost, one finds the following promise: "On Mount Zion and in Jerusalem there will be deliverance, . . . among the survivors whom the LORD calls" (2:32b). This specific analogous reference to the Lord's deliverance of an elect remnant from a plague of locusts in Joel's day underscored what happened on Pentecost when the Lord by the proclamation of the gospel delivered three thousand from the plague of sin. They were baptized and received the gift of the Holy Spirit. With Peter and the earlier believers, they now constituted the true Israel and saw themselves as the inheritors of the promises God had made to his people through the prophets. They almost immediately found themselves separated from that "corrupt generation" (Acts 2:40). Indeed, one could say that those who rejected Jesus and failed to repent thereby ceased to be Israelites (Deut. 32:5; Acts 3:25–26). They had forfeited their covenant relationship with God.

At this point the church begins to take form as a people separated by God to fulfill his purpose for the nations. They are "holy" in the sense that God in his holiness has made his people holy (Exod. 31:13). As Flew has stated:

> Christians are "the saints," first, because they are the true Israel; and second, because they are living in the new order, under the reign of God, and awaiting the return of Christ as Judge. (1960: 102)

Underlying this was the conviction, affirmed by Peter (Acts 2:16–17), that the messianic era had dawned and the last days were at hand. This was confirmed by the gift of the Spirit (Isa. 44:3). But Pentecost was not the very last day, for Peter differentiated between that initial manifestation of the new era and the future "times of refreshing." That day would be the "time . . . for God to restore everything, as he promised long ago through his holy prophets," when the Christ would be sent back from heaven to this world (Acts 3:19–21).

The fundamental characteristic of this new Christ-confessing community was that all its members received the gift of the Spirit. Acts 2:17–18 speaks of his being poured out on "all people," male and female, young and old, slaves and free. The very inclusiveness of this baptism constituted the democratization of the prophetic consciousness. All were empowered to bear witness to the resurrection (2:32). Their new experience of the Holy Spirit was something they shared in common rather than treasured privately, because it transcended the distinctions of sex, age, and caste. As a result, a new corporateness emerged.

These new believers began to express their spiritual oneness by devoting "themselves to the apostles' teaching and to the fellowship, to the breaking of bread and to prayer" (Acts 2:42). So then, from the very first, the essence and vitality of the new community were integral and essential to their confession that Jesus Christ is Lord. The reality of their loving acceptance of one another and their pattern of selfless sharing (koinōnia) was nothing less than the universalization of the ministry of Jesus by the Spirit in and through each member. All sensed his call to participate in the new social reality that the Holy Spirit was sending forth into the world. Their sense of spiritual identity with one another enabled them to affirm their communal relationship "in Christ" by loving service "to anyone as he had need" (Acts 2:45). It was a magnetic fellowship, a corporate participation in the gift of the Spirit that expressed itself in outward acts. These acts constituted the marks of the true church.

We should particularly notice the reference to their "breaking of bread." This oft-repeated symbolic act spoke to them of their new privilege of sharing in the benefits of Jesus' vicarious self-giving on their behalf. Their disciplined reflection on the apostles' teaching must have embraced not only the whole revelation given by Jesus himself (Matt. 28:20) but also the Old Testament and the hermeneutical key he had provided for its correct understanding (Luke 24:27, 44–47). We can well imagine the intellectual wrestling that must have taken place in their midst. They must now regard the Old Testament as mere raw material that had to be reevaluated in the light of Jesus' teaching. They had to take seriously the redemptive as well as ethical implications of his cross. As members of the true Israel, they recognized that the Spirit in their midst had been given to enable them to practice a righteousness wholly consonant with the beatitudes of Jesus, in keeping with his call to childlikeness, forgiveness, nonretaliation, and love.

Pentecost and the Apostolic Gospel

When we analyze Peter's sermon (Acts 2:16–40), we find that it consists of four basic themes:

1. Old Testament prophecy has been fulfilled in the coming of the Spirit (vv. 16–21).
2. Jesus of Nazareth has been vindicated as Lord and Christ (vv. 22–28).
3. Death has been overcome, as evidenced by the presence of the Spirit (vv. 29–35).
4. Forgiveness and the gift of the Spirit are now available to those who repent (vv. 36–40).

We agree with F. F. Bruce that when Peter preached the gospel to Cornelius and his household, he pointedly included another component. He said that Christ had charged the apostles to proclaim that he is the one "whom God appointed as judge of the living and the dead" (Acts 10:42). It is significant that the apostle Paul also included this in his evangelistic preaching (17:31). We dare not minimize the final and complete manifestation of the Kingdom of God, when Christ will be acknowledged by all—redeemed and unrepentant alike—as the Lord of glory (1954: 35).

This summary includes the essentialness of the church and is replete with Kingdom ideas, to which the church is always subordinate. The Word of God, embracing the good news of the Kingdom, creates the church. Luke expresses this axiomatic reality when he states: "The word of God spread. The number of disciples . . . increased rapidly" (Acts 6:7).

A review of all the references in Acts to the Kingdom of God (seven) offers a compelling conviction that the apostles regarded this term as synonymous with the gospel of the grace of God. They did not use it to refer to Israel (1:3–7). They identified it with "the name of Jesus Christ" (8:12) and fully expected that its proclamation would lead to belief in Jesus (8:5). On occasion, when addressing both Jewish and Gentile believers, they stressed its eschatological implications by stating that "we must go through many hardships to enter the kingdom of God" (14:22). In Ephesus Paul's three months of preaching in the synagogue are summarized as "arguing persuasively about the kingdom of God" (19:8), and this is equated with testifying "to the gospel of God's grace" (20:24–25). In Rome Paul proclaimed to the Jews "God's salvation" (28:28), and this activity is defined as testifying to "the kingdom of God and [trying] to convince them about Jesus from the Law of Moses and from the Prophets" (28:23). His ministry of preaching the Kingdom of God and teaching about the Lord Jesus Christ constituted one message (28:31).

Jesus rarely spoke of God as King or of God as ruling. His use of Kingdom language embraced rather the defeat of God's enemies, victory over evil, and the blessing of God's people, that is, God's action leading to salvation. The very infrequency with which the term is found outside the Synoptic Gospels would seem to indicate that the early church "replaced" the Kingdom with "the person in whom the Kingdom was revealed." Their message was about "another king, one called Jesus" rather than about "another Kingdom" (Acts 17:7). Even to identify Jesus as a king ran the risk of misunderstanding. The casual hearer might conclude that the Christian message had subversive political overtones. So great were the suspicions of Caesar that the early Christians deliberately avoided Kingdom language and subsumed the gospel of the Kingdom into "Jesus Christ and him crucified."

However, we should not limit the gospel of the Kingdom to the redemptive dimensions of the cross. God's good news for our generation is not to be confined to his willingness to forgive the sins of the penitent through the merits of Christ's atonement. Whenever one seeks to define the good news of the Kingdom as Jesus and the apostles sought to personalize it, problems arise because of its sheer complexity. Who can exhaust all that is involved in God's bringing his people into a right relationship with himself and in the gracious possibilities of living in this relationship? Richard De Ridder attempted to deal with this when he stated that

> the essence and foundation of the Kingdom is its existence as the inbreaking of the Spirit, power, and justice of God. . . . This Kingdom lies behind, surrounds, and gives meaning to the cosmos, and is in its essence the presence of the God of justice who has called the world into being and placed on the creation the judgment of his sovereignty. (1971: 121)

God "calls [people] out of the dimension of the physical into that of the spiritual, out of the realm of the temporal into that of the eternal, calling [them] to live in God's spiritual world and in his spiritual time even as they continue to live in his world of [humanity] and in the time of history" (Baird 1963: 141, quoted by De Ridder 1971: 139).

What rendered this message most perplexing to the Jews was the role of servant that Jesus adopted and the power of the servanthood that he displayed. This made the Kingdom of God quite upside down, for it not only reflected the complete rejection of the traditional concept of kingdom but was itself its very antithesis.

Conclusion

The advent of the Holy Spirit made possible the beginning of a new era in which God would seek in new ways to covenant with God's people. We recall that in Old Testament times God was revealed as a "warrior" (Exod. 15:3). He promised the Israelites again and again that he would be their Liberator and their Defender, provided their hearts were "fully committed to him" (2 Chron. 16:9). The big test facing the church forever after Pentecost has been whether it would let God be God in its midst or whether it would commit the folly of Israel, turning from trust in God to "depend on flesh for . . . strength" (Jer. 17:5–8). As we press deeper into our study of the New Testament record and review the experience of the apostolic church, we shall be increasingly confronted with all that it means for the church to "fight" this "good fight of the faith" (1 Tim. 6:12).

17

The Jerusalem Church Proclaims
the Kingdom of God

Introduction

When we begin to consider Acts and its contribution to our understanding of the mission of the church, we are confronted with a wide range of problems. These arise from the dimension of mystery surrounding the purposes that Luke had in mind in writing this book. At first glance everything seems obvious. Luke gives us the impression that this volume is merely a sequel to his Gospel. His statement that his Gospel recorded "all that Jesus began to do and to teach" (1:1) gives the impression that Acts will be a continuation of the works and words of Jesus through his apostles. Later when we come upon 1:8, we easily conclude that his theme will be their worldwide witness to the risen Christ.

But when we study Luke's second volume critically, questions arise. For instance, why does he not mention the acts of Matthias (1:26)? And what of the Twelve? He only mentions John seven times and then abruptly leaves him in Samaria (12:2). His references to Peter virtually end with the story of Peter's miraculous deliverance from prison. He entertains us with the very human story of the mix-up in Jerusalem that left the Christians wondering "what had become of Peter" (12:18). Then he makes no further references to him apart from recording his defense of Paul at the Jerusalem Council (15:7–11). Even now in the twenty-first century, we are still wondering what became of Peter! In a similar vein, all references to "the apostles" are confined to the first sixteen chapters. Then silence. But the largest question concerns Paul. Why does Luke devote more than half of Acts to a record of Paul's activities so highly selective that it still frustrates scholars because of its gaps? Ladd rightly concludes that the more one studies Acts, the more convincing becomes the thesis that Luke's "selection of historical data is so controlled by a distinct purpose that he has left scholars with nearly insoluble problems in correlating the data of Acts with the epistles" (1968: 12).

What then were Luke's distinct purposes? Is Acts merely a reflection of Luke's understanding of history and his desire to record what actually happened after

Pentecost? This was a popular view in the nineteenth century: Acts was nothing more than a sequel to the Gospel, an extension of the objective Luke stated in the Gospel prologue (1:1–4). More recently, some scholars have contended that the dominant concern of Acts is to portray the evangelistic and church growth dimensions of the early church. Given the massive literature that has been produced contending for a variety of mutually conflicting theories of Luke's alleged purpose in writing Acts, we will not presume to enter this debate. What concerns us is the contribution of Acts to our understanding of the Christian mission. So then, our selective use of its contents will largely enable us to avoid taking sides on issues that are peripheral to our concern.

Israel

Insight into the "theological history" of Luke-Acts can be gained by contrasting the opening chapters of the Gospel with the closing chapter of Acts. The Gospel begins in a context rich in its Old Testament flavor and allusions. All is familiar ground: synagogue, Temple, and sacrifice; the reiterations of Israel's hope along with the messianic prophecies; the coming redemption and Kingdom blessing for Israel; and even some intimations that Israel's golden age would include Gentiles worshiping the covenant God of Abraham, Isaac, and Jacob (Luke 1:32–33, 54–55, 68–75; 2:30–32; 4:18–21; etc.). But the context of Acts 28 is pagan Rome: the Jews there were rejecting the message of the Kingdom of God while the Gentiles were responsive to the message that Jesus Christ is Lord and Savior (28:31).

It seems that this radical shift in salvation history is what Luke sought to highlight in his two-volume work. He would have us understand theologically those two crucial generations in the first century, when a spiritual movement deep within Jewry emerged and was transformed into a universal religious community largely Gentile in composition. As Ladd summarizes:

> Luke will relate the story by which this radical transformation of the Jewish hope took place. He will indicate how a crucified teacher embodies the true fulfillment of the Old Testament promise of Messiah. He will show how the Gentile church took the place of Israel. He will trace the connection between the Kingdom of God and the Christian church. (1968: 20)

We must underscore the reality and significance of the displacement of Israel by the church. The growing Gentile church, portrayed so vividly in Acts, must be seen as the true people of the messianic era. And there are two sides to this displacement. The negative side of this tragic reality is that although the leaders of Judaism were given repeated opportunities to hear the gospel from the lips of Spirit-filled Jewish believers, they deliberately excluded themselves from the Kingdom of God. This brought upon Judaism the judgment of God and makes Acts sad reading. But the positive side of the displacement is that the gospel, although deeply rooted in

Judaism and although repudiated by Jewish leaders, became both attractive and of surpassing value to non-Jews.

This means that the story recorded in the Gospel of Luke becomes "fulfillment" despite Jewish rejection of it. In Acts Luke sought to reassure the members of the emerging Gentile church that their submission to Jesus as Lord and Savior is the authentic goal toward which God's dealings with Israel were moving. In this connection Maddox perceptively writes:

> The full stream of God's saving action in history has not passed them by, but has flowed straight into their community life, in Jesus and the Holy Spirit. If there are apostates and heretics who have cut themselves off from participation in the Kingdom of God, it is not the Christians to whom such terms apply. . . . With such a message of reassurance, Luke summons his fellow-Christians to worship God with whole-hearted joy, to follow Jesus with unwavering loyalty, and to carry on with zeal, through the power of the Spirit, the chance to be his witnesses to the end of the earth. (1982: 187)

The first indications of this exposition of the Israelite faith in universal terms in Acts are found in Peter's sermon on the day of Pentecost. The prophet Joel had predicted that the Spirit would be poured out on "all people," with primary reference to all the people of Israel, its sons and daughters, its old and young, its manservants and maidservants (Acts 2:17–18). Peter applied these words to a special group within Israel, the followers of Jesus. A faithful remnant had replaced the nation. But in this same sermon (2:30, 34) Peter also reinterpreted Psalm 110. Despite the psalm's center in Jerusalem, from which the Lord sends forth the Messiah (Ps. 110:2), Peter went on to speak of Christ's heavenly enthronement at the right hand of God. As the descendant of David, Jesus now exercises a spiritual reign from heaven that extends to this new and true Israel.

During those first years the church was largely regarded as a messianic sect within Judaism. Its members conscientiously studied the Scriptures, observed the law, worshiped in the Temple, and participated in the religious and social life of the synagogue (Acts 2:46; 3:1; 5:12; 10:14). Despite their confession of Jesus as Lord and Christ, their initiatory rite of baptism, and their possession of the gift of the Holy Spirit, they doubtless understood their new movement largely in Jewish terms. They did not withdraw from association with unbelieving Jews or denounce them as apostates. The breach between nonmessianic synagogues and their house congregations was not very wide. All this was true until the advent of Stephen.

Stephen was probably a Hellenist, a Greek-speaking Jew. Because of this, his perspectives were more akin to those of the Jews of the Diaspora than to those of Palestinian Jews. His "great wonders and miraculous signs" and outspoken witness to the gospel brought him into open confrontation with the Jewish authorities and eventually to a formal hearing before the Sanhedrin. He was charged with speaking "against Moses and against God . . . against this holy place and against the law" (Acts 6:8–15).

Stephen's response constitutes a theological introduction to Luke's narrative of the historic shift in salvation history from Jewish synagogue to Gentile world mission. He largely ignored the charges made against him and concentrated on reviewing God's dealings with Israel outside the land and apart from the Temple. His radical reinterpretation of Israel's sacred moments underscored the fact that God was not limited to the Temple (Acts 7:48). And the possession of the law had not produced a people either submissive to God or productive of the sort of good works that drew the nations to faith in God (7:51–53). In short, Stephen's presentation was a defense of the validity of what happened in Israel in the weeks, months, and years following Pentecost.

Only a remnant responded to the call to repent and follow Christ. Hence, the stage was being set for outreach among the Gentiles, with every expectation that from among them would come those who would believe. Although Stephen was never able to finish his defense, one gets the impression that he was developing a sequence of analogies: Joseph and Moses were both rejected by their brethren; both became mighty among the Gentiles; and subsequently both brought blessing to their own people (Acts 7:17–44). Jesus too was rejected by his people when he first encountered them.

At this point Stephen was silenced, but not before he spoke of the exaltation of the rejected One and thereby intimated the ongoing movement of God's redemptive purpose among the Gentiles. In the eyes of the enraged members of the Sanhedrin, Stephen challenged their much cherished particularism and seemed to be advocating a universal faith that superseded temple worship. Hence, they destroyed him (Acts 7:51–60). We should not minimize this tragic event. It represented the official action of the highest court in Jewry. By it the Jewish leaders revealed once again their implacable hatred of Jesus, whom they had earlier condemned (Mark 14:55–64).

Commenting on Acts 4:1–2, in which Jewish leaders were "greatly disturbed because the apostles were teaching the people and proclaiming in Jesus the resurrection of the dead," F. F. Bruce perceptively observes:

> It is particularly striking that neither on this nor on any subsequent occasion (so far as our information goes) did the Sanhedrin take any serious action to disprove the apostles' central affirmation—the resurrection of Jesus. Had it seemed possible to refute them on this point, how readily would the Sanhedrin have seized the opportunity! Had they succeeded, how quickly and completely the new movement would have collapsed! (1954: 103)

On this occasion Stephen's words (Acts 7:56) so paralleled those of Jesus that the Sanhedrin felt that the movement these two represented posed a threat to the abiding validity of all Jewish institutions. From Stephen's martyrdom onward, official Judaism was determined to destroy all those among the Hellenists who had begun to follow Jesus. And, as would be expected, Luke shows that the movement of the Holy Spirit then shifted away from Jerusalem to Samaria (8:5–25), then to a

Gentile proselyte in Palestine (8:26–40), and on to the borders of Jewry (9:32–43). Soon a whole Gentile household was reached (chap.10), and in Syrian Antioch a largely Gentile church was brought into being (11:19–26). It is this church that became the base of operations for the evangelization of the eastern Mediterranean world (chaps. 13–19).

We should not imagine that all Jewish believers in Jesus were happy over this outward movement. In one sense, they uniformly rejoiced that God was granting to the Gentiles "repentance unto life" (Acts 11:18). But what bothered many was that these new converts were not being circumcised nor were they instructed in the observance of the law of Moses (15:1, 5). This necessitated a special council of "apostles and elders" in Jerusalem to deal with the matter. Luke reported the details of this council rather completely, since they were supportive of his primary thesis that God's intention all along was to bring into being through the gospel a largely Gentile church during this age of the Holy Spirit. It is significant that field reports of the salvation of God reaching Gentiles did not fully resolve the debate (15:7–11). However, the Holy Spirit's activity in visiting the Gentiles and calling out from among them a people for his name (15:14) indicated that God's people were now to be found among the Gentiles.

What clinched the discussion was James' use of Scripture (Acts 15:16–18). He quoted Amos 9:11–12, with its preview of the successive steps in the ongoing development of God's redemptive purpose: (1) the coming of Christ, (2) the rebuilding of the "dwelling of David," and (3) the outreach among the Gentiles. The first step referred to the coming of the Messiah, about which all were familiar. The second step had been earlier interpreted as referring to the restoration of Israel as a sovereign state under Davidic rule but which James reinterprets as being fulfilled in the death, burial, resurrection, and exaltation of the Messiah. The third step can only mean that the true Israel, over whom the greater Son of David reigns, is indeed the church. Hence, James concluded with an unmistakable emphasis on mission: today the rest of humanity may seek the Lord, since the Gentiles are now being called to faith in the resurrected and exalted Messiah. Ladd concludes his discussion of the Jerusalem Council in the following fashion.

> It was on the basis of this amazing and unforeseen fact, that the promises to David were being fulfilled in the church and the Gentiles sharing in David's blessing, that the decision was rendered to accept Gentile converts into the church without imposing upon them Jewish practices. The house of David had indeed been restored, but no longer in terms of Old Testament practices. Even as the enthronement of Jesus on the throne of David had received radical re-interpretation, so the people of God, the true Israel, now finds its realization in the church, which consists of both Jewish and Gentile believers, apart from Jewish practices. (1968: 76)

In the remaining chapters of Acts Luke sought to illustrate this reconceptualization of the largely Gentile church as the true people of God, displacing Israel. This church was no parenthesis or accident of history. Furthermore, in Luke's subsequent selection of certain incidents from Paul's ministry, we should note how often he draws attention to Israel's rejection of Jesus Christ. Not only did official Jewry and many Jews in Jerusalem persist in their unbelief, but in Rome also, the majority of Jewish leaders refused to receive the blessings of the Kingdom. This resulted in Paul's rejoinder: "Therefore I want you to know that God's salvation has been sent to the Gentiles, and they will listen!" (28:28).

Church Growth

In some circles it has been maintained that Acts is primarily concerned with describing and prescribing church growth theory. By this is meant the sort of missionary activity characterized by evangelistic proclamation and the gathering together of the converted into local congregations. Actually, Acts tells us very little about how those early Christians organized their congregations, involved themselves in ministry, defined their creeds, or conducted their worship. Rather, its focus is on the experienced oneness and human togetherness they knew through the new life imparted to them by the Holy Spirit.

Some have sought to make Acts a textbook on "church growth," replete with models and methods regarded as directly applicable to missionary praxis in the twenty-first century. The thesis is that Acts records a continuous success story: how the gospel went from Jerusalem to Rome. Bruce Metzger stated that within Acts one can identify six separate periods of church expansion and that each period concludes with a summary statement of church growth (1965):

1. Throughout Jerusalem (1:1–6:7)—"So the word of God spread. The number of disciples in Jerusalem increased rapidly" (6:7).
2. Throughout Palestine (6:8–9:31)—"Then the church throughout Judea, Galilee and Samaria . . . was strengthened . . . and grew in numbers" (9:31).
3. Beyond Jewish boundaries (9:32–12:24)—"But [despite persecution] the word of God continued to increase and spread" (12:24).
4. Throughout Cyprus and into central Asia Minor (12:25–16:5)—"So the churches were strengthened in the faith and grew daily in numbers" (16:5).
5. To Europe, Greece, and western Asia Minor (16:6–19:20)—"In this way the word of the Lord spread widely and grew in power" (19:20).
6. Paul's journey to Jerusalem, his arrest, and return to Rome (19:21–28:31)—"Paul stayed there . . . and welcomed all who came to see him. Boldly and without hindrance he preached the kingdom of God and taught about the Lord Jesus Christ" (28:30–31).

Enthusiasts for Acts as a textbook on church growth tend to forget that Luke was not concerned with church growth per se but rather with showing the victory of the new, liberating faith as it "breaks through barriers that are religious, racial and national" (Stagg 1955, quoted by Copeland 1976: 13). At first Luke gave particular attention to the numerical growth of the church (1:15; 2:41, 47; 4:4; 5:14; 6:1, 7; 8:6, 12; 9:31, 35, 42; 10:24, 48; 11:21, 24, 26; 13:48–49; 14:1, 21–22; 16:5, 15, 25–34; 17:4, 12, 34; 18:8; 19:7, 10, 17, 26). He used statistics to show that a significant number of Jews came out of Judaism to become the vanguard of the new Israel.

Once this was demonstrated, Luke lost all interest in church statistics, although he shows a penchant for numbering everything else, especially details of chronology. What he continued to note is the diversity of people who entered the church—all ages, both sexes, Jews and Gentiles, individuals and households, the obscure and the prominent, the range of occupations they represented, the people of character and influence who had entered the new faith. He was quick to portray the spiritual power of new converts. They represented quality as well as quantity.

And Luke did not attribute the growth of the church to specific evangelistic methods. When any are converted, God gets the glory because it is the Holy Spirit's work that delivers people from the dominion of darkness and translates them into the Kingdom of his beloved Son (Col. 1:13). The divine superintendence of the apostles was everywhere apparent, often working contrary to their best estimate of what to do next (e.g., Acts 16:6–10 and 22:17–21). And all the while Luke illustrated what Paul later taught (in Col. 1:24–29), namely, that the church does not grow without paying a price. And this price, though paid in suffering, produced the direct return of church growth (see Conzelmann 1973: 34; Copeland 1976: 24; Acts 4:23; 5:40–42; 8:1–4; 14:22).

This, then, is the picture of church growth in Acts. It was qualitative as well as quantitative. The congregations were more heterogeneous than homogeneous in membership, for Luke was eager to show how the "good news of the Kingdom" surmounted the barriers of religion, race, class, sex, and prejudice in its onward march "for the scattered children of God, to bring them together and make them one" (John 11:52).

And everywhere the apostles went, signs of the Kingdom accompanied their witness. Indeed, the manifestations of these signs in Acts remind us again and again of Jesus' ministry and demonstrate the reality of the present dimensions of the Kingdom message. These signs point to the retreat of the devil and "the powers" before the advance of the King. The strong one has been overpowered by the Stronger One at the cross, and his possessions are being taken from him (Matt. 12:29; Luke 11:22).

What are these signs described throughout Acts? We summarize the findings of the Grand Rapids (1982) consultation on the relationship between evangelism and social responsibility (Lausanne 1982: 17–18).

- The *first* sign of the Kingdom was (and still is) Jesus himself in the midst of his people, whose liberating presence brings joy, peace, and a sense of celebration.

- The *second* sign is the preaching of the gospel to all, particularly to the poor, which points people to the Kingdom itself.
- The *third* sign is exorcism; deliverance from all evil, victory over satanic intelligences is possible through the power encounter in which the name of Jesus is invoked.
- The *fourth* sign is the healing and nature miracles, anticipating the final Kingdom from which all disease, hunger, disorder, and death will be banished forever.
- The *fifth* sign is the miracle of conversion and the new birth; converts who have been rescued from darkness to light and from the power of Satan to God are said to have "tasted . . . the powers of the coming age" (Heb. 6:5).
- The *sixth* sign is the people of the Kingdom, in whom is manifested "the fruit of the Spirit." Good works are the signs of the Kingdom; evangelism and social responsibility are indissolubly united.
- The *seventh* sign is suffering: the King suffered to enter into his glory, leaving us an example that we should follow in his steps. To suffer for righteousness' sake, for one's testimony to Jesus is a clear sign of having received God's Kingdom.

Again and again these signs demonstrated the faithfulness of the early church not only to the gospel of the Kingdom but to its conscious acknowledgment that the new era had indeed come. Those early Christians were beginning to enjoy the reality of the Kingdom in all its fullness. Tomorrow was being enjoyed today.

Creative Evangelism

Mention has been made of the preaching of Peter on the day of Pentecost. We have also identified the apostolic gospel as "the good news of the kingdom of God and the name of Jesus Christ" (Acts 8:12). And we have noted that Luke described evangelism in terms of having "declared to both Jews and Greeks that they must turn to God and have faith in our Lord Jesus Christ" (20:21). We shall now examine certain case studies in Acts that underscore the creative ways in which "by setting forth the truth plainly" the apostles sought to "commend [themselves] to every man's conscience in the sight of God" (2 Cor. 4:2).

Cornelius and His Household (10:1–11:18)

Space forbids our reviewing the succession of steps by which God brought a Messianic Jew into the presence of a Gentile and his family who "were devout and God-fearing; . . . gave generously to those in need and prayed to God regularly" (10:2). How impressed Peter must have been with this man. And rightly so! Peter gives generous witness to this, for he could detect the prior activity of God in what Cornelius shared with him. Cornelius had already begun to respond to God—the great Seeker who yearns for all those who bear his image. In every evangelistic encounter we too should look for evidence that God has already been at work in the lives of those we would seek to win.

When Peter arrived at Cornelius's house, a strange thing happened. Cornelius prostrated himself before Peter (10:25). Far from receiving this expression of profound respect, Peter grasped his arm, raised him up, and spoke a memorable word Christians should never forget: "Stand up . . . I am only a man myself" (10:26). Here is the basis for true religious dialogue: the Christian's candid acknowledgment of the commonality of human experience. The Uppsala Assembly of the World Council of Churches spoke of this as an indispensable quality that Christians should cultivate, that is, an accepting attitude toward all people. "In dialogue we share our common humanity, its dignity and fallenness, and express our common concern for that humanity" (WCC 1968: 29). In every evangelistic encounter we too should confess freely our inner awareness of the fallenness all people share, whether Christian or not.

But Peter was not only humble in spirit. He manifested an openness of mind that touched the seeking heart of Cornelius. He gave spontaneous witness to the fact that God was dealing with him through the encounter: "I now realize how true . . ." (Acts 10:34). Peter was receiving enlargement of understanding: God was willing to receive Gentiles as well as Jews! Of course, this was what God had promised Abraham, that through his seed all the families of the earth would be blessed (Gen. 12:3). However, we should not misunderstand Peter's new discovery. When he said, "God does not show favoritism but accepts men from every nation who fear him and do what is right" (Acts 10:34–35), he is not saying that one religion is as good as another. And he certainly is not affirming that Cornelius's religious insights, personal devotion, and acquired morality made him exempt from the need of salvation through Jesus Christ (11:14). Rather, those people manifesting spiritual earnestness are being prepared by God's Spirit to be saved. We too should realize that in every religious encounter we may receive additional insight into the ways God is preparing people to receive his Son.

The story does not end with Peter rejoicing over his enlarged understanding of God and commending Cornelius as an extraordinary Gentile—a very good man, flawless and exemplary in his religious activity. The fact remained that Cornelius was still in great spiritual need. God had already worked "a few minor miracles and changed a few basic heart attitudes," but Cornelius had yet to believe in Jesus Christ, be baptized, and receive the Holy Spirit (La Sor 1972: 161). The Christian bearing witness to Christ must candidly affirm the limitations of all religious activity. This is not to say that Christians have a full understanding of revelation and others do not. Rather, the Christian points gratefully and humbly to Christ, saying: "It has pleased God to reveal himself fully and decisively in Christ; repent, believe, and adore" (Kraemer 1969: 119).

At this point in the encounter, dialogue became proclamation. The climate of mutual acceptance and trust made this possible. In a forthright manner Peter now shared with Cornelius and his household the record of the mighty acts of God in and through Jesus Christ, culminating in his death, burial, and resurrection. It was an honest witness given by a humble though courageous man. Here is faithful dialogue: a truly adequate fulfillment of the missionary mandate Christ had given. It was no mere meeting of two faiths embodied in two friendly devotees. There has to be more than mutual sharing. The gospel has to be proclaimed so as to evoke faith. Jesus Christ is not to be made known just so that he might be admired. The gospel calls for belief; it demands a verdict.

The last scene portrays the Holy Spirit confirming the gospel to Cornelius and his household. They believed the message and received the Spirit's in-working. Gone was the earlier hunger they had experienced despite their devotion, prayers, and almsgiving. They had met the risen Lord Jesus and had received the Holy Spirit. The gospel now became normative in testing all aspects of their lives. And confessing him as Lord meant that henceforth they must live under his direction and for his glory.

Acts shows us that there is a religious dialogue that exalts "the eternal gospel" beyond the level of friendly discussion. The gospel of the Kingdom follows the apostolic pattern of reasoning, explaining, proving, proclaiming, and persuading (to list the action verbs in 17:1–4). Its speech is "always full of grace, seasoned with the salt." Its objective is to give everyone a fitting answer, and its theme is Jesus Christ (Col. 4:6).

Witnessing to Jews (13:16–41)

When Paul was invited to speak in the synagogue at Pisidian Antioch, he found his audience consisted of Jews and some Gentile God-fearers. Even so, his message was not unlike Stephen's address before the council in Jerusalem and consisted largely of a review of God's dealings with Israel from the patriarchs to David. In so doing, Paul followed the Old Testament model since his address narrated "precisely those redemptive acts of God to which the Israelite bore witness in his confessional recital of the works of God" (G. Wright 1952: 76). What is more, Paul moved directly from David to Christ. Indeed, Paul saw in Christ not only the fulfillment of the redemptive history of the Old Testament—God's promises to Israel as a whole—but also the fulfillment of God's promises to David. Although Christ is the reigning Lord now, God's work through him is still incomplete because only at his second advent will the universal Kingdom of God be fully revealed.

When Paul began to identify Jesus as the messianic deliverer of David's house, he used virtually the same narrative form Peter used with Cornelius (Acts 10:37–38). His stress on the resurrection of Jesus also reminds us of Peter's development of this point in his Pentecost sermon (2:24–36). In the end Paul, like Peter, also called for repentance and offered the forgiveness of sins to all who believed.

Luke devotes significant space to recording the varied reactions to this address. There were those who wanted to hear more (Acts 13:42–43). On the following Sabbath "nearly the whole city" gathered to hear the gospel. This probably means that large numbers of Gentiles were interested. This aroused the jealousy of the Jews (13:45), perhaps because Paul said nothing about the necessity of circumcision for those Gentiles who came forward seeking the forgiveness of their sins (13:38).

In response, Paul quoted a great missionary text from Isaiah (49:6), which clearly identified the mission of the Servant of the Lord as extending beyond a guarantee of the security of Israel. He has been given as "a light for the Gentiles." So then, Pisidian Antioch witnessed the tragedy of many Jewish people excluding themselves from the life of God through their unbelief (Acts 13:46, 48). F. F. Bruce vividly summarizes this oft-repeated pattern (e.g., 14:1–7).

> The Jewish communities regarded Paul as one who poached on their preserves, a sheep-stealer who seduced from attendance at the synagogue many well-disposed Gentiles for whose complete conversion to Judaism they had hoped—and seduced them from the synagogue by offering them God's full blessing on what seemed to be easier terms than those imposed by the synagogue on would-be proselytes. Paul's reply to this complaint would have been that it was only the Jews' refusal to receive the gospel light that prevented them from being themselves light-bearers to the Gentiles. (1954: 282)

The record of Paul's efforts to persuade Jews to acknowledge Jesus as their Messiah reflects the unwavering conviction of all New Testament writers that the gospel is as much for Jews as for Gentiles. Indeed, in no uncertain terms they denounced every Jewish hope for acceptability before God that was founded on anything other than the righteousness of Christ imputed to those who received him as Lord and Savior. Reymond summarizes:

> Racial connection with Abraham or Moses counts for nought (Rom. 9:7, 8). A righteousness borne out of good works and the keeping of the law is futile (Gal. 2:16, 21). Even the highest and best of Jewish extra-biblical tradition only makes void the true Word of God (Mark 7:13). Paul was convinced that by their rejection of Jesus the Christ, his kinsmen according to the flesh had called upon themselves the wrath of God "at last" (*eis telos* 1 Thess. 2:14–16). And he was equally convinced that the Jew must give up that very distinctive which separates him from other men, namely, his exalted idea of his own acceptability before God because of his racial relation to the Patriarchs and his obedience to the Torah, if he is ever to know genuine conversion to God through repentance and faith in Jesus Christ. (quoted by Van Til 1968: iv)

Neither "Jewishness" nor Judaism can save the Jew, since neither makes any room for Jesus, who alone is "the hope of Israel" (Acts 28:20). And on no point do present-day Jews differ more markedly from Scripture when they define the Kingdom of God. Leo Baeck in *The Essence of Judaism* states:

> For Judaism the Kingdom of God is not a Kingdom above the world or opposed to it or even side by side with it. . . . It is something which man, as the Rabbis say, "takes upon himself." . . . It is the Kingdom of piety into which man enters through the moral service of God. . . . He who knows and acknowledges God through never ending good deeds is on the road to the Kingdom of God. (1948: 243)

Preaching to Intellectuals (17:22–34)

In his letter to the Colossians, Paul exhorts Christians: "Let your conversation be always full of grace, seasoned with salt, so that you may know how to answer everyone" (4:6). Nowhere did Paul model this better than when he spoke to the Athenians. He found Athens in decline and decay. Philosophy had degenerated into sophistry, political power had passed to the Romans, and yet the city was still the religious and cultural capital of the world with its endless proliferation of statues: gods, demigods, and heroes. The altars were everywhere. It was a city "full of idols" (17:16).

The Epicureans and the Stoics alike taught the folly of idolatry. Their pupils mocked those who thronged the temples. But neither the atheism of the Epicureans nor the pantheism of the Stoics fully satisfied the restless Athenians, who "spent their time doing nothing but talking about and listening to the latest ideas" (17:21).

Prior to his encounter with the Greek intellectuals, Paul contacted the local Jewish synagogue, stark and severe in its monotheism. Its adherents scorned alike the religious life and philosophical debates that swirled about them. They must have been somewhat vocal in their witness as evidenced by the Gentile "God-fearers" ("devout persons") who were drawn to their worship. The word used to describe Paul's encounter with the synagogue implies that he followed the pattern of "reasoning" with its members "from the Scriptures" (17:2–3). However, he did not confine his witness to the synagogue. Indeed, as Paul's eyes ranged from temples to altars to schools to synagogue, he was confronted with three major elements within the totality of human religiosity. It was quite obvious to him that the God he proclaimed was both unknown to them and unthinkable within their worldview. There is a sense in which we confront these same elements today—religion with its rituals, philosophers with their ethical debates, and Jews with their varied forms of Judaism—and we too are obliged to state that all this religious activity and philosophic activity is of no avail. Instead of seeking insight through oracles and idols, cosmogonies and legends, religions or secular philosophies, or strivings to keep the law of Moses, people everywhere are to be confronted with the gospel and pressed to accept the remarkable message of the career and resurrection of a particular human being who was God incarnate.

Restless, unhappy, disoriented people must worship something. The common grace of God prevents them from utterly suppressing the truth. The visible universe is still a source of inescapable knowledge of its invisible Creator. It still bears witness to God's creativity and to his concern for his creatures (14:15–17). However, because all people are blinded by Satan, they cannot interpret aright its witness. "Since man refused in his pride to worship his Maker, he turns the light of divine revelation into the darkness of man-made religion, and enslaves himself to unworthy deities of his own devising, made in his own image or that of creatures inferior to himself" (Packer 1961: 213).

When Paul later stood in the Areopagus (the hill of Ares) and proclaimed Jesus Christ, what did he see? He saw the temples with their altars and the smoke of the incense moving slowly, uncertainly upward into the beyond. People groping, reaching out from themselves, upward, driven by a deep longing for the divine. Many people feel the world is haunted. When they look at themselves, they see insignificance. When they look beyond the earth, the trees, sky, sea, and stars, they experience awe and dread. They are filled with wonder at the mystery of life and of their own existence. This is not their continuous experience. It comes and goes. And yet it is as old as humanity itself. Peoples of every tribe, tongue, and nation have spoken of it—the "imaginative longing" to contact that which seems above and beyond nature. Why? Because of the infinite void, the deep ache within their hearts. People seem possessed with the conviction that contact with what haunts will end their quest. If they fail, life will be devoid of significance. This longing has produced all the religions in this world. We too have experienced the numinous. We have hungered to contact reality. In a sense, we can appreciate why Athens had its temples, its gods, its altars, its up-reaching incense.

At the foot of the Areopagus, Paul saw the marketplace, the schools with their philosophers and disciples. He could imagine the endless debates—arguing about existence, about patterns of life, about the law of nature. Admiring courage, yet conscious of cowardice. Exalting truthfulness, but convicted of double-mindedness and deceitfulness. Defending selfless devotion to principle, yet aware of the constant corrosion of selfishness. Always appealing to an ethical grid that seems part of one's essential makeup. Always aware of personal failure. Mountainous attempts to justify this failure on ethical grounds. Much lofty chatter about exceptions to the basic rules. And yet people seem possessed with the conviction that comprehension of the ethical realities that judge all conduct will bring them peace of heart and mind.

And what did the synagogue signify? Whereas many people in Athens were restlessly reaching out to contact the numinous or seeking to resolve their relation to the ethical, the synagogue represented an exception. Its people stood apart. The very existence and separateness of the Jewish religious experience was the one interruption, the one violation of the uniformity of the ancient world. For in their history the Jews had had a sequence of experiences unrelated to what happened to their neighbors. They came to these experiences in spite of their own inclinations and not because of any particular worth or special genius on their part. At places in their pilgrimage, at Ur, Haran, Bethel, Egypt, Sinai, and in the land of Palestine, successive invasions from "deep heaven" overwhelmed them. Awe gripped them as they related the accounts. Eyes started filling, then shining. So unexpectedly, so undeservedly, so wonderfully had they come to realize that the awesome presence that filled the universe was none other than the moral Governor, the ethical Judge of the universe. Not many gods but one God. Not many rules and philosophies, but one pattern of law. "The Lord our God, the Lord is one," and he has graciously responded to our pitiable condition, without hope and ignorant of his true nature. He has disclosed himself to us. We need no longer drift through life, guessing about life's great questions or dreading the future.

And yet how incomplete is the record of salvation history in the law of Moses, the prophets of Israel, and the rest of the Old Testament. God is! Yes, but his "otherness" makes one tremble. He has taken the initiative to reveal himself to humanity. Yes, but how can one find him? And what of one's guilt before him? Even the worshiper in the Jewish synagogue knows unsatisfied yearnings (Lewis 1945: 1–13).

When Paul faced the totality of Athenian religiosity, he was deeply troubled. He saw only the worship of demons (cf. Acts 17:16 with 1 Cor. 10:20). And as for the philosophers: "The world through its wisdom did not know [God]" (1 Cor. 1:21). The Athenians must turn from these vanities and worship the one true God—the God who is robbed of His glory by all this religious activity. The darkness of Athenian minds and the dissolute character of their lives, when coupled with their idolatry and philosophy, stood in stark contrast to God's ideal for them. An enemy had usurped God's rightful place in their hearts and lives!

Paul's address to the Athenians is full of helpful lessons. The things he left unsaid are worth noting. He saw no point in quoting the Jewish prophets, for they were unknown to his Gentile hearers. Paul did not regard the Word of God as magic, filled with phrases that work wonders whether or not they are suitable to the occasion or intelligible to the audience. He saw no point in descending to the level of his philosophically oriented hearers, to argue from first principles as one of them might have done. The Christian gospel is not just another philosophy, a mere system of ideas. Jesus Christ is a person, not a plan. Hence, Christian witness should not be reduced to the low level of mere intellectual dialogue. Finally, Paul saw no point in blasting the worship of idols, exposing to ridicule its foolishness, and scolding the Athenians for their stupidity. Why give needless offense through assaulting head-on the radical errors of idolatry? Paul wanted to win people, not fight them.

As a result, he spoke with great dignity and courtesy. He commended the Athenians for their deep interest in religious matters. With prudence and tact he told them that they were more divinity fearing than other Greeks. He had not come to proclaim "strange gods." Instead, he went on to describe an altar he had seen within their city. Its inscription—"To an unknown god"—had caught his eye. He felt its agony. Some unknown Athenians had erected this altar. They doubtless listened to the philosophers. They doubtless frequented the temples. But their hearts were still not satisfied. Their quest was not yet ended. Surely somewhere there was some god they had overlooked yet needed to know and honor. Perhaps the unknown god could meet their need. Their altar with its inscription was a wistful confession of ignorance and of unsatisfied longing.

So Paul said in effect that the God who is still a stranger to you, whom you openly confess you do not know, I have come to Athens to proclaim. Paul addressed people, reaching out to the hungry hearted, the groping, those who like the blind confess their blindness. The altar and its inscription revealed to Paul the ultimate agony of idolatry. But it was a hopeful sign. In seizing on it, he accepted the validity of the universal religious consciousness of human beings and the universal ethical concern of humankind. Were he among us today he would say, "Don't preach to

Buddhists, to Muslims, to Hindus. Just preach to people. Reach out to them in the tragedy of their need and you will win them to Christ."

Paul's argument moves swiftly: (1) God is not made by humanity; he is humanity's Maker. He is the transcendent Creator and Lord of the universe. He has been behind the rise and fall of the nations. He rules the world. (2) God doesn't inhabit the material shrines erected by people; he is not dependent on human offerings. In fact, it is he who bestows life on his creatures and provides for their needs. (3) Humankind is a unity by creation. God has made men and women with strong and instinctive longings for himself. Despite people's estrangement from God because of sin, there is something in their nature that makes them grope after God, "since we are God's offspring" (Acts 17:29). (4) God's gracious providence has provided "the exact places where [people] should live" and "determined the times set for them" (v. 26) for their well-being. These are intended to lead men and women to "reach out for him and find him" (v. 27) the more so since they are his offspring. (5) But the days of groping and ignorance are past. While woman and man were still in the shadows, God excused their follies and mistakes. But now in Christ the fullness of the Godhead has been revealed. Valid knowledge of God is now available in the resurrected Jesus Christ.

How should we summarize Paul's message? C. K. Barrett has observed that Paul's speech is closely related to both Stoicism and Epicureanism, though it endorses neither. He states:

> Paul enlists the aid of the philosophers, using in the first place the rational criticisms of the Epicureans to attack the folly and especially the idolatry of popular religion, and then the theism of the Stoics to establish (against the Epicureans) the immediate and intimate nearness of God, and man's obligation is to follow the path of duty and of (true) religion, rather than that of pleasure. But all these propaedeutics come in the end under judgment: men must repent, for God has appointed a day in which he means to judge the world in righteousness, by a man whom he has appointed, and raised from the dead. (1974: 75)

Paul never finished his address. The Athenians listened carefully until he mentioned the resurrection. The "court" then dismissed him as unworthy of serious consideration. To them this idea was as absurd as it was undesirable. The bodily resurrection is still a stumbling block, even in our day. Yet it is still integral to historic, biblical Christianity. Paul desperately wanted to bring the Athenians to Christ. "His preaching comparatively failed at Athens, not because of his method, but in spite of it. . . . The play was a success, but the audience was a failure!" (Gerstner 1960: 216). Some mocked, others temporized with indecision, but a few believed. Paul left Athens a disappointed man. We do not know that he ever cared to return.

Conclusion

We have seen that in the Book of Acts Luke recorded what the Holy Spirit accomplished in transforming a messianic Jewish movement into a universal faith.

In the earliest years of the New Testament church, following its emergence at Pentecost, many Jews came to acknowledge Jesus Christ as their Lord and Messiah. Hellenists in their midst became the vanguard in conceptualizing the gospel so that it also increasingly became good news to the Gentiles. Biblical history increasingly moved from the particular (in Jewry) to the universal (the Gentile world).

Despite all the different situations in which the apostles preached the gospel, calling forth different articulations in response to their assessment of the varied needs of those whom they addressed, they regarded its core as a nonvariable. It contained five distinct elements. John Stott has described them as (1) gospel events: the death, burial, and resurrection of Jesus; (2) gospel witnesses: the Old Testament Scriptures and the apostles themselves; (3) gospel affirmations: Jesus is both Lord and Savior; (4) gospel promises: the forgiveness of sins and the gift of the Holy Spirit; and (5) gospel demands: the acceptance of "repentance ethics" (Padilla) and faith, expressed by submission to baptism (1975: 41–54). Jesus Christ had indeed provided a universal message that began to call forth a new community of faith from the nations, the Jews included.

18

Paul Preaches the Gospel
of the Kingdom
in Jesus Christ

Introduction

We must now place the apostle Paul in the context of the unfolding revelation of the Kingdom of God and the missionary calling. Not only is he to be regarded as a demonstration of what the gospel can accomplish in the heart of an undeserving sinner (1 Tim. 1:12–16). He also demonstrates to the church what it means to be called to the stewardship of this gospel (1:12). Paul's ministry in Christ offers us a pattern or exhibit (v. 16) of what is involved in the apostolic or missionary calling. His life and labors have been the object of study on the part not only of scholars but of all those who have felt themselves constrained by the Spirit to become God's envoys to the unbelieving world. In this chapter we shall review some of the salient details of his missionary principles and practice. Later we will trace his distinct contribution to the theology of the Christian mission.

Saul of Tarsus: His Youth

Although both Jesus and Paul were born in approximately the same decade, the preconversion background of Paul was far more complex. Hans-Joachim Schoeps summarizes the consensus of scholarly thought:

Paul, who sprang from the heart of Pharisaic Judaism and became the pioneer in propagating the Christian gospel among the heathen, had a self-contradictory nature and by his background and course of mental and spiritual development was a product of diverse cultural milieux. (1961: 13)

There is little agreement as to which influence was dominant. Saul (Paul) was born in the Hellenistic city of Tarsus (Acts 21:39; 22:3). His Jewish parents had the rare privilege of being Roman citizens (22:27–28), but his religious and cultural upbringing were such that he could describe himself as having "lived as a Pharisee," the strictest party within Judaism (26:5). There is no reason to believe that as a youth he received any formal training in Hellenic literature or that his knowledge of the Greek language went beyond what he casually picked up through contacts with neighborhood children. His earliest years were dominated by devout parents, the Jewish Scriptures, strict adherence to the ceremonial law and traditions of his people, and synagogue worship. He was an Aramaic-speaking Jew with Aramaic-speaking parents. One would be hard pressed to identify him with the typical Hellenized Jew of the Diaspora.

In a brief allusion to his youth, Paul stated that his "parental home" where he received his early upbringing was in Jerusalem. Under the excellent instruction of Gamaliel of the School of Hillel, he was "thoroughly trained in the law of our fathers" (Acts 22:3). Since no one would be eligible to enter such a school after his thirteenth birthday, some scholars argue that he must have gone to Jerusalem before his tenth birthday (E. Harrison 1975: 334; Conybeare and Howson 1920: 42; see Acts 26:4). After long years of rigorous training he doubtless returned to Tarsus, acquired a trade (weaving cloth of goats' hair), probably married, then became a widower, returned to Jerusalem, and possibly joined the Sanhedrin (Acts 26:10). Years later he summarized his religious development as follows: "I was advancing in Judaism beyond many Jews of my own age and was extremely zealous for the traditions of my fathers" (Gal. 1:14). He could boast that he "fulfilled [his] duty to God in all good conscience" (Acts 23:1). Strange as it is, it would seem that during this period he had no apparent contact with John the Baptist, Jesus of Nazareth, or the beginnings of the Christian movement.

Paul the Disciple: His Conversion

The probability is that when Paul returned to Jerusalem several years after the church began, the Sanhedrin was eager to enlist him in opposing this growing messianic movement (Acts 26:10). At first Paul regarded the followers of "this Way" (22:4) as utterly deceived people. To him they constituted just another troublesome Jewish sect, of which there were many. He believed it would soon disappear despite the fervor, piety, and evident purity of its followers. This was assumed to be the case because of the irrational belief of the members of the movement in the messiahship of Jesus of Nazareth, who had been crucified under Pontius Pilate. However, as long as Jesus' followers remained loyal to the Abrahamic covenant and to circumcision, to the law and its regulations, and to temple worship and its priesthood, Paul had to concede they had a measure of legitimacy. But when he became aware of the way in which many Hellenist Jews were beginning to reconceptualize the great tenets of rabbinic Judaism, he began to sense that this growing movement was a mortal threat to all that he held dear. Perhaps in the synagogue "of those from Cilicia"—whose chief city was Tarsus—Paul initially encountered Stephen and engaged him in debate (6:9), only to be overwhelmed by "the wisdom or the Spirit by whom he spoke" (6:10).

Paul would defend the Temple, but Stephen would insist that "the Most High does not live in houses made by men" (7:48). Paul would insist on the essentiality of circumcision, if one were to be pleasing to God, but Stephen would point out that the promises God made to Abraham and his seed and the spiritual realities they enjoyed antedated the initiation of that rite. Paul would contend that Jesus could not be the Messiah because many of the leaders of Israel did not accept him, but Stephen would reply: "Was there ever a prophet your fathers did not persecute?" (7:52). Stephen would brush aside Paul's focus on Moses and expound the great prophetic texts that spoke of the Messiah, his incarnation, crucifixion, and resurrection. We can well believe that Paul took part in making false charges against Stephen and in bribing witnesses to testify against him (6:11–14).

Then came the trial before the Sanhedrin. Paul was present. There he heard Stephen review the story of God's dealings with Israel in light of "the good news of the kingdom of God and the name of Jesus Christ" (Acts 8:12). All this was completely new; Paul had doubtless never heard such a commentary on God's "saving acts" in the history of his people nor of their relation to God's universal concern whereby all peoples might draw nigh to him. Later Paul would describe it as "the mystery of Christ, which was not made known to men in other generations" (Eph. 3:4–5). Not only did Stephen's exposition confound Paul, it enraged him. In no time at all he joined those who precipitated the hostility that resulted in Stephen's martyrdom (Acts 7:58; 8:1).

> But the light on the martyr's face; that evident glimpse into the unseen Holy; those words; the patience and forgiveness; that peace which enwrapt his mangled body, crushed and bleeding, as he fell asleep—Paul could never forget them. Long years after, when a similar scene of hate was environing himself, he reverted to Christ's martyr, Stephen, and counted it a high honor meekly to follow in his steps. (Meyer 1897: 45, in reference to Acts 22:20)

The stoning of Stephen marked the beginning of a period of ruthless persecution of messianic Jews. Apparently, the Roman authorities did not intervene to check the violence. As Jewish hostility mounted, Paul became extremely active. He himself says that in Jerusalem he not only exercised the power of imprisonment from "the high priest and the Council" but also gave his vote against those who were condemned to death (Acts 22:4; 26:10). We can well imagine his anguish when later he confessed: "Many a time I went from one synagogue to another to have them punished, and I tried to force them to blaspheme. In my obsession against them, I even went to foreign cities to persecute them" (26:11).

All this set the stage for Paul's encounter with Jesus Christ on the road to Damascus. In Acts this event and its surrounding context is recorded three times (9:1–25; 22:1–21; 26:1–23). Actually, more space is devoted to it in the New Testament than to the Pauline teaching on justification by faith. It is significant that the three accounts agree verbatim only in the dialogue by which the glorified Christ identified himself with his church: "Saul, Saul, why do you persecute me? . . . I am Jesus, whom you are persecuting." This supports the general thesis that Luke wrote Acts to demonstrate that the history of the church is the extension of God's redemptive activity in this world. Maddox summarizes:

> Luke celebrates Paul as a great Christian leader of the period between the apostles and the author's contemporaries. Paul embodies the continuity of the gospel. . . . God's salvation has already been fulfilled in what has happened in the mission of Jesus and its sequel in the gift of the Holy Spirit. . . . It is largely Gentiles who have accepted the offered salvation and Judaism which has rejected it. . . . The Kingdom of God is already a present reality, even though it must be consummated in the future. . . . The time of the Church is a time charged with eschatological power; it is characterized by the availability of salvation . . . [and] the church is not led by institutional authorities but by the Holy Spirit. (1982: 182–87)

Whereas the three accounts are in substantial agreement, they have been carefully developed to identify the validating dimensions of Paul's apostolic character. Luke's own account (chap. 9) establishes the fact that Paul really saw the resurrected Christ and hence in this regard was on equal footing with the Twelve (Acts 1:22). Paul's Aramaic address to the Jews (chap. 22) reveals that he alone of the Twelve had the unique experience of seeing the glorified Christ exalted in glory following his ascension. These first two accounts agree that Paul's actual conversion experience took place in Damascus (9:18; 22:16). Paul's Greek address before Agrippa (chap. 26) focuses on his apostolic commission: his calling to the service of extending the knowledge of the gospel and thereby becoming in himself nothing less than an extension of Christ's redemptive activity.

In his letter to the Galatians Paul compresses all the details of his conversion and his early Christian life into a few phrases (1:15–17). Attention should be given to the word received by Ananias: "This man is my chosen instrument to carry my name before the Gentiles and their kings and before the people of Israel. I will show him how much he must suffer for my name" (Acts 9:15–16). Because of this missionary commission—preaching the good news of the Kingdom—Paul would inescapably become involved in spiritual warfare (opposed by the powers), in power encounter (calling people to Christ's lordship), and in suffering (mental as well as physical). Indeed, his theology of the Christian mission would stress suffering as unavoidable, even essential to the sort of fruitful missionary service that "presents . . . the word of God in its fullness" among the nations. Henceforth, Paul would rejoice in his sufferings for the sake of the church. He would fully pay the price to proclaim Christ to the nations. And he knew what this meant. Not the proclamation of some form of cheap grace. Rather, through "admonishing and teaching," through "labor" and "struggling" he would reach for a goal that is nothing less than having every convert "perfect in Christ" (Col. 1:24–2:1).

Paul's Missionary Training

Immediately following his encounter with Christ, Paul was brought into contact with the messianic community in Damascus through the gracious ministry of Ananias, "a devout observer of the law and highly respected by all the Jews living there" (Acts 22:12). Doubtless, Ananias had earlier been in the vanguard of those praying against what this violent man might do to their group. God, however, banished his fears and enabled him to receive Paul. The loving, generous welcome he extended ("Brother Saul") along with the assistance he gave (the recovery of sight and the anointing grace of the Holy Spirit) marked Paul's entrance into the believing community—an experience Paul never forgot. And when he was baptized into its life and fellowship, Paul knew that he had made a final and irreversible break with his past life and his Pharisaic associations. From henceforth he would take up his cross and follow Jesus Christ, glorying in his new role as "his witness to all men of what [he had] seen and heard" (22:15).

We know very little of what happened to Paul during the next few years. Luke merely tells us that "he spent several days with the disciples in Damascus" and that "at once he began to preach in the synagogues that Jesus is the Son of God'" (Acts 9:19–20). Although he was able to confound the Jews in Damascus by his witness, he wanted to be alone to reflect on the implications of his conversion experience. So he shortly left Damascus for Arabia, where he remained for three years (Gal. 1:17–18). He had to think through the entire course of Old Testament revelatory history in the light of the Messiah who had been crucified but was now both resurrected and glorified. He had to separate the chaff from the wheat in the Judaism he knew so well. He had to ponder the tragic blindness of his own people—the mystery of their unbelief (2 Cor. 3:7–18). He had to understand their abuse of the law, making it burdensome to his people. He personally needed deliverance from it, for he had often groaned beneath the unrelieved sense of failure and condemnation it generated. He had to come to the place where he could rejoice that the law was good "if one uses it properly" (1 Tim. 1:8). And since he was commissioned to preach Jesus to the Gentiles, how could this be fitted into his understanding of the Old Testament that only on the last day would the Gentiles be summoned to Jerusalem to hear the law of the Lord (Isa. 2:3)? We cannot believe that he resolved any of these complex issues quickly.

After his time in Arabia Paul returned to Damascus and continued his witness to the messiahship of Jesus. But not for long. Jewish hostility became so great that he had to flee for his life (Acts 9:23–25). He returned to Jerusalem with the deliberate intent of contacting Peter and "stayed with him fifteen days" (Gal. 1:18). Apparently, this was a rather "low key" visit. What particularly encouraged Paul was Barnabas's willingness to sponsor him and give him access to the believers in Jerusalem. Then too, he was strengthened through the discovery that Peter and James the brother of Jesus had nothing essential to add to his understanding of the gospel. Not able to keep silent, Paul briefly witnessed to the Hellenists who had earlier rejected Stephen's witness. But their hostility was such that his life was again in danger (Acts 9:26–29). It is at this point that Paul had his famous controversy with God over his missionary calling. Paul advanced all sorts of reasons why he was uniquely suited to a ministry to the Jews in Jerusalem. The only response was "Go; I will send you far away to the Gentiles" (22:17–21). Apparently, some of his new Christian friends came forward, helped him escape to Caesarea, and "sent him off to Tarsus" (9:30).

Then followed still more years of obscurity. Paul merely says that he "went to Syria and Cilicia" (Gal. 1:21). In all likelihood at this time he experienced the sharp trial of being "disinherited for his Christian confession" and no longer had access to "his ancestral home" (F. F. Bruce 1954: 240). It was a time of testing (2 Cor. 11:23ff.), of revelations (2 Cor. 12:2ff.), and of service. Bruce says, "We may indeed go farther and infer from certain indications in the New Testament that he had begun Gentile evangelization on his own initiative before Barnabas brought him to Antioch" (1954: 241, in reference to Acts 11:25–26). This follows from Paul's own summary of his ministry: "First to those in Damascus, then to those in Jerusalem . . . and to the Gentiles also, I preached that they should repent and turn to God and prove their repentance by their deeds" (Acts 26:20). This was the period in which Paul seriously began to face the Gentile world. Prior to this period he was a thoroughgoing Jew. But now he began to view Hellenism in the perspective of God's revelation in Christ. Being called by God to Gentile evangelization, he now assumed the role of a "task theologian" and sought to resolve the relationship between Jews and Gentiles in the redemptive purpose of God.

Paul and the Great Commission

Paul did not derive his missionary commission from either the church or from the apostles in Jerusalem. Indeed, the reaction of that whole Christian community was one of amazement: "The man who formerly persecuted us is now preaching the faith he once tried to destroy" (Gal. 1:23). But what of the missionary mandate that Christ gave to his disciples in the interval between his resurrection and ascension? What is its relation to the special commission Paul received on the road to Damascus: "You will be his witness to all men of what you have seen and heard" (Acts 22:15)? Max Warren dwells on the importance of Luke's thrice-recorded references to this commission (chaps. 9, 22, 26) and underscores Paul's calling to "break bounds—a particular calling to the world outside the covenant of God's promises to the Jewish people, as he himself hitherto had understood them" (1976: 32).

If we take the New Testament record at face value, Paul was the first apostle who fully understood the Great Commission—what it involved (making disciples of all peoples)—and who sought to obey it (Col. 1:28). Some might question this by calling attention to Peter's witness to Cornelius (Acts 10), although the circumstances surrounding this event hardly reflect a spontaneous witness to this Gentile and his household. Others might refer to the lay witness who reached Antioch with the gospel, but again the details would seem to question conscious obedience to that divine mandate (11:19–23). In this connection it is most significant that in the last chapter of his final letter, Paul speaks of having completed his calling that "all the Gentiles might hear" the gospel (2 Tim. 4:7, 17). The phrase "all the nations" occurs in the Great Commission itself (Matt. 28:19) as well as in Paul's great missionary treatise, the Epistle to the Romans (1:5; 16:26).

Everett Harrison affirmed that when Paul in Romans 16:26 used the phrase "the command of the eternal God," he was directly referring "to the Great Commission which includes all the nations as embraced in the divine purpose" (1975: 171). The probability is that Peter shared its details on the occasion when Paul "stayed with him fifteen days" in Jerusalem (Gal. 1:18). How could it have been otherwise? On that occasion Paul recounted to Peter the commission he had received to bear witness "to all men" of what he had seen and heard.

Paul, who previously had only an outsider's knowledge of the life and ministry of Jesus, must have pressed Peter to tell him the whole story. And who can believe that Peter stopped short of reviewing Jesus' postresurrection issuance of the Great Commission? Probably at that time Peter also recounted his experience in the house of Cornelius when the Spirit of God brought Gentiles into the household of faith, apart from their first becoming Jews via circumcision (Acts 10:44–48).

Under the dynamic of the Holy Spirit the gospel was moving out to all peoples, something that Paul later expressed in hyperbole when he told the Colossians "the gospel that has come to you . . . all over the whole world is bearing fruit and growing . . . [and is being] proclaimed to every creature under heaven" (1:6, 23, a clear echo of Mark 16:15). Paul drew his motivation for his part in the movement of the gospel from Jerusalem to Illyricum and to the regions beyond from his commissioning by Christ, his reception of the Holy Spirit, and his understanding of the explicit components of the Great Commission (Acts 1:8; 9:17, 20; Rom. 15:16).

And yet a problem remains. Why was Luke silent regarding the Great Commission as the object of the conscious obedience of those early Christians? Why, Harry Boer asks, did he not refer to it in the episode of Peter and the conversion of Cornelius and his household (1961: 28–44, in reference to Acts 10:1–11:18)? On three separate occasions prior to this event Peter had spoken of the universal salvific concern of God (at Pentecost, 2:17, 21, 39; in the Temple, 3:25–26; and before the Sanhedrin, 4:12). Should we merely conclude that Peter had only "limited insight" into the implications of his own words and that it was only when the Holy Spirit was poured out on Cornelius and his household that he became truly convinced that the gospel was for Gentiles as well as for Jews (Boer 1961: 40)? To grant this is to underscore the fact that even the best of God's servants, enlightened by his Spirit, perceive truth as "but a poor reflection" (1 Cor. 13:12).

Harry Boer relegates the Great Commission to apostolic oblivion. He contends that old prejudices die hard, despite the best of instructors and their most pointed instruction. And he argues that fortunately the dynamic of the Holy Spirit compelled those parochial Jewish believers to reach beyond their own countrymen and share the gospel with the Greeks (Acts 11:20). Down through the long centuries of the church, however, there have been frequent occasions when this specific mandate to make disciples of all peoples has had to be elevated to remind Christians of their unfinished task. Boer concedes this (1961: 15–27). Even then, the few who responded were invariably those who earlier had been renewed by the Holy Spirit.

However, we should guard against making such judgments as "The Jerusalem Church did not lift a finger to carry out the Great Commission, so understood" (Boer 1961: 46). We must not overlook the fact that the Kingdom belongs to God. Who would dare to say that he was not superintending the fortunes of his people in those early days? Who knows but that it was God's will during that unique period of relative Jewish receptivity to focus the attention of his people on their fellow Jews? In a few years Jewish resistance to the gospel hardened, and so it has remained almost to the present day. When this resistance became widespread, God directed Peter to the house of Cornelius and thereby heightened his awareness that the Gentiles were also to be evangelized.

But a real problem remains: the issue of "making disciples." Should we equate this mandate—so explicit in the Great Commission—with the ministry model Christ gave his disciples? Why is it that the word *disciple*, although common in the Gospels and Acts, is not found in Paul's epistles? And why do we fail to find any reference to "disciple training" after the pattern Jesus followed? The words *church* and *saints* increasingly replace *disciples* or seem interchangeable with the latter term (cf. Acts 5:11 with 6:1–2; 8:1 with 9:1; 11:26, 29 with 13:1; etc.). In this connection George Peters notes:

> A new vocabulary greets us in the language of the Early Church . . . Pentecost introduced a new method of making disciples. The Church of Jesus Christ as the Body of Christ and Temple of the Holy Spirit was born on the day of Pentecost. . . . The maturing and equipping of Christians happened in the Body of Christ and in the Temple of God as manifested in local congregations. This is evident from the very first pages of Acts and the continued practice of the apostles. (1981: 13–14)

Does this mean that the way Jesus trained the Twelve was not to be reproduced intact? Should we argue that the word *disciple,* or *follower,* represents a "disciple-teacher" relationship that is foreign to the understanding of fellowship (*koinōnia*) in the local congregation? If *koinōnia* embraces at its heart the concept of joint participation in Christ in which each member of the body has a distinct role to fulfill, then anything that would introduce a hierarchical dimension would appear contrary to the headship of Christ in the church. Not that the local congregation should be unstructured, so that it has neither leaders nor followers, for this is patently unscriptural (Heb. 13:17). But one looks in vain in Acts and the epistles for the highly structured, small group approach to discipling that characterized our Lord's training of the Twelve. The isolated reference of Acts 14:21—"won a large number of disciples"—must not be extracted from its context: evangelism (14:21), teaching (14:22), and the organizing of local congregations under qualified and available leaders (14:23). Incidentally, the reference to "baptizing" in the Great

Commission followed by the mandate, "teaching them to obey" all that Christ commanded, cannot but imply that the locus of the nurturing process was to be within the local congregation. This is in sharp contrast with the contemporary para-church discipling model of one-on-one training. Interestingly, although Peter was discipled through Christ's person-to-person training method, he never regarded the individual Christian as the key to the Christian movement. His focus was on the structured local congregation: a "spiritual house" made up of "living stones" with "elders . . . serving as overseers" (1 Peter 2:5, 9–10; 5:1–5).

How significant it is, then, that before Paul was called from obscurity in Tarsus and Cilicia to embark on his apostolic calling, he was brought into the life and witness of the dynamic and largely Gentile church in Antioch. Although the various diverse house congregations making up this complex church were actively evangelizing Antioch's people, Paul's main role was that of a teacher of converts in the corporate, not individual, sense (Acts 11:26). Using Great Commission terminology, we would conclude that he "made many disciples," but not after the unique leadership-training pattern Jesus used in training the Twelve. He used Jesus' pattern later when he began to train those who were recruited to serve on his mobile apostolic team.

Paul as Missionary Model

To appreciate the missionary practice of the apostle Paul, we must take into consideration his awareness of the reality of the Kingdom of God and the local church as a sign of that Kingdom. Paul's approach to missionary obedience was devoid of the sort of triumphalism and competition that characterized the religious huckstering of his day. He did not identify the Kingdom of God in terms that reduced it to an institution or structure. The Kingdom rather represented the sovereign gift of God himself to his people (Rom. 14:17). George Ladd affirms that

> if God's Kingdom is the gift of life bestowed upon his people when he manifests his rule in eschatological glory, and if God's Kingdom is also God's rule invading history before the eschatological consummation, it follows that we may expect God's rule in the present to bring a preliminary blessing to his people. (1964: 201–2)

To Paul, then, the sovereign will of God had to be recognized and responded to. If he was to be an apostle to the Gentiles, the initiative had to be God's. It was only after the Spirit spoke to the church in Antioch and then deliberately sent him and Barnabas out from its midst that Paul entered upon his great missionary career. From that time onward he consciously sought to be responsive to the leading of the Spirit. At times the Spirit checked his movements rather dramatically (e.g., Acts 16:6–7). There were also times of special revelation (e.g., Acts 16:9; 18:9–10; 19:21). But once Paul found himself moving along general lines indicated by God, he discussed them with his companions and decisions were made—sometimes collectively and sometimes on his own—without any evidence of the superintendence of the Spirit (e.g., Acts 15:36; 16:10; 18:1). Did he always make the right decisions? Probably not. Charles Bennett says, "Paul must have stumbled and groped with uncertainty for the Spirit's leading, just as we do today . . . and he tried for years to fulfill his personal dream of visiting Spain" (1980: 134).

For this reason, one should not try to perceive Paul as the master strategist whose methods are normative for the church for all time. Even Roland Allen, whose oft-republished classic defends this thesis, commences with a concession:

> It is quite impossible to maintain that St. Paul deliberately planned his journeys beforehand, selecting certain strategic points at which to establish his churches and then actually carried out his designs. . . . In his second journey he followed no predetermined route. . . . On his third journey St. Paul apparently laid his plans and executed them as they were designed so far as Ephesus, but after that he was so uncertain in his movements as to lay himself open to an accusation of vacillation. (1962: 15–17, in reference to 2 Cor. 1:15, 17–18)

This is true only to a certain degree. One cannot review all the twists and turns in Paul's missionary service without coming to the deep conviction that among its variables there were certain methodological principles from which he did not deviate, largely because of his understanding of the nonnegotiable nature of the gospel of the Kingdom he proclaimed. They follow:

The Strategy of Prayer

We have earlier noted that in the Old Testament all significant intimations of the liberating Kingdom that the Messiah would later inaugurate were preceded by the fervent prayer of the people of God. Paul never forgot this. Hence, we can well believe that his use of the "Lord's Prayer" (Matt. 6:9–13) would have been dynamic rather than static. He would have seen in the petition of worship—"hallowed be your name"—the literal construction the Chinese Bible gives it: "O that all peoples might revere your name as holy." This implies the following sequence: first, that each separate people might turn from their idols; then, that they might face and embrace God; and finally, that they might learn of his holiness. This petition is followed by the larger, world-embracing request: "your kingdom come." Paul thereby yearned for the present realization of the liberating Kingdom presence "on earth as it is in heaven." Paul prayed for both the present extension of the Kingdom among the unconverted and for its eschatological consummation, as Jesus had instructed. While he was truly concerned for the Kingdom and its final manifestation in glory, he was equally burdened for the physical, social, and spiritual needs of the peoples of his own generation.

How else can we understand his classic linkage of prayer and God's redemptive purpose in 1 Timothy 2:1–5? In this passage he urges "first of all" that "requests, prayers, intercession and thanksgiving be made for everyone" (2:1). The "thanksgiving" would include celebrating the utter sufficiency of the gospel. Everyone can be addressed and saved through grace! Then he calls for prayer "for kings and all those in authority" (2:2). Paul respected governing authorities as the "servants of God" when they used their authority and power to restrain evil and punish lawbreakers (Rom. 13:1–7). He would have agreed with Luther, who observed that "the lowest realm, that of the sword, serves the gospel by maintaining peace among men, without which it would be impossible to preach . . . and in this manner participate in the ultimate destruction of the prince of this world" (cited in Forell 1954: 114). It should be noted that when Paul expressed the desire "that we may live peaceful and quiet lives in all godliness and holiness" (1 Tim. 2:2), his context is the desire of God that all peoples be saved and "come to a knowledge of the truth" (2:4) because of the universal sufficiency of Christ's redemptive sufferings (2:5–6).

Paul asked his converts specifically to focus their prayers on the extension of the gospel witness. "Pray for us that the message of the Lord may spread rapidly and be honored, just as it was with you" (2 Thess. 3:1; see also Rom. 15:31). But he did not stop there. Their prayers were also needed "that we may be delivered from wicked and evil men, for not everyone has faith" (2 Thess. 3:2; see also 2 Cor. 1:11). At no time did Paul forget that the evangelistic commission given to him on the road to Damascus involved encounter with Satanic power, the power that always opposes the Kingdom of God (Acts 26:18). No wonder Paul stressed prayer. His desire was that his Christian witness should result in converts, not in friendly dialogue. No wonder he did not spare pagan religion, for he saw it as another kingdom set over against the Kingdom of God. To preach the gospel was for Paul to preach the power of God (Rom. 1:16).

Whenever people responded to the gospel and received Jesus Christ as Lord and Savior, Paul would rejoice and give thanks: "We also thank God continually because, when you received the word of God, which you heard from us, you accepted it not as the word of men, but as it actually is, the word of God, which is at work in you who believe" (1 Thess. 2:13; see also Rom. 1:8; 1 Cor. 1:4; Phil. 1:3; 1 Tim. 1:12).

The Strategy of Teamwork

Paul was no "loner." His understanding of the church as the body of Christ—a concept that quite probably first came to him on the road to Damascus (Acts 9:4)—inevitably made him conscious of the reality and value of its unity-in-diversity. Realizing that as apostle to the Gentiles he would be obligated to evangelize all types of peoples (Eph. 3:9), he made sure his companions were not all of the same cultural background. Homogeneity is rarely as creative as heterogeneity. The composition of his team was not unlike the Twelve. Although Jesus only selected Jews, they represented considerable diversity: Galilean fishermen intermingled with a tax collector, an ex-Zealot, and a man from Judea. Paul's companions were similarly diverse and are so described: a Levite (Barnabas, Acts 4:36); a half-Jew (Timothy, Acts 16:1); a Greek (Titus, Gal. 2:3); a non-Jewish physician (Luke, Col. 4:14); a former synagogue ruler (Sosthenes, Acts 18:17); a prophet (Silas, Acts 15:32); several women, such as Phoebe (Rom. 16:1) and Priscilla (Rom. 16:3); a lawyer (Zenas, Titus 3:13); an Alexandrian Jew (Apollos, Acts 18:24);

Macedonians (Gaius and Aristarchus, Acts 19:29); and Asians (Tychicus and Trophimus, Acts 20:4).

From this list one might conclude that the majority of Paul's coworkers were men. But this would be a distortion. He often accepted the assistance of women to spread the faith and worked with them. One recalls Lydia and the church in Philippi that came into being in her house (Acts 16:12–15), and Euodia and Syntyche, who "contended at [his] side in the cause of the gospel" in Philippi (Phil. 4:2) in much the same way that Mary, Tryphaena, Tryphosa, and Persis "worked very hard in the Lord" in Achaia (Rom. 16:6, 12). Because of their presence and status, along with the diverse men who made up his mobile apostolic team, Paul could always demonstrate to non-Christians the reconciled and reconciling nature of the Christian movement. His roving missionary community was a durable demonstration of what the gospel was all about and of the unity-in-diversity that Christ accomplished when he removed the enmity between Jew and Gentile, bond and free, men and women (Gal. 3:28; Eph. 2:14–16).

Paul was a team worker whose letters abound with references to the togetherness he shared with his coworkers in evangelism and church planting (Acts 14:21–27; 15:1–2). He particularly mentions this when referring to their relief work and deeds of consolation (1 Cor. 16:1–2; 2 Cor. 8:16–20), especially when they confronted hardship, persecution, and imprisonment (Rom. 16:17; Col. 4:10). Indeed, when Paul referred to the missionary calling, he invariably described it as a joint responsibility and a joint effort. The gospel of the Kingdom Paul's companions shared with their generation was "our gospel" (1 Thess. 1:5). Paul preferred such words as "we" and "us" to "I" and "me." In his first letter to the Christians in Thessalonica, there are ninety occurrences of plural pronouns and only four references to himself.

One should also note that Paul went out of his way to share the authorship of his letters with his missionary associates (e.g., "Paul . . . and our brother Sosthenes, To the church . . . ," 1 Cor. 1:1–2). We might even say that Timothy and Silvanus were included in the prophetic utterance of 1 Thessalonians 4:13 concerning the second coming of Christ ("we do not want you to be ignorant"). This coresponsibility that Paul and his companions were deliberately sharing was the pattern set by Jesus and his disciples in their proclamation of the gospel of the Kingdom (Mark 6:7).

The Strategy of Adaptation

Paul gloried in the grace of God that had overtaken him on the road to Damascus and confronted him with the risen and glorified Christ (1 Cor. 15:8–10). This grace brought entrustment with the gospel and the calling to proclaim a universal faith to the Gentiles (Gal. 1:11–2:10). From that time onward he knew that he was Christ's bondslave, "obligated both to Greeks and non-Greeks, both to the wise and the foolish" (Rom. 1:14). Constrained by the love of Christ, he felt himself shut off to but one course: preaching this gospel to all peoples and tongues and nations (Eph. 3:9).

The more Paul pondered his own spiritual experience, the more convinced he became of its worldwide horizons. Since Christ had liberated him from the guilt of his sin and from the dominion of darkness, he was a free man, free from himself and from the powers (Gal. 5:1). He could therefore freely become a Jew to the Jews and a Gentile to the Gentiles, adapting himself and his verbalization of the gospel so that it would come as good news to one and all, clothed in the cultural forms that were most meaningful and appropriate. However, since his adaptationist policy arose almost solely out of his theology and was not a methodological expedient, an explanation is in order.

Because of the universal dimensions of the Kingdom of God motif earlier revealed by Jesus, Paul found himself increasingly dislodged from his Jewish particularity. He came to see the profound unity of humankind: all peoples condemned by the law and all included through the gospel within the solidarity of grace, to be appropriated by faith. The darkness in the minds of all peoples could only be dispelled by the light coming from their Creator. Their enmity toward God and one another could only be removed by the Reconciler-Redeemer. The death hold of the powers on all peoples could only be broken by the Liberator who "disarmed" them and triumphed over them through the cross. And the guilt of humankind could only be removed by the one who was made sin for all and who received in himself the judgment all others deserved. So then, Paul saw the inevitability of the Great Commission: the good news concerning the Lord of creation, of redemption, and of the future must be proclaimed to all. Only thereby could the penitent acknowledge the living God, confess his saving name, and worship him in thankful praise.

In the larger context of Paul's description of freedom offered in the gospel and the liberation from all "ways of salvation" variously advanced by Jews and Gentiles (1 Cor. 7:17–24), we find Paul's classical formulation of his adaptationist missionary approach (1 Cor. 9:19–23). In the earlier portion of this chapter he speaks of having deliberately relinquished a wide range of "rights" for the gospel's sake. They involved satisfying bodily appetites (9:4), enjoying romance and companionship in marriage (9:5), and counting on leisure and deserved remuneration (9:6–7), even though he recognized that all these "rights" were legitimate in themselves.

But Paul would make use of none of these rights (9:15). God's necessity was laid upon him. Though free from all, he was constrained to make himself "slave to all" and cried out: "Woe to me if I do not preach the gospel!" (9:16, 19). From henceforth he would curtail his liberties so that his missionary stance with respect to the changeless gospel would reflect the reality that justification is by faith alone. Bornkamm underscores this importance:

> In various religions the idea of indispensable steps and intermediate stations of an *ordo salutis* is customarily linked to the understanding of tradition. That Paul radically abandons all such preconditions is obviously closely connected with his message of justification. (1966: 196)

We must guard against the idea that Paul regarded himself as free to adapt to Jews and Gentiles merely because he was convinced the only valid missionary stance was to be "fiercely pragmatic." One can misunderstand Paul at this point and charge him with unprincipled opportunism: a Judaizer among Jews and a paganizer among Gentiles. Actually, one dominant concern apart from his desire to gain people for Christ (mentioned five times in this passage) was that he might "share in [the gospel's] blessings" (9:23). What he meant was that for him to be true to the gospel demanded that he act the way he did. At stake was his own obedience to the gospel, for this directly involved his own eternal salvation. So then, to follow Bornkamm again we would affirm:

> In the apostle's preaching, theology and mission, Jew and Gentile are seen together. To be sure, from the moment of his conversion and call Paul knows himself to be destined as apostle to the Gentiles. Nevertheless, the gospel which he is to bring to them is the message, developed face to face with the Jewish understanding of law and salvation, of one Lord over all, who bestows his riches upon all who call upon him, Jew and Greek alike. (1966: 199, with reference to Rom. 10:11–12)

Conclusion

We conclude this look at Paul the missionary by reiterating the simplicity and universality of his missionary practice. He believed in the strategy of prayer. The enemy in people's minds and their cultures has to be resisted with the authority and power of the resurrected Christ. Paul also believed in teamwork. He was convinced that if his companions were constantly moving Christward, their diversity would enrich the team and heighten its effectiveness. Paul never forgot the corporateness of the Christian movement. Finally, Paul's strategy called for constant sensitivity to the differences in personality and culture that his hearers represented. He knew that in their spiritual darkness Jews sought signs and Greeks sought wisdom (1 Cor. 1:22–25). Of course, Paul was convinced that what they needed was "Christ crucified: a stumbling block to Jews and foolishness to Gentiles" (v. 23). Nevertheless, he deliberately divested himself of those dimensions that would cause needless offense to Jews and Gentiles. He communicated this message of Christ in ways that were as culturally appropriate as possible. He never deviated from his overriding desire to "become all things to all [people]," that he might "by all possible means . . . save some" (1 Cor. 9:22). We can do no better than to heed his counsel: "Follow my example, as I follow the example of Christ" (1 Cor. 11:1).

19

The Apostolic Church
Embodies Christ's Mission

Introduction

Scholars are divided on whether the New Testament attempts to concretize the structural form of the apostolic church. Some argue from what data exists that the church was congregational in government and that each local congregation was autonomous. Others find evidence of a measure of intercongregational structure and from this contend that its government was either representative or episcopal. One recalls how Bishop Lightfoot contended for the latter on the basis of what he regarded as evidence of settled agreement between the churches on the head covering and hair style of women (1 Cor. 11:16). A matter as controversial as hair styles could not have brought forth Paul's generalization without much interchurch debate and a final decision from the top! Actually, we need to be careful about dogmatism when tempted to describe the actual form of the New Testament church. The New Testament is largely silent about its details.

One could suggest a variety of reasons for this silence. We will only mention two. First, the Jewish synagogue model already existed. And since the first thousands of those who accepted Jesus as Lord and Messiah were Jews, it was inevitable that they utilized this model and adapted it to their corporate needs. When we call to mind Richard De Ridder's evidence of the great cultural variety that existed even among Jewish synagogues in the first century, related to the specific occupations, social classes, and dialects of those making up their membership, we can well believe that messianic Jews in Palestine and throughout the Diaspora likewise gathered in a great variety of Christian synagogues (1971: 79–80; see also Acts 6:9). The synagogue provided believers with a center for informal *koinōnia*, didactic instruction, and communal worship. It was a base for near-neighbor outreach and a community into which converts could be incorporated through baptism and catechetical instruction. The fact that these Christian synagogues were soon called "churches" was not by apostolic invention so much as by simply borrowing a widely used Greek term meaning "assembly."

Second, New Testament silence on the matter of church structure can also be attributed to the cultural diversity existing within the Gentile world. The apostles wrote approvingly of "churches of the Gentiles" in contrast to Jewish churches (Rom. 16:4). This underscores God's intention through the gospel to provide a universal faith for all peoples. Ethnicity and cultural diversity are within his sovereign will for the human race. Hence, we must assume that he intends that his people likewise structure their corporate life in ways congenial to the associative patterns already existing in their separate cultures. And since in this culturally pluralistic world one finds every conceivable form of structural association, ranging from the democratic to the representative to the monarchical, we can well believe that it never was God's intention that one structural form be normative for all the churches. In keeping with this adaptive tendency, an almost infinite variety of differences was bound to appear within the one "church which is his body" (Eph. 1:22–23). A candid admission of this reality is becoming increasingly the witness of theologians even in churches regarded as monolithic (e.g., Küng and Kasper 1973: 28). Granting this, we do well to agree that no pure church form exists anywhere in the world today. Each separate form reflects a measure of admixture of the others. As Leon Morris concludes:

> It is impossible to read back any of our modern systems into the Apostolic Age. If we are determined to shut our eyes to all that conflicts with our own system, then we may find it there, but hardly otherwise. (1960: 127; see also Davies 1962: 208)

The congregational structure was admirably suited to carry out the task of mission in the local context. Linguistic and cultural homogeneity along with the presence of family webs (see *The Bridges of God*, by Donald McGavran) set the stage for the spontaneous expansion of the Christian movement. Assuming the empowering of the Holy Spirit, formal strategy was unimportant. The only requirements one can deduce from Acts are that local leaders, under the authority of God, be willing to act in matters requiring the disciplinary process (Acts 5:3, 9), and that members be so instructed that they were able by word and deed to share the good news of the Kingdom with everyone in every place (1 Thess. 1:3–10).

In Acts 2–12 the story of the expansion of the Christian movement is largely a record of spontaneous growth brought about by the witness of individual Christians (e.g., Peter in 2:14–40; 3:12–26 and Philip in 8:5–13) and, on occasion, by multi-individual activity (e.g., the Hellenists who were driven from Jerusalem and went everywhere preaching the Word, 8:2, 4). In Acts 13–28 the expansion of the Christian movement was achieved through a strikingly different structure—the apostolic team or mission structure. This calls for separate treatment.

The Apostolic Team

Something happened within the church at Antioch (Acts 11:19–30; 13:1–3) that resulted in a structured expression of the church that became "a prototype of all subsequent missionary endeavors organized out of committed, experienced workers who affiliated themselves as a second decision beyond membership in the first structure" (Winter 1974: 123). Concerning this, Allen Thompson has written:

> The New Testament distinguishes between structures, local congregations . . . and the structured apostolic [team] called by God to evangelize the heathen and plant new churches. Whereas the apostles were of the church, their corporate ministry outreach necessitated among themselves patterns of leadership and organization, recruitment and finance, training and discipline, distinct from comparable patterns within local congregations. This significant distinction gives biblical sanction in today's structured missionary fellowship. (1971: 102)

We must take note of the distinctive features of the church at Antioch because it models the missionary church of the apostolic age. It was characterized by evangelistic activity (Acts 11:21). The members of the Antioch church were called "Christians" because of their widespread confession of Christ. At first this was an epithet containing an element of ridicule. Soon it became a name the believers felt honored to bear because it marked the awareness in the Greco-Roman world of a new religion. A variety of words is used to describe the growth of this church (11:21, 24). Its members were well taught in the Scriptures (11:26) and were generous in their response to human need (11:27–30). Most notable was its cosmopolitan character, reflected by the various backgrounds of the "prophets and teachers" who served its various house congregations (13:1). By referring to house congregations in the plural, we are assuming that the biblical data does not demand the existence of only one congregation as constituting "the church at Antioch." The final characteristic of this missionary church was the nature of the burden that caused its various leaders to come together, not just to worship the Lord but to wait before him for the revelation of his will concerning their future service. From the response and instruction given by the Holy Spirit, we infer that their burden concerned a problem they were unable as localized congregations to solve. The fact that fasting is twice mentioned (13:2–3) underscores their sense of urgency. That the Holy Spirit is also mentioned twice indicates the solemnity of this occasion. The Holy Spirit gave specific direction to specific individuals. They were to form a mobile team that would move out into the Mediterranean world, surmounting all the geographic, cultural, and linguistic barriers keeping tribes, tongues, and nations from the knowledge of Christ.

This mandate to form a mission structure whose members were called "apostles" confronts us with a variety of problems. Central is the rather fluid fashion in which the New Testament uses the word *apostle*. It occurs seventy-nine times and is applied rather loosely to a wide range of people (Muller 1975: 128; Harnack 1972: 319–25). Its application ranges from Jesus (Heb. 3:1) to the Twelve (Luke 6:13; Acts 1:24–26) to Barnabas and Paul (Acts 14:14) to unnamed believers (2 Cor. 8:23) and to Junias, a woman (Rom. 16:7). Apostles apparently were the "foundation-laying preachers of the gospel, missionaries, and church founders possessing the full authority of Christ and belonging to a bigger circle in no way confined to the Twelve" (Campenhausen, quoted by Muller 1975: 132). "We may take it as incontrovertible that the missionary commission was an essential part of the primitive Christian apostolate," whereas the Twelve "remained in Jerusalem as eschatological pillars" (Muller 1975: 131, 134). So then, those possessing this gift (1 Cor. 12:28; Eph. 4:11) stood in contrast to prophets, evangelists, and pastor-teachers. This missionary concept of apostle came into its full meaning from this time forward (Acts 13:1–4), with the power of the Holy Spirit working through the church and moving to the very ends of the earth in fulfillment of Acts 1:8 (Hahn 1965: 9–39). The apostolic form has varied down through the ages from the first-century itinerant preacher to the medieval monk, later the friar, and on to the modern missionary. Ronald Bocking of the London Missionary Society describes the abiding apostolic function in the following fashion:

> [Missionaries live] under the continual constraint of crossing the border between belief and unbelief in order to claim the realms of unbelief for Christ. [They are] a microcosm of the church which is apostolic, and being obedient to this call of Christ [they] continually [remind] the church of its essential nature and purpose. In [them] the church reaches out beyond her borders to bring into God's Kingdom the whole world for which Christ died and which as yet does not acknowledge her King. Still the explorer, the missionary does not . . . seek lost countries but lost people. (1961: 24)

This perspective is likewise found in the extensive treatment of the apostolicity of the church by Hans Küng. In his judgment, the church is apostolic not only because it has "direct linkage with the apostles of Christ" (1967: 345) or because it is "founded on the apostles' witness and ministry" (353), but because it possesses a "divine mission, entrusted by Christ to the apostles that will last until the end of the world" (355). The church displays its apostolicity when it "continues in agreement with the witness of the apostles" and also "preserves a vital continuity with the ministry of the apostles" (356). He then adds:

> As an individual Christian, I must become a true successor of the apostles. I must bear their witness, believe their message, imitate their mission and ministry. (1967: 358)

What impresses one in Acts is the manner in which the Twelve are most prominent in its earlier chapters (1:2, 8, 25–26; 2:14, 42; 4:33) but virtually disappear by the time of the Jerusalem Council (15:6). We can only conclude this because they were followed by other apostles, principally Paul and his team. Luke seems to be validating the continuance of God's salvation history. The Twelve go out of existence as an institution but live on as a tradition, and their ministry continues as the abiding missionary tradition of the church (see Wieser 1975: 125–31).

When we inquire into the relationship between the apostolic team and the house congregations at Antioch, we must first recognize that the data is extremely limited, and unfortunately, what data exists has generated great differences of opinion. George Peters concludes that "the local assembly becomes the mediating and authoritative sending body of the New Testament missionary" (1972: 219). He is supported in this by Paul Rees, who says that "for all his apostolic authority, Paul was sent forth by the church (God's people in local, visible congregational life and in associational relationship with other congregations) and equally important, he felt himself answerable to the church" (quoted by Cook 1975: 234). But these inferences are devoid of supporting data. The text merely states that Barnabas and Saul were "sent . . . off" (literally "released") by the "prophets and teachers" in Antioch, but that it was the Holy Spirit who actually "sent [them] on their way" (Acts 13:1–4). Harold Cook regards the position of Peters and Rees as "pure presumption" and then adds that the local house congregations "neither chose them nor sent them, and certainly they had nothing to say about what they were to do, nor how" (1975: 236).

The few clues Luke gives us about the relationship between the several apostolic teams mentioned in Acts and the congregational structures from which they emerged could be interpreted in the following way:

First, team members were called to missionary service directly by the Holy Spirit. They did not volunteer; they were drafted. Even so, the congregations had a part in confirming their call by testifying to their effectiveness in contributing to congregational life and witness (13:1–3; 15:40; 16:2).

Second, the team itself was a voluntary association of Spirit-gifted and like-minded persons and was directly commissioned by the Holy Spirit. (Arndt states that the verb "sent out" in 13:4 implies a specific authoritative commissioning [1957: 647].)

Third, the placing of "their hands on them" (13:3) was a symbolic gesture that conveyed the dual idea of joint participation in the common task and farewell blessing. It is not clear whether the whole church in Antioch participated in this action.

Fourth, there is no indication that the apostolic missionary team was either directed by or accountable to the Christians in Antioch (Cook 1975: 236–37). We state this without qualification, even though upon returning from their first journey, Paul and Barnabas "gathered the church together and reported all that God had done through them and how he had opened the door of faith to the Gentiles" (14:27).

Fifth, there is no indication that the apostles were assisted financially in their travels and work by the church in Antioch, although there is some evidence that they received help from certain of the churches they planted (2 Cor. 11:8 and Phil. 4:15–16; see Cummings and Murphy 1973: 28).

Sixth, within the team an egalitarian spirit based upon mutual trust preserved the freedom of individual members, who moved into and out of its association under what was regarded as the leading of the Holy Spirit. Nevertheless, Paul was invariably regarded as the charismatic leader (16:6–10).

Seventh, the impression is gained that team members either provided or raised their own support, although the team's resources were pooled and shared. When funds were unavailable, team members sought secular employment (18:1–3; 20:33–35).

Finally, although initially the apostolic teams were monocultural in nature, they later became bicultural in composition (Acts 16–19; see Cummings and Murphy 1973: 31).

Although more details could be added, we merely want to note here the distinctives of these two types of structure, congregational and mission. Neither was to be at the disposal of the other. Both were subordinate to the Holy Spirit. Neither was to be an end in itself. Both were to be in wholesome symbiotic relation to each other, as we shall see when we review the mission team's strategy for evangelizing the western Mediterranean. Neither was to be overly upgraded or downgraded. Hence, one should deliberately avoid speaking of "church" and "para-church."

At this point an understanding of the Kingdom comes to our assistance. Although new congregations emerge as a result of missionary work, their emergence cannot be regarded as the end of the story. There is a sense in which each new congregation, as an expression of the body of Christ, is not only a partial manifestation of realized Kingdom but is also an instrument of the Kingdom. Whereas the ultimate goal is that the earth will be filled with the knowledge of the glory of God (Isa. 11:9; Hab. 2:14), we need ever to keep in mind the dynamic possibilities for the Kingdom latent in even the youngest congregation. It too can become "a demonstration of the Spirit's power" through its faithfulness to the gospel (1 Cor. 2:4–5; 4:20).

Apostolic Strategy: The Priority of Receptivity

The idea expressed in the title of Roland Allen's famous book *Missionary Methods: St. Paul's or Ours* has engendered the uncritical acceptance of the thesis that there is something normative in the manner in which Paul pursued his missionary vocation. What is overlooked is the sheer impossibility of using his methods in today's world. The first century no longer exists. We cannot begin our ministry in local Jewish synagogues as he did. The dimension of culture, which Allen overlooked, can no more be ignored today than the twenty centuries that separate Paul from our generation. Furthermore, the painful history of Christian anti-Semitism has tragically prejudiced the synagogue against the church, so that interaction on messianic themes between them is virtually impossible today.

Hence, when we turn to Acts for insight into strategizing the Christian mission, we must guard against focusing attention on Paul's methods and rather search out the principles upon which they were based. However, even here we run into difficulties. It is not that Paul was insensitive to the need for adapting the gospel to his hearers. His preaching was always receptor-oriented, as we have already noted.

For the Jews of Antioch he . . . traced the prophetic line of the Messiah; for the pagans of Lystra, ignorant and superstitious, he . . . made nature an expression of

God; for the Athenians he offered a tactful, correct, yet courageous exposition of Graeco-Jewish thought. (Buckmaster 1965: 133)

But beyond this, Paul's strategizing seems to have but one constant: he concentrated on those places where people were receptive but seems to have little patience with those who resisted the gospel.

True, Paul remained sensitive to the guidance of the Holy Spirit. When the Spirit forbade him to preach in Asia and Bithynia, he obeyed. When he and his company sensed that the Spirit was leading them to Macedonia, they responded (Acts 16:6–10). On the other hand, when Acts reports his launching of what is regarded as his second missionary journey, no mention is made of his seeking the guidance of the Spirit.

Roland Allen creates the image of a Paul who strategized his movements with particular cities in mind.

> All the cities, or towns, in which he planted churches were centers of Roman administration, of Greek civilization, of Jewish influence, or of some commercial importance.... He passed through native provincial towns like Misthia and Vasada in order to preach in Lystra and Derbe—military posts in which there was a strong Roman element. (1962: 13)

And yet this idealization of Paul's strategic planning has been challenged. Donald McGavran argues that Paul chose to visit those places "where his advance information, purified by prayer and guided by the Holy Spirit, led him to believe that a church could be planted" (1955: 29). Perhaps this is the best way to approach the task of strategizing missionary outreach. For, as Max Warren rightly perceives and warns,

> the Holy Spirit, in his operations in history, is strictly incalculable. He is as uncontrollable as the wind. And his fire falls in very unexpected places and upon most unlikely people. Unless the missionary movement can be responsive to the unpredictability of the Holy Spirit, it will soon cease to be a movement. (1978: 194)

So then, we would support consideration of the resistance or receptivity of the receptors in making decisions concerning apostolic missionary strategy. Although Paul sought to preach the gospel as widely as possible, he concentrated his efforts when he found that the Holy Spirit was making his hearers receptive. In Acts, one notes at least six separate instances in which he withdrew from those who rejected his message (13:46; 14:5; 18:1, 6; 19:9; 28:26–28). He did not see his task as the dissemination of information about Jesus or even as explaining what the gospel was all about. He wanted by all means to save people, or as Michael Green succinctly puts it, the apostles "preached a person, proclaimed a gift, and looked for a response" (1970: 150–51). Charles Bennett calls Paul a "big city preacher," for apart from his single diversion into the "surrounding country" of Lystra and Derbe (Acts 14:6), he normally concentrated on cities and sought, through them, to influence the countryside. In Ephesus, for example, he lectured for two years in the hall of Tyrannus during the daily eleven-to-four siesta period, and "all the residents of Asia heard the word of the Lord, both Jews and Greeks" (1980: 137, in reference to Acts 19:10).

This then is the contribution of Acts to our understanding of the apostolic approach to mission strategy. The apostles concentrated their efforts among the receptive within those cultures where they were at home (Aramaic and Greek-speaking). They focused more on households than on individuals. "Acts is pre-eminently a book describing the group approach in missions . . . and speaks a missionary language that is hardly congenial to the individualism characteristic of so much European, Anglo-Saxon, and American Christianity" (Boer 1961: 163). They were not super-strategists who could invariably see the end from the beginning. They were sensitive to local circumstances and shifted their plans accordingly. Although they made no changes in the gospel they proclaimed, their methods and movements were constantly under review for revision and adaptation. In this connection, Charles Bennett concludes:

> Our Western minds, influenced by Greek logic and schooled in scientific method, instinctively attempt to reduce everything to a few basic, unvarying "laws" and "principles." In our study of missionary methods, as in theology, we sometimes "discover" laws and principles in the Scriptures where none, in fact, exist. . . . We might even say that Paul's strategy was to have no strategy. (1980: 138)

The Church's Ministry through Spiritual Gifts

Every society provides a place for the professional religionist, male or female. These individuals are set apart for this service in a variety of ways: by heredity, personal charisma, conferred sacrament, or as a result of training. Their function is to mediate the invisible realm on behalf of the people in the society. Hence, they live in social semiwithdrawal to underscore their linkage with the world of spirit. Their concerns range widely from guaranteeing the fertility of fields, domestic animals, and families to seeking supernatural assistance in overcoming all enemies. Their presence and services are regarded as essential at all milestones in the agricultural year and in the "rites of passage" of individuals: birth, puberty, marriage, parenthood, and death. Every society willingly pays the bill for their services.

Unfortunately, Christian churches have largely and uncritically adopted this model for their career clergy. The ministry has been reduced to a "profession" with one person in each congregation elevated to a monarchial role. He or she alone has the authority to administer properly the sacraments, provide formal proclamation, lead the congregation in worship and prayer, and counsel the needy. Where these services are being rendered, the church is assumed to exist. In contrast, those who serve in mission structures are downgraded. In fact, career clergy are not often prominent in mission structures. As a result, mission structures are often denigrated and made to represent something less than church. Hence the second-class term *para-church*.

When one steps into the world of the New Testament, one finds little that resembles modern churches, with their life and service revolving primarily around the activities of one person, as described in the preceding paragraph. The New Testament speaks about Jesus Christ when it refers to the ministry, about what he does through his church in and for the world. The Montreal Fourth World Conference on Faith and Order (1963) described the work of Jesus Christ under the following headings:

1. "He joins in baptism new members to himself, letting them share in his ministry." We would agree in the light of 1 Corinthians 12:13 with its affirmation that "we were all baptized by one Spirit into one body."
2. "He appointed the apostles to be the pioneers of his church, and his continuing presence draws the whole church into the apostolic ministry." We would want to underscore the fact that Christ continues to appoint apostles, since the missionary function of the church will not end until its missionaries cross every frontier and proclaim to all peoples the message of Jesus Christ (Eph. 4:11–14).
3. "He gives grace to all the baptized, assigning to them their particular authority and function in his ministry." Spiritual gifts are given to all, to be discovered and exercised "for the common good" (1 Cor. 12:7). The New Testament does not speak of the differing services of one "minister" but rather of the different gifts, offices, and ministries of different men and women, with the ideal held before them of working together in unity and for the wholeness of the whole community. So then, the Christian movement should be characterized by driving into oblivion the religionist as a socially recognized profession. It provides no counterpart to the Old Testament priest, for all believers are priests. Nor is there any counterpart to the Old Testament theocracy with its king, for all believers together "reign in life through . . . Jesus Christ" (Rom. 5:17).
4. "He lets the whole Church share in his suffering, calling each member to be spent in his ministry in love and obedience to God and in love and service to men." (WCC 1964: 15–129)

It was only later, when maturing congregations began to sense their need for internal and intercongregational linkage, that the pastoral epistles speak of special, overseeing responsibilities beginning to be placed upon certain persons designated as elders. But there is no evidence in the New Testament of any one "clergy person" ruling over a single congregation.

We have earlier affirmed that the ministry of Jesus during his days "on earth" was nothing less than the Kingdom of God spelled out in human terms. And since the ongoing life and witness of the church is a continuation of his messianic ministry, we would even contend that the doctrine of the church should be regarded as a branch of Christology (Rom. 15:15–19). Indeed, the only "real presence" of Jesus in the church is his Spirit in the midst of his people (Matt. 28:20). This means that the Spirit is truly his vicar, and no mere human person, not even a pope, has the right to so designate himself.

Furthermore, the ministry of the church is primarily to God, because the church is in essence a worshiping community (Titus 2:14; 1 Peter 2:9). The sacraments of baptism and the Lord's Supper express in part this Godward activity. When one realizes that the term *sacrament* comes from the Latin *sacramentum* meaning "oath" or "vow," the meaning of this activity becomes clear. Baptism involves the initial vow one takes while on the threshold of entering the fellowship of the visible church. One vows to forsake the sinful ways of the world, the flesh, and the devil.

Since the Lord's Supper represents the ongoing proclamation by the church of the redemptive death of Jesus Christ, it becomes a visible affirmation of the determination of the people of God to live in the light of this reality. By faith Christians share in Christ's body and blood for their inward spiritual nourishment and growth in grace, as their bodies are nourished outwardly by bread and wine. This is a corporate act because of the joint participation and communal fellowship one shares with all who gather at the table and especially with the crucified Lord in the midst.

Because the sacraments represent, seal, and apply to believers the benefits of Christ's saving work, they are often referred to as "means of grace." But this does not mean that in and of themselves they convey the grace of salvation. Salvation only comes through hearing and believing the gospel, and it is the gospel alone that is the primary channel of grace. Acts never retreats from the sequence: (1) the gospel proclaimed in the power of the Spirit; (2) the reception of that gospel with the hearing of faith; (3) the public confession of faith in Christ by the visible acts of submission to baptism and participation in the Lord's Supper. Should one receive the sacraments apart from faith in Christ, no true *sacramentum*, or oath of allegiance, exists; hence they are of no benefit.

It is significant that during the evangelical awakening of the eighteenth century the sacrament of the Lord's Supper came to be regarded "not simply as a confirming, but as a converting ordinance." In this connection John C. Bowmer writes:

> The Wesleys . . . regarded it as a means of grace to be used at the beginning of the Christian pilgrimage. They were not blind to the fact that it was a means of grace whose full significance is revealed only as the Christian develops the inner life in Christ, and is most precious to those who are most deeply committed to Christian discipleship. . . . At the same time it would be possible to give a lengthy list of early Methodists who were, like Susanna Wesley, the mother of John and Charles, converted at the Lord's Supper. It was the actual experience of the Lord's Supper as a converting ordinance that led the Wesleys so insistently to contend for its use by men and women before conversion. (1951: 107)

So strongly did Wesley believe this that he made the celebration of the Lord's Supper the climax of his preaching missions. At the last gathering of Wesley's preaching missions, the Lord's Supper was utilized to press people to make a decision regarding Christ's gracious offer. Whereas we would recognize the importance of this particular use of the celebration of the Eucharist, we must not forget that it is also at the heart of the ongoing worship of the people of God.

We turn now to consider the ministry in its interrelatedness and diversity. Once again we affirm that the apostle Paul's ideal for the church (Eph. 4:1–17) reflects unity in diversity, strength through maturity, and growth toward wholeness. Its unity is basic: one body, one Spirit, one hope, one Lord, one faith, one baptism, and one Father (4:5–6). This presses Paul to call for an evangelical zeal to maintain the given unity in the bond of peace (4:3). Then virtually in the same breath he speaks of the diversity of ministry gifts (*domata*) "given as Christ apportioned [them]" (*dōreai*) (4:7). Apart from the gift of Scripture, there are only two great *dōreai:* Jesus Christ and the Holy Spirit. Paul can only mean that in these *domata* Christ has given himself back to the church through the Holy Spirit. Through his grace the ministry of Christ is carried on by the church, and even "greater things" than his are thereby made possible (John 14:12).

By the term *ministry (diakonia)* Paul includes both the specific service of material relief and the total range of Christian duties, whether internally to the believing community or externally to the non-Christian world. All are to be involved in ministry. The internal *diakonia* embraces three major types of *domata:* (1) the local congregation's ministry to the Lord in worship by prayer, sacrament, and the hearing of the Word of God; (2) the ministry of its members to one another "for the common good" (1 Cor. 12:7, 11); and (3) the ministry of teaching by which believers are inculcated with the norms of the apostolic tradition (Acts 6:4; Rom. 12:7).

The external *diakonia* likewise embraces three major types of *domata:*

1. the ministry to those in special need—the poor, the sick, the widow, the orphan, the prisoner, the homeless, and "the stranger within the gates" (Rom. 12:7; Gal. 6:10a);
2. the ministry of reconciliation, whereby Christians work for justice and concord among people and nations and within their separate cultures; and
3. the ministry of evangelism and cross-cultural mission.

In the performance of these ministries the Kingdom of God and the mission of the church come together. When the mission of the church is deliberately placed on the track of the Kingdom, specific "signs of the Kingdom" will be manifest to

We serve (*diakonia*) because we are followers of the Great Servant. But we know that the supreme service consists in bringing people to the Servant himself. (1959: 57)

It is an illusion to think that our service can be made so transparent that it will by itself lead those whom we serve to a confrontation with Jesus Christ. (1959: 55)

When every part of the body is "working properly," the result is both bodily growth and spiritual upbuilding "in love" (Eph. 4:16). It should be noted that Paul's phrase "so that the body of Christ may be built up" (Eph. 4:12) employs the same word (*oikodomeō*) found in Jesus' affirmation: "I will build my church" (Matt. 16:18).

Two matters remain. First, one must be grateful for this diversity in spiritual *domata*. The divine intent is that the church be a functioning, completed body. Not only are all believers united to Christ the head, but they are wonderfully related, by joints, to all other members (Eph. 4:16). Paul's use of "joints" must represent all interpersonal relationships, where members touch and "symphonize" with one another. Should we regard the "ligaments" that tie all bodily joints together as the bonds of Holy Spirit love that bind one to all the others (cf. Col. 2:19 with Rom. 5:5)? To express such love is one's covenanted life commitment to all other Christians and must be displayed to the world (John 13:34–35).

The muscles make bodily movement possible. And muscles must always work in tension with one another. Some bend arms; others extend them. No two are alike. If they were, the body would be completely paralyzed, incapable of motion, for all would be pulling in the same direction. Imagine what would happen if the "benders" dominated the "extenders"? No healthy, moving body is ever perfectly balanced. There is always tension between its muscles. Because of this, the body is a very suitable image for the church.

Within the varied ministries in the church one will find some concerned with ardor, others with order; the spontaneous worshipers and the "fixed-form" liturgists; those who stress the traditional versus the advocates of "immediate truth"; the evangelists versus those concerned with social responsibilities; the episcopalians versus congregationalists; the outgoing versus the reflective; the impulsive versus the cautious; the inspirational versus the analytical; and on and on. Be grateful for this diversity! And recognize that it is hardly God's intent that each separate congregation have the same agenda! No two church contexts (or parishes) are ever identical.

But, second, in the midst of this diversity we are not to believe every spirit, but to "test the spirits to see whether they are from God, because many false prophets have gone out into the world" (1 John 4:1). It is no virtue to be uninterested in the grace of spiritual discernment. The Ephesians 4 passage we discussed earlier warns of those who would manipulate and deceive the immature with "cunning and craftiness" (v. 14). There is always the possibility of error coming into the life and thought of the church. In the New Testament twice as much space is devoted to "powers and authorities" as to the Holy Spirit. And the church must always be concerned for its spiritual integrity, for it is plagued with false Christs and false prophets, with wolves in sheep's clothing, with error, heterodoxy, and apostasy. It does Christians little good to be so charitable and irenical that they become indifferent to the issue of truth and treat lightly Paul's warning of "deceitful workmen, masquerading as apostles of Christ" (2 Cor. 11:13).

Conclusion

We have seen that the provision of the Holy Spirit is threefold. The Holy Spirit has structured the church so that it can be expressed either as a local congregation (for near-neighbor mission) or as a mobile team (for frontier or cross-cultural mission). He has also provided spiritual gifts to all the people of God so that all can participate in the church's ministry. Furthermore, as Lord of the Harvest, he sends forth laborers into particular areas and avenues of service and provides them with his guidance and empowering.

However, everyone knows that there is no such thing as spiritually "steady-state" Christians or congregations or missions. As Paul Hiebert has observed:

Any long-range vision for missions must include not only the planting of new churches, but also the renewal of old ones. The former without the latter eventually leads only to lands full of dead and dying churches. The birth of new congregations is no guarantee that they will remain spiritually alive. . . . Spiritual life, like all forms of life, is involved in processes of health and illness, of reinvigoration and decay. (1983: 157)

Because of the crucialness of this problem, the New Testament has much to say about "renewal by the Holy Spirit." Although this phrase occurs only once (Titus 3:5), there are many references to people being either "full of the Holy Spirit" or "filled" with his presence. It is instructive to trace out each reference and inquire why the individuals concerned had occasional experiences of more abundant blessing that went beyond their habitual experience of the Holy Spirit. Paul urged upon Christians the obligation of constantly "being filled" with the Spirit as though they were constantly to be receiving fresh infusions of his power and grace (Eph. 5:18). In no place did he state that this was to be regarded merely as a privilege or an enjoyment or an honor. Those who are not so receptive toward the Holy Spirit are to regard themselves as nothing less than out of the will of God!

Renewal is important for the mission of the church to be fully achieved. Therefore, special attention must be given to the phenomenon of institutionalism, with its attendant tendencies toward bureaucratic rigidity and nominality. The big question is whether renewal can be programmed. Inasmuch as only God can renew his work in the hearts of his people, the key to all renewal activity is constant, focused, fervent prayer after the pattern of Habakkuk: "LORD, I have heard of your fame; I stand in awe of your deeds, O LORD. Renew them in our day, in our time make them known; in wrath remember mercy" (3:2).

20

God Rules Now
Already and Not Yet

Introduction

It is not surprising that Paul would draw upon his character, background, and education to trace out the theological implications of his calling as apostle to the Gentiles. In the process he would review all his rabbinical understanding of the relevant Old Testament passages that referred to God's redemptive concern for the Gentiles. This search revealed a pattern of integration between Old Testament validities and the perspectives that Peter and James shared with him concerning Jesus' teaching on this theme (Gal. 1:18–19). Inevitably, he found that much of the teaching and conduct of Jesus reflected considerable continuity with "the law, the prophets and the writings" of the Old Testament. However, Paul also discovered that continuity did not necessitate identity. There was a dimension of refreshing newness that characterized Jesus' witness to God's intent for the Gentile nations. Paul's task was to put all these different components into a coherent, progressive view of salvation history that was faithful to the historic context of the earlier revelation (Blauw 1962: 68). Paul was too deeply persuaded of the inspiration and authority of the Old Testament to classify it as merely preparatory and hence of only provisional significance. He was also convinced of the normative nature of all that Jesus had said and done. In this section we will trace the sequence by which Paul was to become the great theologian of the Christian mission. We will find him profoundly loyal to the Old Testament witness and deeply responsive to all that Jesus taught ("what is new and what is old," Matt. 13:52 NRSV). Paul also was the recipient of fresh "visions and revelations" (2 Cor. 12:1, 7). He synthesized these varied streams into a coherent whole.

Jesus and the Gentiles: What Is Old

Jesus rigidly confined his ministry and that of his disciples to the "lost sheep of Israel" (Matt. 15:24; 10:5, 6). Yet we also need to recognize that in sending forth the Twelve (10:1–42) on a mission to all "the cities of Israel" (v. 23), he intimated that in the ongoing movement of God's larger purpose they would "be brought before governors and kings as witnesses to them and to the Gentiles" (v. 18). When Matthew placed these two realities in the same passage, he made no attempt to resolve what scholars ever since have regarded as an inconsistency. The lost sheep of Israel were the object of Jesus' redemptive concern, and yet he was also willing to reach out to the occasional "lost" Gentile in anticipation of this larger ministry (15:21–28 and 9:13). Whereas the Kingdom of God was already "at hand" prior to the cross, its full eschatological revelation was possible only after the coming of the Holy Spirit at Pentecost, an outpouring directed to all the surrounding nations listed as examples in Acts 2.

This made sense to Paul. Of course, the Messiah had first to become "a servant of the Jews on behalf of God's truth, to confirm the promises made to the patriarchs" (Rom. 15:8). In fact, in all of Paul's subsequent missionary career he always made sure that he offered the good news of the Kingdom "to the Jew first" (Rom. 1:16), since it had always been the purpose of God that through this one people "all peoples on earth" would be blessed (Gen. 12:3).

It made sense to Paul that the Gentile mission could not be launched before the Lamb of God had been slain (John 1:29). The last Song of the Servant in Isaiah concerning his atoning sacrifice concludes with God assigning him "many" righteous ones for his portion (53:11). Paul understood this as referring to an innumerable host for whom he "made intercession" as he "bore [their] sin" (53:12). Paul doubtless recalled the confirming words of Christ: "I, when I am lifted up from the earth, will draw all [people] to myself" (John 12:32).

Paul understood why Jesus would describe the Gentiles as spiritually ignorant, verbose in their formal religious activity, materialistically inclined, and hostile toward God (Matt. 6:7, 32; Mark 10:33–34). This was identical with the Old Testament witness and, as such, was foundational to Paul's description of the spiritual condition of the Gentiles (see Rom. 1:18–32; 3:10–18).

The continuity of Jesus with the Old Testament revelation could be seen in other ways as well. When Jesus glaringly exposed the flaws of Jewish proselytizing zeal in a devastating fashion because it was hypocritically motivated and evil in its results, Paul would detect a distinctly Sinaitic note (cf. Matt. 23:15 with Lev. 19:33–34; Num. 15:14–16; 1 Kings 8:41–43). Paul agreed with this evaluation and incorporated it in his exposure of the spiritual condition of Jewry (Rom. 2:17–24). Furthermore, the more Paul mingled with Gentiles, the more he identified with Jesus' rejection of Jewish racial and cultural pride. The parable of the Good Samaritan only confirmed Paul's love and esteem for his Gentile coworkers. Paul also recognized Jesus' affirmation that on the last day some Jews and some Gentiles would be saved although many Jews and Gentiles would be lost (cf. Matt. 7:13–14; 25:31–46 with Rom. 10:1–3 and 2 Cor. 4:3). In this connection Paul saw the universal dimensions of Jesus' messiahship. He was the Servant of Yahweh who came "to give his life as a ransom for many" and thereby brought hope to the Gentiles (cf. Mark 10:45 and Matt. 12:15–21 with Rom. 1:14–17 and 1 Tim.

2:3–6). Truly, Jesus' coming into the world had both universal and eschatological dimensions. Paul found no problem with this, nor did he encounter difficulty in relating Jesus' teaching on the universal sufficiency of the Kingdom of God with what he came to describe as "my gospel" (Acts 20:24–25; Rom. 2:16; 16:25).

Jesus and the Gentiles: What Is New

Some of Jesus' statements about the Gentiles mentioned in the preceding discussion would doubtless awaken in Paul a sense of concern, because they could not be easily reconciled with his Old Testament perspectives. And yet upon reflection, Paul came to see that despite Jesus' frequent new ways of expressing these realities, there was no essential departure from what he had earlier been taught. In all this we must recognize Paul's intense desire to identify Jesus' use of the Old Testament (Luke 24:25–27, 44–47) with what he believed about its divine origin (2 Tim. 3:15–17). He had no desire to do what some have done, draw mission significance from a few isolated elements in the older record (e.g., the promise to Abraham in Genesis 12:3; Jonah's oracle against Nineveh; some Psalms, such as the sixty-seventh, and an isolated "universal" passage or two in Isaiah, such as 49:6) and use them to bolster Jesus' Great Commission. The inevitable result of such proof-texting would have violated for him the integrity of the Old Testament and undermined its unique and cumulative revelation concerning the mission of Israel to the nations.

Among Paul's unresolved problems, however, was how he should relate his ongoing mission to the Gentiles to what the rabbis had taught him. They had shown him from Isaiah (2:2–4 and 25:6–9) and Micah (4:1–4) that only in the "last days" would God summon the nations to Jerusalem. Only then would they have contact with God. The focus of their encounter would be the Temple, not Christian missionaries preaching in Gentile towns and villages.

We can be sure that Paul had already sensed the universal implications in Jesus' use of the term "the Kingdom of God." It must include salvation for the people of God throughout all the nations of the world. But how should this be related to the sequence of eschatological events described in the Old Testament? This sequence begins with the epiphany (lit., "appearance") of God in the Temple (Isa. 51:4–5; 60:3; 62:11; Zech. 2:11). Then follows God's summons to the nations (Ps. 50:1; 96:3, 10; Isa. 45:20, 22; 55:5; 66:19) and their march to Jerusalem laden with gifts (Ps. 47:9; 68:30, 32; Isa. 18:7; 19:23; 60:5–20; Hag. 2:7; Zech. 8:21). The nations come to worship God in the sanctuary (Ps. 22:27; 72:9–11; 86:9; Isa. 45:14, 24; 56:7; 66:18; Zeph. 3:9) and then sit down to the final eschatological feast (Isa. 25:6–8). One can well believe that Paul struggled with this imagery and its sequence. It seemed at variance with Jesus' speaking of himself as having "come to seek and to save what was lost" (Luke 19:10) and of his desire to transform his disciples into "fishers of men" (Matt. 4:19).

Paul's resolution of this complex problem involved the exploration of a variety of themes. In the first place, Peter would have shown Paul that Pentecost was an eschatological event and marked the beginning of the day of the Lord. That day was now transformed into a historic era as Joel had predicted (Acts 2:16–21). This meant that the Kingdom of God had an "already" dimension through the coming of the Holy Spirit. Furthermore, Peter showed that the final "time . . . for God to restore everything, as he promised long ago through his holy prophets" awaited a second coming of Christ (Acts 3:20–21). Paul doubtless began at this point to alter drastically his understanding of the eschatological significance of the Incarnation and all that followed.

Second, Paul also would have been encouraged by Peter to reflect more closely on Jesus' teaching and parables. Jesus had spoken of a final summoning of the people of God from all the nations at the end of this era, resulting in their sitting "at the feast with Abraham, Isaac and Jacob in the kingdom of heaven" (Matt. 8:11–12; Mark 13:27). And if the people of God are described as "the light of the world, a city on a hill" (Matt. 5:14), Jesus must have envisioned his people not only proclaiming the Kingdom of God (with its universal implications) but also manifesting its realities in their lives during the historic interval between the present and the last day. Otherwise, what significance would there be to Jesus' words about others who may "see [their] good works and praise [their] Father in heaven" (Matt. 5:16)?

But what of the specifics of "Jerusalem" and the "Temple" from which the "Torah" (lit., "law") would go forth to the nations? We can imagine that these references would give Paul deep concern. He might solve this problem partially by recognizing that the Holy Spirit was poured out at Jerusalem on the day of Pentecost and that the "upper room" in which the 120 were meeting on that occasion was within the Temple precincts (tradition seems to confirm this). And he knew that the Old Testament usage of the word *Torah* could identify something much broader than the Decalogue. It could stand for the redemptive activity of God on behalf of God's people. In this case, it would include the good news of all that Jesus accomplished redemptively to save his people from their sins. All this would be somewhat convincing: identifying the beginnings of the Christian movement with Old Testament imagery.

But problems remained. Paul may have found satisfactory resolution through recalling the charge he heard leveled against Stephen when he spoke against the Temple and predicted its destruction (Acts 6:13–14). Jesus had also predicted the coming invasion of the land (by the "vultures"—Roman legions—Matt. 24:28) and the destruction of Jerusalem. What, then, would this do to the ongoing Old Testament vision of the law going out from Zion and "the word of the LORD from Jerusalem" (Isa. 2:3)? This problem drove Paul to rethink all that Jesus said about these realities, particularly about the Temple.

Paul would have seen immediate significance in Jesus' messianic cleansing of the Temple at the outset of his ministry (John 2:12–25). We are assuming here, of course, that the apostle John's account is chronologically correct. Paul would have been gripped by the cryptic words that Jesus spoke on that occasion, of the destruction of the Temple and of his rebuilding it in three days. He would have begun to identify the Temple with Jesus' body, lifted up on the cross and thereby making provision for all peoples to be summoned to his salvation (John 2:21–22; 12:31–33). Certainly the removal of the animals when Jesus cleansed the Temple could symbolize the end of the sacrificial system under the law. Paul would have been confirmed in this sequence of thought by learning that following the resurrection it was common knowledge among the disciples that Jesus identified the Temple as his own body.

He doubtless also heard that Jesus in an altercation with the Pharisees said that "one greater than the Temple" was present in their midst (Matt. 12:6). Did Jesus mean that the Kingdom of God, present in Jesus, was greater than the Temple? Perhaps at this point Paul recalled the account of what had happened on the Mount of Transfiguration when Jesus was "transfigured" and "his face shone like the sun, and his clothes became as white as the light" (Matt. 17:2). To Paul this must have meant the same Shekinah glory that first appeared when God led Israel out of Egypt (Exod. 13:21), that had covered Sinai (24:16), that then filled the tabernacle (40:34–35), and that later came to Solomon's Temple (1 Kings 8:11). This association vividly confirmed the intimate relation between Christ, the "cornerstone," and the eternal temple of God. That the inner "curtain of the temple was torn in two from top to bottom" the moment Jesus died (Matt. 27:51) would indicate that God was abandoning this flawed sanctuary and that a foundation was being laid for a spiritual temple that would contain the Shekinah Presence forever (Heb. 10:19–25).

In the light of all this we can understand why Paul later confidently declared: "God . . . does not live in temples built by hands" (Acts 17:24). Paul himself was later falsely accused of profaning the Temple because he allegedly brought Gentiles into it (an action forbidden under pain of death). This episode must have doubly confirmed to him that the Temple after Pentecost abruptly lost its relevance to the ongoing purpose of God. It had ceased to be "a house of prayer for all the nations" (Mark 11:17). In fact, God was even prevented by the Jews from bringing Gentiles "to the holy mountain" (Isa. 56:6–8 vs. Acts 21:27–30). Both the Temple and Jerusalem had become unfaithful to their calling and were destined to be destroyed as Jesus had predicted (Matt. 24:1–2; Luke 21:20–24). A new temple with no geographic focus was to be centered in Jesus Christ. Christ's body, the church, must now be formed into a new temple made of "living stones" quarried out of the peoples of every tribe, tongue, and nation. One day in Jesus Christ's glory the New Jerusalem will come to be (Gal. 4:26; Rev. 21:2).

Paul's resolution of this problem was so complete that he never mentions the old Temple in his writings. His single reference to a physical temple is somewhat obscure (2 Thess. 2:4). In contrast, he makes frequent references to a spiritual temple, as already implied in the teaching of Jesus (Mark 14:58). This temple is the Christian individual in whom the Holy Spirit dwells (1 Cor. 6:19) and consists of the church as a whole (1 Cor. 3:9, 16–17; 2 Cor. 6:16; Eph. 2:20–22).

Paul, Mission, and the Church: What Is Unique

We have seen that increasingly Paul came to realize that Jesus' teaching and parables of the Kingdom pointed in the direction of "a new era in the history of Israel and of the world" that began at Pentecost and directed attention "toward a new future" (Blauw 1962: 73, 79). This new era would be characterized by the people of God making Jesus Christ known as Lord and Savior to all peoples. Their central focus would be on him for, in essence, he supremely constitutes the Kingdom. Proclaiming this good news would be akin to scattering good seed. The reaping and ingathering of the final harvest will take place at the end of the times. Following this comes the judgment. In a sense, then, God's final judgment was deferred because judgment was vicariously borne by Jesus at the cross. The new era is to be characterized by proclaiming "the year of the Lord's favor" (Luke 4:19). "The day of vengeance of . . . God" will take place at the end (Isa. 61:2). Paul could now see that all this fitted the symbolism of Isaiah 2:2–4. In fact, as mentioned earlier, the one missing item was the treasures of all nations being brought into the Lord's house. Paul sought himself to fulfill this vision through his preoccupation with "collection tours," that is, collecting offerings and gifts from the Gentile churches on behalf of the poor saints in Jerusalem (Hag. 2:7; Acts 4:32–37; 11:27–30; Rom. 15:25–27).

However, when Paul pondered what was meant by "the people of God," a problem arose. What about the Gentiles who received the gospel, held it fast in an honest and good heart, and brought forth fruit with patience (Luke 8:15)? Were they to be made culturally Jews by being brought under the law and then being circumcised?

We need to remember the insight gained by the early church from Peter's experience in the house of Cornelius when the Holy Spirit came upon Gentile believers as when at Pentecost the Holy Spirit had come upon Jewish believers. This took place apart from either circumcision or baptism (Acts 10:44–48). However, this incident did not answer all Paul's questions. Actually, as the gospel went outward from Jerusalem, those in its vanguard were by no means agreed as to the relation between Gentile believers and the law of Moses. There were Jewish Christians who insisted on its full observance, including circumcision (Acts 11:2). They "belonged to the party [sect] of the Pharisees" (15:5) and were quite antagonistic to Paul. He bluntly describes them as "false brothers [who] had infiltrated our ranks to spy on the freedom we have in Christ Jesus" (Gal. 2:4).

The second group did not insist on circumcision but argued that converted Gentiles must keep some of the Jewish observances. These are the "men [who] came from James" who did not want the Christian movement to lose its Jewish heritage (Acts 15:19–29; Gal. 2:12). The third group was more liberal in that it neither required the Gentiles to be circumcised nor expected them to observe Jewish dietary laws. Paul was its spokesman. It seems he differed with James on the matter of requiring Christians to abstain from food offered to idols (cf. 1 Cor. 8 with Acts 15:20, 29). Some say there was a final group that saw no abiding relevance in the

Jewish cult, its laws, and its feasts. No one in this group would have endorsed Paul's keeping the feasts, worshiping in the Temple, or circumcising Timothy (Acts 20:6, 16; 21:26; 16:1–3). However, we have no textual evidence that such a completely Hellenized group of Jewish believers actually existed. We can believe, however, that these diverse groups of Jewish believers drove Paul to seek a resolution. R. A. Stewart does not overstate its significance when he writes:

> World history was trembling in the balance while Paul and his Judaistic colleagues argued over the circumcision controversy. Had this been made the necessary condition of Christian conversion, candidates might have been few, and world history would have been very different. (1962: 1048)

Fortunately, the gospel emerged triumphant. Entrance into the Kingdom was by grace through faith and apart from the works of the law. And the church as the New Testament expression of the people of God formed at Pentecost became for Paul the focal point of all his subsequent theologizing about the Christian mission. He made no attempt to develop a "theology of mission" as such. His desire was to explore the nature and mission of the church, the community of the Kingdom of God. He saw the church as arising out of God's election of Israel, not as a static religious community but as a dynamic body of people sent into the world to be nothing less than the witnessing and serving presence of Jesus Christ. He was convinced that only thereby could the eschatological dimension of God's purpose for the nations be truly actualized.

To do justice to Paul's development of the nature of the church, we must explore the redemptive purpose of God, the relation of the Jewish law to saving faith, and the unity between Jew and Gentile in Christ. But this would take us far beyond the parameters of this study. Happily, these themes have been thoroughly and satisfactorily explored and definitively stated by others. At this point we will make only a few summary statements.

When Paul spoke about the church, he spoke first and foremost about Jesus Christ: the One who gathered his own to himself (Mark 3:14–15) and instructed them as to their essential oneness (9:34–41). Paul reinforced this in a remarkable fashion by affirming that the offspring of Abraham, the chosen people of God, consists of only one person, and he is Jesus Christ (Gal. 3:16). The church is but one person only. Then, almost immediately thereafter, Paul went on to say that believers are "all one in Christ Jesus" (3:28). They are "heirs according to the promise" (3:29). They have "put on Christ." They are his body. They are "in him."

The apostle John used different imagery, but he described the church in virtually the same fashion. He recorded how Jesus spoke of "the vine," the Old Testament symbol for Israel, the people of God (Isa. 5:1–7), and identified it with himself. His followers constitute the church only in that they are branches of the vine. Without this intimate union with him and thereby with one another, they cannot bear fruit (John 15:1–11). In fact, the whole life of the church is the life of Jesus Christ; and he is not divided. There is but one people of God, a new race, called by one Father in heaven, redeemed by his Son at Calvary, and regenerated by the Holy Spirit, who proceeds from the Father and the Son. There can be only one church, for one can no more multiply churches than multiply God!

But the church is also diversity within unity. Paul emphasized this by comparing it to a human body.

> There is one body . . . the body of Christ, . . . joined and held together by every supporting ligament, grows and builds itself up in love as each part does its work. (Eph. 4:4–16; see also 1 Cor. 12:12–31; Eph. 5:21–33; Col. 1:17–29; 2:19; 3:15; etc.)

No greater diversity within unity can be imagined than that which is represented by the human body with its many different members, each having separate functions to perform for the good of the organic whole. In the light of this unity that necessitates diversity, we approach Paul's great affirmation that in the church "there is neither Jew nor Greek, slave nor free, male nor female; for you are all one in Christ Jesus" (Gal. 3:28). "Here there is no Greek or Jew, circumcised or uncircumcised, barbarian, Scythian, slave or free, but Christ is all, and is in all" (Col. 3:11). Concerning these key texts, Lightfoot states:

> In Christ ye are all [children], all free. Every barrier is swept away. No special claims, no special disabilities exist in him, none can exist. The conventional distinctions of religious caste or of social rank, even the natural distinction of sex, are banished hence. One heart beats in all; one mind guides all; one life is lived by all. You are all one man, for ye are members of Christ. (1865: 150)

In Ephesians 2:11–22 we have Paul's classic statement of this amazing fact. It is through the cross that even the most polarized, the Jews and the Gentiles, have been made one. Not that Gentiles have been brought into Jewish society or that Jews have been brought into Gentile society. Rather, a new unity, a new organism, a new body has been formed of redeemed Jews and redeemed Gentiles in which the old distinctions are forever done away. The "dividing wall of hostility" has been broken down (v. 14).

Paul argued that Christ has brought to an end the Jewish law, which had previously made impossible all fellowship between Jews and Gentiles. But more than this: He has ended the hostility. Twice Paul referred to this hostility (vv. 14, 16). Christ has "put to death their hostility." This means that there should be no barriers of hatred and contempt between those whom he has redeemed. Men continue as males, women as females, and the various groupings of Jews retain their circumcision and distinctive lifestyles. Barbarians and Scythians, slaves and masters—all these diversities remain. But the enmity that used to separate them has been done away. Its prejudices and suspicions can now be surmounted. And in Christ, through mutual acceptance and dynamic interpersonal and intercultural interaction, the most diverse of Christians can develop a oneness that visibly demonstrates they are the one people of God.

This takes us to Paul's central thesis in his Ephesian letter. He began with a description of God's purpose to consummate not only human history but all dimensions of God's creation, in heaven and on earth, in Jesus Christ (especially 1:3–10). To achieve this, a revelatory foundation had to be laid "of the apostles and prophets" (2:20) so that a new people, his church, might be called from a fallen and estranged human race (2:1–10). However, this church does not represent something unrelated to the Old Israel. "Salvation is from the Jews" (John 4:22) as well as among the Jews. Hence, "the dividing wall of hostility" between Jews and Gentiles had to be broken down (Eph. 2:14, within 2:11–22).

This church has been given a task distinctly new in the history of salvation: to issue the call to all the nations to become the disciples of Jesus Christ (Eph. 3:8–10, within 3:1–21). Moreover, this church would perform this task without the assistance of Jerusalem. The strict legalists who argued that Gentiles had to become Jews ("under the law") before they could be saved saw dangerous precedents arising from two sources. One was Peter's amazement when he witnessed the Holy Spirit being poured out upon Gentiles without baptism or circumcision (cf. Acts 10:45 with 11:2–3). The other was in Paul's similar experience of the Spirit working in his ministry "also to the Gentiles" (Gal. 2:8). The Jerusalem church merely sent delegates to Samaria and Antioch to establish linkage with what the Spirit had already begun to accomplish apart from any Jerusalem initiative (Acts 8:14; 11:22). Through Paul's efforts, however, the pattern of compelling Gentiles to live like Jews was brought to a final end in the emerging church (Gal. 2:14).

In Ephesians 3 Paul shows himself as the task theologian, coming to final clarity as to the rationale for the place of Jews and Gentiles in the "already-not yet" period of the Kingdom of God within God's eternal purpose. This mystery was made known to Paul "by revelation" (3:3). Previously, it had not been known precisely how Gentile believers would become "through the gospel . . . heirs together with Israel, members together of one body, and sharers together in the promise in Christ Jesus" (3:6). But now all was clear. Since all along salvation had been bestowed on Jews apart from the law, it is manifestly universal in its scope, God's gift to all peoples (3:7–10). Paul's key word is "now." This age is to be marked by the inclusion of Gentiles into the body of Christ. The time is now! This fact brought a sense of urgency to Paul's missionary obedience and to all missionary obedience from that time onward.

Mission and Israel: The Epistle to the Romans

We have seen that there was a great deal of interaction between the scattered apostles during those early decades. They were deeply involved in proclaiming the gospel throughout the eastern end of the Mediterranean world and in what is now the Middle East. They doubtless shared their letters with one another. We recall that Peter found "some things" in Paul's letters that were "hard to understand" (2 Peter 3:16). Among these "hard-to-understand" things must have been Paul's discussion in Romans 9–11 where the mystery of Israel's rejection of the gospel is related to the salvation of Gentiles. Although no one should presume to have mastered the substance of his complex argument, we feel its thrust should be included in this study. If we keep in mind that the Epistle to the Romans was written by a task theologian at a crucial turning point in his missionary career, we will be able to unravel its mysteries more readily.

"I must visit Rome also," Paul said (Acts 19:21). During Paul's third missionary journey this imperative became increasingly insistent. He sensed that his work in the eastern Mediterranean was over, and he was making plans to evangelize the west, particularly Spain. He needed a new base of operations to replace Antioch, and the only Christian community that had this potential was in Rome. But the church in Rome represented an independent movement with which Paul had no previous contact. This posed two questions: Would it accept Paul's apostolic leadership, and would it support him in outreach as far away as Spain? Rome was not yet fully evangelized; neither was all of Italy. Would the Christians in Rome participate actively in Paul's mission to Spain?

Based on this agenda, when Paul wrote to the Romans he was not particularly concerned to provide them with a comprehensive compendium of Christian truth. He rather desired to awaken them to a sense of missionary obligation. This pressed him to bypass the development of certain major Christian themes (e.g., the person of Christ; the church as the body; the second coming) and select only those that conceivably might transform what was local and vigorous into something world-conscious and missionary-minded. Through the selection and sequence of its themes, the epistle has provided Christians down through the centuries with an apostolic model of missionary motivation. It was written from Corinth in the winter of A.D. 57/58 while Paul was awaiting transport and becomes thereby the most significant letter ever written on a vacation!

At the outset (1:1–7) Paul speaks of all Christians ("we," 1:5) as the recipients of both "grace" (come and believe!) and "apostleship" (go and tell!). His object was to link them with the purpose of God: to bring about "obedience that comes from faith" among "all the Gentiles." The obligation belongs to all God's people.

Paul then becomes quite personal. He does not state precisely why he is writing this letter, only that he is looking forward to visiting Rome. He arouses curiosity as to his real purpose, without revealing prematurely his missionary plans (1:8–13). He concludes the introduction by stressing the universal applicability of the gospel and by summarizing its great themes: faith, righteousness, and life (1:14–17).

The formal argument begins with a most comprehensive portrayal of the lostness of all people, whether Jews or Gentiles (1:18–3:20). To become mission-minded, one must recognize the spiritual need and claims of humankind. After describing the profound sinfulness of sin, Paul speaks of the abounding grace of God to sinners provided through the "righteousness from God," in the Lord Jesus Christ (3:21–5:21). His death was propitiatory and retrospective (3:25), sufficient for all peoples, those living both before and after his coming (3:29–30).

This is fully consistent with the Old Testament revelation. With this gospel of justification by faith, the Christians in Rome are being summoned to take their part in evangelizing the world. Since the gospel offers more than future salvation, Paul then speaks of the abounding grace of God to believers. God has provided for them the possibility of deliverance from the present power of sin (6:1–8:39). The resources he has made available to them for victorious living are found in Jesus Christ and in him alone (6:4–5, 11; 7:24–25). In this section Paul challenges the Romans by sharing his own experience of struggle and victory. He speaks of co-crucifixion with Christ and co-resurrection with him to this life of victory. Though sinning is still possible, it is not necessary. Paul then speaks of the Holy Spirit, who indwells Christians, transforming them to meet all the righteous demands God makes of them (8:1–17). Rightly understood, the Christian life is the "exchanged" life. Then, because of Paul's desire to be realistic, he introduces the concept of suffering, sacrifice, hardship, and persecution involved in the Lord's service (8:18–27). Finally, he concludes with a hymn of triumph. God has so provided for God's people that in the midst of the most adverse circumstances, victory will always be possible (8:28–39).

It is only then that Paul speaks of the Jews and their rejection of the gospel (9:1–11:36). His abrupt introduction of the Jewish question has caused some to downgrade this portion, making it a parenthesis, written merely to help Jewish Christians in Rome (Scofield 1917: 1202). As a Jew and a missionary, however, Paul could never forget that God did not intend Israel to be an end in itself. Actually, when he called Abram out of Ur of the Chaldees, God was concerned with the nations ("all peoples on earth," Gen. 12:1–3). Israel was to be God's means to worldwide blessing. Although Israel as a people largely failed, the Messiah in "the fullness of time" came through Israel and became the Savior of the world. So then, God triumphed despite Israel's failure. The tragedy, however, was that many Jews still remained outside the household of faith. This is Paul's problem. He mourns for his kinsfolk, knowing them to be lost despite their spiritual privileges (Rom. 9:1–5). Indeed, by his very heart anguish, Paul rebukes all easy unconcern for all those who are lost.

But why has this tragedy taken place? In 9:6–18 Paul shows that in every past generation, and even in his own generation, the members of the true Israel were being saved because of God's electing grace. Paul does not challenge God's freedom to make choices. In a very profound fashion he makes no accommodation to what people might think is not fair play (God choosing a people to be saved but not choosing all). He shows that God never condemns anyone who ought to be saved; God saves those who deserve to be lost. One cannot charge God with making people bad and then punishing them for being bad (9:19–33).

All too many Jews sought acceptance with God through self-effort and stumbled at the simplicity of faith in God's provision. They misused the Mosaic revelation, rejected the offer of God's righteousness, substituted their own pretended righteousness, and never became a servant people among the nations. Admittedly, the Gentiles were doubtless less virtuous than the Jews. However, when many heard of Jesus Christ, the gift of God's acquittal and righteousness, they simply met the conditions of repentance and faith (10:1–13).

At this point Paul addresses God's searching missionary questions to the Christians in Rome (10:14–15). How are people to believe in Christ unless they hear the gospel through those sent to bear witness to them about Jesus Christ? And how are they to bear witness unless they are sent? Christians can too easily inquire as to what God will do with those who have not heard of Christ. Actually, God has no alternative plan for bringing God's salvation to people apart from Christians being chosen and sent forth to preach this "good news." If the Jews failed in their calling, certainly the Christians in Rome should ponder this tragedy and make sure they are not similarly indifferent to God's worldwide redemptive purpose.

Paul then relentlessly presses forward with his exploration of the mystery of the Jewish rejection of Christ and the Jews' deliberate abdication of their high calling to be God's light to the nations (10:16–21). In the face of this we underscore the somber reality of much missionary experience: not of peoples' lack of opportunity to hear the gospel, but their unwillingness to respond by repentance and faith. Imagine how jealous Jewish people must be today when they realize that their Scriptures are being proclaimed worldwide, but only occasionally through Jewish lips (10:19).

Paul then begins to round out his argument. The Jews have failed God and have been set aside (chap. 9). Even so, God's missionary purpose for the Gentile world must be pressed with greater energy than ever before, despite the Jewish failure (chap. 10). But do the people of Israel have a future in the redemptive purpose of God? Paul stresses three basic ideas: First, God's rejection of the Jews is not total; every generation of Christians will include Jewish believers (11:1–6). There is always "a remnant chosen by grace." Second, God's immutable laws remain, bringing hardening and blinding to those Jews who remain impenitent (11:7–10). Third, God has overruled the unbelief of many Jews. He has turned from them to bring salvation to the Gentiles, and many Gentiles have responded (11:11–12).

Paul is particularly concerned that the Romans catch the import of this third point, which establishes linkage with God's worldwide missionary purpose (11:13–16). Surprise of surprises! There is triumph in spite of Jewish rejection of Jesus, and this triumph has been incorporated into God's plan! The failure and disaster of Israel in apostolic history actually precipitated the evangelization of the Gentiles. Paul recalled frequent instances of this. His concluding word to the resistant Jews in Antioch of Pisidia was a case in point: "We had to speak the word of God to you first. Since you reject it and do not consider yourselves worthy of eternal life, we now turn to the Gentiles" (Acts 13:46). Although not apparent in his day, Paul then argues that the spiritual blessings Gentiles received stimulate Jews to jealousy and would ultimately result in their conversion, with unprecedented blessing for the whole world.

But Gentile believers should not boast. They can easily fail in their performance of the will of God (Rom. 11:17–24). Furthermore, believing Jews will be grafted back into the olive tree, the people of God. And then where will boasting be? God will indeed show mercy to Israel as a whole, but only after the full number of Gentiles has been incorporated into Christ as a result of the worldwide missionary outreach of God's people (11:25–26a). This engrafting of Jews will not be gradual; it will necessitate divine intervention (11:26b–27), thereby fulfilling a frequently stated Old Testament prophecy (e.g., Isa. 27:6; 59:20–21; Jer. 31:33–34). Although most Jews are now the enemies of God as regards God's election, their nation is beloved and will yet be shown mercy (11:28–32). Paul concludes with praise to God because God is the source of all good and all grace. And God will in the end be fully vindicated (11:33–36).

The final sections of this letter focus on practical matters regarding Paul's concern to see the Christians in Rome transformed into a missionary-minded community: a sending base eager to participate with his apostolic band in the evangelization of Spain. He begins by calling them to a new commitment to God and God's will for their lives (12:1–2). Since all are to be involved in one way or other with the Christian mission, it follows that God's provision of various spiritual gifts for one and all should be taken very seriously. All are to be diligent in their exercise of their spiritual gifts (12:3–8), and are to seek harmonious relations not only with one another but also with non-Christians (12:9–21). Since a distinction must be made between this pattern of Christian love for all human relationships and the duty of governments to execute judgment, Paul introduces a section on the relations of Christians to the state (13:1–7). Christians engaged in mission must respect the civil authorities, but not to the point of failing to "give . . . to God what is God's" (Mark 12:17).

Paul concludes this practical section by calling for love: the only valid cement for human relations (Rom. 13:8–15:13). He calls for personal holiness (13:8–14), an avoidance of the judgmental spirit that disrupts harmony when Christians differ over "disputable matters" (14:1–23), and a concern to "please [one's] neighbor for his good, to build him up" (15:1–6). Paul then issues an ecumenical invitation to receive all those whom God has manifestly received, because of their profession of Jesus Christ as Lord (15:7). True, there may be serious differences between them, but these can be resolved by following the example of Christ. That means listening and sharing in love. They are only to avoid those who "cause divisions and put obstacles in your way" (16:17–20). This section concludes with a review of God's redemptive purpose, beginning with the patriarchs and moving into the Gentile world in their day (15:8–13). This review points to God's abiding concern for the nations. Paul uses many Old Testament texts to demonstrate this concern that Gentiles are to be included with Jews in God's redemptive plan.

At this point Paul repeats his conviction that the Roman Christians (1:8) were to be vital in their Christian experience, vigorous in their witness, and knowledgeable about the truths contained in this letter (15:14–15). They knew that the human race was lost (chaps. 1–3), that Jesus died for all (chaps. 3–5), that God's salvation brought liberation and victory as well as eternal life (chaps. 6–8), and that the Jews had failed God but that there was still a future for them in his eternal purpose (chaps. 9–11).

Paul then speaks autobiographically about his own missionary effectiveness. From Jerusalem to Illyricum (the present-day Balkan countries) and "by what I have said and done," he had "fully proclaimed the gospel of Christ" (15:18–19). Where previously there had been neither Christians nor churches, there now were both. His work in the eastern Mediterranean was over, but his ambition remained undiminished: he must preach the gospel where Christ was not known (15:20). That meant Spain, where he would be helped by the participation of the Christians in Rome. "I hope to visit you while passing through [as I go to Spain] and to have you assist me on my journey there, after I have enjoyed your company a while" (15:24). Paul fully expected the Christians in Rome to say: "If you are going to Spain, we are going with you." Rome would become his new base of operations. The Christians there would outfit him for his journey. Notice also Paul's request that the Christians in Rome pray for him (15:30–33). Even though his mission plans were scripturally based and realistic, he wanted to ensure that all future steps would be of the Lord. Hence, by seeking their prayers he entrusted his plans to God.

Actually, when Paul later was in the process of delivering a Gentile contribution to the poor saints at Jerusalem (Acts 15:25–29) while hopefully en route to Rome, he was seized and imprisoned. Acts 21–26 tells the story. Two years later he reached Rome, but in chains. Then followed two more years of house arrest there. Among the early church fathers, only Clement of Rome seems to intimate, in a vague statement, that Paul eventually reached Spain. In a very real sense, however, what happened to Paul does not concern us here. The abiding relevance of this epistle is that it shows us how to impart to local congregations a missionary concern. Only by solid Bible teaching on the great themes of redemption and the eternal purpose of God can this be accomplished.

Conclusion

In the closing words of this epistle Paul summarizes God's redemptive concern for the Gentiles. Although "hidden for long ages past," it is now being "made known . . . [to] all nations," and this is in accordance with "the command of the eternal God" in order "that all nations might believe and obey him" (Rom. 16:25–27). There is a deep unity to both covenants, old and new. Jesus Christ is indeed the fulfillment of Scripture. Salvation is only available through faith in him. Indeed, apart from him there is no salvation. And the time is now to proclaim this message to the nations. The coming of the Holy Spirit at Pentecost gave birth to the church, mobilizing and empowering the church to be God's primary instrument for announcing the Kingdom of God among the nations of the earth.

In part 6 we will review three major New Testament themes of God's mission that will continue to impact our mission today and into the future: Christ and the powers, the uniqueness of Christ in relation to religious pluralism, and John's missiological perspective in the Book of Revelation with reference to the end of time.

PART 6

GOD'S MISSION EXTENDS TO THE END OF TIME

21

God's Kingdom Extends over the Powers

Introduction

We have seen the dimension of power encounter in the unfolding record of the coming of Jesus into the world, his public ministry, vicarious death, and resurrection triumph. All this is relevant to the subsequent New Testament teaching concerning the mission of the church in relation to the powers. The gospel of the Kingdom that was proclaimed to Jews and Gentiles alike after Pentecost was nothing less than good news about One who had demonstrated by word and deed that he had become the worthy recipient of all authority in heaven and on earth. As the divine Liberator, Jesus had conquered the power of Satan, destroying his works and his ways and bringing people out from under his bondage. As the divine Savior, Jesus Christ fulfilled the law, and through his death he reconciled the world to God. His resurrection gave tangible evidence of this victory.

From his baptism onward, Jesus was the object of relentless attack, since he represented the invasion of God onto the human scene. When God identified Jesus as "my Son, whom I love; with [whom] I am well pleased" (Matt. 3:17), open warfare began. It was inevitable that Satan would immediately counterattack after such an identification. Though he was quickly repulsed, his assaults were in those areas where people are most vulnerable: the physical-economic sphere (stones into bread), political power games (kingdoms of the world), and sensual religious display (signs and wonders, Luke 4:1–13). Even the demons joined in the struggle, for they too had heard the voice, and they trembled over its implications (Mark 1:24). The more Jesus proclaimed the coming of the Kingdom—by deeds as well as by words—the more apparent it became that the dominion of darkness was being penetrated, the strong man was being bound, and his prisoners were being released. We must not forget that Jesus' acts of healing and exorcisms were "mighty acts of reclamation, mighty acts of reestablishing his rule in areas where earlier God-opposing forces had held sway" (Kallas 1968: 155). Late in his ministry Jesus began also to proclaim the necessity of his crucifixion (Matt. 16:21–23; 17:22–23; 20:17–19; etc.). Since death is Satan's greatest weapon, that weapon must be taken from him if he and his works are truly to be overcome and if the people of God are truly to be liberated (Heb. 2:14–15). So then, the Gospels are replete with events that can only be understood under the motif of spiritual conflict. Moreover, the conflict mounts in intensity, reaching its climax at the crucifixion (Luke 22:53). But Jesus wins! The empty tomb and the resurrected Christ underscore the subsequent affirmation that he had invaded Satan's seat of power (through the cross and his descent into hell) and decimated Satan's weaponry (guilt and death) by crossing the boundary between "death's prison" and the land of the living (resurrection).

To summarize: demonological-eschatological motifs are at the very core of all that Jesus said and did, and they culminate in his resurrection. When we get to the writings of the apostle Paul and to a lesser degree the general epistles and Revelation, we find the powers and their subjugation by Christ related to the church and its mission.

The Powers: General Remarks

G. B. Caird has demonstrated that some mention of the powers is found "in every (Pauline) epistle except Philemon" (1956: viii). It is Satan who seeks relentlessly to frustrate Paul's missionary work (2 Cor. 12:7; 1 Thess. 2:18). The nations he would evangelize are being impelled by "the secret power of lawlessness" to open revolt against God (2 Thess. 2:7). "Hollow and deceptive philosophy" has penetrated all cultures and social structures, enslaving Jews and Gentiles alike in legalisms, mysticisms, and esoteric superstitions (Col. 2:8, 20). The "god of this age" blinds people to the gospel (2 Cor. 4:4). The "ruler of the kingdom of the air" is at work among the disobedient (Eph. 2:2). The "rulers of this age" crucified the Lord of Glory (1 Cor. 2:6). The "powers and authorities" keep people from experiencing the love of God (Rom. 8:20, 38). And Christians must contend with the "the powers of this dark world" if they are to serve their generation in the will of God (Eph. 6:12–13). After Caird summarizes the complex variety of spirit beings referred to in Paul's writings, he concludes:

> The concept of world powers reaches into every department of his theology. So much so that it cannot be dismissed as a survival of primitive superstition . . . Paul is describing spiritual realities with which he and his missionary companions have personal acquaintance. (1956: x)

When one steps back into the world of the Old Testament, however, the reality of menacing spiritual powers and related forces is only infrequently encountered (e.g., Gen. 3:1–5; 6:1–4; Deut. 4:19; 17:2–7; 18:10; 1 Sam. 28:13; Job 1:6–12; 2:1–7; Ps. 89:6–7; Isa. 8:19; Dan. 10:13, 20). All false gods appear to be personalized manifestations of rebellious powers, craving the worship of ancient humanity in much the same way that totalitarian ideologies seek to dominate people today. But exegetical support for this is scarce. In contrast, the Palestine of the first century was virtually quivering with their presence and activity, and the New Testament reveals that Christians in the early church were quite preoccupied with them (Schlier 1961: 12). Since we cannot believe that they have not always existed, we must seek out reasons for this abrupt shift in emphasis from the Old Testament to the New.

Many biblical scholars agree that the New Testament's angelic- and demon-related terminology and its underlying concepts were influenced by Jewish apocalyptic writings in the pre-Christian era. Both Jesus and Paul accepted the basic presuppositions of the apocalyptic-eschatological tradition of their day. But they rejected its cruder implications and recast the concept to deliberately discourage either philosophizing about the existence of evil or defining its exact nature. Both took a very pragmatic position, being concerned solely with the actual influence of the powers on individuals, on history, and on the cosmos.

A major thrust in Paul's epistles concerns the evils of the present age and the transforming eschatological victory of Christ at the cross, to be revealed in the last day. He perceived in the church's present proclamation of the good news of the Kingdom to Jew and Gentile alike its triumphant declaration to principalities and powers in heavenly places that the reconciling wisdom of God is in fact bringing about the final triumph of God in history (Eph. 3:10–11).

But this is only part of the picture. Whereas all New Testament writers perceived their age to be in the grip of evil supernatural powers, we must keep in mind that they also spoke of benevolent spiritual beings (angels) who "give to God the perfect service in heaven for which we are to pray on earth" (Bromiley 1969: 42, in reference to Matt. 6:10). Although their mission in heaven is to worship God and do his bidding, angels also take part in the cosmic struggle on earth. God sends them forth as "ministering spirits . . . to serve those who will inherit salvation" (Heb. 1:14).

Actually, the nature of the invisible world remained largely hidden from the writers of the Old Testament. This may in part reflect the desire of all evil powers to avoid exposure lest the source of their activity be made the focal point of spiritual counterattack. When Christ came in the flesh, inaugurated the Kingdom, and confirmed its presence by sending the Spirit upon the church at Pentecost, the cosmic struggle erupted into vivid prominence.

Before the cross, the powers found no alternative but to oppose him, for they somehow sensed that he had come "to destroy the devil's work" (1 John 3:8). Hence, they determined to disarm him first. The crucifixion represented the ultimate in their implacable hostility to God (1 Cor. 2:8). What they least expected was that by the cross they themselves would be overcome and stripped of their power (Col. 2:15). Christ's subjugation of the powers while making redemptive satisfaction for all sin is at the heart of Pauline theology. And Christ's victory over the grave made possible his being seated at his Father's "right hand in the heavenly realms, far above all rule and authority, power and dominion, and above every title that can be given, not only in the present age but also in the one to come. And God placed all things under his feet" (Eph. 1:20–22). Furthermore, the Father made all God's people "alive with Christ . . . and raised [them] up with Christ and seated [them] with him in the heavenly realms in Christ Jesus" (2:5–6).

So then, although "spirit" beings and the invisible "princes" of the Gentile nations are only barely alluded to in the Old Testament, they are fully exposed in Paul's writings. Despite their defeat at the cross, he was careful to point out that their present activities are not peripheral to the cosmic struggle between "the dominion of darkness . . . and . . . the kingdom of the Son [God] loves" (Col. 1:13). They represent a primary source of resistance to the church. Yet they function more by bluff and illusion than as reality. It is strange that in most theologies of mission the powers are either overlooked or minimally treated. Sin brings bondage as well as alienation, and salvation through Christ provides liberation as well as forgiveness. When one realizes this, it becomes apparent that a biblical theology of the Christian mission based on the Kingdom motif must grapple with the extensive Pauline data on the powers. Let us consider the main lines of his thought.

The Powers: Their Creation and Nature

[Christ] is the image of the invisible God, the firstborn over all creation. For by him all things were created: things in heaven and on earth, visible and invisible, whether thrones or powers or rulers or authorities; all things were created by him and for him. (Col. 1:15–16)

This statement clearly indicates that the powers are created beings, a fact of tremendous significance. It means that they not only owe their very existence to God but also were created in and through Christ. The purpose behind their origin was not that they might exist unto themselves in an autonomous fashion, but that they might bring glory to God. In terms of the functions they were to perform, these beings were originally good. The power they represented was God-given and God-reflecting. They did not stand in opposition to his will, but were positive in their contribution to his creation. When their original purpose is understood and the full measure taken of what happened as a result of the Fall, we find ourselves confronting realities of great missiological significance.

Satan is at the center of all biblical references to the powers. He has various names (e.g., the devil, Beelzebub, Belial), various representations (e.g., serpent, dragon, lion), and is variously described as to his activity (e.g., accuser, tempter, destroyer, adversary, enemy). He is both "strong" and "wicked." He is ultimately behind all the evil in the world. The "signs" of his kingdom are sin, sickness, disease, and death (Rom. 5:12; 2 Cor. 12:7). The diversity of language used to describe Satan is characteristic of references to the other powers. Indeed, one quickly gains the impression that Paul and the other New Testament writers were not particularly interested in classifying or analyzing them. This discourages speculation as to the nature of these realities and their hierarchies. But Paul's descriptions of their deliberate activity are such that we must regard them largely as "personal" beings having both intellect and will. Some of the passages in which they are mentioned convey the impression that they might even be regarded as collective representations of "power." In this connection Schlier observes:

They do not merely possess power and other attributes, they are power. They are not just something or somebody, and also have power. They exist as power. That is what they are called, and they get these names because that is how they manifest themselves and their being. That is why St. Paul enumerates them in the same breath with such phenomena as life, present, future, height and depth. Evidently while they are powers of existence—dominating, embracing, determining powers—they have something in common with these other enumerated phenomena. That common element is their nature as power, as threatening superior power. (1961: 20)

When first created, they all had positive roles to fill, being instruments in the rule of God over his good creation. Whereas Scripture says that it is by Christ that the whole of his creation hangs together (Col. 1:17), the powers apparently served to effect this coherence, each in its proper and intended place under his lordship. As Hendrikus Berkhof suggests:

The powers served as the invisible weight-bearing substratum of the world, as the underpinnings of creation . . . the linkage between God's love and visible human experience. They held life together, preserving it within God's love and served as aids to bind men fast in His fellowship; intermediaries, not as barriers but as bonds between God and man. As aids and signposts toward the service of God, they formed the framework within which such service must needs be carried out. (1962: 22)

In other words, the powers originally served as "dikes with which God encircled his good creation, to keep it in his fellowship and to protect it from chaos" (H. Berkhof 1962: 23). Even though we can only infer the manner in which they accomplished this prior to their initial revolt, there are some intimations of it in those passages in the Old Testament that look forward to the "golden age." Surely then, all unfallen angels will participate fully in its consummation. At that time friendship, plenty, and peace will be universal; full harmony will exist between the redeemed and all creatures, great and small. The Kingdom of God will be upheld with justice and righteousness. All peoples will know the Lord—his knowledge and glory filling the earth as the waters cover the sea (Isa. 32:18; Hos. 2:18; Amos 9:13–14; Hab. 2:14).

Although Paul was virtually silent about the powers in relation to the future, he was quite specific about their activity since their revolt. Apparently, at that time particular powers irrevocably fell: Jude, not Paul, stated that they "did not keep their positions of authority but abandoned their own home" (v. 6; see also 2 Peter 2:4). They became "independent and autonomous, egocentric and self-willed" (Schlier 1961: 38). We might say that although they retained their God-given power, they began to exercise it as though it were self-achieved. The bent of their natures came to be opposition to God and was expressed by seeking to achieve dominion over the world and over all peoples. They became as gods (Gal. 4:8), posing as ultimate realities and intruding between God and his creation. Instead of continuing as the channels of his love, they abruptly became usurpers, seeking the worship that belongs to God alone. In order to achieve this they cast a deluding spirit upon people, causing them to adopt false perspectives on all circumstances and institutions of life and particularly on all spiritual realities. Through their activity evil is enabled to exist as a force in the world, transforming the powers into "the world rulers of darkness" (Caird 1956: 53).

All things have their coherence in Christ, but the powers help people create "false coherences" that rest on human institutions such as traditions and laws. Thus, people are deceived into thinking they can fulfill God's will by keeping a system of external religious, ethical, cultic, and social rules (H. Berkhof 1962: 60). They may even come to accept the deception that a valid worldview is one which holds that the whole of human existence is bound to the movement of the stars or the signs of the zodiac (Drenth 1977: 59).

At this point we must introduce the subject of culture. The term *culture* embraces the totality of the response of any people to their environment. It includes all deliberately defined religion, mores, and social organization. It is the integrated, organized, and distinctive way of life that distinguishes one people from another people. Its components are the technological, the sociological, and the ideological—not merely the tools, weapons, and techniques by which a people sustain their corporate life and exercise their will over other peoples. Culture is not just the rules by which a people operate within the diversity of their personal conduct and interpersonal relationships. Culture also includes the ideas, mythologies, legends, folk wisdom, and commonsense knowledge a people express in articulate speech (their own language) or by means of other symbolic forms. Culture consists of all the learned patterns of behavior that are socially transmitted from one generation to the next.

When we seek to relate the phenomenon of culture to biblical categories, we are arrested by the New Testament word *kosmos* ("the world"). This word has a wide range of meanings: the universe; the center of human history; humankind as God's creation; the totality of human society and activity; and finally, people in their fallenness and alienation from God. George Ladd concludes that *kosmos* embraces the totality of culture, for it

> includes the whole complex of human earthly relationships in which marriage, joy and sorrow, buying and selling, i.e., the totality of human activities are included . . . not merely the world of men but the world system and complex of relationships that have been created by men . . . structures that are transitory and destined to pass away. (1974: 399)

We would add that the evil connected with the *kosmos* is not of the essence of the world, but arises from the attitude of autonomy it engenders in fallen human beings unwilling to live under God's rule and for his glory. This fact of autonomy helps us link the activity of fallen powers to all that comes under the rubric of culture. When Paul spoke of "weak and miserable principles" or "human commands and teachings" (Gal. 4:9; Col. 2:22), he was referring to the spirit of autonomy that has invaded human traditions and relationships, shaped all religions and ethical systems, and defined the nature of the political state and its coercive functions. One gains the impression that Paul believed the powers have incarnated themselves in all of the interrelated elements of culture. The ethos and structure of a culture stand in resistance to God and his love. Indeed, no culture has escaped the demonic element; all are to a greater or lesser degree "in the control of the evil one" (1 John 5:19). As Hendrikus Berkhof has stated:

> No longer do the powers bind [humans] and God together; they separate them. They stand as a roadblock between the Creator and his creation. (1962: 23)

It is because of the powers' overarching pervasion of all human existence that Paul could make the universal declaration that before people come under the liberating lordship of Christ, they follow "the ways of this world and of the ruler of the kingdom of the air, the spirit who is now at work in those who are disobedient" (Eph. 2:2). The domicile of the powers is "in the air." The powers dwell within the invisible, higher sphere of influence from which the affairs on earth are ordered.

This does not mean that we should dismiss all the achievements of human culture as utterly satanic. Total disintegration and chaos would characterize the human scene if it were not for the positive benefits of corporateness and the constructive values that characterize human societies. But it must be reaffirmed that the powers make sure that no society reaches out to God. Hendrikus Berkhof sounds the right note when he states that it should not be difficult for us to perceive today in every realm of life that the powers that unify men and women nonetheless separate them from God. He adds:

> The state, politics, class, social struggle, national interest, public opinion, accepted morality, the ideas of decency, humanity, democracy—these give unity and direction to thousands of lives. Yet precisely by giving unity and direction they separate these many lives from the true God; they let us believe that we have found the meaning of existence, whereas they really estrange us from true meaning. (1962: 26)

From the preceding discussion it will be apparent that despite their fallenness, God uses the powers to enclose people in supportive relationships that function partly for their best interests. Although fallen humans deserve only the judgment of God because of their sin and their desire for an existence separate from him, by means of the powers God graciously preserves them in reasonably stable societies and cultures. This reality is detailed in Galatians 4:1–11. We would conclude, however, that whereas life apart from Christ can have its good features, Paul regarded it as slavery and not to be favorably compared with the liberation that Christ brings.

The Powers: Conquered by Christ

In the context of describing the redemptive work of Christ, the apostle Paul states that Christ "disarmed the powers and authorities . . . [and] made a public spectacle of them, triumphing over them by the cross" (Col. 2:15). By this affirmation Paul goes beyond the familiar New Testament thesis that Christ's redemption delivers his people from the guilt of sin. Rather, Paul speaks of Christ as the One who also liberates his people from their previous slavery and bondage to the powers. Jewish legalisms and pagan regulations have lost their power to tyrannize; social and religious mores that tend to alienate people from God have lost their "pull" (2:16–23). It is the crucifixion that has made this abundantly clear. As Paul says elsewhere: "None of the rulers of this age" (the scribes and the Pharisees, the priests and Pilate) understood God's wisdom, "for if they had, they would not have crucified the Lord of glory" (1 Cor. 2:8). The fact that these representatives of Jewish law and Jewish piety, the Jewish priesthood and Roman justice, unitedly crucified Christ vividly demonstrates their very real bondage to the powers.

Furthermore, Jesus Christ was "declared with power to be the Son of God in power by his resurrection from the dead" (Rom. 1:4). The resurrection demonstrates the reality of his triumph over the powers themselves. They have been unmasked and stripped of their ultimate weapon, death. Their ancient grip on people has been broken. What remains is merely the capacity for colossal deception. The powers have been disarmed or rendered ineffective. Although they will continue to divert people from openness to God, their activity is now devoid of substantial power. All is bluff and illusion. It is as though by the cross Christ deliberately disconnected all the linkages within cultures by which the powers previously held people in bondage. Finally, the powers have become completely powerless when it comes to separating the people of God from God's love (Rom. 8:38–39).

We must not underestimate the intensity of the struggle whereby Christ "disarmed" the powers. Gustaf Aulen has underscored this for us. He describes Christ's atoning death in terms of divine conflict and victory:

> Christus Victor fights against and triumphs over the evil powers of the world, the tyrants under which [humankind] is in bondage and suffering, and in him God reconciles the world to himself. (1951: 4)

> For my own part I am persuaded that no form of Christian teaching has any future before it, except such as can keep steadily in view the reality of evil in the world, and go to meet the evil with a battle song of triumph. (1951: 159)

Christ's complete victory over the powers presses Alan R. Tippett to encourage Christians not to draw back from the power encounter that biblical evangelism demands. His challenge is without qualification:

> Sinful [humanity] is bound. Christ came to unloose [humans]. . . . There is no way out in this war, no compromise, no friendly agreement to engage in dialogue, no mere Christian presence. . . . When we ask ourselves why there had to be an incarnation, a death and a resurrection, we see that there was no other way of overcoming Satan, his works and his authority. (1969: 89–90)

So then, we repeat: by the cross Christ made "a public example" of his victory over the powers. No longer are they permitted to pose as the most basic and ultimate realities of human existence. He dealt decisively with their subtle claim that they were the regents of this world. Hence, the final manifestation of the Kingdom of God in power will not take place until Christ has "destroyed all dominion, authority and power" in the sense of rendering them inoperative so that all will know of the completeness of his redemptive sufferings and resurrection victory (1 Cor. 15:24). This is the good news of the Kingdom we announce in word and deed. This is the church's mission.

Incidentally, the Revised Standard Version uses the word *destroy* in this verse, implying the total annihilation of the powers so that their cohesive function in culture would come to a complete end. But this would mean the end of culture—something that the Revelation emphatically denies when it portrays Christ as the eschatological King of kings and Lord of lords (i.e., "of all the peoples [pl.] of God," 17:14; 19:16; 21:3). A more precise translation would be "to render inoperative." Because of the cross, their power to enslave and seduce the people of God has been broken—especially when the good news of the Kingdom is being publicly affirmed.

When Jesus confronted evil spirits in the course of his earthly ministry, they trembled at his ability to drive them from the presence of those whom they had bound or tyrannized. Their cry was: "Have you come here to torture us before the appointed time?" (Matt. 8:29). At the cross the time was fulfilled; they were rendered inoperative. From then onward the church in its missionary advance has the right to expect that even the most evil manifestation of their presence cannot hinder Christ's using even their opposition to further the ongoing of his Kingdom. This was, in essence, the deep conviction of Christians in Jerusalem when they sought boldness from God to preach the gospel:

> Indeed Herod and Pontius Pilate met together with the Gentiles and the people of Israel in this city to conspire against your holy servant Jesus, whom you anointed. They did what your power and will had decided beforehand should happen. (Acts 4:27–28)

Mission and the Powers

The New Testament and the record of church history bear ample witness to the fact that despite the cross and the nullification of the real threat of the powers, they still dominate all people to a greater or lesser degree. They relentlessly attack the church and seek by every means to hinder the church's missionary obedience. Their abode remains "in the heavenly realms" surrounding the visible world (Eph. 3:10). From there they venture forth to menace, seduce, and in other ways thwart the ongoing movement of the Kingdom of God among the nations. Often they do this through incarnating themselves in existing structures in society and in cultural traditions and religious institutions. On occasion, however, they assault individuals directly.

It is interesting to note the various ways in which scholars regard the powers in the context of mission. Oscar Cullmann wants to focus attention on the cosmic powers almost solely in terms of the demonic nature of the state (1950: 199–200). Markus Barth interprets them as "the world of axioms and principles of politics and religion, of economics and society, of morals and biology, of history and culture" (1959: 90). Hendrikus Berkhof wants us to see their relation to the "secularization" process (1962: 47–54).

Whether the powers may be interpreted in our time as personal or social maladjustment, political or economic determinism, religious or cultural axioms, existential or empirical disharmony—whatever names may be attributed to them—as long as they separate us from the love of God in Christ Jesus our Lord, they are the cosmic powers.

Since the powers exist by deceit and operate by deceit, we can well believe that they continually use new and varied disguises, depending on time and place. Hence, the early Christians dared to challenge Satan at their baptism early on Easter morning and cry into the darkness of the receding night: "I renounce you, Satan, and all your service and all your works!" This primitive affirmation claimed for oneself the victory of Christ's irrevocable defeat of the powers of darkness (J. Stewart 1951: 294). It also underscored their conviction that these invisible beings "in some way . . . stand behind what occurs in the world" (Cullmann 1950: 192).

It is particularly in animistic societies that the cosmic struggle between Christ and Satan is most apparent. There one encounters widespread servitude to unseen spirits coupled with an almost universal fear of what they might do if not served aright. MacGregor quotes Schweitzer in this connection.

> For the African, Christianity is the light which shines in the night of fear. It assures him that he is not in the power of nature-spirits and ancestral ghosts, but that in all that happens the will of God maintains its sovereignty. Thus he turns from terror to trust, from an unethical to an ethical worldview. (1954: 25)

But it would be a mistake to speak of power encounter—Christ versus the powers—only in terms of animistic societies. The powers are everywhere, and Calvin speaks to us all when he states:

> If the glory of God is dear to us, as it ought to be, we ought to struggle with all our might against him who aims at the extinction of that glory. If we are animated with proper zeal to maintain the Kingdom of Christ, we must wage irreconcilable war with him who conspires its ruin. (1960: 14)

At this point we must remind ourselves that through the church's witness to the gospel, both friendly angels and hostile powers come to understand the wisdom of God's eternal, redemptive purpose (Eph. 3:10). But what does this mean particularly for the powers? Apparently, they are to perceive something in this witness that demonstrates the reality of their having been conquered by Christ, undercutting whatever they might seek to do to thwart the progress of the Christian movement. All too often Christians tend to overlook this dimension and proceed directly to Paul's instruction in Ephesians 6:10–20, feeling that the "spiritual warfare" it describes is where the action is. Actually, however, the church is to be a witness or demonstration to the powers of Christ's victory before the church is to resist their hindrances to the advance of the gospel. This follows because of the reality of "the dominion of darkness" and "the kingdom of Son" in diametric opposition to each other during this era (Col. 1:13).

The good news of the Kingdom is that the whole of Christ's work is a work of liberation from the rule of sin, Satan, and death. Hence, the church must reflect liberation from the influence of the "dominion of darkness." Ellul develops this thesis in the following fashion (and we summarize here his lengthy argument). Unfallen Adam knew nothing of necessity, obligation, and inevitability. When he obeyed God, he did so freely. Necessity only appeared when he broke his relation with God. Then he became subject to the order of obligation: the order of toil, hunger, passion; the struggle to do otherwise. But when the liberating reality of Christ's salvation became available, then true freedom became possible. The order of Christ rose up against the order of necessity. The person who does not know freedom in Christ cannot understand the word of freedom Paul spoke in the midst of temptations to submit to the order of necessity: "We are hard pressed on every side, but not crushed; perplexed, but not in despair; persecuted, but not abandoned; struck down, but not destroyed" (2 Cor. 4:8–9) (Ellul: 1969:127–45).

What this means is that Christians in the world have a role to fill that non-Christians cannot possibly fill. They have to break the fatality that hangs over the world through reflecting in every way the victory that Christ gained over the powers. They are to be a sign of the new covenant, a demonstration that a new order has entered the world, giving meaning, direction, and hope to history. This means that Christians dare not uncritically and automatically reflect even the best of the world's patterns of conduct, social amelioration, and service. The world's agenda and the world's methodology are not to be theirs, largely because the motivation behind their activities will shape their service differently. And the powers must be confronted with this.

Indeed, the powers will not be confronted by "the wisdom of God" if the people of God today resort to the "normal" means that the Israelites frequently used to resolve their conflicts in Old Testament times prior to the cross. The Israelites too often relied on weapons, chariots, horsemen, alliances, diplomatic maneuvers, and revolution (for example, Jehu). Even then, God pled with them to put their trust in his Word and in his faithfulness. Had he not pledged to be their warrior (Exod. 14:13–14; 15:3, 18)? How much more now—after Christ's conquest of the powers—should the church reject all these "normal" means, particularly the resort to physical or psychological violence. The church in our day must be called back to "true spiritual violence, based on earnest faith: faith in the possibility of a miracle, in the Lordship of Jesus Christ, and in the coming of the Kingdom through God's action." This means "faith in all of the promises" implied and guaranteed by the resurrection (Ellul 1969: 166–71). Paul summarized this call to the violence of love by encouraging the church not to be overcome by evil, through playing evil's game by using the world's weaponry of necessity. Rather, the church is to "overcome evil with good" (Rom. 12:14–21). Of course, the church is to serve as the advocate of the poor and the oppressed and is to challenge all injustice in society. But this is to be done only through nonviolent means.

On the practical level this means that the church is to be a radical presence in society. It is always putting itself in true repentance wholly into God's hands, submitting to God's revealed will in Scripture and trusting in his mercy. The church also seeks constantly to reflect its liberation through Christ. By its identification with society's victims and its bold protests against all oppressors, the church creates a climate of doubt, insecurity, and bad conscience among these oppressors. By its conduct it shows that it has truly been set free.

The world is dominated by "mammon"—the power behind acquisitiveness. In response, the church lives by using its resources in the service of the needy. The world is torn by racism, but the church sees all individuals in all racial groups as bearing the image of God and treats them as such. The world is enslaved by the powers that produce injustice, oppression, and authoritarianism, exalting sexism, scientism, and secularism. In response, the church makes itself the servant of all, respecting human dignity and reflecting the contentment that only Christ can bring. So then, we need to take the full measure of the intention of God: that the church by its liberated stance in the world will convince the powers that they cannot prevail against God's Kingdom (Matt. 16:18). Furthermore, since the church has been given "the keys of the kingdom," it is responsible to be involved in the eternal destinies of all peoples (Matt. 16:19).

This brings us to Paul's classic instruction on the powers in Ephesians 6:10–20. The context is his personal need for boldness to preach "the mystery of the gospel" and thereby fulfill his missionary ambassadorship (6:19–20). This is the context in which faithful witnesses to Christ often find themselves. Their aspiration is Peter's, "that the Gentiles might hear from my lips the message of the gospel and believe" (Acts 15:7).

With this in mind, we find Paul calling us to wrestle against the powers that "flesh and blood" obey. He begins by stressing the importance of being personally clothed with the defensive armor of God. First, is "truth," sincerity and integrity in one's dealings with God and with oneself. But truth must be supplemented with "righteousness." Paul is thinking not only of moral rectitude (as in Rom. 6:13) but also of a passion for the justice of God (Mic. 6:8). Then follows "the readiness that comes from the gospel of peace." This means more than one's movements being determined by opportunities for gospel witness. Paul is also stressing "the desire to be zealous, that is, courageous like soldiers for the peace which Jesus brought for all [humans]" (Ellul 1969: 165). Then comes "faith," which in this context means the sort of personal trust in God demonstrated not only by an indifference to public opinion but also by a life of sacrifice. By "salvation" Paul is thinking of God's expected interventions consciously anticipated at every turn in the struggle.

Note that when Paul lists the Christian's weaponry, he confines himself to the sword of the Spirit, the Word of God, and to prayer. No lance, no bow and arrows, no spear! No triumphant seeking to bring the powers to their knees! Christians are called merely to stand at a distance from their seduction and enslavement in the quiet conviction of Christ's victory. As Schlier summarizes:

> The aim [of the members of the church] must be to defeat the principalities in faith and loyalty, in works of justice and truth, in unceasing prayer, sober and vigilant, with the gift of the discernment of spirits. They must also endeavor through sacrifice to create in the church a place free from their domination, as a sign of the new heavens and the new earth which are to come. (1961: 68)

The struggle is against the powers incarnated in very concrete forms, in institutions, in governments, in coercive bodies, and in ideologies. Christians are to live out the full reality of what it means to belong to the body of Christ. To do so demands an encounter with the structures of political power. It necessitates a stance of courageous resistance to those societal patterns and prejudices that discriminate via class, race, sex, and age. It also involves encouraging the healing of all relationships, whether psychological, economic, social, or political. To proclaim that Jesus is Lord is to remind governments that their authority is not absolute and that they are accountable to God for the ways in which they treat his creatures and his creation.

By this holistic witness we recognize that our use of the weapons of truth—the Word of God and prayer—involves not only political action but aggressive action. In this connection Sider reminds us of the incarnation whereby God himself stepped into history to join battle with the forces of evil.

> As the Body of Christ, we are to continue the mission of the Incarnate One in the world today and that includes an ongoing offensive against the fallen principalities and powers, a vigorous, active use of power in the search for greater justice in society. (1980: 17)

Mission: Signs and Wonders

We cannot conclude this study of the powers without relating it to what has come to be called "power evangelism." It has been argued that "presence evangelism" is not enough, for it only represents Christians carrying out the cultural mandate that people may see their good works and glorify the Father, who is in heaven (Matt. 5:14–16). Even if this is supplemented with "proclamation evangelism," the results will be minimal, since the gospel will then allegedly come to people "in word only." And even if these two efforts are further supplemented with "persuasion evangelism," in which people are challenged to respond to the claims of Christ, something will still be lacking. What is needed, it is argued, is "power evangelism" in which the apostolic pattern is fully followed and there is the "demonstration of the Spirit's power" (1 Cor. 2:4). This is affirmed because "the kingdom of God is not a matter of talk but of power" (4:20). It is pointed out that Paul claimed that Christ enabled him to lead the Gentiles "to obey God by what I have said and done—by the power of signs and miracles, through the power of the Spirit" (Rom. 15:18–19). Power evangelism represents the added influence that is needed to communicate the gospel effectively; the gospel must be perceived and demonstrated as "power" as well as "word."

At this point the issue of "signs and miracles" is introduced, supported by appealing to the pattern of the Lord Jesus. Not only did he work miracles, but when he sent forth the Seventy he conferred on them the authority to heal the sick, tread on serpents and scorpions, and have authority over all the power of the enemy (Luke 10:9–19). Their spiritual authority and existential power made it possible for them to overcome demons in Jesus' name (10:17). Since this provision is being extended to Christians today—the argument runs—there is the possibility of an ongoing pattern of power evangelism in the church.

It has also been argued that in many parts of the world today people seem to be more power conscious than truth conscious. Following this line of reasoning, the conviction has grown that in order to get the attention of non-Christians, the church must display "signs and miracles" through healings and exorcising ministries. Such demonstrations of God's activity allegedly will precipitate the sort of power encounter that proves that the Christians' Jesus is more powerful than other gods. This paradigm of precipitating power encounters is popularized by appealing to Elijah's confrontation of the prophets of Baal on Mount Carmel (1 Kings 18:20–40).

We regard this as an unwarranted analogy. Judging from the passages of Scripture we examined earlier in this discussion, this approach would seem to seriously distort the New Testament mission of the church. We should be cautious about precipitating such encounters. We are to pray, to serve, to witness, and to persuade. If the enemy reacts with power, we can trust God to overcome him by the violence of our love and faith.

When Christians get sick, they pray. And when their Christian friends get sick, they pray for them. No one argues that God does not heal the sick. No one rules out the possibility of God working miracles today. Jesus' miracles authenticated his messianic role. In Acts the conspicuous workers of miracles were Peter and Paul. As apostles they wrought miracles: specifically, these were "the things that mark an apostle" (2 Cor. 12:12). But gospel proclamation must not be reduced to promoting a form of Christian magic. Whenever we seek to coerce God to do our bidding through the use of a religious formula of one sort or another, we are in danger of yielding to that residue of fallenness in us that desires to be in control, rather than to submit to God's will. The central thrust of biblical faith is the recognition that we are to worship God and to identify with God's purposes and will.

We must refuse to concede that any preaching of the gospel that does not include "signs and miracles" is somehow sub-biblical. The gospel itself is "the power of

God for the salvation of everyone who believes" (Rom. 1:16), and to proclaim it is power evangelism par excellence! How significant that in Paul's argument in Ephesians he makes no mention of "signs and miracles" in connection with preaching the good news of the Kingdom.

To make "signs and miracles" the only or even the most important theme for mission is not biblical. The church's mission of announcing the Kingdom of God must also include seeking justice for the poor and minority peoples; opposing all forms of racism, sexism, and exploitation; and promoting disarmament and world peace. These matters are also integral aspects of the church's proclamation of the Kingdom of God.

Conclusion

We draw this brief study to a close by reiterating the primacy of prayer, if the powers are to be overcome and this generation is to be evangelized. "Prayer: Where Word and Deed Come Together" is the title Harvie Conn gives to a crucial chapter in *Evangelism: Doing Justice and Preaching Grace,* a chapter that significantly emphasizes the centrality of prayer.

> Bringing men and women to Christ in faith and gaining victory over unjust principalities and powers do not come simply, or even primarily, or even to start with, by swamping our senators with letters and petitions, looking for new bandwagons to jump on, holding one more successful church seminar, or joining marches to the Pentagon. Changes begin with petitionary prayer, the elect crying to God day and night about [the issues that affect their nations]. (1982: 88)

Paul would have us avoid dismissing any "ism" as harmless, for this would be to underestimate the strengths of the powers. And he would warn us against regarding any "ism" as incorrigible, for this would be to underestimate the victory of Christ over all powers. For the sake of the mission priority, Paul called for persevering and believing prayer, calling on God to open doors of opportunity and give courage and faith to proclaim "the mystery of the gospel." Indeed, the church that fails to discern the spirits and stand against them in the name of the Lord Jesus will do little to make him known, loved, and served throughout the world.

Admittedly, a paradox of massive proportions is constantly before us. This arises when we place the conviction that the powers were decisively defeated by Christ alongside the reality that they currently exercise a devastatingly destructive and evil influence in the world. We are constantly faced with the "not yet" existence of the Kingdom of God. But we should guard against the temptation to deny the scope of Christ's victory by allowing ourselves to be deceived by the heresy that the devil is alive and well in this age. And we must never attribute all evil to misguided human activity, thereby denying that the powers as supernatural intelligences actually exist. The paradox is resolved by Christians when they consciously participate in the sufferings of Christ (Col. 1:24–29). As they follow Christ's example of loving service and courageous witness, exposing themselves thereby to the hatred of the powers, they are indeed carrying out the mission of God. All the while Christians are conscious that the powers, for all their hatred of God and hindrance to this mission, bear the marks of Christ's victory over them. And he would have his people never forget his unqualified words: "I will build my church, and the gates of Hades will not overcome it" (Matt. 16:18).

22

There Is Salvation in Only One Name
Jesus Christ the Lord

Introduction

We have seen that the Epistle to the Romans deals with several themes basic to the Christian mission: Jews and Gentiles are equally guilty in God's sight; Christ's redemptive sacrifice is sufficient for all peoples; the church is under obligation to proclaim this gospel; and the apostolic ministry ascribes priority to the regions "where Christ was not known" (15:20).

One section in this epistle, however, is of particular importance (1:18–31). It represents the most comprehensive treatment in Scripture of non-Christian religion and its bearing on the Kingdom of God. Since we have previously made only infrequent references to this complex subject, we must now bring together the various strands of related truth scattered throughout both the Old and New Testaments, integrating them with this passage.

It has long been held that when one turns to the Old Testament in search of positive estimates of other religions, the search is in vain. Schlette speaks of the Old Testament witness as "extremely negative" (1966: 25; he quotes such texts as 1 Kings 11:1–13; Isa. 40:18–20; 44:9–20; 46:1–7; and Jer. 2:26–28; 10:1–16). Dewick says its predominant note is "hostility," although he qualifies this somewhat by saying there are some "notable exceptions but they are the exception rather than the rule" (1953: 63). We are in essential agreement with these two observations. However, this element in the divine revelation can only be appreciated if one keeps in mind the redemptive purpose of God touching the nations.

Actually, there never was a time from the Fall onward when the human race was in a situation totally without divine grace, what might be called exclusive perdition. Following the judgment of the Flood, we find the record of God's covenant with Noah and his sons (Gen. 9:1–17), in which he pledged his grace and providential care. The New Testament repeatedly states that God wills the salvation of all peoples (1 Tim. 2:1–6; 2 Peter 3:9; etc.).

Religion in the Old Testament

From the call of Abraham onward, however, the focus in the Old Testament shifts from the universal to the particular. In order to bless the nations, God chose a particular people as his channel and sought to prepare them for this task. Emil Brunner dismisses as wholly untenable the popular opinion that the biblical witness to this divine disclosure has its parallels in other religions. He contends:

> The claim of the revelation . . . possessing universal validity in the history of religion is rare. The claim of revelation made by the Christian faith is in its radicalization as solitary as its content: the message of atonement. It is this: only at one place, only in one event has God revealed himself truly and completely—there, namely, where he became man. . . . No other religion can assert revelation in the radical unconditional sense in which the Christian faith does this, because no other religion knows the God who is himself the Revealer. (1946: 235–36)

We should not be surprised then that Scripture describes other religions as a constant threat to what God was seeking to do with Israel throughout the whole Old Testament era. How could it have been otherwise? God's people were so few in number, so lacking in moral courage, and so wayward in their regard for God that they were tragically vulnerable to almost every blandishment that came from their pagan neighbors, whether social, political, or religious. At times God had to go to great lengths to guard the growing deposit of truth he was giving them. They tended to treat it lightly and regard him with ingratitude, even contempt. All the while God was seeking to bring them to the place where they would willingly embrace their God-appointed role as his priestly-servant people among the nations. He treated them not as robots to be manipulated, but as free moral agents to be discipled. As a result, there were times when they would reap the fruit of their folly, even though this appeared to put God's own saving purpose for the nations in great jeopardy.

When the Israelites completed their wilderness wanderings (Num. 14–32) and began their conquest of Canaan, they were commanded to utterly destroy all aspects of Canaanite religion (Num. 33:50–56; Deut. 7:2–5). This intolerance in part grew out of God's expressed hostility toward the low level of morality practiced by the Canaanites. But it also grew out of the conviction that all other gods were at best shams and lies, pretending to be what they were not. The Israelites in their particularity never imagined that God revealed himself to other branches of the human family. They firmly believed that they alone of all peoples had the true revelation of God and that other religions were essentially demonic (Lev. 17:7; Deut. 32:17; 2 Chron. 11:15; Ps. 106:37).

All in all, the writers of the Old Testament were uninterested in the nature and meaning of pagan religion, if we are to judge from their silence on the subject. They only record a scattering of names of some of the gods the pagans worshiped (e.g., Baal, Ashtoreth, Chemosh, Milcom, Bel, Nebo). They focused attention not on the gods as active beings but on the idols that represented them. The gods themselves were not deliberately denied existence; they were simply ignored. One searches in vain for any reference to the popular myths associated with these gods. When the prophets inveighed against the worship "of all the starry hosts," they were explicit in referring not to any astral deities but to the cultic worship of the actual heavenly bodies (e.g., Deut. 4:19; 17:3; 2 Kings 17:16; 21:5; 23:5). In fact, when the Old Testament refers to the conflict between God and the "gods of the nations," in every case it is the idols that are the objects of his fury. When magic and sorcery are mentioned, the idols are regarded as the bearers of occult powers and deserving of God's wrath. The sole argument advanced against pagan religion is that it is a fetish-dominated worship, a senseless deification of wood and stone, what the anthropologists would call "mana belief."

Idolatry, then, is regarded in the Old Testament as the foolish belief that divine and magical powers inhere in certain natural or man-made objects and that humans can activate these powers through fixed rituals (Kaufmann 1960: 64). The prophetic denunciation of idolatry is largely confined to taunts against fetishism. It has no place for serious reflection on what might be called "authentic paganism." "All who make idols are nothing, and the things they treasure are worthless" (Isa. 44:9). Because inanimate objects cannot be gods, it would appear that God had no rivals apart from these graven images. And yet idolatry posed a tremendous challenge to Israel's God. Associated with all idols were demonic spiritual forces that constituted a positive menace to Israel. Hence, they were simultaneously nonentities and dangerous spiritual forces. All who worshiped them inevitably became infected with a deadly blindness of heart and mind. Therefore, we should not minimize idolatry, even though the Old Testament contains no polemic against the essence of polytheism or belief in other gods, much less any repudiation of the pagan myths that clustered around these gods. Idolatry is regarded as perverted worship. As Louis Bouyer states:

> When false gods are declared powerless, or even called nullities by the prophets it is false to interpret this as a rationalistic denial of their existence. It is rather a question of vehement dispute about the divinity attributed to them. (1965: 23)

Monotheism, as we meet it in Scripture, is not merely the view that there is a single God who is an all-powerful, eternal Creator. Such a belief was variously held throughout the ancient world. Rather, monotheism is the concept of a God who is the source of all being. He is not emergent from a preexistent primordial realm of power but is free of all limitations that magic and mythology forge around the gods. Schmidt and Langdon's "high gods," discovered in the legends of many primitive peoples, should not be automatically regarded as irrefutable demonstrations of the original biblical monotheism. More often than not, they were shrouded in mythology, revealed as dependent on the world, and manipulable by self-operative forces external to themselves. In contrast, the Old Testament speaks of only one God, and he is supreme over all. He is subject to no laws or forces that transcend him. He is completely free from mythological traits. He is not surrounded by a heavenly court of angels and demons metamorphosed from gods and goddesses, whom he overcame in earlier cosmic struggles.

Of God's own life we know nothing. Scripture focuses solely on his relationship to his creation. It says nothing about fate. It knows but one fundamental and supreme law: the will and command of an absolutely good and utterly holy God. Perhaps for this reason the Old Testament is devastating in its denunciation of the confidence of sinful people in human wisdom. Yehezkel Kaufmann in *The Religion of Israel* says:

> The biblical religious idea is of a supernal God, as above every cosmic law, fate and compulsion; unborn, unbegetting, knowing no desire, independent of matter and its forces; a God who does not fight other divinities or powers of impurity; who does not sacrifice, divine, prophesy, or practice sorcery; who does not sin and needs no expiation; a God who does not celebrate festivals of His life. An unfettered divine will transcending all being—this is the mark of biblical religion and that which sets it apart from all the religions of the earth. (1960: 121)

Although the Old Testament neither approves of pagan religion nor suggests that it possesses any "religious value," it needs to be underscored that it does teach that God is just and impartial in his dealings with all peoples (e.g., Amos 1:3–2:5). Furthermore, it contains many intimations of God's outgoing concern for non-Israelite peoples (e.g., Jonah 4:11). In a moving passage in Amos, Yahweh reminds Israel of his unconditional sovereignty in dealing equally with Israel and with neighboring nations: "'Are not you Israelites the same to me as the Cushites?'" declares the LORD. "'Did I not bring Israel up from Egypt, the Philistines from Caphtor [Crete] and the Arameans from Kir?'" (9:7).

God is also concerned with justice and mercy. His expressed goodwill toward the Gentile nations culminates in the promise that they will be converted and incorporated into the family of his people. Isaiah discloses the heart of this universal concern.

> Foreigners who join themselves to the LORD, to serve him, to love the name of the LORD, and to worship him . . . these I will bring to my holy mountain and give them joy in my house of prayer. Their burnt offerings and sacrifices will be accepted on my altar; for my house will be called a house of prayer for all nations. (56:6–7)

Religion in the Witness of Jesus Christ

We have no evidence in the Gospels that Jesus ever expressed a judgment about non-Jewish religions. All we know is that he gave unquestioned allegiance to the

Old Testament. He came not to abolish the law and the prophets but to fulfill them (Matt. 5:17). He saw no possibility of other gods besides the one he knew as his Father in heaven (Mark 12:32–34). He believed that his coming into the world to bring redemption to Israel and salvation to the nations was in fulfillment of Old Testament prophecies. It is virtually impossible to contend that his attitude to other religious systems would have been at variance with the Old Testament perspective summarized in the preceding discussion.

And yet Jesus used the Old Testament in a selective and original fashion to attack the dogma and practice of the various Jewish sects of his day. For instance, he warned against the teaching of the Pharisees and Sadducees (Matt. 16:12) and exposed and rebuked their self-righteousness, religious externalism, and exclusive nationalism. On the other hand, he told his disciples to "practice and observe" whatever the Pharisees told them, so long as one avoided their hypocrisy (Matt. 23:2–12). He was particularly adamant against the legalistic use Jews made of the law in hope of bartering with God to secure his favor. As Baago rightly affirms:

> He accepted and rejected at the same time the religion of his forefathers realizing that man can never relate himself to God without religious forms (symbols and rites, worship and institutions) but also realizing that it is man's temptation to absolutize these forms in order to win security for himself. (1966: 327)

In the Gospels Jesus is portrayed not only as controversial but also as a controversialist. He was not reluctant to issue warnings against the false teachings of some of the religious leaders of his day (Matt. 16:6). On one memorable occasion he told them that they were "in error" and then went on to state they were "badly mistaken" (Mark 12:18–27) because they were ignorant of the Scriptures and of the power of God. He linked his confessed lordship with the issue of truth: "You call me 'Teacher' and 'Lord,' and rightly so, for that is what I am" (John 13:13). He spoke his convictions without hesitation, apology, or diffidence; with self-conscious authority he claimed to be *the* Teacher and *the* Lord of all humankind. "My teaching is not my own. It comes from him who sent me" (John 7:16). "Why do you call me, 'Lord, Lord,' and do not do what I say?" (Luke 6:46). He made the most dogmatic claims with quiet, unabashed finality: "His message had authority" (Luke 4:32; see also Matt. 7:28–29). And those who confessed him as Lord made no attempt to substitute their opinions for his or to adopt any other stance than to contend earnestly for the faith he delivered to them.

We are not surprised, then, that Jesus balanced his criticism of Jewish externalism with commendations of those among the Jews who served God faithfully. Although he regarded the Samaritan offshoot of Judaism as inferior (John 4:22), he commended individual Samaritans for their personal morality and social concern (Luke 10:25–37; 17:16). He also rejoiced over the genuine faith of a Roman centurion (Matt. 8:10). Because of Jesus' willingness to speak positively of all who were outgoing in their love and who were devoid of the spirit of retaliation toward others, the early church fathers came to recognize that "all that is good, true and beautiful, wherever it is found, comes from the Holy Spirit" (Schlette 1966: 36).

The question naturally surfaces. Does Jesus offer us any guidelines to follow with respect to other religions? Whereas he did not make any comprehensive statement about non-Jewish religions, he did comment on the Gentiles' futile patterns of repetitious prayer (Matt. 6:7). He did not challenge the Old Testament witness against gods other than the God of Abraham, Isaac, and Jacob. It is impossible to contend that his attitude to other religious systems would have been at variance with the commandment: "You shall have no other gods before me" (Exod. 20:3). His Father was supreme and unique; the service of other gods was totally forbidden. Hence, we cannot believe that he would endorse the postmodern openness to toleration of religious pluralism, nor would he have encouraged his followers to regard all religious systems as relative or to make as their priority the deepening of mutual understanding between them. Of course, he was concerned that all peoples in their interrelation with one another attain the proximate goals of social harmony, civil justice, and the alleviation of poverty. But his constant stress on the ultimate goal of the Kingdom of God led him to conclude and in a very real sense climax his ministry with the mandate that his people make disciples of the peoples of every tribe and tongue and nation (Matt. 28:19). This was his response to the issue of religious pluralism.

The Apostle Paul and Religion

When we turn to the letters of the apostle Paul, we gain insight into additional dimensions of this complex subject. First, he exposes the part played by "the powers" in the religious activity of people. In the previous chapter we discussed the fact that when Satan along with other invisible intelligences challenged God's sovereignty, a result was that they incarnated themselves within the creaturely existence of human societies—within customs, institutions, ethical mores, the ordering of the state, and religious patterns. Their unvarying objective has been to keep people from the love of God. Hendrikus Berkhof argues:

> This understanding is especially illuminating when we think of the religio-social structures by which the world outside Christ has been and is carried along. . . . We may point to Shintoism in Japan, to the Hindu social order in India, to the astrological unity of ancient Babel, to the deep significance of the *polis* or city-state for the Greeks, or to the Roman state. It is no less evident that the modern world as well is ruled by the *stoicheia*. However pointedly the Bible teaches us to see this as slavery, we should not forget that it is still a part of God's preserving mercy holding life in line where men do not know Christ's liberation. . . . Paul can help us with the problems of comparative religions. To see the pre-Christian faiths as a life in subjection to the powers, following Galatians 4, will preserve us from illegitimate rapprochements with Christian faith (for example, as if it were the "highest form" of religiosity), as well as from an equally illegitimate condemnation of "blind heathendom." (1962: 27–56)

One might cite Pauline texts that stress the mental, hence religious, activity of people as being to a greater or lesser degree dominated by the powers (e.g., Eph. 2:2–3, 11–13; 4:17–21; Col. 1:21–22; 1 Tim. 4:1). In our day of careless tolerance and religious relativism, we can all too easily dismiss this witness. Doubtless the Christians in Ephesus did not like to have Paul tell them that they once had "followed the ways of this world and of the ruler of the kingdom of the air, the spirit who is now at work in those who are disobedient" (2:2) and that all their religious activity prior to conversion had been locked into a system dominated by intelligences hostile to God.

Strange as it may seem, when Paul gave his most comprehensive exposition of the spiritual plight of humanity in his Epistle to the Romans, he mentioned neither Satan nor the powers. His focus was rather on the fallenness and guilt of the human race. They are "without excuse" by virtue of their own conduct (1:20). He attributed false religion to the human heart. Because his exposition is crucial to our understanding of the role religion plays in the context of human interaction with God, we will summarize its major emphases.

- The gospel of Christ is of universal relevance. "It is the power of God for the salvation of everyone who believes: first for the Jew, then for the Gentile" (1:16–17).
- The wrath of God—what could be described as God's love at work against sin"—is likewise universal in that it has brought all peoples under judgment (1:18).
- The whole of God's creation is the vehicle whereby God deliberately discloses "his eternal power and divine nature," and the only worthy response of his creatures is worship and obedience (1:19–20).
- The fallenness and guilt of all peoples is vividly apparent in their unconscious and unintentional resistance to what "God has made plain . . . to them" (1:19) and their suppression of it (1:18–21).
- The judgment of God is apparent in the way in which he gives people up to the destructive dynamics of their reprobate minds (1:24, 26, 28).
- The religions of people reflect feverish preoccupation with the distortions that have surfaced in their minds following the suppressing of all valid clues of God's existence and nature and their preoccupation with God's creation but not with God himself (1:23).
- This religious activity gathers to itself the self-deception and self-exaltation that spawn all manner of immorality, perversion, nonsocial behavior, and implacable hatred toward God himself (1:24–32).

We dare not dilute the stark reality of this picture. Bavinck's understanding of this passage is most insightful. When the truth of God's everlasting power and divinity is exiled to the recesses of a person's subconsciousness through his or her wickedness (Rom. 1:18), it does not vanish forever.

Still active, it reveals itself again and again. But it cannot become openly conscious; it appears in disguise, and it is exchanged for something different. Thus all kinds of ideas of God are formed; the human mind as the *fabrica idolorum* is not intentional deceit—it happens without man's knowing it. He cannot get rid of them. So he has religion; he is busy with a god; he serves his god—but he does not see that the god he serves is not God Himself. An exchange has taken place—a perilous exchange. An essential quality of God has been blurred because it did not fit in with the human pattern of life, and the image man has of God is no longer true. Divine revelation indeed lies at the root of it, but man's thoughts and aspiration cannot receive it and adapt themselves to it. In the image man has of God we can recognize the image of man himself. (1966: 122)

We cannot conclude the discussion of Romans 1:18–32 without asking, What was Paul describing in this passage? Admittedly, his larger objective in 1:18–3:20 was to show the whole world under the judgment of God. However, was he merely concerned with describing how contemporary pagan society became corrupt and idolatrous? Or was his canvas larger and embraced "the origin of all religions—even of religion itself?" In this connection Andrew Walls adds, "Does he assume the wilful rejection of a universal primitive monotheism?" then concludes the discussion: "It is such questions as these, or rather, the assumed answers to them, which underlie much of the debate arising from Christian evangelization" (1970: 348).

Over the centuries many in the church were convinced that Paul was portraying the origin of all idolatrous systems in the ancient world and indicating that all have depraved overtones. But not all scholars have accepted this interpretation. One recalls Justin Martyr's arguments to establish the thesis that men such as Socrates and Seneca, in their opposition to idolatry and their loyalty to high ethical standards, were illuminated by the eternal Logos. However, in the nineteenth and twentieth centuries, as the missionary movement became truly global and many undertook the careful study of non-Christian religions, many came to feel that Paul had been vindicated. The great German missiologist Gustav Warneck (1834–1911) contended that paganism often reflected a tenuous memory of a primeval revelation: "Dispassionate study of heathen religions confirms Paul's view that heathenism is a fall from a better knowledge of God" (quoted by Walls 1970: 354). What we should avoid is the temptation to superimpose on Paul's words the thesis that he condemned out of hand all the activities of people in their quest of what they perceived to be transcendence. Actually, Paul's objective was to state that people in their fallenness suppress the clues of God's invisible nature and gracious providence in the created world and in human conscience and history. They do not honor God and rather give themselves to unseemly passion. And the religions that they create and to which they give their allegiance reflect only in part their reaching for God. Examined carefully, their god or gods focus on individuals, not on the God and Father of our Lord and Savior, Jesus Christ. Against such evil the wrath of God is plainly revealed.

We must interject into this sequence of thought what the apostle Paul said regarding the Jewish people and their standing before God (Rom. 2:1–3:8).

Because God had in the past shown special favor to them, they had come to the conclusion that they were exempt from condemnation, believing that their Abrahamic lineage automatically granted their salvation. But Paul countered with the reminder that God's judgments are always based on the principle of justice, on what people do, that is, their works. "To those who by persistence in doing good seek glory, honor and immortality," God will give eternal life, but "for those who are self-seeking and who reject the truth and follow evil, there will be wrath and anger" (2:7–8). God shows no racial partiality in judging sin. This does not mean that salvation is by works, that persons will be saved when they conform completely to the law's demands. In 2:12–16 Paul states that God's judgments will depend upon the light under which people have lived: whether the revealed law of Moses that the Jews received or the law of nature and conscience, marred through their sin, that the Gentiles know. In any event, both Jews and Gentiles will perish, since both have sinned (2:12). As John Murray states:

> It would violate all canons of truth and equity to suppose that the sins against law naturally revealed and specially revealed would be ignored. By faith in the grace of the gospel sins are blotted out but other sins are not waived by unbelief of the gospel. Hence law in the utmost of its demand and rigour will be applied to the judgment of those in this category—they will be judged according to their works. (1959: 78)

In Athens (Acts 17) Paul encountered Greek polytheism. On this occasion he deliberately avoided a debate on religion. He did not blast the worship of idols. Rather, he accepted the validity of the universal religious consciousness and quest of people. As a result, he did not see his hearers as the devotees of this or that god, but only as hungry-hearted people groping and tragic in their need. Hence, he did not engage in philosophical disputation. He refused to demean his witness to Jesus Christ to the level of mere intellectual dialogue. And he was confirmed in this approach, for through his proclamation of Jesus Christ he saw some turn from their idols to the living God (17:34).

Conversion and the Kingdom

The church has long understood its mission to involve working for the conversion of non-Christians. Disciples must be made of every people. Not a few biblical texts underscore this obligation. However, in our day influential voices have challenged this and argue that the conversion of non-Christians is neither necessary nor desirable. The reasons they advance are formidable.

First, nationalist movements in many countries regard Christianity as too closely identified with Western colonialism. To become a Christian is to identify oneself with something foreign and denationalizing. Why should citizens who love their country join a religious system prominent among those who exploited it in the past?

Second, people are increasingly aware that there is much of ethical and social value to be found in non-Christian ethnic faiths. Hence, the Christian missionary must look "with sincere respect upon those ways of conduct and of life, those rules and teachings which, though differing in many particulars from what she holds and sets forth, nevertheless often reflect a ray of that Truth which enlightens all [people]" (Vatican II, Abbott 1966: 662). This has caused some to speculate: If the Spirit of Truth has already been at work in these religions, the probability is that they more adequately meet the spiritual needs of their peoples than a foreign, Western faith. Christian missionaries should help them become more aware of the treasures they possess and more willing to utilize them for the humanization of their societies.

Third, disillusionment with the institutional church has become so widespread that the simplistic call has been widely heard and fervently accepted: "Forget the church! Join hands with those supporting the poor and the oppressed in their struggle for social justice and human values! That's where God is and that's where the action is!"

As a result of this ferment, the religious debate on conversion has shifted in many circles from individual conversion to Christ, followed by incorporation into the church, to speaking of "conversion" as involvement with a socially concerned community, whether or not its members profess any allegiance to the person of Jesus Christ. Cultural pluralism and religious relativism have diverted many from making Jesus Christ the center of their approach to the subject of conversion. Admittedly, there is a sense in which, as Stephen Neill has said, "Every person really needs three conversions—to Christ, to the church and to the world." By being converted to the world Neill means that the Christian needs to face outward and move "back to the world in witness and devoted service." He then adds:

It is an observable fact that these conversions may come in any order. One man first finds himself challenged to surrender by the recognition of Christ as the supremely lovable and adorable Master. Another first finds the reality of Christian faith in the shared fellowship and mystery of the church. A third finds himself overwhelmed by the sorrows and sufferings of humanity and discovers in Jesus of Nazareth the pattern and the inspiration for a life of service. (1957: 50)

At this point we do well to turn to the Scriptures for their witness to the reality of, and need for, conversion. A key to its place in both testaments is found in the appearance of John the Baptist and his summons to radical repentance in view of the imminent approach of the Kingdom of God. Repentance was marked by submitting to baptism. Since John's preaching and baptism represented the continuation of the Old Testament prophetic call to return to the Lord—to turn back, to be converted—any biblical discussion of conversion should begin with a review of this tradition.

The prophets were essentially revivalists who sought to call the people of God to renew their covenant obligation to Yahweh. Although their call was to the people as a corporate unity, it resulted increasingly in the emergence of a remnant comprised of individuals who personally responded by "turning" (involving repentance) and recommitting themselves to the ordinances of worship and to the ethical standards of the Sinaitic covenant. The Israelites were originally converted to God when they accepted his purpose for them to turn from their slavery in Egypt and become his servants (Exod. 19:4–8). Generally speaking, specific expressions of obedience were involved in every reaffirmation of their covenant relationship to God (for example, their reconversion as in Hezekiah's day, 2 Chron. 29–30). On occasion we come upon the record of a king (e.g., Manasseh in 2 Chron. 33:12–13) going through a turning around (turning back) conversion experience. Since the prophets were invariably messengers of future hope, the thrust of their call to a conversion experience was to focus attention on the ongoing movement of God's redemptive purpose toward its glorious consummation in the day of the Lord. This forward-looking stance characterized John the Baptist, with his proclamation that the Kingdom of God and the advent of the Messiah were "at hand."

Nothing is more important at this point than to take the full measure of the call to conversion uttered by Jesus following the imprisonment of John. He inaugurated the Kingdom as "already" and "not yet" with his proclamation that the time was fulfilled, that one and all should repent and believe the gospel. Lesslie Newbigin helpfully amplifies this proclamation in the following fashion: "Turn around! Look the other way! Believe what I am telling you, namely that God's righteous reign is at the door" (1966: 32). Jesus' call to conversion involved turning around, accepting the reality of God's rule, and then willingly becoming an expression and extension of that rule in participation with a local congregation of his people.

These three elements demand expansion. First is the spiritual reorientation of a person turning in repentance and faith from all unworthy allegiances to Christ's lordship. One turns "to God from idols" (1 Thess. 1:9). Second, there is the behavioral transformation in which one consciously begins to participate in the activity of God, what Paul defined as "to serve the living and true God" (1 Thess. 1:9). Finally, there is the dimension of community. Solitary, individualistic Christianity has no place in the New Testament record. From this time onward—and underscored by the reference to baptism in the Great Commission—the call to conversion issued by the apostles involved radical repentance, submission to Jesus Christ, and baptism into a visible fellowship.

The proclamation of the universality of Christ's lordship over all nations and over all creation should not be confined only to God's provision of the forgiveness of sins (Luke 24:47). Since the Great Commission primarily concerns "the kingdom of God" (Acts 1:3), conversion to Christ does not mean that the nations should be left as they are. Individual Christians and corporate congregations are to be "signs of the Kingdom." And this can only mean being so responsive to the rule of Christ that they reflect in every way God's tomorrow in the world of today. The Kingdom in its final glorious manifestation will reflect the fullness of peace, justice, truth, and holiness. It follows, then, that God's people today are to be peacemakers, concerned for reconciliation between all types of warring factions. They are to be involved in the struggle for social justice, deeply concerned to extend the knowledge of the truth of God worldwide. Finally, they are to be in themselves unmarred reflections of his holiness and his love. This is what conversion is all about! And it brings great rejoicing not only in the presence of God but among his people on earth (Luke 15:10 and Acts 15:3).

Individual Conversions in the Book of Acts

So then, the biblical data is explicit. Conversion involves the decisive, Godward reorientation of a person's inner world. Conversion not only changes the relationship of people with God but also enlists them in becoming a sign of the coming Kingdom.

Luke records in Acts the conversion experiences of five people of different background, nationality, temperament, prior religious experience, and sex: the Ethiopian eunuch (chap. 8), Saul the Pharisee (chap. 9), the Italian Cornelius (chap. 10), the merchant Lydia (chap. 16), and the Roman jailer (chap. 16). Although their encounters with Christ are markedly different, we find striking similarities in the sequence of events that brought about their conversion. None was directly challenged to "convert to God," yet all were found by him in the context of the apostolic evangelistic witness that God had reconciled the world to himself through Jesus Christ and was calling men and women to himself as an expression of his universal concern (Kummel 1963: 18).

First, all went through a period of preparation: the Ethiopian read the Scriptures (8:28). Saul understood Judaism and the law (22:3; 26:5) and heard of the doctrine of those he was persecuting (7:2–53; 9:2; 22:4; 26:9–11). Cornelius was a God-fearer and a man of prayer (10:2). Lydia was a synagogue worshiper who had cultivated the habit of prayer (16:13–14). And the Roman jailer doubtless heard the witness of Paul and Silas during the considerable period ("several days") before they were imprisoned (16:12).

Second, all either heard preaching about Jesus or experienced his presence. Philip explained the good news of Jesus to the Ethiopian (8:35); Jesus himself formed the content of Saul's vision on the road to Damascus (9:5; 22:8; 26:15); Peter reviewed with Cornelius the highlights of Jesus' words and deeds (10:34–43; 11:14); Paul bore witness to Lydia (16:13); and Paul and Silas "spoke the word of the Lord" to the jailer and his household (16:32–34).

Third, all made some sort of response, generally an inquiry, in the process of their movement toward conversion. The Ethiopian questioned Philip about the passage he was reading (8:34); Saul sought the glorified Christ's identity (9:5; 22:8; 26:15) and, in one account, requested a commission from him (22:10); Cornelius asked the "angel" for an explanation of his vision (10:4); and the Philippian jailer put the key question to Paul and Silas, "Sirs, what must I do to be saved?" (16:30).

Fourth, prominence is given to the activity of God. The Spirit is associated with the ministry of Philip and became the agent in the Ethiopian's conversion (8:29, 39). Saul encountered the glorified Christ directly (9:4–6) and, at the hands of Ananias, prompted by God (9:10–16), received the Spirit prior to his baptism (9:17–18). Cornelius saw an angel of God in his vision (10:3, 30–32) and also received the Spirit before being baptized, evidenced by his speaking in tongues (10:44–48; 11:15; 15:8). The Lord opened the heart of Lydia (16:14). And everything about the unlikely conversion of the Roman jailer bears witness to God's intervention (16:25–34).

Fifth, the convert in each case received baptism (8:38; 9:18; 10:47–48; 16:15, 33). This belonged inseparably to them all with its implicit confession of faith and its vivid representation of their having embarked on a "resurrection life" made possible through the risen Christ. It should be noted that none made an explicit confession of faith apart from baptism. Scholars are largely agreed that Acts 8:37 is a late interpolation.

Finally, in each case one cannot but note the evident results of the conversion experience. The Ethiopian and the jailer rejoiced (8:39; 16:34); Saul proclaimed that Jesus is the Son of God (9:20, 22; 26:22–23); Cornelius spoke with tongues, extolling God (10:46); and Lydia and the jailer displayed the Christian virtue of hospitality (16:15, 34; cf. 1 Peter 4:9).

Despite the limitations of the biblical data, certain features are sufficiently common to these five accounts for us to make the following deductions. It is clear that the spiritual experience in question is more than simply the work of a moment. Conversion is a process. Also, conversion is frequently occasioned by all that the New Testament includes under the rubric of "preaching." It can be affirmed that some kind of intellectual activity, however elementary, takes place in the process and that Christian conversion involves the total personality, not merely intellectual apprehension. Further, the convert is normally brought into the total life of the church through baptism, and this is often directly related to the gift of the Holy Spirit. It is fundamental to all that may be said about conversion in the New Testament that this work is, from first to last, a response to the *opus Dei* (Smalley 1964: 193–210).

Viewed externally, conversion involves a process, turning, reviewing, moving forward. More is involved than mere repentance over the past and new resolutions about the future. There is the deliberate disposition of heart and mind to surrender to the will and power of God through encounter with Jesus Christ and then, under his direction, to turn away from the things that are not of God. This reorientation of the whole life and personality is the sine qua non of entrance into the Kingdom of God (John 3:3). Paul struck a parallel with the death and resurrection of Christ: the convert has been "baptized into his death" and "raised . . . [to] a new life" in the Spirit (Rom. 6:2–4; Col. 2:12). And the conversion paradigm of repentance and faith, of death and life, becomes the subsequent pattern of the Christian life ("as you received Christ Jesus as Lord, continue to live in him," Col. 2:6).

Baptism is central to the total conversion experience. Bishop Stephen Neill has pointed out the radical discontinuity involved in the conversion process by calling attention to the fact that admission to the churches of the apostolic age was "by faith *and baptism*" (his emphasis) and added: "The New Testament knows nothing of membership in the church by faith alone, without this accompanying act of obedience and confession" (1964: 188). Luke's summary of Paul's ministry in Corinth was: "Many of the Corinthians who heard him believed and were baptized" (Acts 18:8) and his definition of a Christian would be one who confesses Jesus Christ as his Lord and Savior, who is baptized, who regularly shares in the Lord's Supper, who abides in the teaching of the apostles through faithful study of the Scriptures, and who participates in the local *koinōnia* of the people of God, sharing in their common life and service (2:42).

Furthermore, at every level of the biblical evidence conversion demands commitment to conduct that is reflective of the coming Kingdom of God. This means the commitment to constructive action in history—the proclamation of the knowledge of God accompanied by those activities in society that anticipate and move forward God's purpose for his creation—the Kingdom in its full realization, not mere membership in a saved community but participating as an agent of the work of God in history, which is not complete until all things have been summed up in Christ (Newbigin 1969: 112).

Conclusion

No issue in mission theology or in mission methodology is as crucial as the issue of religion and conversion. We dare not be content merely to describe the gospel of the Kingdom. To preach it adequately is to issue a call to conversion. Of course, the gospel assures us the new heavens and the new earth will certainly come and replace all that is old. But God's judgment must precede this glorious manifestation of the Kingdom. Hence, the importance of preaching repentance today and calling for the conversion of the heart—today!

So then, we close this chapter by repeating Jesus' words to Nicodemus on the essentiality of the conversion experience:

> I tell you the truth, no one can see the kingdom of God . . . no one can enter the kingdom of God unless he is born of water and the Spirit. (John 3:3–5)

If Nicodemus, a well-trained Jewish rabbi, was given this stark and pointed statement of his spiritual need, who can say it is without universal application? Is it not also true that persons who are not born again may on the day of judgment wish that they had never been born at all?

23

The Whole Bible
Announces God's Rule

Introduction

We have discussed the spiritual destiny of the human race in terms of those who are the sons and daughters of the Kingdom and those who are not. We now turn to the final events in salvation history, related to the triumph of the Kingdom of God in history—the ushering in of the new heavens and the new earth. We shall find that this complex subject is incomprehensible unless related to the mission of the church on behalf of the nations. Our primary information comes from a person named John, written in the context of his imprisonment "on the island of Patmos because of the word of God and the testimony of Jesus" (Rev. 1:9).

Who was this John? Because the language of Revelation is somewhat different from the Gospel and epistles of the apostle John, some scholars have questioned whether he could have been one of the twelve apostles: the son of Zebedee "whom Jesus loved" (John 13:23). Apparently, the author was widely known among the churches of Asia and did not object to the designation of "prophet" (Rev. 22:9). Because several early Greek fathers (e.g., Justin Martyr and Irenaeus) attribute this book to the apostle John, we believe it was written in his old age (c. A.D. 95, in the reign of Domitian), when the church in certain parts of the Roman Empire was entering a period of persecution. It portrays the church struggling for its spiritual integrity and suffering under satanic assault. It thereby reflects many of the concerns of John's earlier writings. We see no need to invent an unknown John as its author.

The apostle John doubtless remembered Jesus' prediction that the people of God would always be treated with hostility by the world (John 15:18–20; 16:33). But did this new outbreak of Roman persecution have eschatological significance? He personally needed an answer. And the church has always needed insight into the whole course of God's Kingdom history in the midst of world history, particularly because it was believed that just before the end the church's tribulations would greatly intensify. How fitting, then, that this last book of the canon should be given to the people of God as they face this darkening future.

Revelation and the Kingdom

John had known Jesus and the sequence of his earthly ministry: the year of renewal ministry; the year of Kingdom inauguration with its crowds and signs and wonders; and the year of growing opposition (and diminishing signs!) leading to the cross, resurrection, and ascension. John had also been active in the early years of the church age. He experienced the outpoured Holy Spirit at Pentecost. He rejoiced over the thousands of Jews who believed soon afterward. He marveled at the new signs and wonders of the Kingdom. And he participated in the evangelistic penetration of the Mediterranean world. Toward the end of the century, however, John was in prison, and the church in the region where he served was facing what seemed to be total catastrophe. As persecution mounted and the climate of oppression became more widespread, there was an apparent absence of miraculous deliverances. The churches were beginning to cry out: "For your sake we face death all day long; we are considered as sheep to be slaughtered" (Rom. 8:36). The inevitable question was "How long, Sovereign Lord, holy and true, until you judge the inhabitants of the earth and avenge our blood?" (Rev. 6:9–10). Rousas Rushdoony captures the scene:

> Revelation depicts the world as a turbulent sea, restless, always moving, not its own master but acted on by the winds of heaven, an area without foundation, security, or stability. The saints feel the impact of the world and its fever, are buffeted by its storms, and feel the fever of its restlessness, helplessness, lust for power and security, and its shapeless mutability. They feel driven, abandoned to the storms of a wild and restless sea, and wonder at the place of God in all this. (1978: 87)

It was Jesus Christ himself who gave to John the answer (Rev. 1:1). The church has always believed that Revelation was written for Christians in every age to assure them that God is working both in their day and particularly when the tempo of persecution intensifies just before the end. God will not turn back from his goal of consummating his purpose in his time and in his way.

Before this final triumph and the full manifestation of the Kingdom can take place, however, there must be a resolution of the cosmic struggle between God and Satan. Hence, it is not without reason that Revelation opens with an affirmation of who Jesus Christ is: "The faithful witness, the firstborn from the dead, and the ruler of the kings of the earth" (1:5). Through his death he has demonstrated his integrity in carrying out what he promised to do: "To give his life as a ransom for many" (Mark 10:45). By his resurrection he showed himself the omnipotent One, fully qualified to rule the earth. All earthly power is under his control. He is also portrayed in prophetic vision (Rev. 1:12–16), dressed in robes reflecting his judicial and kingly power and having the keys (i.e., total control) of Hades and death. His glory exceeds that of the sun in its strength (1:16), and he is constantly present in the world, particularly in the midst of his church (1:12, 20).

This vision sets the stage for all that is to follow. Indeed, Revelation claims an inspiration, integrity, and authority unmatched by any other book in the canon

(1:1–3; 22:18–20). It has but one central purpose. It is to declare that the Kingdom of God is triumphant today, will triumph throughout time, and will be so revealed in eternity. Christians always need this message. The Christ who is currently hidden from the world is not only the enthroned King of creation but the exalted Head of the church and the Lord of history.

Lest one think Revelation represents only signs and symbols, we must hasten to state that it is radically historical, for it speaks pointedly of the coming of the sovereign Christ and the New Jerusalem into history. Hence, as many have done before us, we must strike the parallel with Genesis, an equally historical book. As Rushdoony summarizes (1978: 90):

Genesis	Revelation
Paradise lost	Paradise regained
Creation of heaven and earth	A new heaven and a new earth
The curse enters: sin, sorrow, suffering, death	No more curse: no more sin, sorrow, suffering, death
Tree of life guarded	Tree of life restored
Four rivers watering the garden healing the nations	A pure river of water of life available to all
Communion destroyed	Communion restored
Work cursed	Work blessed
People out of harmony with nature	People at peace with nature

This parallelism underscores the lordship of Christ over creation and the certainty of his ultimate triumph within it. It is not without reason that his past victories are recalled through the affirmation: "'I am the Alpha and the Omega,' says the Lord God, 'who is, and who was, and who is to come, the Almighty'" (1:4, 8). This reminds us of the revelation given to Moses prior to the Exodus (Exod. 3:14). Furthermore, John's portrayal of the Lord as the One who through his cross has "made us to be a kingdom and priests to his God and Father" (Rev. 1:6) reflects a similar promise made to the redeemed children of Israel at Sinai (Exod. 19:6). Christ's atonement marked the beginning of a greater Exodus. Not only did it deliver the people of God from the bondage of sin and introduce them to a pilgrim life in this world, but it also pointed to the ultimate "power and glory" manifestation of the Kingdom of God in history. We now turn to the unfolding of this theme via a succession of visions.

The Churches and the Kingdom (Rev. 2–3)

The first vision portrays the triumphant and exalted Christ in the midst of seven churches. These seven have been selected possibly because they were representative of the churches of the apostolic age and in some way are representative of churches in every age. Certainly, they contain no problems that churches today are not facing. The church in Ephesus (2:1–7) was orthodox and hardworking but lacked love, the absence of which made all its other qualities worthless. It was possibly so busy hunting heresy that it lost the capacity for witnessing with outgoing love. The church in Smyrna (2:8–11) was hard pressed by the sharp testing of its political loyalty and by the slander of hostile Jews. Although materially poor and in constant trouble, one gains the impression its members were fearless and optimistic.

The church in Pergamum (2:12–17) was obliged to function in a context where the influence and power of Satan were rampant and where martyrdom was a possibility. Some compromised the faith; others condoned false teaching and even open immorality. The church in Thyatira (2:18–29) was a strange mixture of Christian love, genuine faith, and diligent service, but it was intermingled with the sort of sentimental toleration of false teaching that led to all manner of wickedness. The church in Sardis (3:1–6) was virtually dead, having only a facade of godliness, and was devoid of any commendation from Christ. It offered nothing to him, hence was called to remember its past, to repent of its sin, and to keep the commands of God.

The church in Philadelphia (3:7–13) was small and weak but faithful to Christ. As a result, he promised to keep it in the hour of testing and to open to it a door of evangelistic opportunity denied the rest. Finally, the church in Laodicea (3:14–22) was spiritually bankrupt. The risen Christ was unsparing in his condemnation of its spiritual indifference ("neither cold nor hot") because this had brought it blindness and insensibility toward all the noble aspects of life.

The binding lessons of this first vision emphasize the fact that Christ is renewal-oriented in his dealings with his people. He is fully knowledgeable of the state of the churches in every age. He regards each congregation as a "lampstand," a potential center of light, a witness to the gospel in a dark world. He is quick to commend all evidence of loyalty to truth, obedience to mission, and purity of life. But he severely rebukes coldness of heart, indifference to truth, and carelessness about sin; these can misrepresent his kingship and blunt the appeal and attractiveness of the gospel to non-Christians. Although Christ threatens to remove congregations from their opportunities for witness and service (2:5), he nowhere calls for the withdrawal of the faithful from defiled or largely unbelieving congregations in order to form "separatist" and competing congregations. Every effort must be put forth to express the unity of the people of God and through forthright witness to "strengthen what remains" (3:2). As Head of the church, Christ's abiding concern is for the renewal of his people, not for their fragmentation. Only thereby can they avoid repeating the failure of Israel under the old covenant and become what Israel never was: a serving presence and a guiding light in a dark and needy world.

So then, every local congregation should be a sign of the Kingdom of God through its worship and submission to the Lord in its midst, as well as through its outgoing service and witness under his direction. Each local expression of his body is to be a visible demonstration today of the good things Christ has promised for tomorrow when the Kingdom is finally revealed. This demands that churches in every generation take to heart the exhortation concluding each of the letters to the seven churches: "He who has an ear, let him hear what the Spirit says." Christians dare not be indifferent to the presence of the devil, the distortions of false prophets, the negative influence of disobedient Christians, and their own faithless propensities when they review their responsibility to pray and work for church renewal.

Mission and Mounting Conflict (Rev. 4–16)

Revelation now moves to its major theme: the ominous fact that there will be a relatively short period in which Christians will face terrible evil and severe persecution just prior to the end. This second vision presents in a most comprehensive and vivid fashion the cosmic conflict between the Kingdom of God and the kingdom of the devil. It begins with the portrayal of an ultimate and eternal fact: the enthroned Sovereign of the universe is secure in his power, authority, and control (chap. 4). The symbolism reflects the purity of heaven sharply separated from the sinfulness of earth. In God's presence are heavenly hosts and his redeemed people. The focus is on a sealed document that records the unfolding of history, particularly the final events of judgment and salvation (chap. 5). The question is raised: Who is worthy to carry to completion its details? The answer is given by setting the stage for the emergence of Jesus Christ, the triumphant Lamb. All heaven breaks forth into singing as he takes the document and commences to break its seven seals. Singing replaces mystery because apart from him, human history is an enigma. He is its key.

The first four seals, when broken, reveal that Jesus' perspective of history is subsumed under the images of four horsemen (chap. 6). The last three horsemen represent the sequence of war, famine and pestilence, and death: the ravages of human evil. But the first horseman is different. Because of its color (white), George Ladd concludes we should look for some interpretation that associates it with Christ. He then points out that in his Olivet Discourse Christ singled out the mission of the church as the one positive element in human history. After quoting Matthew 24:14 and Mark 13:10, Ladd comments:

> The course of the age is not to be one of unrelieved evil when God's people are surrendered helplessly and passively into the bands of hostile powers. While the Kingdom of God will not be established until the return of the Son of man, the age will be one of tension: tension between evils which characterize history and afflict particularly the followers of Jesus, and the active and aggressive proclamation of the gospel of the Kingdom by those same disciples. . . . The rider is not Christ himself but symbolizes the proclamation of the Gospel of Christ in all the world. (1972: 98–99)

Christians desperately need this vision of the victorious character of their mission to the nations. The accompanying symbols of bow and crown mean that despite every form of opposition, the church will effectively and completely carry out its mission. Victories will be won, peoples will be evangelized, converts will come forward, churches will be planted, and the gospel will victoriously manifest its power as it is increasingly proclaimed throughout the whole world. Not that those bearing witness to the gospel will not experience opposition, persecution, and even martyrdom (6:9–11). All too often, suffering has largely characterized the church throughout its long history, especially on the frontiers of missionary advance into non-Christian lands.

Inevitably, the vision enlarges at this point, and we are given intimations of innumerable peoples down through the centuries who will be won to Christ's allegiance through this sacrificial missionary effort (chap. 7). God reveals his personal knowledge of and concern for his elect, whether from Israel or the Gentile nations, and he seals them all as his very own.

This sealing is anticipatory of the heightening tempo of the cosmic conflict as history moves to its climax (chap. 8). The opposition of the enemy increases, only to be met by the beginnings of the outpouring of God's wrath. But his wrath does not touch those with the seal of God upon their foreheads (9:4). Indeed, this portrayal of God's missionary purpose moving forward (chap. 9) tends to refute those who seem to delight in superlatives when they characterize the last days by speaking of a totally triumphant Satan, a world of unrelieved evil, an apostate church, and an unfinished missionary task. Certainly, Revelation goes on to speak of dark days ahead and of the final efforts of Satan and his cohorts seeking to frustrate the will and purpose of God. But "in the last days" God has promised that he "will pour out [his] Spirit on all people" (Acts 2:17). This promise should not be forgotten. To quote Ladd:

> The last days will be evil, but not unrelieved evil. God has given us a gospel for the last days, and he has given a power to take that gospel into all the world for a witness unto all the nations: then shall the end come. This must be the spirit of our mission in this evil age. We are not rosy optimists, expecting the gospel to conquer the world and establish the Kingdom of God. Neither are we despairing pessimists who feel that our task is hopeless in the face of the evil of this age. (1959: 139)

There will be suffering. The people of God will cry out for justice and for deliverance. They will sense the growing tempo of intensity in God's cosmic struggle with Satan. The earth, sea, rivers, and sky will be stricken (chap. 8). Furthermore, toward the end, evil superhuman powers will desperately seek opportunities to frustrate God and his church. Plagues will follow. In their midst God will seek to bring the unbelieving to repentance, but to no avail (chap. 9). In the midst of their anguish, the last trumpet will prepare to sound that there will be no more delay (chap. 10). But before this takes place and no more opportunity for repentance remains, there will be an interlude in which a variety of pictures will be held before us of things to come. They portray God watching over his own (11:1–2); his faithful witnesses in the midst of the final terror (11:3–6); the emergence of the Antichrist (11:7–10); the conversion of Jews (11:11–13); and the first intimation of the final triumph of Christ (11:14–19).

The focus then turns from Christ himself (12:1–7) to the final banishment of Satan from heaven (12:8–12) and to his intensified warfare against the people of God (12:13–17). Satan is assisted in this by two agents, who, together with Satan, form a trinity of evil. First is the beast out of the sea of unbelieving nations (13:1–10), the Antichrist who takes the state apparatus that God has made for human welfare and transforms it into an instrument for oppression. Since this beast represents anti-Christian states and cultures in their grasp for the authority and sovereignty that properly belong to God and in their centralization and manipulation of human power, Christians need to keep in mind that Satan's power is more illusory than real. The coming of Christ into the world to "destroy the devil's work" (1 John 3:8) proved to be his death stroke (John 12:31; Col. 2:15). And yet the beast continues. "The fatal wound was healed," so much so that "the whole earth was astonished and followed the beast" (Rev. 13:3). Albertus Pieters writes: "The deadly wound is healed. In the days of St. John it was evident that the brute was by no means dead, and this healing of the wound was, no doubt, a sore trial to him and his friends" (quoted by Rushdoony 1978: 174). And yet he knew that Satan was truly doomed, by virtue of Christ's death and resurrection.

The second agent is the beast out of the earth (13:11–18). He is the false prophet who perverts religion and by it presses all people to worship the Antichrist. Christians have always encountered difficulty in accepting the darker implications of both the state (Caesar) and false religion (which often includes apostate churches). Christians love their countries and are all too prone to render to Caesar far more than he deserves. Furthermore, they love their churches and are not always alert to the church's temptation to drift from a Christ-centered salvation to one that is people centered and achievement oriented. When religious persons uncritically place fallen people and their potential in the center of the stage, they are not consciously rebelling against God. But too often their preoccupation with humankind eventuates in an overly moralistic humanism preoccupied with human works and human law. Thus, the second beast is described as lamblike (13:11) and that by "great and miraculous signs" (v. 13) it "deceived the inhabitants of the earth" (v. 14).

At this point light shines into the bleak picture. Just when the power of the satanic triumvirate seems all conquering and the people of God are being overcome—their witness to Christ virtually extinguished—assurance is given that all is well (chap. 14). The Lamb remains enthroned, and the consummation of history is seen as firmly in his hands. The godless civilization of the Antichrist (Babylon) will be judged, and the saints of God will be brought to their eternal salvation. Especially the martyred dead are reminded that their efforts to extend the knowledge of Christ have not been in vain (14:13); the final harvests are gathered in. These harvests are twofold: the redeemed from all corners of the earth (cf. Rev. 14:14–16 with Mark 13:27) and the impenitent to face the wrath of God (cf. Rev. 14:17–20 with Matt. 24:30). The final portents reveal God in heaven in the midst of his victorious people (chap. 15) and the outpouring on the earth of the seven last plagues: the seven bowls of his wrath (chap. 16).

Babylon Falls and God Triumphs over Satan (Rev. 17–20:3)

The third vision focuses on the judgment of what can only be called eschatological Babylon and the triumph of Christ. Babylon is introduced as the epitome of all the idealistic dreaming of humanistic states ("the human lust for a paradise without God and in contempt of God" [Rushdoony 1978: 194]). Since it mimics the Kingdom of God and tempts fallen people to believe that unaided by God they can perfect human society, Babylon is rightly called a whore. She is depicted as sitting on the waters of "peoples, multitudes, nations, and languages" (17:1, 15). She is "the great city that rules over the kings of the earth" (17:18). It now becomes crystal clear that the "disciple-making" mission of the church was nothing less than God's chief instrument in liberating people from satanic bondage. All through history various forms of these awesome realities have drawn their power from fallen peoples and from "the kings of the earth" through enticing them to become preoccupied with themselves, their immoralities, their acquisitions, their exploitations, and their defiance of the laws of God. Now, at the end, the Antichrist experiences sudden and total destruction. Utter confusion overtakes all that is satanic. Christ emerges as the conqueror and is exalted as Lord of lords and King of kings (17:14). "Even as the first Adam destroyed paradise by his sin, the second Adam destroys the counterfeit paradise by his righteousness" (Rushdoony 1978: 197).

Babylon's judgment is so far-reaching that all heaven bursts into a great hymn of thanksgiving and praise to God (19:1–5). This leads directly to the proclamation of the signs of the final triumph of the Kingdom of God and the consummation of God's redemptive purpose.

First, the private marriage of the Lamb takes place (19:6–10). His bride is the one people of God, whether from Israel or the nations. They are revealed as having been steadfast in their endurance. They kept the commandments of God and persevered in their faith in Jesus (14:12).

Second, all witness the public manifestation of the conquering Christ (19:11–16). He is revealed as faithful and true, as righteous in his conquest of evil, as the Word of God, fully embodying the totality of God's redemptive purpose. His people share in his victory and in his sovereignty.

Third, all hear the shout of triumph because the Antichrist has been conquered (19:17–21). This is Armageddon: the final battle. No struggle takes place. Christ's victory is total, and the armies of the Antichrist completely capitulate. The victory that had been announced earlier (16:12–16) now finally takes place. Amazingly, to the very end great numbers of people remain obstinate in their resistance to God and his righteousness. Inevitably, on them his wrath and judgment finally fall.

The fourth element in this sequence is the precautionary binding of Satan (20:1–3). His power is deliberately and drastically curbed. The ease with which Christ accomplishes this confirms his earlier conquest of Satan at the cross. The defeated Satan is incarcerated in the abyss from which the demonic locusts earlier emerged to torment the human race (9:1–6). He is thereby prevented from deceiving the nations for one thousand years. At their end he is released and initiates another revolt against God (20:7–10). But to no avail. He encounters God the third and final time, is overcome, and then banished forever to "the lake of burning sulfur" (20:10; see also Matt. 25:41).

The First Resurrection and the Final Judgment (Rev. 20:4–6, 11–15)

The triumphant though martyred people of God are now raised from the dead and commence their millennial reign with Christ. They serve as "priests of God and of Christ." It is in this sequence that we turn to Paul for insight into the unraveling of the complexities of the end.

> For as in Adam all die, so in Christ all will be made alive. But each in his own turn: Christ, the firstfruits; then, when he comes [Parousia], those who belong to him. Then the end will come, when he hands over the kingdom of God the Father after he has destroyed all dominion, authority and power. For he must reign until he has put all his enemies under his feet. The last enemy to be destroyed is death. For he "has put everything under his feet." Now when it says that "everything" has been put under him, it is clear that this does not include God himself, who put everything under Christ. When he has done this, then the Son himself will be made subject to him who put everything under him, so that God may be all in all. (1 Cor. 15:22–28)

This passage describes the successive stages by which God finally and fully destroys all his enemies and realizes his perfect reign throughout the whole universe. Paul begins with Christ's resurrection; he is the firstfruits of this final victory (15:23). Jesus Christ then reigns at his Father's right hand, subduing his enemies (15:24). This is the church age. Afterward comes his future return (the Parousia) and what is called the first resurrection, when all those who have shared his life will rise from the dead. Since the last enemy to be destroyed is death (15:26), we posit that this takes place at the end of the millennial age, when the rest of the dead are resurrected to respond to Christ's summons to stand before the final judgment (Rev. 20:11–15). With scrupulous justice, divine judgment is then administered in accordance with deeds done in this life (Rom. 2:6). Death is finally overcome, sin is forever removed, and the way is now prepared for Christ to deliver up the Kingdom to God the Father (1 Cor. 15:28) that he might be "all in all."

It needs to be recognized that there is another way of looking at the one thousand-year reign of Christ. It begins with the assumption that in a highly symbolic book (Revelation) one should not take literally these few verses. Rather, one should regard the period of the New Testament church to be the true millennium, in which Christ reigns through his people in their mission as they bring individual men and women and the nations under his dominion. This view states correctly that mission is God's activity in Christ. Through the church, God gathers God's elect. By the gospel he also extends his sovereignty over his creation. This view also stresses that Christ's triumph at the cross resulted in Satan being cast out of heaven and being bound "to keep him from deceiving the nations anymore" (Rev. 20:3). The first resurrection is seen as the spiritual regeneration of the people of God. The release of Satan at the end of the millennium (20:7–10) results in the intensification of the persecution and suffering of Christians just prior to the end. Because the reference to the destruction of Gog and Magog (20:8) at the end of the one thousand years is in stark contrast to the parallel account in Ezekiel 39:1–8, where it takes place before the Kingdom era, legitimacy has been found in believing that there will be no actual millennial reign following the Parousia of Jesus Christ.

Many things could be said about the "amillennial" approach to this admittedly complicated passage. We will make but two observations. Whereas we will grant that Christ is sovereign in history and that "in all things God works for the good of those who love him" (Rom. 8:28), his present rule is hidden. It is neither seen nor recognized by the world. Even so, hidden or not, we know "he must reign until he has put all his enemies under his feet" (1 Cor. 15:25). But Scripture seems to indicate that this reign will be "with power and glory" and will be universally recognized by all creation, with every knee bowing and every tongue confessing his lordship (Phil. 2:10–11). This phase of his reign has yet to take place.

Second, we should ask, Will human history never see "righteousness reign"? Or, putting the question differently: Must the nations be told that even with Christ triumphant there will never be the realization of that for which so many have dreamed and struggled down through the centuries—for peace, plenty, social justice, and the end of all exploitation? This is the basic flaw in the amillennial view: it awakens no hope in Christ's glorious reign on earth. Although it claims that the earth and the nations will enjoy their jubilee, it provides no assurance that this will ever take place. Imagine the violence of the twentieth century having been part of the millennium.

All Things New (Rev. 21–22)

We now reach the point wherein the new heavens and the new earth take the place of the old (21:1–8), and perfected fellowship with God is enjoyed by the redeemed: "The first heaven and the first earth had passed away." The bride, the wife of the Lamb, is then revealed in all her glory (21:9–22:5). The city of God also is revealed in all its glory with the Lord in his temple and the Lamb like a flame providing its light and splendor. The river of life flows there freely, and the leaves of the tree of life serve "for the healing of the nations."

At this point Revelation comes to its formal ending since "the conflict of the ages" is no more. Its "signs" have spoken of realities that only dimly express their fullness. They never completely unveil the mysteries to which they have been pointing. But of one thing we can be sure: God will triumph in history—finally and absolutely!

The Destiny of Non-Christians

In any discussion of the final judgment of God and the consummation of salvation history, questions are inevitably raised concerning the eternal destiny of those who during their lifetime were either ignorant of Jesus Christ or who refused to acknowledge him as their Lord and Savior when confronted with the demands of the gospel. According to the biblical data already examined, it is apparent that the gospel arises from the unique historical event of the death, burial, and resurrection of Jesus Christ. No other founder of a religion claimed to be the eternal Son of God, the only supreme deity. No other religious teacher ever had the audacity to claim, as Jesus claimed, that to deny his deity was to incur the certainty of dying in one's sins (John 8:24). Scripture concurs with the judgment of Stephen Neill: "Jesus' life, his methods and His message do not make sense unless they are interpreted in the light of his own conviction that he was in fact the final and decisive word of God to people. For the human sickness there is one specific remedy, and this is it. There is no other" (1961: 16–17).

The Christian faith by its own claim to truth casts the shadow of falsehood, or at least of imperfect truth, on every other system. Its "claim to universal validity cannot quietly be removed from the gospel without changing it into something entirely different from what it is" (Neill 1961: 16). The fundamental issue is truth. The Bible states that an event took place in history when "God was reconciling the world to himself in Christ" (2 Cor. 5:19). This event opened the possibility for a new and permanent relationship between a holy God and the sinful human race. All peoples may have access and are thereby invited into God's presence and friendship. This great achievement neither needs to be repeated nor can be replaced. It stands sufficient for all time and for all generations of people. On this the biblical witness is unequivocal and unambiguous. In Jesus Christ and in him uniquely, people can "find the road to God, the truth about God, and the life of God" (J. N. D. Anderson 1970: 96).

There are those who would challenge these affirmations. They readily admit that in earlier generations of the church, the view that ultimately all people would be redeemed was totally unacceptable. It was dismissed as heresy by the Synod of Constantinople, a judgment that was confirmed by the Council of Constantinople in A.D. 553. Even so, they contend that the universalist option is more reflective of the spirit of this generation. Furthermore, they appeal to three distinct lines of scriptural witness to support this "larger view." First, the universality of God's redemptive purpose (e.g., "I, when I am lifted up from the earth, will draw all [persons] to myself," John 12:32, or "One act of righteousness was justification that brings life for all men," Rom. 5:18). Second, the universality of God's salvific will (e.g., "God . . . wants [everyone] to be saved and to come to a knowledge of the truth," 1 Timothy 2:4 or ". . . not wanting anyone to perish, but everyone to come to repentance," 2 Peter 3:9). Third, the universality of Christ's vicarious atonement (e.g., "He is the atoning sacrifice for our sins, and not only for ours but also for the sins of the whole world," 1 John 2:2, or "[He reconciled] to himself all things, whether things on earth or things in heaven, by making peace through his blood, shed on the cross," Col. 1:20).

Taken in their contexts, these affirmations are hardly conclusive. They demonstrate the utter sufficiency of Christ's redemptive achievement and the breadth of God's universal concern, but they do not establish the certainty that the grace of God will fully and finally triumph in every person.

Another line of argument is to advance those texts that describe the love of God in universal and superlative terms. It is reasoned that it would be unthinkable to such a God to be eternally separated from great numbers of those who on earth have borne his image (2 Thess. 1:7–9). As Nels Ferre says:

> A theology based on sovereign love will uncompromisingly stand for universal salvation. Anything less would be inconsistent with God's sovereignty and would impugn God's love. If he is sovereign love, the question as to the outcome is completely closed. Love will win unconditional surrender from all that is not love, and God will rule everywhere and forever. (quoted by Griffiths 1980: 120)

But these texts must be balanced by those that affirm God's holiness and justice and his concern that people be free to decide either to obey him or to live their lives apart from him. Choices made in this life are determinative. If a person refuses to live with God and his people in this life, would such a person not find eternity intolerable since it involves this linkage in an eternal sense? The fact remains that a God of love has allowed sin to enter the world with all its destructive tendencies and its injustices. God has allowed people to suffer as a consequence. Michael Griffiths concludes:

> The co-existence of hell with the God of love would seem a moral necessity if man is to have freedom of choice. We know all too sadly even in human experience that love may be rejected and that a person may persist in wilful hatred and estrangement, even when it is not in his interests to do so. Human pride can keep a man in hell. (1980: 132)

What concerns us at this point is not whether there is both a heaven and a hell. Jesus Christ was most explicit on this point (Luke 10:20; 12:5). Nor are we concerned to refute the contention that all people will be saved. The most carefully contrived arguments in support of universalism cannot stand before the strong witness of Scripture. Our concern is at the primary level of gospel communication and human response, with the focus on what constitutes a Christian. How much does one have to believe in order to have "saving faith"? What are the outward signs of the genuine encounter with God?

If we are to judge from the prophetic witness in Old Testament times, the sine qua non of saving faith was a heart attitude of repentance toward God because of an awareness of one's sinfulness. This was accompanied by bringing a prescribed sin offering to God. When the sin was so grievous to God that no specific offering could cover it, the penitent could only cry out for forgiveness in much the same way as David when he became aware of his sins of adultery and murder (e.g., Ps. 51). Later, the apostle Paul confirmed that whereas no animal sacrifice could take away specific sins, the offering of any God-appointed sacrifice accompanied by sincere repentance and the plea for forgiveness reflected faith in the final sacrifice of Christ for human guilt and shame (Rom. 4:7–8). In a similar vein, the writer to the Hebrews says that that sacrifice "set them free from sins committed under the first covenant," thereby assuring repentant and believing Jews prior to Jesus the forgiveness and salvation of God (Heb. 9:15; see also Rom. 3:24). The cross of Christ is of timeless, eternal significance in the redemptive purpose of God.

However, Scripture is also clear in its witness that faith comes by hearing the Word of God (Rom. 10:17). What then does one do about related matters concerning which Scripture is silent? What about the eternal destiny of those millions who, through no fault of their own, never heard the gospel? Do they stand condemned on the basis of their fallenness and their probable failure to respond to the tokens of God's self-disclosure in the world he has created ("without excuse," Rom. 1:19–20)? Or should we rather adopt the sequence of thought popularized by J. N. D. Anderson (1970: 98–106)? Our summary of its basic postulates follows:

1. Those saved under the old covenant ("by grace through faith") only dimly perceived the implications of offering "the same sacrifices repeated endlessly year after year," which were unable to "make perfect those who draw near to worship" (Heb. 10:1, 10).

2. Whereas their knowledge was limited, their turning to God in repentance and their offering the prescribed sacrifice (or casting themselves on God's mercy when no sacrifice was deemed appropriate to cover major moral sins) meant that they obtained a forgiven status identical with ours.

3. Since salvation is never achieved "by works," we must be adamant in denying its possibility to the followers of other religions just because they seek to be religious and strive to be moral.

4. However, if people realize their sinfulness and cast themselves on the mercy of God with a sincerity reflected in righteous conduct, may we assume that they are in a relationship to God different from Paul's description in Romans 1:32 (that all people know something of the judgment of God against sin, but that many treat this possibility with scorn)?

5. Only through postulating that grace may be extended apart from any knowledge of the gospel can we resolve the question raised by the silence of the Bible on the minimal amount of knowledge necessary to salvation, that is, that ignorance of the gospel disqualifies one for the grace of God.

6. If, by the inner working of the Holy Spirit, a man or woman cries out for the mercy of God, he or she will find it. It is recognized, of course, that the only empirical evidence we have comes from Christians who have contacted these penitent ones and have shared with them the gospel that alone brings assurance.

7. This sequence of thought would substantiate the biblical stress on the necessity of seeking God if one is to find him (Lam. 3:25; Ps. 53:2–3; Prov. 8:17; Luke 11:9–10; Acts 17:27; Heb. 11:6; etc.). Because in the natural world no one seeks God (Rom. 3:11), we must presume that the Spirit of God is at work wherever people seek him.

Since we have endorsed this sequence of argument, it would hardly do to say that all non-Christian religions are either totally demonic or totally of human contrivance or a mixture of both. We must not forget the light that enlightens everyone (John 1:9). Anderson, after rich missionary experience in Egypt, could only conclude:

I have never met a Muslim convert who regards the God he previously sought to worship as a wholly false God; instead he is filled with wonder and gratitude that he has now been brought to know that God as he really is, in Jesus Christ our Lord. (1970: 110)

Perhaps the best way to conclude this discussion is to see greater significance and broader application in the parable Jesus told of the publican in the temple who cried out: "God, have mercy on me, a sinner," and who "went home justified" (but not inwardly assured, Luke 18:9–14). It will be wise if evangelicals follow John Wesley and not countenance the wholesale condemnation of the non-Christian world to eternal damnation.

Let it be observed, I purposely add, to those that are under the Christian dispensation; because I have no authority from the Word of God "to judge those that are without;" nor do I conceive that any man living has a right to sentence all the heathen and Mahometan [Muslim] world to damnation. It is far better to leave them to him that made them, and who is "the Father of the spirits of all flesh," who is the God of the heathens as well as the Christians, and who hateth nothing he hath made. (1872, vol. 7:353)

Conclusion

We have traced the steps leading to the consummation of God's redemptive purpose with the Kingdom safely and finally in his hands. At last, all his servants "see his face" (Rev. 22:4). This calls forth their spontaneous and joyous worship. As they worship, they gladly enter his higher service and begin to "reign for ever and ever" (22:3–5).

However, when the apostle John finished detailing this glorious climax, he could not lay down his pen. He had to call attention to the variety of voices authenticating the themes of Revelation and insisting on their urgency. In quick succession he wrote of Christ himself proclaiming a benediction on all who "keep the words of this book" (22:9). Further, he noted that Christ then lingered at his side, encouraging one and all with a thrice repeated pledge of his "soon" coming

(22:7, 12, 20). He also spoke of his abiding concern for all people. Repentance will be forced on none (22:11). However, whether people experience salvation or judgment will depend on whether they have sought his cleansing or persisted in their sin (22:12, 14–15). Christ's reiteration is clear: there is only one way into the paradise of God. Some will enter it, but many will not. The tree of life will not be accessible to the impenitent.

Then John sought to worship at the feet of the angel who had served as his intermediary throughout the inscripturation of these visions. But he was pointedly told: "Worship God!" (22:9). This prompted another warning: Revelation is one piece! One incurs the wrath of God by treating it lightly, either by adding one's own speculations or by deleting segments of its exclusive and pointed affirmations (cf. 22:18–19 with Deut. 4:2).

Before John concludes with a benediction on "God's people" (22:21), he heard a final appeal wistfully yet urgently coming from the Spirit and the bride. Together they cry out, "'Come!' . . . Whoever is thirsty, let him come; and whoever wishes, let him take the free gift of the water of life" (22:17). And their invitation is repeated: "Come!"

That the Holy Spirit and the church in union should beseech men and women to be reconciled to God, and that this should be virtually the final word addressed to the human race in Holy Scripture is most significant. It points up what Charles Van Engen has defined as a new word for defining the essence of the church: a deep "yearning" to gather all peoples around the cross and around the throne of the Lamb and into its unity, its holiness, its catholicity, its apostolicity, and its witness (1981: 486–505).

How natural that this insistent word, "Come!" should be the final appeal from the Spirit and the church at the close of the Word of God written. Indeed, all who have come to vital faith in Jesus Christ must ardently desire that all others experience this liberating reality. They will rejoice at every report of the growth of the church throughout the nations. As the apostle John so vividly expressed:

> We proclaim to you what we have seen and heard, so that you also may have fellowship with us. And our fellowship is with the Father and with his Son, Jesus Christ. We write this to make our joy complete. (1 John 1:3–4)

Indeed, we must agree with Lesslie Newbigin that "where this desire and this rejoicing are absent, we must ask whether something is not wrong at the very center of the church's life" (1978: 142).

We conclude this study with the vivid impression that our understanding has been partial and that our glimpses of truth are neither perfect nor complete (1 Cor. 13:9, 12). On occasion this has involved our confrontation with paradox, seeing truths that have appeared to conflict and not being able to understand fully the connections between them. But we trust that what has been written conveys the impressions of an honest and sincere effort to listen to the Word of God in the canonical text of Holy Scripture.

Works Cited

Aalen, Sverre
    1961   "'Reign' and 'House' in the Kingdom
            of God in the Gospels." *New Testa-
            ment Studies* 8:215–40.

Abbott, Walter M., ed.
    1966   *The Documents of Vatican II.* Trans-
            lated by Joseph Gallagher. New York:
            Geoffrey Chapman.

Albright, William Foxwell
    1946   *From the Stone Age to Christianity:
            Monotheism and the Historical Process.*
            Baltimore: Johns Hopkins University
            Press.

Aldwinckle, Russel F.
    1982   *Jesus: A Savior or the Savior?* Macon,
            Ga.: Mercer University Press.

Allen, Roland
    1962   *Missionary Methods, St. Paul's or Ours?*
            Grand Rapids: Eerdmans.

Anderson, Bernhard
    1957   *Understanding the Old Testament.*
            Englewood Cliffs, N.J.: Prentice-Hall.
    1977   "The Babel Story: Paradigm of
            Human Unity and Diversity." In *Eth-
            nicity,* edited by Andrew M. Greeley
            and Gregory Baum, 63–70. New
            York: Seabury Press.

Anderson, Gerald H.
    1974   "The Church and the Jewish People:
            Some Theological Issues and Mis-
            siological Concerns." *Missiology: An
            International Review* 2, no. 3:279–93.

Anderson, James Norman Dalrymple
    1970   *Christianity and Comparative Religion.*
            Downers Grove, Ill.: InterVarsity
            Press.

Archer, Gleason
    1964   *A Survey of Old Testament Introduc-
            tion.* Chicago: Moody.

Arndt, William F., and F. Wilbur Gingrich
    1957   *A Greek-English Lexicon of the New
            Testament.* Cambridge: Cambridge
            University Press.

Atkinson, Basil F. C.
    1953   "The Gospel of Matthew." In *The
            New Bible Commentary,* edited by F.
            Davidson, 771–805. Grand Rapids:
            Eerdmans.

Aulen, Gustaf Emanuel Hildebrand
    1951   *Christus Victor.* Translated by A. G.
            Hebert. New York: Macmillan.

Baago, Kaj
    1966   "The Post-Colonial Crisis of Mis-
            sions." *International Review of Mis-
            sions,* 55, no. 219 (July): 322–32.

Baeck, Leo
    1948   *The Essence of Judaism.* New York:
            Schocken.

Baird, J. Arthur
    1963   *The Justice of God in the Teaching of
            Jesus.* Philadelphia: Westminster.

Bamberger, Bernard J.
    1939   *Proselytism in the Talmudic Period.*
            New York: KTAV.

Barclay, William
    1962   *Jesus as They Saw Him.* New York:
            Harper & Row.

375

1975   *The Gospel of Luke.* Rev. ed. Philadelphia: Westminster.

Barker, Glenn W., with William L. Lane and J. Ramsey Michaels
1969   *The New Testament Speaks.* New York: Harper & Row.

Barrett, C. K.
1974   "Paul's Speech on the Areopagus." In *New Testament Christianity for Africa and the World,* edited by Mark E. Glasswell and Edward W. Fashole-Luke, 69–77. London: S.P.C.K.

Barth, Christoph
1991   *God with Us: A Theological Introduction to the Old Testament.* Grand Rapids: Eerdmans.

Barth, Karl
1957   *Church Dogmatics.* Vol. 2, *The Doctrine of God.* Translated by Geoffrey W. Bromiley et al. Edinburgh: T. & T. Clark.
1961   "An Exegetical Study of Matthew 28:16–20." In *The Theology of the Christian Mission,* edited by Gerald H. Anderson, 55–71. New York: McGraw-Hill.
1962   *Church Dogmatics.* Vol. 4, *The Doctrine of Reconciliation.* Translated by Geoffrey W. Bromiley and T. F. Torrance. Edinburgh: T. & T. Clark.

Barth, Markus
1959   *Broken Wall: A Study of the Epistle to the Ephesians.* Philadelphia: Judson.

Bavinck, Johannes H.
1960   *An Introduction to the Science of Missions.* Translated by David H. Freeman. Philadelphia: Presbyterian & Reformed.
1966   *The Church between the Temple and Mosque.* Grand Rapids: Eerdmans.

Beals, Alan R., with Harry Hoijer and Ralph C. Beals.
1977   *An Introduction to Anthropology.* 5th ed. New York: Macmillan.

Bennett, Charles T.
1980   "Paul the Pragmatist: Another Look at His Missionary Methods." *Evangelical Missions Quarterly* 16, no. 3:133–38.

Ben-Sasson, H. H.
1976   *A History of the Jewish People.* Cambridge, Mass.: Harvard University Press.

Berkhof, Hendrikus
1962   *Christ and the Powers.* Translated by John Howard Yoder. Scottdale, Pa.: Herald.
1964   *The Doctrine of the Holy Spirit.* Richmond: John Knox Press.

Berkhof, Louis
1946   *Systematic Theology.* 3d ed. Grand Rapids: Eerdmans.

Blauw, Johannes
1962   *The Missionary Nature of the Church.* New York: McGraw-Hill.

Bocking, Ronald A. H.
1961   *Has the Day of the Missionary Passed?* London: London Missionary Society.

Boer, Harry
1961   *Pentecost and Mission.* Grand Rapids: Eerdmans.

Bonhoeffer, Dietrich
1953   *The Cost of Discipleship.* New York: Macmillan.

Bornkamm, Gunther
1966   "The Missionary Stance of Paul in I Corinthians 9 and in Acts." In *Studies in Luke–Acts,* edited by Leander E. Keck and J. Louis Martyn, 194–207. Nashville: Abingdon.

Bosch, David J.
1969   "'Jesus and the Gentiles': A Review after Thirty Years." In *The Church Crossing Frontiers,* edited by Peter Beyerhaus and Carl F. Hallencreutz, 3–19. Studia Missionalia Upsaliensia XI. Uppsala: Gleerup.

Bouyer, Louis
1965   *Dictionary of Theology.* New York: Desclee.

Bowler, Maurice G.
1973   "Do Jews Need Jesus?" *Christianity Today,* 58, no. 2:12–14.

Bowmer, John C.
1951   *The Sacrament of the Lord's Supper in Early Methodism.* London: Daere.

Breslaner, S. Daniel
1984   "Universalism–Jewish View." In *A Dictionary of the Jewish-Christian*

Dialogue, edited by Leon Klenicki
and Geoffrey Wigoder, 198–201.
New York: Paulist.

Bright, John
1953 *The Kingdom of God.* Nashville:
      Abingdon.
1967 *The Authority of the Old Testament.*
      Nashville: Abingdon.
1972 *A History of Israel.* Philadelphia:
      Westminster.
1976 *Covenant and Promise: The Pro-
      phetic Understanding of the Future
      in Pre-exilic Israel.* Philadelphia:
      Westminster.

Bromiley, Geoffrey W.
1969 "Angel." In *Baker's Dictionary of
      Theology,* edited by Everett F. Har-
      rison, 41–43. Grand Rapids: Baker.

Bruce, Frederick F.
1954 *Commentary on the Book of the Acts.*
      Grand Rapids: Eerdmans.
1956 *Second Thoughts on the Dead Sea
      Scrolls.* Grand Rapids: Eerdmans.
1968 *The New Testament Development of
      Old Testament Themes.* Grand Rapids:
      Eerdmans.
1978 *The Time Is Fulfilled: Five Aspects of
      the Fulfilment of the Old Testament in
      the New.* Grand Rapids: Eerdmans.

Brunner, H. Emil
1946 *Revelation and Reason: The Christian
      Doctrine of Faith and Knowledge.*
      Translated by Olive Wyon. Philadel-
      phia: Westminster.

Buckmaster, Henrietta
1965 *Paul, a Man Who Changed the World.*
      New York: McGraw-Hill.

Buttrick, George A.
1951 "The Gospel according to Matthew."
      In *The Interpreters' Bible,* vol. 7,
      230–625. Nashville: Abingdon.

Caird, George Bradford
1956 *Principalities and Powers: A Study in
      Pauline Theology.* Oxford: Clarendon.

Calvin, John
1960 *Institutes of the Christian Religion.*
      Edited by John T. McNeill. Philadel-
      phia: Westminster.

Carson, D. A.
1981 *Divine Sovereignty and Human
      Responsibility.* Atlanta: John Knox
      Press.

Carson, Herbert M.
1962 "Stranger." In *The New Bible Diction-
      ary,* edited by J. D. Douglas, 1219.
      Grand Rapids: Eerdmans.

Childs, Brevard
1970 *Biblical Theology in Crisis.* Philadel-
      phia: Westminster.

Clemens, Lois Gunden
1971 *Woman Liberated.* Scottdale, Pa.:
      Herald.

Clines, David J. A.
1976 *A Biblical Doctrine of Man.* Lon-
      don: Christian Brethren Research
      Fellowship.

Cole, R. Allen
1973 *Exodus: An Introduction and Commen-
      tary.* Downers Grove, Ill.: InterVarsity
      Press.

Conn, Harvie M.
1982 *Evangelism: Doing Justice and Preach-
      ing Grace.* Grand Rapids: Zondervan.

Conybeare, W. J., and J. S. Howson
1920 *The Life and Epistles of St. Paul.* Lon-
      don: Longmans, Green.

Conzelmann, Hans
1973 *History of Primitive Christianity.*
      Translated by John E. Steely. New
      York: Abingdon.

Cook, Harold R.
1975 "Who Really Sent the First Mission-
      aries?" *Evangelical Missions Quarterly*
      11, no. 4:233–39.

Copeland, E. Luther
1976 "Church Growth in Acts." *Missiol-
      ogy: An International Review* 4, no.
      1:13–26.

Corell, Alf
1958 *Consummatum Est.* London: S.P.C.K.

Costas, Orlando E.
1982 *Christ outside the Gate.* Maryknoll,
      N.Y.: Orbis.

Cullmann, Oscar
1950 *Christ and Time.* Translated by
      Floyd V. Filson. Philadelphia:
      Westminster.

1957   *The State in the New Testament.*
        London: SCM; New York: Harper &
        Row.
1970   *Jesus and the Revolutionaries.* Trans-
        lated by Gareth Putnam. New York:
        Harper & Row.

Cummings, Norman, and Edward Murphy
1973   "The Ministry and Organizational
        Development of Overseas Crusades as
        an Apostolic Team." Research paper,
        Fuller Theological Seminary.

Daane, James
1973   *The Freedom of God.* Grand Rapids:
        Eerdmans.

Davies, William D.
1962   *Christian Origins and Judaism.* Phila-
        delphia: Westminster.
1974   *The Gospel and the Land.* Berkeley:
        University of California Press.

de Dietrich, Suzanne
1960   *God's Unfolding Purpose.* Philadelphia:
        Westminster.

Deist, Ferdinand
1977   "The Exodus Motif in the Old Testa-
        ment and the Theology of Libera-
        tion." *Missionalia* 5, no. 2 (August):
        58–69.

De Ridder, Richard R.
1971   *Discipling the Nations.* Grand Rapids:
        Baker.

Derwacter, Frederick Milton
1930   *Preparing the Way for Paul: The Pros-
        elyte Movement in Later Judaism.* New
        York: Macmillan.

de Santa Ana, Julio
1977   *Good News to the Poor: The Chal-
        lenge of the Poor in the History of the
        Church.* Geneva: World Council
        of Churches, Commission on
        the Churches' Participation in
        Development.

Dewick, Edward Chisholm
1953   *The Christian Attitude to Other Reli-
        gions.* Cambridge: Cambridge Uni-
        versity Press.

Dodd, Charles H.
1936   *The Apostolic Preaching and Its
        Developments.* London: Hodder &
        Stoughton.
1938   *History and Gospel.* New York:
        Scribner's.

Drench, Cecelia
1977   "The Central Theological Issues
        Related to Paul's Evangelism of Jews
        and Gentiles." M.A. thesis, Fuller
        Theological Seminary.

Dunn, James D. G.
1970   *Baptism in the Holy Spirit.* London:
        SCM.
1977   *Unity and Diversity in the New Testa-
        ment.* Philadelphia: Westminster.

Edersheim, Alfred
1949   *The Bible History: Old Testament.*
        Grand Rapids: Eerdmans.

Eichrodt, Walter
1951   *Man in the Old Testament.* London:
        SCM.

Eller, Vernard
1973   *King Jesus' Manual of Arms for the
        "Armless": War and Peace from Genesis
        to Revelation.* Nashville: Abingdon.

Ellison, Henry L.
1976   *From Babylon to Bethlehem: The Jew-
        ish People from the Exile to the Messiah.*
        Exeter: Paternoster.

Ellul, Jacques
1969   *Violence: Reflections from a Christian
        Perspective.* New York: Seabury Press.

Ferre, Nels Fredrick Solomon
1951   *The Christian Understanding of God.*
        New York: Harper & Brothers.

Flew, Robert Newton
1960   *Jesus and His Church: A Study of the
        Idea of the Ecclesia in the New Testa-
        ment.* London: Epworth.

Forell, George W.
1954   *Faith Active in Love.* Minneapolis:
        Augsburg.

Fuller, Daniel P.
1969   *Hermeneutics.* Course Syllabus: Fuller
        Theological Seminary.

Fuller, Reginald H.
1954   *The Mission and Achievement of Jesus:
        An Examination of the Presuppositions
        of New Testament Theology.* Chicago:
        Allenson.
1960   *The Book of the Acts of God.* Garden
        City, N.Y.: Doubleday.

Gerstner, John H.
1960   "Acts." In *The Bible Expositor*, edited by Carl F. H. Henry, vol. 3. Philadelphia: Holman.

Gibbon, Edward
1952   *The Decline and Fall of the Roman Empire*. 2 vols. Chicago: Encyclopedia Brittanica.

Glasser, Arthur.
1974   "What Is 'Mission' Today? Two Views." In *Mission Trends No. 1*, edited by Gerald H. Anderson and Thomas F. Stransky. Grand Rapids: Eerdmans.
1984   "Missiology." In *Evangelical Dictionary of Theology*, edited by Walter A. Elwell. Grand Rapids: Baker.
1985   Foreword to the American edition of *The Mission of the Church in the World*, by Roger Hedlund. Grand Rapids: Baker.
1992   *Kingdom and Mission*. Privately published.

Goodall, Norman
1953   *Missions under the Cross*. London: Edinburgh House Press.

Goppelt, Leonhard
1970   *Apostolic and Post-apostolic Times*. Translated by Robert A. Guelich. New York: Harper & Row.

Gottwald, Norman K.
1979   *The Tribes of Yahweh: A Sociology of the Religion of Liberated Israel, 1250–1050 B.C.E.* Maryknoll, N.Y.: Orbis.

Green, Michael
1970   *Evangelism in the Early Church*. Grand Rapids: Eerdmans.

Griffiths, Michael
1980   *The Church and World Mission*. Grand Rapids: Zondervan.

Gross, Heinrich
1970   "Peace." In *Encyclopedia of Biblical Theology*, edited by J. B. Bauer, 648–51. London: Sheed & Ward.

Gutierrez, Gustavo
1973   *A Theology of Liberation: History, Politics, and Salvation*. Maryknoll, N.Y.: Orbis.

Hahn, Ferdinand
1965   *Mission in the New Testament*. London: SCM.

Hare, Douglas R. A.
1967   *The Theme of Jewish Persecution of Christians in the Gospel according to St. Matthew*. Cambridge: Cambridge University Press.

Hare, D. R. A., and Daniel J. Harrington
1975   "Make Disciples of All the Gentiles." *Catholic Biblical Quarterly*, vol. 37:359–69.

Harkness, Georgia
1974   *Understanding the Kingdom of God*. Nashville: Abingdon.

Harnack, Adolf
1972 [1902]   *The Mission and Expansion of Christianity in the First Three Centuries*. Translated by James Moffatt. Freeport, N.Y.: Books for Libraries Press.

Harrison, Everett F.
1975   *Acts: The Expanding Church*. Chicago: Moody.

Harrison, Roland K.
1969   *Introduction to the Old Testament*. Grand Rapids: Eerdmans.

Hartenstein, Karl
1939   "The Biblical View of Religion." In *The Authority of the Faith*, Madras Series, vol. 1, 117–36. New York: International Missionary Council.

Hendry, George S.
1956   *The Holy Spirit in Christian Theology*. Philadelphia: Westminster.

Hiebert, Paul
1983   "Missions and the Renewal of the Church." In *Exploring Church Growth*, edited by Wilbert R. Shenk, 157–67. Grand Rapids: Eerdmans.

Hort, Arthur Fenton
1914   *The Gospel according to St. Mark*. Cambridge: Cambridge University Press.

Hoskyns, Edwyn C., and Noel Davey
1947   *The Riddle of the New Testament*. London: Faber & Faber.

Howell, Leon
1983   "Conversion: For the Sake of the World." *International Review of Mission* 72, no. 287:365–72.

Hubbard, David A.
  1983   "Hope in the Old Testament." *Tyndale Bulletin*, no. 34:33–59.

Ingram, T. Robert
  1975   "The Grace of Creation." *The Westminster Theological Journal*, 37, no. 2:206–17.

Jacob, Edmond
  1958   *Theology of the Old Testament.* New York: Harper & Row.

Jeremias, Joachim
  1968   *Rediscovering the Parables.* New York: Scribner's.
  1982   *Jesus' Promise to the Nations.* Philadelphia: Fortress.

Jewett, Paul K.
  1975   *Man as Male and Female: A Study in Sexual Relationships from a Theological Point of View.* Grand Rapids: Eerdmans.

Jocz, Jakob
  1961   *The Spiritual History of Israel.* London: Eyre & Spottiswoode.
  1981   *The Jewish People and Jesus Christ after Auschwitz: A Study in the Controversy between Church and Synagogue.* Grand Rapids: Baker.

Josephus, Flavius
  1957   *The Life and Works of Flavius Josephus.* Translated by W. Whiston. Philadelphia: Winston.

Kaiser, Walter C.
  1981   *Toward an Exegetical Theology: Biblical Exegesis for Preaching and Teaching.* Grand Rapids: Baker.

Kallas, James G.
  1968   *Jesus and the Power of Satan.* Philadelphia: Westminster.

Kaufmann, Yehezkel
  1960   *The Religion of Israel.* Translated and abridged by Moshe Greenberg. Chicago: University of Chicago Press.

Kidner, Derek
  1967   *Genesis: An Introduction and Commentary.* Chicago: InterVarsity Press.
  1973   *Psalms 1–72: An Introduction and Commentary on Books I and II of the Psalms.* London: InterVarsity Press.

Knight, George Angus Fulton
  1959   *A Christian Theology of the Old Testament.* London: SCM.

Kraemer, Hendrik
  1969   *The Christian Message in a Non-Christian World.* Grand Rapids: Kregel.

Kraus, Clyde Norman
  1974   *The Community of the Spirit.* Grand Rapids: Eerdmans.

Kraybill, Donald Brubaker
  1978   *The Upside Down Kingdom.* Scottdale, Pa.: Herald.

Kuhns, Dennis R.
  1978   *Women in the Church.* Scottdale, Pa.: Herald.

Kummel, Werner Georg
  1963   *Man in the New Testament.* Translated by J. J. Vincent. London: Epworth.

Küng, Hans
  1967   *The Church.* New York: Sheed & Ward.

Küng, Hans, and Walter Kasper, eds.
  1973   *Polarization in the Church.* New York: Herder & Herder.

Ladd, George E.
  1959   *New Testament Theology.* Grand Rapids: Eerdmans.
  1962   "Introduction to Matthew." In *Holman Study Bible*, 911a–911b. Philadelphia: Holman.
  1964   *Jesus and the Kingdom.* New York: Harper & Row.
  1968   *The Young Church: Acts of the Apostles.* London: Lutterworth.
  1972   *A Commentary on the Revelation of John.* Grand Rapids: Eerdmans.
  1974   *A Theology of the New Testament.* Grand Rapids: Eerdmans.

La Sor, William Sanford
  1972   *Church Alive.* Glendale, Calif.: Regal.

Lausanne Committee for World Evangelization, World Evangelical Fellowship
  1982   *Evangelism and Social Responsibility: An Evangelical Commitment.* Exeter: Paternoster.

Lewis, Clive Staples
  1945   *Mere Christianity.* New York: Macmillan.

Lightfoot, Joseph Barber
    1865   *The Epistle of St. Paul to the Galatians.* Grand Rapids: Zondervan.

Loffler, Paul
    1965   "Conversion in an Ecumenical Context." *The Ecumenical Review* 19, no. 3:252–60.

MacGregor, G. H. C.
    1954   "Principalities and Powers: The Cosmic Background of Paul's Thought." *New Testament Studies,* vol. 1 (summer): 17–28.

MacKinnon, Donald M.
    1906   "Commission." In *Dictionary of Christ and the Gospels,* edited by J. Hastings, 347–49. New York: Scribner's.

Maddox, Robert
    1982   *The Purpose of Luke–Acts.* Edinburgh: T. & T. Clark.

Marshall, I. Howard
    1971   *Luke: Historian and Theologian.* Grand Rapids: Zondervan.

Martens, Elmer A.
    1981   *God's Design: A Focus on Old Testament Theology.* Grand Rapids: Baker.

Mavis, Walter C.
    1947   "Jesus' Influence on the Pastoral Ministry." *Theology Today* 4, no. 3:357–67.

McCarthy, Dennis J.
    1968   *Kings and Prophets.* Milwaukee: Bruce Publishing Co.

McGavran, Donald A.
    1955   *The Bridges of God.* New York: Friendship Press.
    1989   "Are Seminaries Shortchanging Evangelism?" *Missions Tomorrow* (spring/summer): 22–26. Excerpted from D. McGavran, *Effective Evangelism: A Theological Mandate* (Phillipsburgh, N.J.: Presbyterian and Reformed, 1988).
    1990   *Understanding Church Growth.* Grand Rapids: Eerdmans.

McKenzie, John L.
    1974   *A Theology of the Old Testament.* Garden City, N.Y.: Doubleday.

McLeish, Alexander
    1952   *Christ's Hope of the Kingdom.* London: World Dominion Press.

Metzger, Bruce
    1965   *The New Testament: Its Background, Growth and Content.* Nashville: Abingdon.

Meyer, F.
    1897   *Paul: A Servant of Jesus Christ.* New York: Revell.

Michaels, J. Ramsey
    1981   *Servant and Son: Jesus in Parable and Gospel.* Atlanta: John Knox Press.

Minear, Paul S.
    1976   *To Heal and to Reveal: The Prophetic Vocation according to Luke.* New York: Seabury Press.

Miranda, Jose
    1974   *Marx and the Bible.* Translated by Jean Eagleson. Maryknoll, N.Y.: Orbis.

Morris, Leon
    1960   "Church Government." In *Baker's Dictionary of Theology,* edited by Everett F. Harrison, 126–27. Grand Rapids: Baker.

Morrison, Clinton
    1960   *The Powers That Be: Earthly Rulers and Demonic Powers in Romans 13, 1–7.* Naperville, Ill.: Allenson.

Muller, D.
    1975   "Apostle." In *The New International Dictionary of the New Testament,* edited by Colin Brown, vol. 1, 126–35. Grand Rapids: Zondervan.

Murray, John
    1959   *The Epistle to the Romans.* Vol. 1. Grand Rapids: Eerdmans.

Neill, Stephen
    1957   *The Unfinished Task.* London: Edinburgh House Press.
    1961   *Christian Faith and Other Faiths.* London: Oxford University Press.
    1964   *The Interpretation of the New Testament: 1861–1961.* London: Oxford University Press.

Newbigin, Lesslie
    1966   "Conversion." *Religion and Society* 13, no. 4 (December): 30–42.

1969   *The Finality of Christ.* Richmond: John Knox Press.

1978   *The Open Secret.* Grand Rapids: Eerdmans.

Packer, James I.
1961   "Christianity and Non-Christian Religions." *Christianity Today* 4, no. 6 (December 21): 211–13.

Padilla, C. Rene
1982   "The Kingdom of God and the Church." *Theological Fraternity Bulletin,* no. 1:1–23.

Peters, George W.
1972   *A Biblical Theology of Missions.* Chicago: Moody.

1981   *A Theology of Church Growth.* Grand Rapids: Eerdmans.

Pieters, Albertus
1950   *Studies in the Revelation of St. John.* Grand Rapids: Eerdmans.

Pilgrim, Walter E.
1981   *Good News to the Poor.* Minneapolis: Augsburg.

Ramm, Bernard L.
1954   *The Christian View of Science and Scripture.* Grand Rapids: Eerdmans.

Rees, Paul S.
1974   "More on the Muddle." *World Vision* 18, no. 4:23.

Ringgren, Helmer
1956   *The Messiah in the Old Testament.* London: SCM; Chicago: Allenson.

Rosenberg, Stuart E.
1986   *The Christian Problem: A Jewish View.* New York: Hippocrene Books.

Rosin, Hellmut H.
1972   *Missio Dei.* Leiden: Interuniversity Institute for Missiological and Ecumenical Research.

Rowley, Harold H.
1939   *Israel's Mission to the World.* London: SCM.

1944   *The Missionary Message of the Old Testament.* London: Carey Press.

1956   *The Faith of Israel: Aspects of Old Testament Thought.* London: SCM.

Rushdoony, Rousas John
1978   *Thy Kingdom Come.* Edited by Stanley J. Samartha. Fairfax, Va.: Thoburn Press.

Russell, David S.
1978   *The Method and Message of Jewish Apocalyptic, 200 B.C.–A.D. 100.* Philadelphia: Westminster.

Sanders, James A.
1972   *Torah and Canon.* Philadelphia: Fortress.

Schattschneider, David Allen
1975   "'Souls for the Lamb': A Theology for the Christian Mission according to Count Nicolaus Ludwig von Zinzendorf and Bishop Augustus Gottlieb Spangenberg," 75–78. Ph.D. diss., University of Chicago.

Schlette, Heinz Robert
1966   *Towards a Theology of Religions.* New York: Herder & Herder.

Schlier, Heinrich
1961   *Principalities and Powers in the New Testament.* New York: Herder & Herder.

Schmidt, Karl Ludwig
1964   "*Ethnos, ethnikos.*" In *Theological Dictionary of the New Testament,* vol. 2, edited by Gerhard Kittel, translated by Geoffrey W. Bromiley, 364–72. Grand Rapids: Eerdmans.

Schoeps, Hans Joachim
1961   *Paul: The Theology of the Apostle in the Light of Jewish Religious History.* Translated by Harold Knight. Philadelphia: Westminster.

Schoonhoven, Calvin Robert
1966   *The Wrath of Heaven.* Grand Rapids: Eerdmans.

Schweizer, Eduard
1956   "*Pneuma.*" In *Theological Dictionary of the New Testament,* vol. 6, edited by Gerhard Kittel, 389–455. Grand Rapids: Eerdmans.

Scofield, C. I.
1917   *The Scofield Reference Bible.* New York: Oxford University Press.

Scott, Waldron
1978   *Karl Barth's Theology of Mission.* Downers Grove, Ill.: InterVarsity Press.

Senior, Donald, and Carroll Stuhlmueller
1983   *The Biblical Foundations for Mission.* Maryknoll, N.Y.: Orbis.

Sider, Ronald J.
1980 "Christ and Power." *International Review of Mission* 69, no. 273 (January): 8–20.

Skydsgaard, Kristen E.
1951 "Kingdom of God and Church." *Scottish Journal of Theology* 4, no. 4:383–97.

Smalley, Stephen
1964 "Conversion in the New Testament." *The Churchman* 78, no. 3 (summer): 193–210.

Snaith, Norman H.
1944 *The Distinctive Ideas of the Old Testament*. London: Epworth.

Snyder, Howard A.
1983 *Liberating the Church: The Ecology of Church and Kingdom*. Downers Grove, Ill.: InterVarsity Press.

Stagg, Frank
1955 *The Book of Acts: The Early Struggle for an Unhindered Gospel*. Nashville: Broadman.

Stern, Menahem
1976 "The Period of the Second Temple." In *A History of the Jewish People*, edited by H. H. Ben-Sasson, 185–295. Cambridge, Mass.: Harvard University Press.

Stewart, James S.
1951 "On a Neglected Emphasis in New Testament Theology." *Scottish Journal of Theology*, vol. 4 (fall): 292–301.

Stewart, R. A.
1962 "Proselyte." In *The New Bible Dictionary*, edited by J. D. Douglas, 1047–48. Grand Rapids: Eerdmans.

Stott, John R. W.
1975 *Christian Mission in the Modern World*. Downers Grove, Ill.: InterVarsity Press.

Sundkler, Bengt
1965 *The World of Mission*. London: Lutterworth.

Talmage, Frank Ephraim, ed.
1975 *Disputation and Dialogue: Readings in the Jewish-Christian Encounter*. New York: KTAV.

Thompson, Allen
1971 "Mission/Church Structures." Paper read at Interdenominational Foreign Missions Association Board meeting.

Tippett, Alan R.
1969 *Verdict Theology in Missionary Theory*. Lincoln, Ill.: Lincoln Christian College.

Toynbee, Arnold
1957 *Christianity among the Religions of the World*. New York: Scribner's.

Trepp, Leo
1982 *Judaism: Development and Life*. Belmont, Calif.: Wadsworth.

Van Engen, Charles
1981 *The Growth of the True Church*. Amsterdam: Rodophi.

Van Ruler, Arnold Albert
1971 *The Christian Church and the Old Testament*. Translated by Geoffrey W. Bromiley. Grand Rapids: Eerdmans.

Van Til, Cornelius
1962 *Christianity and Barthianism*. Grand Rapids: Baker.
1968 *Christ and the Jews*. Philadelphia: Presbyterian & Reformed.

Verkuyl, Johannes
1978 *Contemporary Missiology: An Introduction*. Grand Rapids: Eerdmans.

Vicedom, Georg F.
1965 *The Mission of God*. Saint Louis: Concordia.

Visser 't Hooft, Willem Adolph
1959 *The Pressure of Our Common Calling*. Garden City, N.Y.: Doubleday.

Von Rad, Gerhard
1961 *Genesis: A Commentary*. Philadelphia: Westminster.
1972 *Wisdom in Israel*. Nashville: Abingdon.

Vos, Geerhardus
1948 *Biblical Theology: Old and New Testaments*. Grand Rapids: Eerdmans.

Walhout, Edwin
1963 "The Liberal-Fundamentalist Debate." *Christianity Today* 7, no. 2:3–4.

Walls, Andrew F.
1970 "The First Chapter of the Epistle to the Romans and the Modern Mis-

sionary Movement." In *Apostolic History and the Gospel,* edited by W. Ward Gasque and Ralph P. Martin, 346–57. Grand Rapids: Eerdmans.

Warren, Max
1976   *I Believe in the Great Commission.* Grand Rapids: Eerdmans.
1978   "The Fusion of IMC and WCC at New Delhi: Retrospective Thoughts after a Decade and a Half." In *Zending Op Weg Naar De Toekomst: Essays Aangeboden aan Prof. J. Verkuyl,* edited by Jerald D. Gort, 190–202. Kampen: J. H. Kok Uitgeversmaatschappij.

Webber, Robert E.
1978   *Common Roots.* Grand Rapids: Zondervan.

Westermann, Claus
1969   *Isaiah 40–66: A Commentary.* London: SCM.

Wieser, Thomas
1975   "Notes on the Meaning of the Apostolate." *International Review of Mission* 64, no. 254:129–36.

Wilson, Marvin R.
1989   *Our Father Abraham: Jewish Roots of the Christian Faith.* Grand Rapids: Eerdmans.

Winn, Albert Curry
1981   *A Sense of Mission: Guidance from the Gospel of John.* Philadelphia: Westminster.

Winter, Ralph D.
1974   "The Two Structures of God's Redemptive Mission," *Missiology: An International Review* 2, no. 1:121–39.

World Council of Churches, Department on the Laity
1964   "The Redemptive Work of Christ and the Ministry of His Church," "Christ's Ministry through His Whole Church and Its Ministers." *Encounter,* vol. 25:105–29.

World Council of Churches, Fourth Assembly
1968   *Uppsala Report: Official Report of the Fourth Assembly of the World Council of Churches, Uppsala, July 4–20, 1968.* Edited by Norman Goodall. Geneva: World Council of Churches.

Wright, Christopher J. H.
1984   "The Ethical Relevance of Israel as a Society." *Transformation* 1, no. 1 (January–March): 11–20.

Wright, G. Ernest, ed.
1952   *God Who Acts: Biblical Theology as Recital.* London: SCM.
1969   *The Old Testament and Theology.* New York: Harper & Row.

Zwemer, Samuel M.
1943   *Into All the World.* Grand Rapids: Zondervan.

Scripture Index

Subject Index

Made in the USA
Las Vegas, NV
11 March 2023

68895417R00223